UNCERTAIN PASSAGE

A. Doak Barnett

UNCERTAIN PASSAGE
China's Transition to the Post-Mao Era

THE BROOKINGS INSTITUTION
Washington, D.C.

Copyright © 1974 by
THE BROOKINGS INSTITUTION
1775 Massachusetts Avenue, N.W., Washington D.C. 20036

Library of Congress Cataloging in Publication Data:

Barnett, A Doak.
  Uncertain passage: China's transition to the post-Mao era.
  Includes bibliographical references.
    1. China—Politics and government—1949–
I. Title.
DS777.55.B333   320.9'51'05   73-22482
ISBN 0-8157-0820-3
ISBN 0-8157-0819-x (pbk.)

To my wife
JEANNE BADEAU BARNETT

THE BROOKINGS INSTITUTION is an independent organization devoted to nonpartisan research, education, and publication in economics, government, foreign policy, and the social sciences generally. Its principal purposes are to aid in the development of sound public policies and to promote public understanding of issues of national importance.

The Institution was founded on December 8, 1927, to merge the activities of the Institute for Government Research, founded in 1916, the Institute of Economics, founded in 1922, and the Robert Brookings Graduate School of Economics and Government, founded in 1924.

The Board of Trustees is responsible for the general administration of the Institution, while the immediate direction of the policies, program, and staff is vested in the President, assisted by an advisory committee of the officers and staff. The by-laws of the Institution state, "It is the function of the Trustees to make possible the conduct of scientific research, and publication, under the most favorable conditions, and to safeguard the independence of the research staff in the pursuit of their studies and in the publication of the results of such studies. It is not a part of their function to determine, control, or influence the conduct of particular investigations or the conclusions reached."

The President bears final responsibility for the decision to publish a manuscript as a Brookings book or staff paper. In reaching his judgment on the competence, accuracy, and objectivity of each study, the President is advised by the director of the appropriate research program and weighs the views of a panel of expert outside readers who report to him in confidence on the quality of the work. Publication of a work signifies that it is deemed to be a competent treatment worthy of public consideration; such publication does not imply endorsement of conclusions or recommendations contained in the study.

The Institution maintains its position of neutrality on issues of public policy in order to safeguard the intellectual freedom of the staff. Hence interpretations or conclusions in Brookings publications should be understood to be solely those of the author or authors and should not be attributed to the Institution, to its trustees, officers, or other staff members, or to the organizations that support its research.

Foreword

CHINA'S GROWING ROLE in the world has made increasingly apparent the need for greater knowledge and better understanding of the forces influencing its policies. For Americans, this need is especially clear because, after two decades almost without diplomatic or trade contact with the People's Republic of China, the United States is now attempting to develop an entirely new relationship with it. Both Washington and Peking are adjusting their Asian policies in important ways, and both have committed themselves to "normalizing" their bilateral relations.

Realistic policies toward any nation must be based on an understanding of that nation's polity and society, the characteristics of its leaders, the goals they pursue, the problems they face, and the determinants of their policies both foreign and domestic. Acquiring such understanding about a huge, complex, and changing nation such as China is no easy task.

China is now in the midst of a historic transition. The turmoil of the Cultural Revolution in the late 1960s left a legacy of problems that China's leaders are still attempting to solve, and the approaching post-Mao succession poses many uncertainties about the future. This study examines the nature of the current transition and analyzes the forces that will influence events in China in the post-Mao era.

A. Doak Barnett's interpretations and judgments are based on more than a quarter-century of intensive study of China. He also draws on his own broad experience in dealing with Chinese affairs as newspaperman and government official as well as scholar. The book is primarily the product, however, of his recent research on the changing situation in China today, and he focuses on the further changes likely or possible in the future. He was fortunate, while writing this volume, to be able to

ix

revisit China during the winter of 1972–73, and the insights thus gained contributed to many of his conclusions.

The author has also benefited from the research and writings of his fellow specialists in Chinese affairs. His notes mention books and articles by his colleagues that he has found particularly perceptive and useful. He wishes to express special thanks to those who read and commented on portions of this study in early drafts: Robert W. Barnett, Lester R. Brown, Parris Chang, Ralph N. Clough, Alexander Eckstein, Harold P. Ford, Angus M. Frazer, James P. Grant, Harold C. Hinton, Donald W. Klein, Ernest W. Lefever, Henry Owen, Dwight H. Perkins, Ralph L. Powell, Lucian W. Pye, Carl Riskin, Thomas W. Robinson, Robert A. Scalapino, Ezra F. Vogel, Allen S. Whiting, and William W. Whitson. The comments of all of them contributed significantly to the study, although none, of course, bears any responsibility for the views expressed in it.

The author would also like to express his gratitude to Susan E. Swannack for assistance of many kinds, including the typing of numerous drafts. The index was prepared by Florence Robinson.

The Institution is indebted to the Ford Foundation for partial support of the study. As in all Brookings books, the views expressed here are those of the author, and should not be ascribed to the Ford Foundation or to the trustees, officers, or other staff members of the Brookings Institution.

KERMIT GORDON
President

October 1973
Washington, D.C.

Author's Preface

IN THE PAST twenty-four years China has experienced one of the greatest revolutions in history, and today, while by no means a superpower, it is clearly a power of first rank that is playing an increasingly important and active role in international affairs. The need for sober, objective analysis of its problems and prospects is especially urgent now, because China is in the midst of an extremely important period of change.

Basically, China today is in a transition period of political reconstruction, adjustment, and preparation between two watershed events, one past and one still to come. Its leadership is still recovering from the trauma of the Cultural Revolution of the 1960s, trying to restore unity at the top level of Party and government and to rebuild its institutions, meanwhile searching for a new balance of domestic political forces and ideological consensus. At the same time, the country is poised in anticipation of the approaching post-Mao succession, which will clearly mark the end of one era and the beginning of another.

How Chinese leaders cope with these difficult challenges will shape both the nature of the Chinese regime and the direction of its domestic and foreign policies in the period ahead. Other nations seeking to deal effectively with China in coming years must base their policies on realistic estimates of the likely direction of political trends. This requires identification of the problems that the Chinese leadership faces, assessment of alternative ways these problems may be handled, and analysis of the possible effects of external events on the policies the Chinese pursue both at home and abroad.

Despite the recent increase of travel to China, the outside world still has relatively little detailed knowledge about the functioning of the country's polity and society. More than most countries, China has projected dramatically conflicting images of "reality" in recent years. Even to the visitor—at least to this writer—the political situation and mood in the country in early 1973 seemed significantly different at different levels of the system.

It is at higher levels in the system that doubts about what the succession may bring are greatest. Among senior officials, there is a subtle but pervasive atmosphere of tentativeness and uncertainty about leaders and institutions in China—even as the regime pursues pragmatic new policies of reconstruction with considerable vigor and seeming self-confidence. Serious conflicts, marked by periodic purges, have continued to plague the top leadership, and the rebuilding of the leadership and the Party and government bureaucracies, so weakened by the Cultural Revolution, is far from complete. Problems continue to plague relations between civilian leaders and the military establishment, and between central and local authorities. The search continues for an effective long-run economic development strategy for China that will take into account both Mao's egalitarian values and the imperatives of growth as seen by many technocratically inclined leaders. Many of the social tensions and conflicts that broke into the open during the Cultural Revolution have left lasting scars, and segments of the elite probably harbor deep resentment about their treatment in recent years. All of these factors constitute a part of the "reality" of the situation in China today.

Yet at the lowest level of society, among ordinary Chinese, the keynote for some time has been a "return to normalcy." The passions and struggles of the Cultural Revolution appear to have been pushed into the background, and at least for the moment the general mood seems to be one of political relaxation. Except in fields that involve China's intellectuals, educators, and cadres still undergoing reform, it is difficult, in fact, for a visitor to China today to find convincing evidence at the "basic" levels of society of drastic or lasting institutional or value changes, of the kind that Mao hoped to achieve by the revolutionary turmoil of 1966–68. In many respects the situation appears to have returned essentially to the status quo ante—that is, to what prevailed in China before 1966. The mass of Chinese workers and peasants are back at work, orderly, disciplined, patient, and purposeful, yet at the same time notably subdued, and they are going about their business in a matter-of-fact fashion, albeit in a society where Spartanism and austerity shape the dominant mood.

Which of these conflicting images should one use as a starting point for attempting to project future developments? Should it be the image of a country with serious leadership problems, struggling to cope with the confused legacy of the Cultural Revolution, and uncertain about the long-term implications of the impending succession, or the image of a nation hard at work, purposeful, and coping with considerable success with many of its immediate problems?

Clearly, both of these faces of reality must be taken into account in any attempt to look ahead. The danger of basing one's estimates solely or even primarily on impressions of observable current conditions and the surface appearance of things is apparent if one looks back at the Chinese regime's history since 1949—and the record of foreign specialists who have attempted to project future trends in China over the years. The regime's performance has been a mixed one of successive ups and downs, accomplishments and setbacks, and successes and failures. Predictions by foreign scholars and journalists of the onset or outcome of these twists and turns have been a good deal less than infallible.

Throughout most of the first decade of Communist rule of China, the regime functioned with impressive effectiveness and made rapid progress toward many of its basic goals. There seemed at that time good reason to believe that the character of the regime and the direction of its policies could be projected fairly far into the future. Then came the Great Leap Forward, Mao's highly personalized response to complex pressures and problems that outside observers poorly understood at the time. During the surge of frenetic activity that took place during the Great Leap, some students of Chinese affairs were skeptical of the regime's claims of accomplishments under Mao's new policies, while others concluded that perhaps China had indeed discovered a new and unique path to extraordinarily rapid development. The post-Leap depression and the severe economic and political crises associated with it quickly made it clear that in this instance the skeptics were right. The fact that China was in deep trouble in the early 1960s was soon evident to everyone.

Few analysts were prescient enough, however, to foresee the next turn of the wheel. Economic recovery after the Great Leap took place more rapidly than most observers expected, but the social and political conflicts that evolved in its aftermath proved to be much deeper and more serious than was generally recognized. These set in motion developments that culminated in the Cultural Revolution, a period of chaotic struggle that no one had predicted. Perhaps the Cultural Revolution was inherently unpredictable, since it was the result not only of problems and conflicts that had been developing for many years but also—in a basic sense—of the responses of one man, Mao Tse-tung, to them. Nevertheless, hindsight suggests that foreign observers would have better understood the dynamics of change in China in those years of rising tension if they had probed more deeply under the regime's rhetoric and surface appearance to analyze the basic political, economic, and social forces at work.

Once the Cultural Revolution was well under way, it became clear that China was experiencing an upheaval that would have a profound impact on the country's political and social order. Once again, however, the ability of outside observers to predict the future proved inadequate. Few specialists on Chinese affairs believed in 1968 that an atmosphere of order, relative "normalcy," and purposeful activity could be restored as rapidly as it has been, especially at the lower levels of society, since 1969.

Perhaps students of China should not be excessively criticized for their shortcomings as prognosticators. Students of other societies—including the United States, about which data are almost unlimited—have not been notably successful in recent years in predicting the future either. In the modern world, the complexities of the political and social forces at work in major nations are so great and the tools of social science used to analyze them still so primitive that anyone attempting to look ahead must frankly acknowledge that in a fundamental sense the future is indeterminate. It is essential, nevertheless, in the search for more rational responses to the forces at work in the contemporary world to attempt to analyze the major factors that will help to shape future developments in China. That is the premise that underlies this study.

My aim in writing this volume has been limited and specific, and perhaps it is wise, here at the start, to define what the study is and what it is not. It is not a broad analysis of all aspects of the Chinese regime, although it does attempt to highlight some of its characteristics as they have undergone change over time. It is not a general history of the past quarter-century of Communist rule in China, although it does examine the recent historical background of the specific questions examined. It is a study that focuses primarily on some of the major problems China faces now and in the period ahead. In treating these problems, I attempt to evaluate the regime's successes as well as its failures. The study is not, fundamentally, a research monograph presenting a large body of new factual data, although it is based on, or takes into account, a great deal of the research done on China by American specialists—including myself—

over the past two decades, as well as facts and impressions that I gathered on a trip to China in 1972–73, my first such trip since I observed the Communist takeover in 1949. (For further details on sources, see the introduction to the Notes, page 334.)

Essentially, the study is an interpretive and analytical essay, focusing on selected problems that will be of crucial importance, in my view, in shaping the overall course of China's development and the character of its policies at home and abroad in the transitional years of the 1970s that lie ahead.

Chapter 1 examines some very broad questions concerning underlying conflicts of values and the problem of institutional stability in China, and provides a context for the analysis of problems in specific areas in the later chapters. Chapter 2 analyzes the political roles of the military and the changing character of civil-military relations. This is an area in which far-reaching changes have occurred since the mid-1960s, and the Chinese leadership's ability to deal with the problems that these changes have created will clearly be a major factor shaping the regime's nature and policies in the future. In Chapter 3, the discussion focuses on the regime's developmental problems and policies and the interrelationships of politics and economics. The extent to which the regime is able to resolve these problems and the economic strategies it pursues will also be determining factors affecting the regime's capacity to achieve its goals both at home and abroad. In Chapter 4, I examine problems related to leadership, authority, and the approaching succession which, as much as anything else perhaps, will be a primary determinant of broad trends in China in the period immediately ahead. In Chapter 5, I discuss China's foreign policy and its interaction with the outside world, and attempt to assess how Peking is likely to act on the international stage in the period ahead. The concluding comments summarize briefly some of the implications I would draw from my findings for U.S. policy toward China.

In attempting to look ahead, I have tried to shed some light on long-term trends, but the specific time span that has concerned me most in this study is the medium-range future—essentially the remainder of the 1970s. In some respects, the time span I have chosen is particularly difficult. An experienced journalist may project current situations and trends ahead for a matter of weeks or months with some degree of confidence—although even such short-term prediction is frequently confounded by sudden and unexpected developments. If one adopts a historian's perspective and looks decades ahead, certain long-run trends and developments can be set down as highly likely. In the case of China, for example, one can assert with considerable confidence that "over the long run," despite ups and downs, the processes of modernization and growth now under way are probably not reversible and in time are likely to result in an increasingly strong, modernized, and developed nation that will play a growing role in world affairs. Moreover, whatever happens in the short run, a number of basic postrevolutionary trends are likely to occur in the long run, including a decline in ideological dogmatism, increased institutionalization, and related changes. But in attempting to look ahead a few years rather than a few weeks or a few decades, it is the ups and downs that are crucial—and it is precisely these medium-range trends that are most difficult to foresee with accuracy.

In undertaking this study, I have not believed that I could or should try to set forth a blueprint of China's course of development in the years immediately ahead. My aim has been much more modest. Above all, I have tried to identify certain major problem areas, define the nature of the problems, and analyze the post-1949 background required to understand them. In relation to certain problems, I have attempted to outline future trends that I believe are most likely, but for others, I have merely set forth a variety of possible developments, examining factors that will help to determine what actually occurs. All projections must be viewed as tentative and subject to revision as events actually unfold. As any serious student of Chinese affairs knows, the one thing that is certain about China is that one must expect the unexpected. The most one can do is estimate, on the basis of present evidence, what seems possible, or in some cases likely, to occur in the future. That is what I have tried to do in this volume in regard to the problems that have been the primary focus of my concern.

It is my hope, nevertheless, that this book will assist the reader seeking to understand the problems China will face in the years of transition and change that lie just ahead.

A. D. B.

October 1973

Contents

I. **Values and Institutions in Crisis**   1

From Consensus to Uncertainty 1
The Future Role of Ideology: Possible Trends 26
The Problem of Institutional Stability 35

II. **The Changing Political Roles of the Military**   67

The Historical Context 68
The Changing Military-Civilian Balance 84
Problems and Tensions within the Military 91
Military Issues and Priorities for the 1970s 109
Probabilities and Uncertainties 113

III. **Strategies for Economic Development**   117

The Major Economic Periods: Shifting Strategies 118
Basic Problems and Issues 129
China's Performance in Quantitative Terms 166
Future Prospects 179

IV. **Problems of Future Leadership**   185

Mao Tse-tung and the Succession Problem 186
Rebuilding the Top Elite 202
The Uncertain Future 242

V. **China and the World**   245

Chinese Foreign Policy, 1949-73 246
Continuing Issues and Persistent Patterns of Behavior 279
Probable Future Trends 300
Continuing Uncertainties 308

VI. **Summary and Implications for U.S. Policy**   316

Implications for U.S. Policy 328

Notes   334

Index   379

Tables

1. *Estimated Economic Performance of China, 1949–71* 168
2. *Estimated Production of Selected Industrial Commodities in China, 1949–70* 174
3. *Production of Selected Industrial Commodities in China during Key Periods* 176
4. *Two Sets of Estimates of China's Grain Output, 1949–71* 177

I

Values and Institutions in Crisis

ANY ATTEMPT to examine future trends in China requires an analysis of many specific military, economic, and leadership problems that will have a crucial impact on the nature of the regime and its policies in the critical transition period ahead. The bulk of this book—in Chapters 2, 3, and 4—will focus on these specific problems. It is not sufficient, however, to deal with economic issues, problems of military-civilian relations, or leadership differences in isolation. They must be assessed in the context of the overall process of political change in China and the continuing search for a viable political order.

Today, in the aftermath of the extraordinary upheaval of the late 1960s called the Cultural Revolution and as the Maoist era draws to its inevitable close, basic questions must be asked about the crisis of both values and institutions that the Chinese political system has experienced in recent years and about the nature and functions of ideology and organization in the period ahead. In late 1973, almost five years after the winding down of the Cultural Revolution and immediately after completion of the Party's Tenth Congress, the effects of the crisis China has been through in the last decade may not seem quite as apparent as they did when the country was in turmoil in the late 1960s. Both the society and the polity appear on the surface to have recovered more rapidly from the nadir of 1967–68 than many observers expected. But the situation is still changing and uncertain, and the regime is still searching for formulas to achieve and maintain genuine ideological consensus and institutional stability in the post-Mao era.

From Consensus to Uncertainty

When the Communist Party achieved power in 1949, its leaders shared a deep-rooted consensus about goals and, in general, how to go about achieving them. Inspired by a strong ideological faith, they were firmly committed to the task of carrying out a far-reaching revolution that would establish a new political system, alter the basic character of Chinese society, develop the economy, and create a strong, modern, socialist nation. They set about doing so in a systematic fashion. Drawing on their own experience in ruling large areas of rural China before 1949 and on the Russians' experience in the Soviet Union, as well as on the concepts of their ideology, they proceeded rapidly and with remarkable success to restructure the institutional basis of the Chinese political system, build an entirely new leadership, and redistribute power in a fundamental fashion. This swift political revolution provided them with the necessary power and the organizational mechanisms to begin remaking Chinese society, through programs aimed at altering the structures of China's social and economic organization, mobilizing the nation's resources for rapid modernization and development, and indoctrinating the Chinese population in order to "remold" their thinking and transform the prevailing patterns of personal motivation and social behavior.

The new political system built by the Communists in the years immediately after 1949 was, like previous Chinese governments, highly authoritarian, hierarchical, and centralized, but in fundamental respects it was vastly different from anything in China's past.[1] It was "totalitarian"—or, to use a term less loaded with debatable semantic content, totalistic—in the sense that it was designed to penetrate and politicize every segment of society, at all levels, in a way that would enable the regime to plan and control all social activities. China's new leaders were fully committed to collectivism, and they systematically proceeded to undermine the old pattern of social institutions, reorganize the population into new social groups subject to close central direction, and subordinate local and individual interests to collectivist goals. To an extent unprecedented in China, the new system was one geared to achieve extensive mass mobilization of the population and political participation by everyone. The leadership was determined to draw the entire population into the political process for the first time and, through mass mobilization techniques, to use all the nation's resources in working toward the regime's principal revolutionary and developmental objectives. Like most modern Chinese leaders who had preceded them, the Communists were motivated by a strong sense of nationalism, and they were committed to building China into a powerful modern nation-state; as they saw it, this required sweeping measures to subordinate particularistic interests to the nation's needs and to harness the energies of the entire population to fulfill China's ambitious national goals.

The new political system built by the Communists was rooted in principles borrowed from the Soviet Union but substantially adapted to fit conditions in China. Leadership was concentrated in a disciplined Party elite, backed by a strong politicized army. The regime claimed, however, to represent a broad "class coalition," and it rapidly involved the "masses" in new institutions designed to ensure intimate contact between the country's elite and China's vast population of peasants and workers.

The speed with which the Communists were able to build a strong and effective new political system based on Marxist-Leninist principles was impressive. In view of the enormous size of China's territory and population, it constituted one of the most remarkable political achievements of any group of revolutionary leaders in history, testifying both to the power of the Communists' ideology and to the effectiveness of their organizational principles and skills. Within less than a decade after achieving power, they had made an indelible imprint on China. Their early accomplishments altered the fundamental nature of politics and the fabric of social and economic life in ways that were both far-reaching and, in many respects, certain to be permanent. Whatever happened in the future, there could be no simple reversion to the past or any restoration of the status quo ante. This is still a valid assessment despite all the uncertainties created by some dramatic shifts of course in recent years. For the foreseeable future, China will almost certainly have a Communist political system, led by men who, despite many differences, share a commitment to totalistic, collectivist, mobilizational, and nationalistic goals.

What is not clear, in the light of recent developments, is precisely what kind of Communist system China is likely to have in the future, what priority values will move its leaders, and what institutional changes are yet in store. One fundamental cause of this uncertainty is the major— even if only temporary—breakdown of the system during 1966–68. For a time during the height of the Cultural Revolution, China seemed to be in almost total disarray. Political reconstruction has come a long way since 1968, but China is still living with the legacy of that upheaval, and the problem now is to try to assess the extent to which the pattern that existed before the Cultural Revolution is reemerging or the extent to which recent developments will result in important and lasting changes. This is extremely difficult to judge, in part because the situation in China is still highly fluid and in part because of the coming succession. Nevertheless, both past developments and current trends provide important clues about the future.

Revolutionary Theory and Practical Problems

A basic problem faced by any ideologically motivated group of leaders is how to translate theory into practice—how to apply ideology to particular problems. The link between ideology and policy is a subtle one. Ideology defines certain general values and goals, ways of analyzing situations, and methods of approaching problems. It sets parameters to the range of acceptable policy choices. But it does not provide concrete answers to specific issues at any particular time. Even men sharing common ideological beliefs obviously can and do differ greatly in their policy prescriptions.

Policy preferences are influenced by a myriad of factors. The experience, roles, and personal predilections of particular policy makers affect them. So too do the institutional, local, and other interests that they represent. Yet Marxist-Leninist ideology demands that there be only one "correct" view on major policy issues at any particular time. Once a "correct" policy is defined for a given period, all others are "deviationist," and are generally labeled either "leftist" or "rightist."

There is always the danger that major differences on specific policy problems will be transformed into ideological conflict, but so long as there is a reasonably broad consensus on policy questions—which tends to be the case when a regime's policies appear to be successful in achieving the leadership's goals—ideological strains can usually be contained. When policy differences grow and then power conflicts emerge, however, these frequently become associated with ideological conflicts. This is precisely what occurred within the Chinese leadership between the mid-1950s and the mid-1960s.

Although one cannot understand the course of events in China in recent years without reference to basic conflicts of values, it is no simple matter to relate these to broad political trends, or even to analyze the value conflicts in clear and unambiguous terms. If there had been open ideological debate in China, involving clear-cut doctrinal positions, the problem of analyzing value conflicts and their political effects would be easier, but there was no such debate.

By the time the Cultural Revolution had erupted, Maoist ideologues were describing the conflict in terms of a struggle between "two lines"—a dichotomy between "true Marxist-Leninists" loyal to Mao and those allegedly supporting a "capitalist road," a category into which all who questioned Mao's judgment were lumped. The ideological "debate," however, consisted solely of Maoist propaganda glorifying the infallibility of China's supreme leader and bitter attacks against any sign of dissent or deviation. Lacking access to the apparatus of mass communication, Mao's opponents were given no opportunity publicly to rebut the attacks made against them.

When the Maoists asserted that the struggle in China was between "two lines"—a struggle that allegedly had crystallized as early as the 1950s—they seriously distorted the realities of the situation. In fact, until Mao and his supporters chose to define the struggle in dichotomous terms and stressed the polarization between "two lines," the conflicts within the Chinese leadership, whether over military, economic, or other issues, were not for the most part based on fundamental ideological differences. Not only did China's leaders share a strong common faith in the basic doctrines of Marxism-Leninism, most of them were also prepared from the 1940s on to acknowledge that Mao was China's most authoritative interpreter of doctrinal questions.[2] When significant policy differences eventually and inevitably began to emerge, they first developed over concrete policy questions, not broad questions of values and goals.[3] For the most part, these differences concerned immediate and short-term problems—what priorities to give to various objectives, how fast the pace of change should be in a given area, what institutional changes were desirable, how existing resources should be allocated. Differences were shaped by the particular roles played by individual leaders and the responsibilities they carried, their institutional interests, their power bases, their personal ties and group affiliations, and, not least important, their personal styles and idiosyncrasies.

Over time, however, the range of policy differences affecting virtually all policy fields gradually widened. This was in part a result of the increased difficulty encountered in solving actual economic, social, and political problems, and in part a consequence of the increasing complexity of the bureaucratic structure of the regime. The more deeply the regime became involved in modernization and development, the less clear it was that there were any unchallengeable answers to the nation's problems. And the steady differentiation of roles, division of labor, and specialization of tasks within the leadership inevitably increased the range of perspectives and differences over priorities and policies.

As divisions multiplied and deepened in leadership councils, Mao showed an increasing propensity to initiate dramatic and "radical" policy innovations of his own to attack the nation's problems. As will be discussed further in Chapter 4, the uniqueness of Mao's outlook, as well as his position at the pinnacle of authority in China, had increasingly set him apart from the rest of the leadership. He held the power to make ultimate decisions, and he made them, but he became less and less involved in the regime's day-to-day operations and less able or inclined to manage its burgeoning bureaucracies. China's other senior leaders assumed primary responsibility for the actual functioning of most of China's institutions dealing with specific sectors of the society.[4]

The gap between Mao and the top bureaucratic leaders of the regime widened from the late 1950s on, and it was the events associated with Mao's Great Leap Forward and Commune program (and the depression and crisis they produced) that first highlighted the relationship between specific policy differences and deeper schisms over broad development strategy. Thereafter, specific differences over policy gradually led to ideological polarization and power conflicts which culminated in the Cultural Revolution.

The Clash of the "Two Lines"

This does not mean that the fundamental causes of the Cultural Revolution were essentially ideological. That is too simple an explanation. It is extremely difficult, in fact, to link cause and effect in the chain of events that led to the Cultural Revolution crisis. It was the end result of a complex social process "caused" by many factors: basic socioeconomic and political trends in China, underlying tensions in society, leadership failures, policy disputes, power struggles, and personality clashes, as well as accidents of history.[5]

Viewed in these terms, China's crisis in the late 1960s must be traced to varied problems that began to emerge at least by the middle or late 1950s.[6] Some were the result of the fundamental intractability of the social and economic conditions with which the leadership had to deal in trying to revolutionize and develop such a huge, complex, and tradition-rooted society. Others were the almost inevitable result of the steady growth in the size and functions of the regime's bureaucracies.

Still others did, however, reflect conflicts between revolutionary values and competing priorities.

After the initial period of rapid revolutionary change, despite the remarkable changes that had taken place, some traditional attitudes and patterns of Chinese behavior gradually reemerged. The modernizing process itself created new groups whose attitudes diverged, and this began to alter the nature of the regime and the society in disturbing ways. For reasons to be discussed in Chapter 3, the prospects for sustained economic growth became increasingly problematic toward the end of the first Plan period (1953–57), and economic dilemmas were high on the list of problems preoccupying China's leaders. The steady growth of bureaucratism as the huge apparatus of the regime grew more and more complex, the emergence of complicated new patterns of social stratification,[7] and the appearance of elitism in various guises created new problems for the revolutionary regime. To some leaders in Peking, the Party's cadres appeared to be developing into a dominant "new class." Economic development and modernization programs encouraged trends toward increased specialization and professionalism among the elite, and these trends seemed to Mao and others to be weakening the commitment of Party cadres to broad revolutionary goals. As the complexities of the regime's bureaucratic structures increased, so too did tendencies to promote particularistic and parochial interests. Bureaucratic politics became increasingly complex.[8] In the regime's first years in power, there had been great social mobility, but as time went on those in power clung to their positions; there was a disturbing decline in opportunities for upward social mobility, and little infusion of new blood occurred at higher levels. As the years went by, moreover, signs of dissatisfaction and alienation were evident among intellectuals and youth resentful of restrictive bureaucratic controls. Age-old problems created by the wide urban-rural gap in China persisted, despite all efforts to solve them.

Ideologically, there was clearly a decline in revolutionary fervor and a tendency toward ritualized behavior rather than dedicated pursuit of the regime's long-term goals. As Mao himself put it as early as 1957, "It seems as if Marxism that was once all the rage [in China] is not so much in fashion now."[9]

All these problems contributed to the process that led to the Cultural Revolution, but they alone do not explain the nature of the crisis that ultimately occurred. If China's leaders had remained united in their general outlook and had agreed on ways to adapt and modify their policies to cope with changing conditions, the course of events might have been very different. The crisis of the late 1960s resulted, fundamentally, from the leadership's inability to agree on ways to adapt the regime's policies to meet new problems. It was the steady erosion of unity that finally led to open policy splits and bitter power struggles, and ultimately to the temporary political breakdown of 1966–68.

In a sense, in fact, the Cultural Revolution can be viewed as the outcome of a violent clash between the unique revolutionary vision of one man, Mao Tse-tung, and the predispositions and views of the majority of the Party's other top leaders. Mao himself was responsible to a considerable degree for the polarization between "two lines." He insisted on the correctness of his views, and it was the radical actions he took to impose his values on the regime and society that caused an explosive polarization of the leadership.[10] Without Mao, China probably would not have experienced the kind of crisis the Cultural Revolution produced.

In a literal sense, of course, no one man can move a nation as large as China. Mao could not have survived if he had not been able to mobilize significant support. By the mid-1960s, however, he no longer represented the common will of a united leadership; instead, he found himself in the minority. He was nevertheless determined, and able, to impose his views on those Party leaders who disagreed with him.[11] When he did, his enormous prestige as the supreme leader of the revolution, reinforced by the success he achieved in obtaining army support and in mobilizing the nation's urban youth against the established bureaucracies, enabled him to launch the Cultural Revolution and to oust his principal enemies. But his ability to control the nature and consequences of the struggle was limited.

Basic Maoist Values

What have been the essential differences in ideological values and priorities that have divided China's leaders over the years and caused what the Maoists have labeled "the struggle between two lines"? What have the Maoists regarded as their "true Marxist-Leninist" line?[12]

Many labels have been used to characterize Mao's strategy of revolutionary development and the basic assumptions, predispositions, values, and goals that presumably have motivated his actions. All involve great oversimplification, and none is therefore wholly satisfactory. Yet most of them have a certain validity. Terms such as revolutionary nationalism, idealism, radicalism, romanticism, populism, and egalitarianism highlight distinctive characteristics of his thought, but each of these labels is also misleading in some respects when applied to Mao.

Perhaps the best word to use, in this discussion, is simply the term "Maoist."[13] One must immediately point out, however, that the ideas one can legitimately call "Maoist" have not been Mao's alone; others have contributed to and helped to articulate them. Moreover, Mao himself has not always been consistent, and at times—including the most recent period, since 1969—it would appear that he himself has not been an undeviating Maoist in the sense that he has endorsed or at least tolerated policies shaped by values other than those most commonly associated with his name. Nevertheless, one can identify a special set of interrelated values that help to explain the character of such unique Maoist phenomena as the Great Leap and the Cultural Revolution and that can be regarded as the essence of what is generally considered to be Maoism.

One fundamental concept in the Maoist approach to China's problems has been that of "uninterrupted revolution."[14] Chinese theoretical writings have tried to resolve an intellectual problem long debated by Marxist-Leninists by asserting that revolution can and should be *both* "uninterrupted" and "by stages." While prepared to acknowledge that revolution must proceed by stages, the Maoists in practice have insisted that everything possible should be done to promote rapid and continuous change, to combat tendencies toward retreat or backsliding, and to sustain revolutionary momentum. Repeatedly, the Maoists have pushed for radical change—and dramatic leaps forward—to spur both economic development and institutional and "cultural" change. They have usually viewed with deep suspicion compromise policies calling for more gradual incremental change or "realistic" accommodation to intractable problems.

Mao's approach to China's problems has been strongly rooted in dialectical thinking. The Marxist-Leninist concept of "contradictions,"[15] which he reinterpreted and modified in the 1950s to suit his own purposes, has been fundamental to his view of the entire revolutionary process. All reality, Mao has asserted, is rooted in conflict between opposing forces—expressed, above all, in society, in class struggle—and the problem for revolutionary leaders is to understand these contradictions correctly, to identify those that should be viewed as the "principal" ones at any time, and then to manipulate existing contradictions successfully to foster continuous change. These contradictions, Mao insists, constitute a permanent feature of society, destined to continue even after socialism and communism have been achieved.

On a theoretical level, Mao's contribution to the concept of contradictions lies in the special stress he has placed on differences between "antagonistic" contradictions (i.e., basic social conflicts that require coercion to defeat the "enemies" of the revolution) and contradictions "among the people" (which are less serious and should be resolved by nonviolent methods of persuasion and "thought reform"). This distinction helps to explain his persistent attempts to differentiate between clear-cut enemies, who should be openly attacked, and misguided individuals and groups, who can and should be ideologically "remolded."

Mao's stress on the crucial role of contradictions in society has also led him to act on the premise that a state of continuing dynamic tension in society is both necessary and desirable in order to sustain "uninterrupted revolution." He has viewed with great concern any tendencies on the part of others to relax, to moderate the intensity of class struggle, or to blur distinctions between competing groups and ideas. In the past, he has generally opposed, therefore, policies that place primary emphasis on conciliation, the achievement of consensus through compromise, and the traditional Chinese impulse to stress harmony in social relations. He has tended to regard such tendencies as dangerous signs of a decline of revolutionary commitment and fervor that could lead only to retrogression and a loss of revolutionary momentum.

Another crucial element in Mao's revolutionary outlook has been his faith in the potentiality of the masses, which has been one of the most distinctive and important features of his approach to China's problems. Mao has not merely given lip-service to the idea that the masses constitute the principal motive force of history; he has insisted that actual policy be based on this faith. His "mass line,"[16] summed up in the phrase "from the masses, to the masses," has glorified the virtues (collective, not individual) of the common man, and he has argued that the masses should be directly involved in every aspect of the political process.

Mao has also been labeled a "populist," and for good reasons.[17] His rural orientation and primary focus on the historical role of China's peasants, his faith in the wisdom and potential of the masses in general, his emphasis on the need to stimulate initiative and spontaneity in every citizen, and his distrust of bureaucrats, technocrats, intellectuals, urbanites, and elite groups generally have all reflected, in different ways, an outlook that can legitimately be termed populist.

Mao has also placed great stress on "voluntarism"[18]—on the belief that sheer human will and determination can move mountains, overcome all obstacles, and mold the course of history. Men, he has repeatedly proclaimed, are more important than machines, weapons, special expertise, or "techniques." Human will is the key to progress, and the masses—the common man—acting collectively, can accomplish miracles if properly motivated and inspired.

In the light of these "populist" and "voluntarist" predispositions, it is not surprising that, in organizational terms, Mao has put his faith above all in mass mobilization techniques rather than in regularized bureaucratic administration. The most effective way both to revolutionize and to develop society, as he has seen it, is through massive mobilizational "movements" or "campaigns," not through rationalized, routinized bureaucratic institutions and techniques.

This does not mean that Mao has been antiorganizational. In some respects, he has been what one writer has called a "natural Leninist,"[19] with a genius for creating new types of mass organization and devising new techniques of mass mobilization. Because he has been strongly antibureaucratic in his basic outlook, however, one can legitimately describe Mao as anti-institutional. He has feared—not without justification—that stable institutions tend to foster elitism and support a new status quo rather than serve as instruments of continuing change. Consequently, whenever he has believed that institutions were settling into regularized, routinized patterns of organizational behavior, he has favored shaking them up. The tendency of large institutions to become "bureaucratic"—in the pejorative sense—has also been regarded by Mao as anathema. He has repeatedly initiated steps to combat institutional complacency and—as was dramatically indicated during the Great Leap and Commune period—has periodically favored radical experiments to promote continuing institutional change, to try to ensure that existing institutions will be responsive to the leadership's goals and will serve as effective instruments for revolutionary change.

Mao's disillusionment with trends toward increased bureaucratism developed into something close to an obsession in the early 1960s. In part, this was due to his growing differences with the Party leaders who actually ran China's bureaucracies and to his inability to control and use the bureaucracies for his purposes. The obsession was also fed by the Sino-Soviet split and Mao's belief that, unless effective steps were taken to halt existing trends, Chinese society would become "degenerate"—as he maintained Soviet society already had.[20] He believed profoundly that the growing size and rigidity he observed in the bureaucracies of both Party and government would gradually subvert his basic revolutionary ideals.

One of the most eloquent and damning Maoist indictments of China's bureaucrats is contained in a Cultural Revolution document that purported to summarize the Chairman's views on "twenty manifestations of bureaucracy in China."[21] Whether or not this document actually originated with Mao himself, it almost certainly reflected the kind of views he held that, by this time, had moved him to unleash a major political assault on China's established bureaucracies.

The document asserted that China's bureaucrats "are divorced from reality, from the masses, and from the leadership of the Party." It inveighed against "authoritarian bureaucracy" (run by bureaucrats who "force orders" and "maintain blind control"), "brainless, misdirected bureaucracy" (led by men guilty of "routinism"), "bureaucracy of the overlords" (in which "egoistic" bureaucrats "cause people to become afraid"), "dishonest bureaucracy" (in which cadres try to "deceive those above them and fool those below them"), "irresponsible bureaucracy" (staffed by people who "push things off onto others"), and "the bureaucracy of those who work as officials" (rather than as revolutionaries).

The document also attacked the "bureaucracy of government offices" ("offices grow bigger and bigger" and "there are more people than there are jobs"); the "bureaucracy of red tape and formalism" (staffed by cadres preoccupied with "documents" and "meetings"); and the "bureaucracy for the exceptional" (in which the tendency is to "engage in back door deals; one person becomes an official and the entire family benefits"). Finally, China's bureaucrats were accused of building a "disunited bureaucracy" ("a plural leadership cannot be harmoniously united"; they "try to crowd each other out"), a "sectarian bureaucracy" (whose members "engage in factionalism" and "form cliques"), a "degenerate bureaucracy" (in which cadres "worry about their individual interests" but "do not worry whatsoever about the national interest"), and a "bureaucracy of erroneous tendencies and reaction" (led by men who "do not differentiate between the enemy and ourselves").

Mao and his supporters clearly exaggerated the bureaucratic evils in China in the period before the Cultural Revolution in order to attack their enemies, but there is no question that strong and genuine feelings of antibureaucratism and antielitism—and a strong positive commitment to egalitarianism—lay behind many of Mao's policies. By the time of the Cultural Revolution, he not only attempted to bypass and then partially dismantle the established bureaucracies; he stressed the need for a direct link between himself and China's "masses." For a brief time, in fact, there appeared to be an element of anarchist thinking in his emphasis on the need to stimulate "spontaneous" mass action and abandon hierarchical organizational patterns in order to overcome the conservative inertia associated with established bureaucratic institutions.[22]

The Cultural Revolution highlighted another important facet of Mao's thinking that was deeply rooted in his earlier revolutionary experience. Despite his belief that institutional change is a necessary part of the revolutionary process, Mao has long been convinced that the real key to successful revolution is a spiritual transformation of values, a revolution in men's minds.[23] Creating "new socialist men" is even more important than building new social institutions, although of course the two tasks are linked. Some would argue that Mao has turned traditional Marxism-Leninism on its head. Marx, and most subsequent classical Marxist-Leninist ideologues, asserted that human values are fundamentally shaped by the nature of the social base of society, and that revolutionizing society's institutions, modes of production, and patterns of social relations is a prerequisite to lasting change in "the superstructure" of society.

As the revolutionary process unfolded in China, Mao seemed increasingly to believe that priority must be given to "revolutionizing" the "superstructure" of society—the creation of a new political "culture." Perhaps this derived in part from his realization that even such far-reaching institutional changes as those involved in collectivization, socialization, and even communization had not suddenly or completely transformed old patterns of thought and motivation. Mao has therefore devoted primary attention to propaganda and indoctrination, and to revolutionizing education and the arts, with the aim of changing basic values. In his view, "politics," not economics, must be "in command," and the inculcation of a new ideology and new values in the entire population must be given the highest possible priority.

By the late 1960s, Mao was quite prepared to disrupt the normal functioning of China's political institutions as well as its economy if this could help to revolutionize values and to create new attitudes. These were the primary aims of the new political programs he pushed at that time—first in the "Socialist Education Campaign" begun in 1963, and then in the Cultural Revolution. As Mao saw it, although China's institutions had been revolutionized, the attitudes of the population— both leaders and led—had not. The crucial arena of conflict now, therefore, was in the realm of ideas, and the need was to embed firmly in the thinking of all Chinese the essential values required for a genuinely revolutionary sense of morality and ethics.

The slogan that in some respects best sums up Mao's conception of the essence of the revolutionary morality and ethics needed in China is "serve the people."[24] For a nation to be genuinely revolutionary, Mao believes, each citizen must be willing to subordinate self to the collective good. The people must be activist, wholly dedicated, and willing to make any sacrifice for the revolutionary cause. Like good soldiers (whom Mao has repeatedly held up as models for society as a whole), the citizenry must, at one and the same time, observe discipline, show initiative, be fearless, and act with selfless dedication to the common goals of society as defined by society's top leaders.

The values that have been at the heart of Mao's conception of revolutionary morality, therefore, have been unselfishness, activism, and egalitarianism. Since the root of exploitation is selfishness, everyone in a revolutionary society must subordinate individual desires to collective goals; compromise with selfish goals can only lead to dangerous bourgeois and capitalist tendencies. Passivity and inertia are equally dangerous; everyone must work hard and participate. And since it is only when a society realizes genuine egalitarianism, in both thought and behavior, that it can be said to have really accomplished its revolutionary goals, every sign of special privilege and elitism must be opposed.

If one understands the intensity of Mao's dedication to populist, egalitarian, antielitist, and antibureaucratic values, the basis for many of his other economic views and policy preferences—and prejudices—

becomes clear. He has consistently been uneasy about economic incentives because of his belief that men should be motivated by ideology and not material gain; the problem is how to inspire dedicated work primarily by the use of nonmaterial incentives. He has repeatedly, and increasingly, shown strong biases against professionals and specialists, against intellectuals in an even broader sense, and against urbanism as a general phenomenon.[25]

Mao obviously has recognized the need for technical expertise in modernizing China, the crucial role that intellectuals play in shaping a society's values, and the great importance of urban centers in nations undergoing rapid development. At the same time, he has feared that growing professionalization and specialization would endanger the egalitarian values that he has believed to be essential for a genuinely revolutionary society. In his view, too many of China's intellectuals have persistently clung to individualistic and "bourgeois" values that must be eradicated. And he has felt that the predisposition of many Chinese leaders to stress urban development has tended to perpetuate a serious urban-rural gap, thereby endangering many of his basic populist goals. Mao has repeatedly insisted that the regime must take vigorous steps—including intensive reindoctrination of all elite groups, universal participation in manual labor, the transfer of educated persons from cities to the countryside, and emphasis on development of health, education, and other services in rural rather than urban areas—that break down the barriers between intellectual activity and physical labor and narrow the gap between city and country dwellers. Goals such as these, rooted in his particular mix of revolutionary values and reflecting his special vision of the good society, have been basic to the Maoist strategy of revolutionary development.

"Non-Maoist" Values

If these are some of the distinctive values characterizing Mao's Thought, how should one characterize the values of those Chinese leaders who have disagreed with him? Difficult as it is to apply simple labels to Mao, it is even more so in the case of his opponents. The term "anti-Maoist" is not valid. While the ultimate victims of Mao's purges have been men who have opposed him politically, few of them really challenged Mao's ideological values openly. In one sense, all of China's leaders since 1949 have been, at least in some degree, Maoist. Many of them have been "non-Maoist," however, in the sense that they

have seriously questioned the priority Mao has often given to certain
of his values and the way he has tried to achieve his goals. Non-Maoists
have tended to give high priority to certain values that Mao has been
inclined to deemphasize or denigrate.[26]

Many different kinds of leaders in China have been non-Maoist in
this sense. They have included members of such diverse groups as the
"organization men" in the Party who have exercised operational control of the regime's major institutional hierarchies, both civilian and
military, and the economic planners, managers, scientists, and technocrats who have borne the main responsibility for managing the nation's
economic affairs. They have also included many writers, artists, and
other intellectuals who have persistently sought (within the framework
of Marxist-Leninist ideology) for greater recognition of the importance of individual creativity and have resisted the regime's demands
that individual talent be subject to rigid controls designed to ensure
total conformity to Maoist values.[27]

Men of such diverse types have by no means held identical views, of
course, or even shared a single set of non-Maoist values.[28] Some have
been motivated primarily by what might best be labeled the Party's
"organizational ethic," which has stressed the need to build strong and
stable bureaucratic institutions. Others have been strongly motivated
by the "ethic of professionalism," which emphasizes the importance of
values and standards associated with professional competence and
scientific and technological expertise in particular fields. In varying degrees, many Chinese doubtless have—as the Maoists have charged—
clung to certain old patterns of thought, both traditional and bourgeois,
inherited from the past. In sum, the mix of values motivating different
non-Maoist individuals and groups has varied greatly, and when they
have favored strategies and policies different from Mao's, the reasons
have been diverse. Nevertheless, it is possible to identify certain values,
which can be labeled "non-Maoist," that have characterized the opposition to Mao.

In general, the men who have been the targets of Mao's attacks have
favored, at least in comparison to Mao, a relatively gradual and incremental approach to revolutionary development. They have questioned,
and sometimes they have clearly opposed, Mao's propensity to move
China forward by initiating "radical" policy innovations and by intro-
ducing dramatic institutional changes. In the view of some of them,
Mao's attempts to foster rapid change through sudden "leaps" have

created at least as many problems as they have solved.[29] In contrast to Mao, they have tended to stress the need for more orderly, cautious, and gradual policies of development, and to favor policies that would consolidate accomplishments at each stage before pushing for further change.

As good Marxist-Leninists, as most of them have been, they have not denied the validity of the dialectical approach to revolution or the need to analyze the contradictions in society and base the regime's policy on such analysis, but some of them have argued—for example, in the period following the completion of collectivization and socialization—that because the basic struggle between "socialism" and "capitalism" in China has been essentially won, the regime's policies should no longer be designed to maintain a high degree of social tension in society but should deemphasize class struggle and try to harmonize social relations to a greater extent.[30]

Many non-Maoists, especially those most directly responsible for managing China's economy, have been inclined to put economics, not politics, in command. They have accorded high priority to the goal of increased production—that is, to economic growth as such—and have been less concerned than Mao with possible side effects that might compromise egalitarian values; their tendency, therefore, has been to judge a policy primarily on the basis of the extent to which it is likely to spur growth rather than its potential for transforming people's attitudes.

Many Chinese leaders have been less "populist" than Mao and less strongly motivated by faith in the potentialities of the masses. While supporting the basic concepts inherent in Mao's "mass line," China's bureaucratic leaders have been preoccupied with strengthening the regime's bureaucratic institutions. They have placed their faith in regularized administrative approaches rather than mass mobilization to achieve the regime's basic goals. This is not to say that they have been unaware of the problems of bureaucratism and elitism; they clearly have been, and have adopted many measures to combat them. Nevertheless, most of the leading non-Maoists, who themselves have been powerful bureaucratic leaders, have never lost faith, as Mao obviously did in the 1960s, in the capacity of China's established institutions to manage the revolutionary process.

Virtually all of China's bureaucratic leaders seem to have shared Mao's view that the maintenance of ideological orthodoxy is important, and that to this end continuous and intensive indoctrination of both the elite and the mass of the population is essential. But many non-Maoists have had less confidence than Mao that a basic spiritual transformation, which would revolutionize the nation's values, can be rapidly accomplished in a country whose traditions reach as far into the past as China's. They have often been predisposed, therefore, to give a lesser priority to ideology per se and a higher priority to practical steps designed to increase the efficiency of China's institutions, mobilize the country's resources, increase production, and promote growth. In short, their approach has tended to be more pragmatic and empirical than Mao's. They have generally put a greater stress than he has on the importance of concrete material incentives to spur the population to work hard and efficiently. Technical and professional competence has rated high in their scale of values, and they have been predisposed to give fairly high priority to the fostering and rewarding of specialized knowledge and skills.

In sum, they have tended to stress the crucial importance of "expertise" even at the expense of "redness," or ideological purity. They have positively favored rather than opposed the values embodied in the "professional ethic," accepting that the price for this might be a society that is less egalitarian and more elitist than the Maoist ideal. Nor have they shared—at least not with Mao's intensity—the Maoist bias against cities; their tendency, in fact, has been to place high priority on urban industrialization in the quest for rapid economic growth.

To oversimplify, the non-Maoists, in contrast to Mao, have tended to stress economics over politics, the growth of production over the transformation of values, professional technocratic competence over egalitarian goals, material rather than ideological incentives, institutional rather than mass mobilization approaches, and orderly incremental change in preference to dramatic sudden leaps. They have usually been more willing than the Maoists to compromise when the regime has encountered serious obstacles and more predisposed to adjust their goals to intractable social realities. In this sense, they have generally been less visionary and more empirical, pragmatic, and "realistic" than Mao. It is probably correct in many respects to say, as the Maoists have repeatedly asserted, that the non-Maoists have been less "revolutionary" than Mao, at least in purist Maoist terms. While the non-Maoists have focused their attention on solving short-range, concrete problems, Mao's overriding concern has been the pursuit of broad and long-term revolutionary goals. And while Mao's inclination has been to insist that what is desirable in order to achieve the good society in the long run must be made to work in the short run, the non-Maoists have implicitly argued that if a particular approach is workable today and contributes to both growth and stability it is good, even if it requires some compromises in terms of ultimate goals.

Modernization and Revolutionary Change

The conflicts over values in China ultimately came to reflect broad differences in outlook toward the basic problems of modernization. All of China's Communist leaders have been strongly committed to the achievement of political and economic modernization as well as social revolution. But they have differed on the strategies China should pursue to achieve both modernization and revolution, and also on the relative priorities of modernization and revolutionary social change. Whereas the Maoists have tended to give priority to revolutionary change designed to achieve the goal of a highly egalitarian "just society," many leaders have tended to give priority to less ideological goals—especially economic growth—similar in many respects to those of other already-developed or developing societies, both Communist and non-Communist. The Maoists have deliberately attempted to avoid many of the consequences of modernization in other countries—including large-scale urbanization, mushrooming bureaucracies, specialization, increased group differentiation, bureaucratic or professional elitism, and the tendency to stress secular values rather than ideology per se—because they have believed these developments would compromise fundamental Maoist revolutionary values. In contrast, the non-Maoists have been much more inclined to accept such trends, perhaps because they may have viewed them as intrinsic and unavoidable aspects of the modernization process.

An intriguing parallel can be drawn between Mao's dilemma and that of China's nineteenth century leaders who wrestled with the problem of how to borrow needed technical knowledge from the outside world without compromising the basic values inherent in traditional Chinese culture. Many of China's nineteenth century reformers proceeded on the assumption that, while it was necessary to borrow utilitarian practical learning (*yung*) from the West, it was important to preserve the essential values (*t'i*) embodied in Confucianism.[31] Their goal was to obtain the results of the modern scientific and technical revolution without accepting the intellectual and social underpinnings of modernization in the West.

In a somewhat analogous fashion, Mao has argued that China's scientific and technical modernization can and should be carried out without compromising the essential ideological and social values of Marxism-Leninism in its Maoist form. He made this explicit in a particularly interesting statement to a Party meeting in December 1965 in which he referred directly to the parallel between China's post-1949 problems and the problems faced by China's nineteenth century reformers:[32] "Toward the end of the Ch'ing Dynasty, some people advocated 'Chinese learning for substance and Western learning for application.' 'Substance' is like our general line which cannot be changed. The 'substance' of Western learning cannot be applied . . . only the techniques of the West can be applied." What he was arguing, in effect, was that the modernization of China must take place within the context of China's new revolutionary culture and that, while it is necessary to develop modern science, technology, and industry, it is equally vital to ensure the integrity of China's Marxist-Leninist-Maoist "general line" and to oppose many of the intellectual and social changes associated with modernization elsewhere, both in bourgeois Western societies and in "revisionist" Communist nations such as the USSR.

The Changing Role of Ideology

To simplify matters, the discussion above has treated the value conflicts underlying the political conflicts in China in recent years in terms of distinctive Maoist and non-Maoist outlooks held by opposing individuals and groups. In reality, however, these conflicts have existed to a greater or lesser degree in the minds of most Chinese leaders. As indicated earlier, China's non-Maoist leaders at times have been Maoist in their approach to many problems, and even Mao has been non-Maoist at times.[33] The question that each leader—as well as the leadership as a whole—has had to face in approaching specific problems has been how best to balance the demands of conflicting values, in particular how much stress to place on ideology and rapid revolutionary social change or on pragmatic problem solving and more orderly, incremental development.

During the Cultural Revolution, the propaganda campaign to promote Maoist values reached an unprecedented intensity, and all competing values were bitterly attacked. In ideological as well as power terms, it appeared at the time that Mao had won an unqualified victory. And yet in retrospect it seems fairly clear that the gap between ideology and policy widened between 1966 and 1968. In certain fields—above all, education and culture—the immediate impact of Maoist concepts on policy was very great during the Cultural Revolution. But in the field of economic policy, Mao and his followers did not seriously attempt to introduce radical policy changes of the kind that Maoist values had inspired a decade earlier, during the Great Leap Forward. Despite the rhetoric of radicalism, the regime did not reduce material incentives to any significant extent, did not reorganize institutions at the "basic" level (for example, at the Commune level) to conform to purist Maoist concepts, and did not initiate any great new economic mobilization effort to produce a new "leap." This led some foreign students of Chinese affairs—especially in Japan—to assert that, despite the glorification of Maoist values, China's concrete policies during the Cultural Revolution represented not Maoism but "Liuism without Liu." While this overstated the case, it did contain an important element of truth. The fact that Mao's main concerns now focused on ideology and politics rather than on economics or other fields may help to explain his tolerance of many "Liuist" policies dating to the 1960s, but the explanation doubtless also lay in his inability to translate his values into concrete policies in many fields.

The role of ideology in China underwent subtle but significant changes during the Cultural Revolution period. Although the importance of ideology was stressed perhaps even more than before, its relevance as a guide to policy appeared to decline significantly. The prime functions of ideology during the Cultural Revolution were several. Perhaps most important, it was an instrument used to bolster the cult of Mao in an extreme form; both Mao and his Thought were portrayed as infallible and unchallengeable. Secondly, profession of belief in Maoist values became a basic loyalty test in the complex political struggles of the time. How effective a test it was in practice, however, is arguable, since virtually everyone in China, whatever his real views, claimed to be a good Maoist. Instead of clarifying differences of outlook, the pressure to give verbal support to the Thought of Mao sometimes simply obscured and blurred genuine value conflicts. And for the ordinary Chinese, the prime function of ideology now appeared to be simply that of defining basic standards of revolutionary ethics and public morality. Much of the content of the "little red book," *Quotations from Chairman Mao Tse-tung,* which purported to distill the essence of Maoist Thought, consisted of pithy aphorisms defining rules for proper social conduct. This small volume became the basic catechism for promoting Maoism as a secular religion.

From the Cultural Revolution to the Tenth Congress

Mao's effort in the Cultural Revolution to assert his personal power and vision, shake up China's bureaucracies, and revitalize the nation's revolutionary values resulted in a shattering of the leadership's unity. Not only were a large number of the top Party and government bureaucrats who had guided the country during the regime's first decade and a half in power purged; in effect, there was a temporary breakdown of the political system and a dramatic shift in the internal balance of power in favor of the military.

The first major attempt to restore national cohesion occurred at the Ninth Party Congress in 1969. Minister of National Defense Lin Piao, who had provided Mao with crucial military backing during the Cultural Revolution, was officially designated as the Party's only Vice Chairman and Mao's successor, and the new Central Committee and Politburo selected at that time gave overwhelming predominance to the military. The weakened Party and government bureaucracies were badly underrepresented. Lin's political report to the Ninth Congress formally endorsed Mao's general Party line and his revolutionary values, but it was extremely vague about the concrete policies that the Party was to pursue, and in reality a swing of the pendulum was already under way, with Premier Chou En-lai gradually leading the regime toward more pragmatic and moderate policies both at home and abroad.

The attempt of the Ninth Congress to consolidate a new leadership and achieve a new national consensus regarding the road China should now follow was a failure. Intense factional strife continued, and by 1971 the shaky balance at the center had broken down. Lin Piao's death, allegedly while fleeing China after an abortive coup against Mao, and the purge of most of the top military men on the Politburo in 1971 were followed by another widespread shakeup at lower levels.

The principal burdens of political reconstruction then fell upon Chou En-lai. What he attempted to do, as will be analyzed in greater detail later, was to rebuild China's political institutions and create a viable new collective or coalition type of leadership, representative of varied views and interests. Gradually, he rooted out those loyal to Lin Piao. In dealing both with China's military leaders and with its most radical leftists, he avoided direct confrontation, attempting to work out new relationships while gradually cutting back their power and influence. In evolving new policies, both domestic and foreign, Chou steadily led the regime in the direction of greater pragmatism and flexibility. In doing so, he appeared to have Mao's blessing, or at least acquiescence, even though the thrust of China's new policies clearly involved a major retreat from the Maoist extremes of the Cultural Revolution.

In August 1973, a new Party Congress—the Tenth—was convened.[34] Its main accomplishment was to endorse and legitimize the changes that had occurred during the previous two years and the general direction of Chou's policies. As will be discussed in more detail later, the very fact that the Tenth Congress finally took place represented an important step in the long process of repairing the damage to China's leadership and institutions that had resulted from the Cultural Revolution. The shortest and most secretive of the four Congress meetings held since the Party won power in 1949, the Tenth Congress was strangely undramatic in some respects, yet it was a major milestone. Its task was to define the Party's course for the difficult transition into the post-Mao period. The Congress was Chou En-lai's show. Mao appeared briefly, to "wave to the delegates," and the Congress reaffirmed his symbolic and titular position as China's supreme leader, but Mao's actual role at the Congress appeared to be minimal (although he clearly continued to play an important role offstage).

The brevity of the meeting suggested that there was little detailed discussion of major policy issues, and neither the communiqué nor Chou's political report to the Congress had very much to say about concrete policy issues confronting the regime. Chou devoted much of his report to bitter criticism of the Soviet Union abroad and of the late Lin Piao and his "anti-Party clique" at home. As was to be expected, he gave lip service to the "great victories" of the Cultural Revolution and emphasized the unchallengeable validity of "the theory of Marxism-Leninism-Mao Tse-tung Thought." He asserted that "Chairman Mao has laid down for our Party the basic line and policies for the entire historical period of socialism," and declared that the "struggle between two lines" must still be continued. He called for steps to prevent a "restoration of capitalism," vigilance against the dangers of "revisionism," and continued revolution in the fields of literature, art, education, and public health. The tone of the report on a new Party constitution delivered by Wang Hung-wen—a young newcomer at the top of China's hierarchy—was more ideological than that of Chou's report, and the new Party constitution presented by Wang stated that new Cultural Revolutions would "have to be carried out many times in the future."

Yet a close reading suggests that Chou's endorsement of Maoist concepts was almost pro forma. While embalming Lin Piao and enshrining Mao, he said relatively little about specific revolutionary policies. In his few comments relevant to concrete domestic policies in the period ahead, he stressed the need to restore "Party leadership," strengthen "planning and coordination," observe "rational rules and regulations," "pay close attention to questions of economic policy," show concern for "the well-being of the masses," and "fulfill or overfulfill" the regime's economic goals. In reiterating well-established themes regarding China's foreign policy, he carefully stressed the importance of "necessary compromises."

There is good reason to believe, however, that many policy differences persist in China. Chou's own preoccupation, in his political report, with the Lin Piao affair and its aftermath revealed continued uneasiness about potential threats from that quarter to the delicate political balance achieved in the new coalitional leadership in Peking. In the months just before the Congress, renewed leftist sniping at Chou, which implicitly criticized him for rehabilitating so many old cadres and for favoring educational policies that stressed professional standards rather than ideological values, indicated continuing pressure on Chou from China's radicals. Immediately after the Congress, an intense propaganda campaign to denigrate Confucius and glorify Emperor Ch'in Shih-huang suggested that such pressure was increasing. It was evident that many important policy issues in China remained unresolved, including not only problems concerning China's intellectuals and educational institutions, but also basic issues relating to civil-military relations, economic policy, the balance between central and local power, and probably foreign policy as well.

In the wake of the Tenth Party Congress—more than four years after the climax of the Cultural Revolution—what can be said about the effects of the apotheosis of Mao and his values that occurred during the years 1966–68?

Mao clearly remains the country's one and only ideological sage, and he is constantly quoted and universally glorified throughout China. Yet one senses that, for many working-level cadres as well as ordinary people, he is now a fairly remote figure. There is no question that propagation of his cult has been steadily muted. The "little red book" has virtually disappeared, and many other symbols of the cult that were ubiquitous during the Cultural Revolution—such as the Mao buttons that were then worn by everyone—are less and less in evidence. Some new symbols have appeared to glorify the Chairman. But many of these—such as the widely distributed reproductions of his calligraphy —seem to symbolize Chinese cultural pride and nationalism more than politics and ideology.

Except in the fields of education and culture—where something like the Cultural Revolution continues (now under the slogan "the revolution in education"[35]) and the effort to indoctrinate intellectuals in Maoist values is still intense—China, at the grassroots level, entered a period of relative political and ideological relaxation in 1969, comparable in many respects to similar periods following revolutionary outbursts in the past. The indoctrination of cadres in the so-called May 7 schools[36] and of ordinary people in regularized small study groups continued, but the intensity of the effort appeared to have substantially declined. More and more, in fact, indoctrination and political activity for most people seemed to be relatively routinized, with little resemblance to the frenetic efforts of 1966–68. The recent propaganda campaign focused on Confucius obviously represents an attempt by some Chinese leaders to halt these trends, but whether it will be successful remains to be seen.

The dominant political slogans in the country are still quotations from Mao, and many are ones that date from the Cultural Revolution period. But many concrete policies appear to have relatively little relation to the slogans, and the gap between theory and practice—or rhetoric and policy—seems to have widened rather than narrowed. Moreover, even in the rhetoric there is a subtle and confusing interplay of ideological crosscurrents.

Since 1968, the general thrust of the regime's key policies, both at home and abroad, has become increasingly flexible and "realistic," and the influence of Maoist values—at least in their most extreme and radical forms—seems steadily to have declined. In the prevailing atmosphere of gradual political relaxation, there has been much less stress than in the late 1960s on the need for uninterrupted revolution, class struggle, and dynamic tension. As the regime has moved to restore routine administration, mass mobilization has declined; not since 1968 has there been a nationwide mass campaign or mobilization effort to stir up the majority of ordinary people. Although the current anti-Confucius and anti–Lin Piao campaign in China could develop into such a mobilization effort, so far it has not.

One senses, however, not only in the declarations of the Tenth Congress, but also in discussions with lower-level cadres in China, continued sensitivity to the ideological differences and value conflicts which persist at the highest levels of leadership in the country. The current line, emphasized at the Tenth Congress and articulated by all cadres, is that the "struggle between two lines" is not only fundamental in understanding China's past, but is alive today and still unresolved. There has always been such a struggle in China, it is said, and the struggle will continue into the future, both during and after the succession.

The gap between Maoist rhetoric and the essentially pragmatic policies of 1973 creates inevitable tensions, uncertainties, and ambiguities. Local cadres as well as top leaders denounce not only "rightist" tendencies, against which the Cultural Revolution was directed, but also "ultraleftist" tendencies, on which the excesses of the Cultural Revolution period are now blamed. It is doubtful that many have forgotten, however, that Mao was responsible for many of the tendencies now labeled "ultraleftist." The slogan "Let A Hundred Flowers Bloom," which in the past has always been a signal for relaxation of political pressures on China's intellectuals, has reentered the approved political vocabulary, but it is difficult for anyone to define precisely what it means in the context of the situation in 1973. Despite the general trend toward ideological relaxation, China's intellectuals, especially in its universities, remain the principal targets of continuing efforts to revolutionize society and inculcate Maoist values.

The Future Role of Ideology: Possible Trends

China today is in a period of change ideologically as well as in other respects. What direction is the change likely to take? Is the present trend toward more moderate policies and essentially pragmatic approaches to problems likely to persist? Or should one expect a swing of the pendulum toward greater emphasis on Maoist ideological values?

Are the value conflicts that have divided the leadership being genuinely resolved? Or are they simply temporarily submerged?

Is it likely that in the period ahead there will be renewed ideological polarization? If so, will either Maoist or non-Maoist values emerge triumphant? If non-Maoist values triumph, should one expect a clear renunciation of the Thought of Mao—a process of "de-Maoification"? Or is it likely that a subtle process of gradual compromise will take place, resulting in a new consensus among China's leaders based on a complex mix of values?

Any observer of China who has watched the cyclical changes of policy over the past two decades is likely to reject a projection of the future that excludes the possibility of continued oscillation between periods in which the relative emphasis placed by the regime on Maoist or non-Maoist values shifts significantly. Yet it is now plausible to believe that dramatic swings comparable to the most extreme ones in the past are less likely after Mao dies. The great revolutionary upsurges in the period since 1949 have for the most part originated with Mao, and they have reflected his very personal revolutionary vision and style.

In the context of the present balance of forces in China, one cannot predict whether an aging Mao—eighty years old as of December 26, 1973—will be able to launch another major revolutionary upsurge again before he dies, or whether if he tried he would then be able to mobilize sufficient support to carry it out successfully. Immediately after the succession, successful implementation of extreme Maoist policies would seem to be unlikely, however. There is no major political figure on the horizon who seems to have the potential to pursue Mao's revolutionary vision in the same way he has, even if so inclined. As will be discussed in Chapter 4, the collective leadership which now seems likely to emerge after Mao's death will probably be under strong pressures to seek compromise and pursue "centrist" policies during the transition period.

There is little reason to believe, however, that the underlying conflicts of values in China have yet been fundamentally resolved—or that they will be in the foreseeable future. The continuing emphasis, at all levels, on the "struggle between two lines" indicates that the Chinese themselves do not believe basic value conflicts have been finally resolved and do not rule out future ideological struggles.

Among those within the regime's top hierarchy who might try to spearhead a future drive for a return to increased emphasis on radical Maoism are the surviving members of the Cultural Revolution Group who continue to be influential in the regime's propaganda apparatus. Conceivably some of the newcomers who are rising in the Party hierarchy may fit into this category. At present, however, they appear to be a minority. The majority of the top leadership today appears to consist of civilian and military leaders who are inclined toward either centrist or conservative positions, and who seem to favor policies stressing orderly incremental development rather than rapid revolutionary change. A succession struggle involving intense ideological conflicts would probably increase the chances that an alliance of military and bureaucratic leaders, composed of men who would react strongly against ideological pressures from the left, would come to the fore.

Much will, or could, depend on the role Mao himself chooses to play between now and the succession. If he were suddenly to try to throw his weight once again behind a strong drive for more radical policies, the chances for ideological polarization and conflict would increase greatly. However, as stated already, it seems unlikely that ideological radicals could win out today in any open conflict because of the powerful opposition they would encounter.

In any case, since 1968 Mao seems to have given his personal support to many policies that are essentially centrist and pragmatic, in contrast to the radical policies that he was promoting in the late 1960s. It is debatable whether this represents a temporary retreat on Mao's part (similar to those he has made in the past after almost every great mobilization effort), a more basic shift toward the center, or simply a reluctant recognition that however much he may have wished to promote radical revolutionary policies it has simply not been possible for him to do so. Whatever the explanation, Mao's support is now being invoked by moderates at the helm of government operations to move China in generally non-Maoist directions. If this continues until his death, it should increase the likelihood that present trends will continue after the succession. If not, the future is more uncertain.

The Possibility of Renewed Conflict

It would clearly be unwise to exclude entirely the possibility that acute ideological polarization could occur, during or after the succession, with open conflict between leaders favoring extreme Maoist positions and those who are basically non-Maoist. It is possible to conceive of various situations in which this might happen.

For example, if what emerges is a new kind of collective, centrist leadership, there could be serious dissatisfaction not only among influential Maoist ideologues but conceivably also among certain powerful military and bureaucratic leaders who do not achieve membership in the top collective leadership. If the latter were to decide to challenge Mao's successors, and were to search for vulnerabilities to attack, they might conclude that the most promising prospect would be to claim that the existing leadership was abandoning Maoist principles and thereby forfeiting the mantle of legitimacy. In such a situation, whether or not the principal challengers were in fact strongly inclined toward Maoist values, they might ally themselves with Maoist ideologues in challenging those occupying the principal seats of power. While it seems unlikely that Maoist ideologues alone could seriously challenge a post-Mao collective leadership based on an alliance of bureaucratic and military leaders, an alliance of disaffected military and civil leaders and alienated ideologues could pose a challenge of a different order of magnitude, which might lead to renewed ideological polarization and heightened conflicts over basic values.

The Probability of Compromise

While such a turn of events is possible, it is not probable. What seems likely, especially in light of the results of overall domestic political trends, is that there will be strong pressures after the succession to achieve political compromises and avoid ideological extremes. If this is so, it seems unlikely that in the immediate postsuccession period there will be either an attempt to reassert Maoist values in an extreme way or to reject them in any open or sweeping fashion.

The principal reason that no new upsurge based on extreme Maoism seems likely is that a large majority of China's leaders will probably believe that any repetition of upsurges comparable to the Great Leap or Cultural Revolution might severely threaten China's stability and harm its prospects for growth.

A dramatic swing of the pendulum toward open denigration of Mao and repudiation of his Thought—in short, a process of "de-Maoification"—seems equally unlikely. Primarily this is because Mao, as the supreme leader of the revolution for almost four decades, has acquired a unique historical position that is virtually unassailable. Post-Mao leaders, whoever they may be, will probably believe it essential to present themselves as the true inheritors of Mao's mantle to establish their legitimacy. One could conceive of certain circumstances in which this might not be true. For example, if certain Party leaders purged during the Cultural Revolution—most notably Liu Shao-ch'i and P'eng Chen— were to regain power, they might be strongly tempted to carry out a campaign to denigrate all of Mao's ideas and policies. But while this is conceivable in theory, in reality it seems unlikely.

What seems probable is that the kind of trends that have character- ized the post–Cultural Revolution period are likely to characterize the overall direction of change after the succession. If so, future leaders will doubtless continue to pay obeisance to the Thought of Mao, but at the same time they will probably pursue policies directed primarily toward the solution of immediate problems and the achievement of medium-range developmental goals through relatively flexible means.

There will unquestionably be significant conflicts of values, how- ever, manifesting themselves in important differences over priorities and specific policies. Not only will functional groups within the leader- ship and society have differing concerns; individual leaders will be con- fronted by many choices involving serious value conflicts within their own individual scale of values. It seems likely, in time, that value con- flicts will increasingly be approached and dealt with on an issue-by- issue basis, in a relatively undramatic fashion, rather than through bitter confrontation between irreconcilable and polarized "general lines" or strategies. In many instances, moreover, the outcomes will probably represent complicated compromises between conflicting values rather than the clear dominance of some over others. In sum, China's leaders in the immediate post-Mao era will probably try to blur the distinc- tions between "two lines"—in practice if not in theory—rather than highlighting them as Mao did in the late 1960s.

As is the case today, certain values are likely to be more influential in shaping policy in some sectors of policy and other values will be more important in other sectors. While non-Maoist pragmatic impulses now dominate in economic policy (see Chapter 3), Maoist values con- tinue to be a primary influence on policies toward intellectuals in gen- eral, and educators in particular. One should expect, also, that there may be some general swings of the pendulum in the future as in the past, but, as already stated, it seems likely that these will involve rela- tively limited, restricted shifts in emphasis, and not the drastic fluctua- tions of the recent past.

Even if all the above projections are valid, it still remains to be seen whether, and if so how, a genuine new consensus on values can be achieved, one that somehow compromises or reconciles the extreme differences of the past. There will probably be strong pressures to try to work toward such consensus, however, and in the course of the search it seems likely that post-Mao leaders will gradually and cautiously reinterpret and adapt the Thought of Mao to serve their new needs and the new situation in which China finds itself (just as Mao himself adapted and reinterpreted ideological concepts imported from abroad in earlier years). It would not be surprising, for example, if future leaders, motivated by the desire to use the Thought of Mao to justify relatively pragmatic policies, decide to put increasing emphasis on the elements in Mao's writings that stress pragmatic approaches and to deemphasize those of his writings that have favored more radical and utopian goals. This would not be difficult, since Mao's writings, like most bodies of doctrine produced by prolific political leaders, contain material that can be used to justify or support widely differing policies. Particularly in his earlier years, Mao placed great stress on the necessity of relating "theory and practice." If future leaders wish to shift the emphasis of Mao's Thought, they can easily do so by emphasizing the importance of certain of his writings (for example, "On Practice") and deemphasizing others (such as "On Contradiction").

The Erosion of Ideology

Another trend to be anticipated in the period ahead is an almost certain, albeit gradual, decline in the general force of ideology in China. The experience of revolutionary regimes elsewhere suggests that, while dedicated leaders may be able to sustain a high level of ideological intensity for a considerable period, a slackening of ideological fervor seems destined to occur eventually, as the memory of the revolutionary struggle for power recedes into the background and as postrevolutionary pressures toward stabilization and institutionalization increase. Perhaps the tremendous stress Mao has placed on continuing indoctrination to inculcate his revolutionary vision, and on dramatic measures (including the Cultural Revolution) to revitalize revolutionary values, may slow this process in China; but Mao was probably right when he sensed as early as the late 1950s that a process of ideological erosion had begun. While he may have checked the trend, there is little reason to believe that he halted it permanently or reversed it.

On the other hand, there is every reason to expect that, in a fundamental sense, Marxism-Leninism and the Thought of Mao will provide the basic ideological underpinnings of the Chinese polity and Chinese society for the foreseeable future. No serious ideological competition is on the horizon, and the development of real ideological pluralism is not in prospect. Throughout their long history, the Chinese seem to have been strongly predisposed to believe that an ordered, stable society must be based on a well-defined body of political and social doctrine. Virtually all Chinese leaders—modern as well as traditional, non-Communist as well as Communist—have used the power of the state to enforce ideological orthodoxy. With the exception of some of China's most notable independent intellectuals, the majority of Chinese —both leaders and led—seem to find it difficult to live with ideological pluralism in politics or with situations in which there is open competition of political ideas and values. In this sense, the Communists have not broken with the past; they have simply perpetuated a long tradition. The intensity of their effort to inculcate and enforce their new orthodoxy has surpassed that of any rulers in the past, however, and there is good reason to believe that Marxism-Leninism-Maoism has been firmly established as the ideological foundation of China's political culture for the foreseeable future.

Maoism and China's Political Culture[37]

To say that Marxism-Leninism-Maoism will remain China's ideological foundation does not rule out significant change in the role of ideology in general, and of the Thought of Mao in particular. If Maoist prescriptions become decreasingly useful as a guide to practical policy making, the primary role of the Thought of Mao may become that of a secular religion, defining certain ultimate truths and goals and outlining the basic standards of revolutionary morality and ethics held up as a guide to social behavior. This would not mean that ideology would have no influence on policy, but it probably would mean that policy would be shaped just as much, and probably more, by other influences and factors.

It is extremely difficult to judge, however, the impact Mao's Thought has had as a secular religion on China's fundamental political culture and general patterns of thought and behavior. Assessments differ widely. Some observers appear to believe that an extremely far-reaching and long-lasting "transformation" of values has already occurred in China, while others are more skeptical about the extent of fundamental and permanent change. The former can point to some important observable changes in Chinese behavior—for example, the relative absence of corruption and the apparent willingness to work hard for collective goals. The skeptics can point to some significant variations in mass Chinese behavior in different periods (notably, the lack of fervor and mass activity of the citizenry under the loosened controls during the depression of the early 1960s as compared with the emotional demonstrations during the Cultural Revolution period). When intense indoctrination and tight political control prevail, it is difficult to judge the extent to which behavior is determined by internalized values or external sanctions and pressures.

Because the data available today are simply not sufficient to support confident conclusions on the extent of real value change in China, any judgments must be tentative, impressionistic, and somewhat subjective. My own estimate is that there have been some very significant changes in certain patterns of Chinese thought and behavior as a result of indoctrination in Maoist values, but these changes probably fall far short of the sweeping transformation assumed by some to have occurred; in certain areas of thought and behavior they have probably only begun to alter deep-rooted traditional patterns.

It is beyond the scope of this discussion to elaborate on this judgment in any detail, but it can be illustrated by two observations, based in part on impressions received on a visit to China in 1972–73 as well as on more conventional research data. There is strong evidence to support the view that the regime's attempts to raise the general level of national and social consciousness in China have achieved considerable success. The Chinese people today almost certainly think and act, more than ever before in China, on the basis of an awareness of obligations to collectivities beyond the family. For many, "serve the people" doubtless is not simply a slogan but a concept that has real meaning and significantly influences their behavior.[38]

In contrast, despite the great stress placed upon egalitarian values in Maoist Thought, the deep-rooted traditional Chinese proclivity to think in terms of differentiated authority, status, and hierarchy has been as yet only qualified and not fundamentally changed.[39] The stress on egalitarianism has inhibited the reemergence of extreme forms of elitism; it may well have also had important effects, qualitatively, on the character of relationships between Chinese of different status or rank. But there is ample evidence, which direct observation in China strongly supports, that the society continues to be highly stratified, and that Chinese today as in the past are strongly inclined to think in terms of status and hierarchy, to defer and submit to authority, and to conform to whatever social roles are expected of them.

This is not really surprising. In periods of radical revolutionary change, there can be major changes of some values, and this quite clearly has occurred in China. But it is also true that in a society that has a centuries-old legacy of certain patterns of thought and behavior, some values are very resistant to change. The political culture that will ultimately emerge from this revolutionary period in China will undoubtedly be a mixture of old and new. How much it will be influenced by Maoist values still remains to be seen, and it is wise to reserve judgment on this until one can assess the impact of post-Mao developments and the direction in which China ultimately moves in the postrevolutionary period.

One prediction can be made with confidence: whatever conflicts between Maoist and non-Maoist values persist, nationalism will continue to be a powerful motivating and unifying force in China. Throughout the modern period, Chinese leaders of all political persuasions, and increasingly the mass of ordinary Chinese as well, have been moved as much (or more) by nationalistic impulses as by any other ideological forces. Mao—and most other Chinese Communist leaders as well—was a nationalist before he became a Communist, and there is good reason to label him, as some have, a "revolutionary nationalist."[40] The sense of cultural identity and national pride shared by the majority of China's population has been strongly reinforced under Communist rule, and there is considerable evidence that the importance of nationalist values in motivating both the leaders and the society as a whole has become more rather than less important in recent years.

Whatever mix of Maoist and non-Maoist values eventually emerges as the basis for a new national consensus and political culture in China, nationalism will be a crucial component that will have an enormous influence on both the regime's policies and the population's behavior. Even if there are renewed polarization and conflict, precipitated by differences over certain political values and priorities, nationalism will be an important force working for unity and in favor of consensus. Alone, it will obviously not be sufficient, in the future any more than it has been in the past, to ensure consensus, but it could be an extremely important factor reinforcing others operative in the post-Mao period that should move China in the direction of ideological compromise and unity rather than polarization and conflict.

The Problem of Institutional Stability

The political crisis experienced by China during the Cultural Revolution raised serious questions about the future of the regime's institutions as well as about the values shaping the country's development. For a time, in fact, it appeared that the basic institutional structures of the regime, built up so carefully over nearly two decades, had to a considerable extent been dismantled. One of Mao's primary aims in initiating the Cultural Revolution was to revolutionize the bureaucratic "establishment" in China as well as to seize power from the men who had previously dominated it. The Maoist-inspired assaults on Party and state institutions created a situation of such extreme instability that it was unclear at the height of the struggle whether or not an entirely new organizational structure would emerge.

The Maoist attacks on the regime's bureaucratic leaders and institutions can be analyzed, if one chooses to do so, primarily in terms of the factional power struggles that erupted in 1966. But in a fundamental sense, these attacks were also the climax of complex policy disputes and the underlying ideological and value conflicts discussed earlier in this chapter. As indicated earlier, Mao became obsessed with the belief that trends toward institutionalization and bureaucratization were undermining the revolutionary character of the regime, and concluded that the revolution could be revitalized only by subjecting the entire organizational establishment to a drastic shakeup. The Cultural Revolution was, in part, a conflict over the degree to which the revolution should be institutionalized, what kind of institutions China should have, and what roles they should play.

It has now been roughly seven years since the Red Guard and Revolutionary Rebel assaults of 1966–67 temporarily paralyzed both the Party and state bureaucracies, placing their future in doubt, and almost five years since the Cultural Revolution drew to a close and serious efforts at political reconstruction began. What can be said about the consequences of that extraordinary upheaval?

As for structural institutional change, the results appear to be considerably less far-reaching than many observers expected them to be.

The most radical and utopian of the ideas that surfaced during the Cultural Revolution—for example, the notion, briefly mooted, that the entire Chinese political system should be restructured on the Paris Commune model, and even the subsequent effort to ensure that political power should be exercised by "three-way alliances" in which "representatives of the masses" would genuinely share power with Party cadres and military leaders—appear to have left relatively little lasting imprint. As political reconstruction has progressed, many of the institutional structures gradually rebuilt have begun to look very similar to those existing before the Cultural Revolution.

There is no doubt, however, that the disruptions of the 1966–68 period have left a legacy of serious problems. The process of institutional reconstruction has been painfully slow, and conditions of instability may continue for some years. China still has a considerable way to go before it can achieve a degree of institutional cohesion comparable to that of the pre-1965 period. Especially at the upper levels of the regime, the situation has continued to be fluid and transitional in many respects, and many institutional arrangements are obviously still experimental and ad hoc. Not only is the structure of many institutions still evolving; even more important, the roles of specific institutions and the pattern of relationships among them are still undergoing change.

The lack of institutional stability has been both a cause and an effect of other unresolved problems that plague China in this period of transition from the Maoist era to the post-Mao period. The regime may not be able to achieve real institutional stability again until after the succession is past and until a new leadership, a new balance of forces, and new policies crystallize. To the extent that this proves to be true, Mao's attempt to prepare China for the future will have made the transition after his death more rather than less difficult than it might otherwise have been.

The Institutional Structure before 1966

To appreciate the institutional problems that China faces in the 1970s requires at least a minimal understanding of the basic character of the structures built during the regime's early years—and the traumatic impact of the Cultural Revolution on them. Many volumes have been written on the organization of the Chinese Communist polity in the pre–Cultural Revolution period, and no attempt will be made here to portray it in any detail.[41] A few of its characteristics must be kept in mind, however, if one is to have a baseline on which to judge the consequences of the political turmoil of recent years.

The new political structure built with such impressive speed by the Communists after 1949 combined, in a remarkably effective way, highly centralized decision making by a unified Party elite, coordinated policy implementation by the disciplined cadres staffing multiple organizational hierarchies (the Party, government, military, and mass organizations), which functioned under close Party direction, and unprecedented involvement of the population in closely controlled "basic" cellular units and mass organizations operating under the supervision of the Party-led hierarchies.

The key to the operation of the system—apart from such sources of strength as the unity of the decision-making elite and the consensus that existed on ends and means in those early years—was the crucial role of the Party. Authority and power were effectively concentrated in the Party as an institution, and it was able to exercise firm control over the entire system. Consisting of a carefully recruited, thoroughly indoctrinated, and highly disciplined elite, the Party penetrated every area of the country and every sector of society, down to the lowest grassroots level, and at every level its authority as the ultimate center for decision making was unchallenged.

Enjoying uncontested primacy, the Party controlled and directed all of the complex institutional hierarchies in the society, and through them the population as a whole, to a degree that no political authority in China had ever attempted previously. Under Party direction and control, a workable division of labor and reasonably stable interrelationships were maintained among the regime's various institutional hierarchies. The army gave the Party essential backing and, as will be discussed in Chapter 2, performed a variety of political and economic as well as military functions; but there was no doubt about Party primacy, and the army did not pose any threat to the Party's ultimate authority. Similarly, the government was effectively controlled by the Party, and the state bureaucracy served as the Party's principal administrative arm for ruling the country.

The apparatus for maintaining political control and social order included a strong nationwide public security system; while a part of the government, the security system also operated under close Party control. Police power was usually employed with considerable restraint, however, and the Party's main instruments for political control, ideological indoctrination, and mass mobilization at the grassroots level of the society were the Party's own "basic organizations," plus the numerous Party-organized and Party-led mass organizations that encompassed virtually the entire population. The mass organizations were crucially important as "transmission belts" between the Party and the masses and played critical roles during the great mass campaigns periodically organized by the Party in pursuit of its priority goals.

The Party also exercised direct and effective control over rural Communes, urban enterprises, and the entire structure of state and collective organizations that ran the economy. At the lowest levels of society, virtually everyone belonged to Party-directed cellular "small groups" of various sorts, organized in every locality in the country and within all major institutional structures. These, in effect, were the foundation stones on which the entire society and policy were built. Like every important element in the system, they functioned as instruments of Party rule, not as autonomous units.

The essential characteristics of this system took shape rapidly. Within a relatively brief period after 1949, its major institutional elements were firmly established and the basic relationships among its components crystallized.[42] From then until the Cultural Revolution it was generally assumed—not only by foreign observers but perhaps just as much or even more by the majority of Chinese—that China's institutional structures and relationships had stabilized on a basis that would persist indefinitely.

This is not to say that these structures and relationships did not evolve and change as time passed. They obviously did, in important ways, and some of these changes contributed to the forces and trends that ultimately produced the Cultural Revolution. As noted earlier, there was a tremendous growth over time in the size and complexity of the bureaucracies operating within the general framework of centralized Party control, inevitably resulting in complicated bureaucratic politics—involving numerous conflicts of interest, policy disputes, and power rivalries. But none of these trends suggested that any basic change in the system itself was imminent; in fact, few people in or out of China thought that any such change was possible. The essential structures and relationships based on the theory and fact of Party primacy appeared to be firmly established, stable, and unchallengeable.

Impact of the Cultural Revolution

The extraordinary fact about the Cultural Revolution was that it involved a direct attack by Mao and his allies against the Party and other Party-directed civilian bureaucracies they had created and called into question the entire pattern of institutional structures and relationships that had previously existed. In this sense, Mao's "revolution within a revolution" was an unprecedented historical phenomenon. Where else has a supreme leader of a revolution not only purged the majority of his former colleagues, but also incited sweeping attacks on the basic institutional structures of a regime that he himself had done so much to conceive and build?

As several excellent and detailed analyses of the Cultural Revolution have made clear,[43] the 1966–68 struggle was an incredibly complex one, unfolding in a step-by-step fashion. It was based on ad hoc decisions made as the leadership confronted each new problem. Neither Mao nor anyone else foresaw how it would or should evolve or what its outcome would or should be. Mao himself admitted, after the Cultural Revolution was well under way, that he had not anticipated many of the consequences of unleashing the forces that he did.[44] But there is no doubt that Mao consciously attempted not simply to purge his opponents but also to shake up and alter the institutional foundations of the regime. He viewed the fact of institutionalization, and in particular the increasingly bureaucratic character of the Party, state, and mass organizations, as basic obstacles to continued revolution.

In essence what Mao did was to assert his individual authority as the supreme charismatic leader of the revolution over the institutionalized authority of the Party and other civilian bureaucracies. With the support of key elements in the military, he bypassed the established institutionalized structures of the regime and directly mobilized the youth of the country, inciting them, under the slogan "it is right to rebel," to attack the regime's major bureaucratic leaders and institutions. In doing so, Mao threw the entire political system into turmoil. The carefully built structure of authority temporarily broke down, and for more than two years China's population, especially in its major urban centers, was caught up in a chaotic and frequently violent political struggle.

The immediate results of the Cultural Revolution were so complex and traumatic that they defy simple generalizations. Yet if one strips away the complicated details, one can identify several crucial aspects of its initial impact on the regime's institutions. For a time the Party and state bureaucracies—the civilian hierarchies that had constituted the core of the regime—virtually ceased normal operations.[45] The majority of the bureaucratic leadership, especially at the top levels, was purged, and millions of ordinary cadres at lower levels were subjected to intense political attacks. At the climax of the struggle, huge numbers were sent to the newly established May 7 schools for prolonged reindoctrination.

The Party Committees at all levels, previously the nerve centers for decision making throughout the country, stopped normal functioning in 1967 when Red Guard and Revolutionary Rebel groups invaded their offices throughout China to carry out "power seizures." This is not to say that they all went completely out of operation. In many places, some cadres continued to work, and certain routine activities were carried on. In other areas (it is difficult to know how many), the Party Committees as such ceased to exist, but small rump groups of former members—"leading groups" or "core groups"—continued to operate and to make some decisions.[46] (Later, in 1968–69, such leading groups were formed in virtually all of the Revolutionary Committees established during 1967–68 and took the lead in rebuilding the Party Committees.) But for all practical purposes, the Party Committees, as they had previously existed, went out of existence for two years or more; many of the organs under them ceased operations, and vast numbers—probably a majority—of working civilian cadres ceased to perform the Party tasks previously assigned to them.

The state organs were similarly attacked, and a high proportion of their leaders were ousted as a result of the "power seizures" that occurred. The impact of the struggle was somewhat less severe on many government agencies than it was on the Party apparatus, but it was disruptive enough. Some ceased all normal operations for a period of time. Others retained a core of personnel who continued to perform some routine functions. But as a result of the mass purging, the prolonged factional struggles among competing groups within the bureaucracy, and the priority given to political debates and indoctrination, most government agencies were unable to perform more than minimal functions during the height of the struggle.

The major Party-led mass organizations—the labor unions, organizations for youth and women, professional associations, and the like —were also subjected to severe attacks and ceased normal operations. Mass politics at the lowest levels in China now centered in hundreds of new revolutionary organizations that sprang up all over the country, particularly in urban areas. With the encouragement and moral support of Mao and his allies in Peking, there was a degree of spontaneity —although exactly how much is difficult to judge—in the formation of many Red Guard units, which were composed largely of college and middle school students, and Revolutionary Rebel units, which were made up of activist workers. There was no clear chain of command subjecting them to effective centralized control and direction.[47] They all attempted to build local bases of support and tried to ally themselves with, or obtain support from, competing authorities at higher levels. Many received logistical support from local military units, with competing groups often supported by different military leaders.

While attacking the established bureaucratic institutions, these new mass organizations also engaged in violent factional struggle among themselves. The resulting conflict and confusion contributed significantly to the weakening of the regime's entire structure of order and authority. Eventually, the Maoist leadership in Peking, as well as local military and political leaders, attempted to group them into "alliances," subject them to discipline, and bring them under centralized control. But once let loose, the genie of "spontaneous" local action was extremely difficult to control, and in the end the regime was compelled to use strong methods against them. By late 1968 Peking undertook to suppress most of the groups, sending their leading members out of the cities into the countryside or to remote provinces.

When the original power seizures occurred in 1967, paralyzing the principal Party and state organs, the Maoist leadership and the military tried to fill the vacuum and build a new civilian institutional structure by supporting the formation of Revolutionary Committees in every area and in all major institutions in China. These Revolutionary Committees were viewed for a time as a new kind of political entity, combining the previous roles and functions of both the Party Committees and the top decision-making and administrative bodies of the government (or other institutions). Revolutionary Committees were supposed to be based on "three-way alliances" and therefore to have representatives from the most important revolutionary mass organizations, as well as the army and "revolutionary cadres" (i.e., Party men who had survived the initial assaults on the bureaucracies and had proved their political acceptability in the new situation).

The process of forming Revolutionary Committees was extremely difficult and slow, however. Because of the breakdown of previous channels of communication and authority, bitter factionalism emerged almost everywhere at the local level. There was intense competition for power, resulting in unstable relationships and shifting alliances among mass organization representatives, old Party cadres, and military men—with complicated divisions within each of these major groupings. The Revolutionary Committee structure slowly took shape, built from the bottom up, but it was roughly two years before the process was completed. The final provincial-level Committees were formed in late 1968.

Throughout this two-year period, China continued to suffer from an extremely high degree of institutional instability. There was continuing uncertainty about the appropriate organizational structure and functions of the new Revolutionary Committees, and great variations existed from place to place. The lack of clarity about lines of authority linking local bodies with higher levels of authority was compounded by the complicated power struggles and the unclear distribution of power at the center. In the absence of clear lines of authority to the top and with the continuation of factional strife and political struggles at the local level, power relations everywhere were extremely fluid and constantly shifting. For considerable periods, social order broke down in many of China's major cities, latent social tensions erupted to the surface, and there was widespread urban conflict involving considerable violence.

This situation persisted until the army finally moved in to reestablish order, suppress conflict, and impose overall control. By that time a major redistribution of power had occurred. At all levels, there had been a serious fragmentation and diffusion of authority. There had also been a significant de facto shift of power from central authorities to local centers of power. Most important, the military had moved into a predominant political position at the expense of civilians. However, although the military clampdown resulted in suppression of the most militant mass organizations, old Party cadres gradually began to make a comeback.

By the time the Cultural Revolution reached its peak, the impact of two years of turmoil on the institutional structure of the regime had been so severe that the ability of any central leaders to formulate and implement policies effectively on a nationwide basis was in doubt. It was even unclear what the new civilian bureaucratic structures would be. The dismantling of the major mass organizations appeared to reduce the ability of the regime to control and mobilize the general population, and some observers speculated that after two years of undisciplined local struggles many Chinese at a grassroots level might either resist the restoration of centralized control or, disillusioned, retreat toward political passivity.

Then, starting in late 1968, soon after the army had reestablished overall control, China entered a new phase, and the process of institutional reconstruction was given primary emphasis. The crucial task now was the rebuilding of the civilian bureaucracies. Understandably, the reconstruction of the Party received very high priority, and this was pushed energetically from 1969 on.

Because the previous balance of political forces in China had been so seriously destabilized during 1966–68 and because widespread factional competition and power struggles continued, the rebuilding of a nationwide structure of Party Committees proved to be just as difficult and time consuming as the previous effort to establish Revolutionary Committees. In this instance, the first dramatic move was directed at the top rather than the bottom level of organization. In April 1969, the Ninth Party Congress—the first in more than a decade —elected a new Central Committee, which in turn chose a new Politburo and Standing Committee.[48] The intention, obviously, was to try to stabilize the top leadership so that the process of Party reconstruction could proceed in an orderly fashion at lower levels. But in a fundamental sense, this step proved to be premature. In the past, Party Congresses had generally ratified existing power relationships that had already been worked out; but in this case, as the discussion in Chapter 4 will indicate, the effort to create a stable top leadership failed. Within a short time, power struggles resumed and the newly designated leading Party groups were decimated by further purges.

The new Party constitution adopted by the Ninth Congress to replace the one under which the Party had operated since 1956 was an extremely short and vague document,[49] containing few details about the proposed new Party structure, particularly at the center. There was clearly no genuine consensus on many organizational issues. Although the constitution stated that "a number of necessary organs which are compact and efficient" should be established under the Politburo, no mention was made of a Party Secretariat or any other specific organizations under it. The constitution had one remarkable, and unprecedented, provision in which Lin Piao was named as Mao's successor. Instead of solving the succession issue, however, the inclusion of this provision rendered the entire constitution obsolete when Lin was purged a little more than two years later.

While the Ninth Party Congress failed to resolve the key institutional as well as power issues at the top, the very fact that such a meeting was held spurred Party building at lower levels, and the effort to reconstruct the Party proceeded simultaneously at several levels from early 1969 on. Special stress was placed at the start on the reestablishment of Party branches at the lowest levels of society; in a sense, therefore, the rebuilding of the institutional structure—once the national Congress set the process in motion—occurred from the bottom up. By late 1969, it was possible to start forming new County Party Committees, and when substantial progress had been made at this level, the task of organizing new Provincial Party Committees began.

This process, like the previous effort to establish Revolutionary Committees, proved to be excruciatingly difficult and slow, and the final Provincial Party Committees were not formed until December 1971. Although the intensity of factional disputes and power struggles gradually abated, they did not end; in many instances, in fact, the strife continued even after the new committees had been established. The reestablishment of each Party branch and committee, moreover, had to be preceded by a time-consuming process of selecting, screening, and reindoctrinating local Party members. In theory, great emphasis was placed on weeding out undesirable members and bringing in new blood; in fact, however, as will be indicated below, old cadres persistently reasserted themselves, and by the time the process had been completed it was clear that relatively few old Party members had been permanently ousted at "basic" levels.

The rebuilding of the state apparatus was also energetically pushed during this same period. As suggested earlier, while many government agencies that had previously run day-to-day affairs in China were badly damaged and disrupted during the Cultural Revolution, they retained a greater capacity than the Party to resume something approaching normal operations.

The first effort to reorganize and simplify the central apparatus occurred during the Cultural Revolution. Military representatives (sent, according to some reports, by the Party's Military Affairs Commission) took charge of most ministry-level organizations, often setting up supervisory Military Control Commissions within them. By the end of the Cultural Revolution, however, many if not most of the ministry-level bodies were being managed by "revolutionary leading groups," in which old cadres with specialized knowledge and skills had gradually made a comeback, although in general military men still held key positions.

In line with Mao's belief that all bureaucratic institutions should be reduced in number and size, steps were taken to cut back the central state machinery and simplify its organs. Many institutions were cut in size and reduced in status (e.g., bureaus downgraded to sections, and so on) and there was a major reduction of personnel. One way this was accomplished, toward the end of the Cultural Revolution, was by sending huge numbers of cadres to May 7 cadre schools for two to three years of reindoctrination.[50] Large numbers of them continued on the rosters and payrolls of their original units, however, and by 1971 or 1972, many had begun to return to their units.

Although all the central state organs had been put through a wringer by 1969 and were still engaged in "struggle, criticism, and transformation" involving continued efforts at reorganization and intense "rectification" and indoctrination of all cadres, they nevertheless were beginning to restore normal operations. Another period of fairly drastic administrative reorganization—reportedly on Mao's own instructions—started in late 1969 and continued through most of 1970[51] under the slogan—which dated to the Yenan period—of "better troops and simpler administration." By the end of this second reorganization, the number of ministry-level bodies had been cut, largely as a result of mergers, from almost fifty before the Cultural Revolution to roughly twenty. This severe shakeup was completed more rapidly than the first, however, and by the second half of 1970 the central ministries began to operate again—on a new basis—with an increased degree of effectiveness. Only then, for the first time since before the Cultural Revolution, did the regime announce new appointments to ministry posts.

As these changes were occurring at the center, a similar process of governmental reorganization and personnel retrenchment took place at lower levels of the state bureaucracy, especially at intermediate levels, from the provinces through the subprovincial districts (which, under a new title, ti ch'u, were now regarded as regular governmental levels rather than simply branches of the provinces as in the past) and down to the counties.[52] It is difficult to judge precisely how durable the changes were. There were many reports, during and immediately after the Cultural Revolution, of drastic institutional changes and huge cutbacks of cadres at lower levels (sometimes to a quarter, or less, of previous levels). Many of the changes may have been much more extreme on paper than in reality, however, since old patterns appeared gradually to reemerge at lower levels when the situation began to settle down.

At the highest levels of the state bureaucracy, the leadership situation continued to be extremely fluid and unstable during the 1969–70 reorganization, but by the fall of 1970 China's leaders apparently decided that it was time to take steps to crystallize and try to stabilize the new state structure. A new state constitution was drafted, to replace the constitution of 1954, and it was reportedly presented to the Ninth Central Committee's second plenary session in August–September 1970 and then circulated through Party channels for nationwide discussion.[53]

Like the 1969 Party constitution, the 1970 draft state constitution was much shorter and simpler than the document it replaced. But it did at least outline the overall government structure and describe the functions of major state organs at all levels, taking into account the major changes since 1954, especially the establishment of the Communes and the Revolutionary Committees.[54] (No official version of the 1969 draft constitution has ever been issued, but the unofficial versions that became available in 1970 probably were reasonably accurate.)

The Revolutionary Committees were now described as basic governmental organs, replacing the old People's Councils. The draft constitution left unanswered almost as many questions about the new state structure as it answered, however. It did not even mention any formal posts equivalent to the former positions of State Chairman and Vice Chairman. Instead it described Mao, by name, as "head of state" and "supreme commander" of China's armed forces, and Lin Piao as "successor" to Mao and "deputy supreme commander."[55] Mao reportedly opposed restoring the formal position of State Chairman, while Lin pushed for it.[56] The draft contained no mention of previous consultative bodies such as the Supreme State Conference and the National Defense Council.

It was almost certainly the top leadership's intention in 1970 to move fairly rapidly to adopt the new state constitution, convene a new National People's Congress (NPC), and try to restore some stability and normalcy to government operations. This proved to be impossible, and three years later the draft constitution had still not been published, the NPC meeting had not been held, and the regime had been unable to formalize the new state structure. The fundamental reason was that continued power struggles at the top in China—and in particular the civil-military crisis that reached a climax with the purge of Lin in 1971 —made it impossible to take these actions. As long as the internal balance of power remained unstable and the pattern of relationships among the major political forces in China continued in a state of flux, it was simply not possible to stabilize a new institutional structure on any lasting basis.

The Situation in Late 1973[57]

In the two-year period from the Lin Piao affair in 1971 until the convening of the Party's Tenth Congress in August 1973, Premier Chou En-lai took the lead, with Mao's backing, in rebuilding the country's political institutions as well as its leadership. By mid-1973, when reports began to filter out of China that a new Party Congress and National People's Congress were in the offing, it was apparent that considerable progress had been made. Yet it was also evident that the process of reconstructing and stabilizing China's political institutions on a new basis continued to be extremely difficult in many respects. This was reflected in the regime's inability—or unwillingness—to reveal, even to its own population, not only who led and staffed the country's major institutional hierarchies but even the character of their organizational structures. As of mid-1973 the situation was still a changing and evolving one.

Gradually, however, in the period leading up to the Tenth Congress, certain basic characteristics of the situation and of current trends could be pieced together from fragmentary data obtained from interviews with Chinese officials as well as from published Chinese data. Although progress had obviously been made in the direction of institutional reconstruction and stabilization, numerous problems remained unresolved. This picture was not basically changed by the information released at the time of the Tenth Party Congress in August 1973. While holding the Congress clearly represented an important step toward greater stabilization of the political situation, particularly in regard to the regime's top leadership but also institutionally as well, the Congress revealed little that was new about the present state of China's reconstructed political institutions. Further details undoubtedly will become known, especially about the present government structure at the top, when a new National People's Congress is convened, possibly in the near future. But there is good reason to believe that this will basically reinforce rather than alter the general picture that has emerged during the past two years.

One of the striking characteristics of the institutional situation as of late 1973 is the significant difference between conditions and attitudes at "basic" levels of the society and those at higher levels of the regime. What is notable now about the situation at the lowest levels—to judge from what visitors can observe as well as from published information—is the degree to which the Party and government structures as they existed before the Cultural Revolution appear to have been restored, how little fundamental organizational change seems to have occurred as a result of all the political turmoil of recent years, and how resilient the institutional structure has proven to be. At higher levels in the regime, in contrast, a subtle but pervasive mood of tentativeness and uncertainty has continued to characterize China's institutions, as well as its leadership, and one has the impression that many institutional arrangements are still provisional, ad hoc, and transitional.

For some time, the keynote at the lowest levels in China has obviously been a "return to normalcy." Rural Communes, urban Street Committees, Residents' Committees and Groups, and industrial and other enterprises appear, from all one can learn, not only to be operating much as they did before 1966 but to be remarkably unchanged in institutional terms from the pattern that existed before the Cultural Revolution. At this level, moreover, there is some evidence to suggest that the composition of leadership groups underwent far less change than at higher levels.

The pattern at the grassroots level now, as before 1966, is one of strong Party leadership (though with continuing military supervision in many places), tight political control, and thorough organization of the population. In the cities, now as before, the lowest levels of government are the Street Committees, which are funded by and operate under the direction of the Municipal Districts. Under the Street Committees the population is grouped into Residents' Committees (or in some places, such as Shanghai, Lane Committees), which theoretically contain 100 to 600 households but may actually have more; and under them the entire population is organized into Residents' Groups consisting of roughly 15 to 40 households. The top leadership group at the Street Committee level is the Party Committee, which shares control of several sections or groups with the local Revolutionary Committee, the basic administrative organ of local government. These local committees function under the direction of district-level Party and government organs and in cooperation with local Public Security Substations. The Residents' Groups are theoretically "mass organizations," but in reality they function as branches of the Street Committees. Each is led by a Party Branch and a Residents' Group Revolutionary Committee, which share control over a common set of "groups" or sections with responsibilities in specific fields such as public security affairs, political propaganda, production and livelihood, welfare, and public health. The public security affairs group, operating under the local Public Security Substation's supervision, helps ensure public order and supervises ostracized or disenfranchised groups (the "four [bad] elements"), which sometimes constitute 1 or 2 percent or more of the local population (a small percentage, which may nevertheless be a sizable group).[58] Each Residents' Group at the lowest level is directed by a group leader.

The rural Communes, which vary tremendously in size but average over 8,000 members each, are divided, as before the Cultural Revolution, into Production Brigades, which in turn are divided into Production Teams. In reality, the Communes and Brigades are now, as they have been since the early 1960s, essentially levels of local government, roughly comparable in many respects to the pre-Commune rural Districts and Administrative Villages, while the Teams, which are "accounting units," are responsible for organizing production and distributing net income to members. The Teams, in short, are the basic "collective" units, comparable to the pre-Commune Advanced Producer Cooperatives. Most Teams are rooted in traditional "natural villages." At the Commune level, as in the past, a Party Committee is the leading decision-making group, and an administrative body, the Revolutionary Committee, is comparable to the previous Management Committee. At both levels, there are a number of subsidiary organs (sections, groups, or offices) or designated personnel (operating under both Party and Revolutionary Committee direction) responsible for various functional fields—such as production, finance, military affairs (or militia work), security, education and health, youth work, and women's work. The Teams, consisting of several dozen households, have a much simpler structure, with only a few cadres (who are active farmers), including a head, a deputy or deputies, and specialists in functions such as accounting and recording work points.

Industrial and other nonagricultural economic enterprises vary in organization, as one would expect, but they too are tightly structured and are closely directed by Party cadres. In a large factory, there is both a Party Committee and a Revolutionary Committee at the top. The Party Committee appears now, as in the past, to be the most powerful leadership body, with the notable difference that military men often occupy key positions in Party Committees today. There is a high degree of overlap of personnel between the Party Committee and the Revolutionary Committee. As has been the general pattern everywhere since the end of the Cultural Revolution, these two Committees operate under "unified leadership" and have working under them a single set of organs (called divisions, sections, or departments, but now sometimes simply called *tsu*, or groups) responsible for various functions that, before the Cultural Revolution, might have been divided between the Party and the local administration. These functions include organizational work, political propaganda (or propaganda and education), security, militia affairs, various planning and production tasks, and general administration and welfare. The organization of the production force at lower levels obviously varies, depending on particular local needs, but commonly a factory's personnel are divided into a number of large Workshops, under which the workers are organized into numerous small Production Groups, as needed. Party organization almost always extends down to the Workshop, or equivalent level, where the basic Party unit is the Party Branch or General Branch, whereas frequently there are no subsidiary Revolutionary Committees below the top factory level.

This institutional network is very similar in essentials to the kind of basic structures that existed before the Cultural Revolution, and the evidence available suggests that the nature of Party control, the hierarchical pattern of authority, the general structure of production organization, the methods used to maintain effective political and ideological controls, and the essentially bureaucratic nature of the basic organizations (despite all the efforts to encourage mass participation and mass mobilization) have probably not undergone any very profound or fundamental change as a result of the Cultural Revolution.

The degree to which basic Party, administrative, and production units at the grassroots level—in both urban and rural areas—seem to be operating once again with a reasonable degree of normalcy and apparently with so little structural change from the past, goes far toward explaining why the mass of China's population appears once again to be orderly, disciplined, and hard at work, despite the instability of China's institutional structure at higher levels.

One wonders, in fact, whether the organization and functioning of the majority of "basic-level" political and economic institutions, in urban as well as rural China, were ever as greatly affected by the widespread political conflict in China during 1966–68 as has sometimes been assumed. The Cultural Revolution was primarily an urban rather than a rural phenomenon, which helps to explain why relatively little change occurred in the Communes. It now appears that many of the grassroots units in China's cities were less extensively changed than was at one time believed. In the area of one Lane Revolutionary Committee that I visited in Shanghai in late 1972, for example, the organizational pattern was obviously similar in essentials to what it had been before 1966, and local leaders told me that only one Party member in the entire area had been permanently purged as a result of the Cultural Revolution.

What happened to the mass organizations is a different matter. Almost all of them ceased normal operations for extended periods of time, and the evidence available indicates that the leadership of most mass organizations was extensively purged, even at the lowest levels in many places. The new structures that are emerging appear to be very similar to those that existed previously (although under new names in several cases), but they are only gradually regaining their former organizational strength, prestige, and power. The mass organizations that the regime has been concentrating on rebuilding over the past two or three years have included the Party's youth subsidiary (the Young Communist League), the labor unions, and various organizations for students and schoolchildren.[59] The reconstruction of the Young Communist League has paralleled that of the Party and is now well advanced. The process of rebuilding the others lagged somewhat, but was accelerated during the first half of 1973.

Most of the mass organizations were renamed when the reconstruction process began. The labor unions were now called Worker Representative Congresses. At the university level, student associations continued under their old titles, but at the middle school level they were now called Red Guards. These were very different, it should be emphasized, from the undisciplined Red Guard units of the Cultural Revolution period, which were composed of both university and middle school students. In primary schools, the former Pioneers, operating under Party and Young Communist League direction, were renamed Little Red Soldiers.

As of mid-1973, the organization of the lowest-level units of labor, women's, and student organizations appeared to have been completed —or nearly completed—in most enterprises and schools. A number of provincial congresses were held in the spring of 1973, and the building of a leadership hierarchy at the national level appeared to be imminent. In late 1972, cadres in China stated that the principal mass organizations would be rebuilt during 1973, and developments in the first half of the year made this appear likely.

Other Chinese mass organizations with local units operating again, at least in many places, are the Women's Federation and the Poor and Lower Middle Peasants' Associations, but one hears relatively little about them and they seem to be less important now than when they were first established in the 1960s. One can learn almost nothing, moreover, about most of the numerous smaller "people's organizations" that, before the Cultural Revolution, were the principal Party-led instruments for directing and controlling the activities of virtually every identifiable professional and social group in China, including artists, writers, and journalists. It is unclear whether these will eventually be reconstituted, and if so, when.

In sum, the previous all-pervasive network of mass organizations is still in the process of being rebuilt, and clearly it is less extensive or effective than before 1966. The process of restoring normalcy at the local level in China, which has involved a restoration of effective political controls, the reinstitution of fairly routinized bureaucratic administration, and the resumption of established patterns of productive activity, appears to have been achieved above all by the regime's basic Party, administrative, and economic units, rather than by the old mass organizations. The relative scarcity of dramatic mass mobilization efforts since the end of the Cultural Revolution has almost certainly been related in part to the delays in restoring China's mass organizations to their former strength and influence, as well as to the inhibitions many of China's leaders must now have, in the aftermath of the excesses of the Cultural Revolution, about pursuing the regime's goals primarily through nationwide mass campaigns.

In contrast to the trend toward restoration of something very much like the status quo ante at the grassroots level, recovery from the Cultural Revolution appears significantly less advanced at the higher levels. As of mid-1973, on the eve of the Tenth Party Congress, the upper levels of the regime were still permeated by uncertainty, and there was a continuing sense of transition and tentativeness. The process of "struggle, criticism, and transformation" was still under way at higher levels, and changes of organizations as well as of personnel continued. Cadres constantly emphasized that institutional structures were still experimental. Not only were many leading cadres at higher levels identified simply as "responsible persons" or "leading persons" in a particular body, instead of by more specific institutional titles, but many organizational units were simply called "groups," a term that suggested arrangements that might prove to be provisional and ad hoc rather than permanent. To foreign visitors, leading Party or Revolutionary Committee cadres would sometimes describe the structure of political organizations in their area of jurisdiction and then volunteer the observation that if the visitor were to return a year later he might find that the structure had changed.

Broadly speaking, the roles and relationships of the most important institutional hierarchies in China—the Party, army, and government—still appeared to be undergoing a difficult transitional process, and the future pattern of their relationships remained a matter of speculation.

The new relationships evolving between military and civil authorities are discussed in Chapter 2. Here it is only necessary to note that, while the political roles of the military have been slowly reduced since the peak of military dominance during the Cultural Revolution and the roles of civilian cadres and institutions gradually strengthened, military personnel nevertheless continue to occupy extremely influential leadership positions in the Party and government at many levels (perhaps most of all at provincial and other intermediate levels). The People's Liberation Army still directs the public security apparatus in many areas, and it still exercises important supervisory functions in a wide range of economic, educational, and other institutions.

In this situation, the differentiation between the functions of the military and of Party and state cadres remains imprecisely defined, and the balance of power among the major institutional hierarchies appears to be a delicate and evolving one. As long as this situation exists at the leadership levels, the pattern of military-civil relationships throughout the society will continue to be ambiguous.

It is less generally known that a somewhat analogous situation has existed, and probably continues to exist today, in the relationships between the Party and government at all levels below the center.[60] From the province down, the leading bureaucratic organs operating under the top Party and government decision-making bodies are now merged in a single structure, which suggests that the roles of the Party and the government are less distinct or differentiated than in the past.

As in other Communist countries, there was a large overlap of Party and government personnel in China before the Cultural Revolution—especially in the principal leadership bodies, the Party Committees and People's Councils. And while leading Party men dominated the key posts in the government, the Party nevertheless maintained a distinct and separate bureaucracy of its own, consisting of various functional "departments" operating under the Party Committees, which were separate from the organs of the state bureaucracy and were responsible for monitoring, directing, and controlling them. Today, the situation is different. At the decision-making level, the structure is comparable to the pre-1966 pattern, with separate and distinct Party Committees and Revolutionary Committees (the latter being essentially the same as the former People's Councils); in fact, the degree of overlap between the two is, if anything, greater than before. But there are no longer separate bureaucracies beneath these two bodies. Instead, under the slogan of "unified leadership," a hybrid structure of functional "groups" performs both Party and government tasks, and the old basic structure of the state bureaucracy operates under these groups. The number of such groups varies from place to place. In some places, there are only four or five principal ones (usually including at least a unit for general office administration, a political work group, a security group, and a production group). In other places there are more; in Shanghai, for example, there were ten as of early 1973. The Shanghai structure included, besides an office-administration group, an organization group (which probably handled security work), a planning group, a foreign affairs group, an industry and communications group, a finance and trade group, a culture and education group, a science and technology group, a District group, and a Suburbs group.[61]

The emergence of this unusual hybrid Party-government structure was probably not preplanned, and it can doubtless be explained in part by ad hoc decisions made following the initial paralysis of both the Party and state bureaucracies during the Cultural Revolution. In early 1973, however, leading cadres, in explaining the rationale for the new structure, emphasized its advantages for "improved coordination" under "unified leadership" and the elimination of redundant organizations and personnel. The fact remains that it clearly violates a fundamental Communist Party premise that the Party should maintain a distinct elite group that can effectively direct state operations without itself getting too directly involved and bogged down in day-to-day bureaucratic administration. It is ironic, in a sense, that one of Mao's prime aims in the Cultural Revolution was to purify the Party and check all tendencies toward bureaucratism, yet the institutional structure that emerged from his purification drive is one in which the Party appears to be even more directly linked to day-to-day administration, and thereby exposed to the dangers of bureaucratism, than in the past.

It is by no means clear, however, that the present structure will prove to be permanent. When pressed as to whether it does, in fact, represent the shape of the future, cadres in China frankly stated in early 1973 that they did not know; they emphasized, as they do about so many things in China today, that much is still experimental and provisional.[62]

Neither the new Party constitution adopted by the Tenth Congress in August 1973 nor the major reports delivered at the Congress shed any new light on the institutional structure or relationships evolving at lower levels. The two brief sections of the new constitution dealing with local and "primary" Party organizations were almost identical with those in the 1969 document that it replaced and were no more enlightening than the earlier constitution on the leadership's thinking about appropriate future Party relationships with other institutional structures at lower levels of the regime. This ambiguity about the future relationship between the Party and government at subnational levels highlights, like so many other factors already discussed, the transitional character of the present period.

Conceivably the present pattern of relationships could settle into a lasting one—there is a certain logic to it—but the overall organization of the polity would then be significantly different from the past. It seems more likely that growing pressures will in time result in the separation and differentiation of the Party and government to a greater degree once again, and the restoration of the dual structure of parallel bureaucracies that previously existed. In either case, numerous concrete issues relating to a reasonable division of functions and an acceptable balance of power between the two have yet to be resolved.

Because of the ambiguities at the top, it is difficult to know how to characterize present Party-government relationships at subnational levels. One might argue that the Party Committees are simply creatures of the Revolutionary Committees and that the Party has not yet fully re-established its own distinct identity. The Revolutionary Committees were, after all, established first; their core groups took the lead in creating the new Party Committees, and their leading members generally assumed the dominant leadership roles in the Party Committees once they had been formed. A much more plausible interpretation is that the reverse is true—that the Party Committees have steadily reasserted Party primacy and the Revolutionary Committees are now creatures of the Party Committees, clearly subordinate to them. It was, after all, Party leaders (whether military or civilian) within the Revolutionary Committees who set up the new Party Committees, and everyone in China today stresses that the Party is again the prime leadership group, responsible for policy making. (Chou En-lai strongly stressed to the Tenth Congress the need "to strengthen the centralized leadership of the Party.") It could be that neither of these descriptions accurately portrays the subtleties of an ambiguous situation, and that the process of sorting out roles and clarifying relationships is still far from complete.

Despite the continuing uncertainties about the respective roles and relationships of the army, Party, and government, it has become increasingly clear that fewer members of the Party were ousted during the Cultural Revolution than was originally believed to be the case. The mass of rank-and-file Party and Party-government bureaucrats who came under attack in 1966–68 have been gradually rehabilitated as the structures of the state at subnational levels have been steadily rebuilt. Premier Chou En-lai has stated that the Cultural Revolution purges permanently ousted less than 1 percent of the total Party membership[63] (which would mean that those purged amounted to only 200,000 or so of the 1966 Party membership of roughly 20 million). This figure may or may not be accurate, but accounts by cadres of developments affecting their particular units make it at least plausible.

Apparently, most of the huge numbers of rank-and-file cadres who seemed to have been purged during 1966–68 were simply sent to May 7 reindoctrination schools for one, two, or more years—or were transferred to posts at lower levels. In the last two years, as noted earlier, many of these have been returning to their original units. By early

1973, it became evident that even many of the highest-ranking old cadres victimized in the Cultural Revolution were being rehabilitated. These included, for example, former Politburo members such as Teng Hsiao-p'ing, Ulanfu, T'an Chen-lin, and Li Ching-ch'uan, all of whom were elected to the new Central Committee chosen by the Tenth Congress (although not to the Politburo). At lower levels, the rehabilitation of old cadres has been far more extensive.

In addition, the Party energetically recruited new members in the period following the end of the Cultural Revolution. The extent to which the Party was being expanded was not apparent at the time. As late as the fall of 1972, U.S. government specialists on China believed that the number of new recruits since the Cultural Revolution was probably not more than slightly over a million. When the Tenth Party Congress met, however, it was revealed that the actual expansion of Party membership had been very substantial indeed; Chou in his political report stated that total membership had risen to 28 million.

One important question—another one about which one can venture only tentative judgments—is how the attitudes of most of these old cadres have been affected by the course of events since 1966. The regime's attempt to eradicate bureaucratic tendencies may have checked elitist trends somewhat, yet one does not have to be a cynic to doubt that the deep-rooted tendencies of the Chinese to think in terms of hierarchical, authoritarian, bureaucratic relationships will be easily erased. Perhaps the previous gap between the regime's bureaucrats and "the masses" has been narrowed to a degree and some of the alienation of ordinary people from the authoritarian structures of power may have been reduced, but it is very doubtful that the indoctrination in populist, participatory, antibureaucratic, and egalitarian values has had its full intended effect.

Indeed, some of the most important effects on the attitudes of rank-and-file cadres may have been ones quite different from those intended. One senses, in talking with both middle-level and low-level cadres in China today, uncertainty and caution about the overall political situation in China, as well as about their own political positions in the future. Events of the past eight years have underlined the dangers and risks of playing active political roles or possessing authority in China, and many cadres today impress one as predisposed to "play it safe" rather than to show individual initiative. It is impossible to judge how widespread this attitude may be, but it would not be surprising if many of those who were attacked during the Cultural Revolution and then sent to May 7 schools for reindoctrination were traumatized by the experience. If so, the consequences could be that large numbers of cadres will be inclined to pursue cautious strategies of political survival rather than show the kind of activism Mao and his supporters hoped to inspire.

As an increasing number of old cadres have returned to their former posts, the size and complexity of the state bureaucracy at lower levels appear to have been steadily growing once again. Although the data available are still insufficient to form confident judgments about the results, there is evidence that in some areas at least the governmental structure may be approaching its former state. To cite one example. the Shanghai Municipality (a provincial-level unit) had by the beginning of 1973 roughly forty specialized bureaus under its Party and Revolutionary Committees, covering virtually all the major areas of activity that the government had concerned itself with in the period before the Cultural Revolution.[64] Although no information was available on the total number of cadres employed, the experience of one agency in the Shanghai government may be indicative of recent trends. According to a cadre on its payroll, this agency had a staff of roughly a hundred before the Cultural Revolution. When large numbers of cadres were first "sent down" to May 7 schools, the total actually working in Shanghai dropped to roughly sixty (although those sent to May 7 schools remained on the agency's payroll).[65] In the two years 1971–72, the number slowly but steadily increased until by late 1972 it had reached eighty— and it was still growing. Of these, sixty were cadres who had worked in the agency before the Cultural Revolution and only about twenty were new.

It is not possible to say how typical this particular agency in Shanghai may be; nevertheless its experience supports a general impression, with which some local cadres in China say they agree, that the state bureaucracy at levels below the "center" has been moving steadily, in terms of structure and the numbers of cadres employed, back toward the situation that prevailed before the Cultural Revolution. This trend may be stronger at subnational levels than at the center because of the regime's emphasis on decentralization. The degree of economic decentralization may be less than is sometimes assumed (see Chapter 3), but there seems little doubt that local authorities now carry greater responsibilities. This probably helps to explain the seeming restoration of relative normalcy in routine government operations at the provincial level and below.

The greatest uncertainties today concern the structure, operations, and interrelationships of political institutions at the center. It is extraordinary that, as of mid-1973, it had been impossible for eight years to find in the public record any comprehensive listing of the structures of the Party, army, or state apparatus in Peking. If one were to judge the situation during this period simply from the lack of published official data, it would be logical to conclude that the situation continued to be so fluid that the bureaucracies at the national level found it almost impossible to operate; clearly, this has not been the case. There has been ample evidence for some time that the central apparatus is again functioning, that important policy decisions are being made, and that major programs are being implemented. Despite grave difficulties—and there have been many—the regime at the top leadership level is obviously a "going concern." But the inability of China's leaders over a period of eight years to reveal, even to the Chinese people, any clear picture of the regime's institutional structure at the top or to announce publicly what bodies have existed, who has staffed them, what their respective roles and functions have been, and how they have interrelated does indicate how difficult it has been to crystallize the situation into a genuinely stable pattern.

Second-level cadres in China emphasized to visitors in early 1973 that the Party Politburo was again—or still—the body in which the regime's most important policy decisions were being made. But it was impossible to delineate the broad structure of decision making at the center or define the relationships among the various centers of decision making in Peking. Clearly, the processes of decision making have been less well defined, and more diffuse, than in the past.

As of mid-1973, it was still impossible, moreover, to say who constituted the Politburo. It had been apparent for some time that the Politburo's membership included a mixture of at least three identifiable groups apart from Mao himself—a group of state leaders associated with Premier Chou En-lai, a number of national and local military leaders who survived the Lin Piao purge, and several "leftists" such as Chiang Ch'ing and Yao Wen-yuan. But what balance existed among these was impossible to say.

It was even less clear what relationships have existed, and how such relationships may have affected the decision-making process, between the Chairman's own office (and his "palace guard" of personal retainers and supporters) and the Politburo as an institution, or, for that matter, between Chou (and the State Council which has traditionally been his main institutional base) and the Politburo. As of mid-1973, in fact, no one could yet describe exactly the composition of the Party bureaucracy. The old Secretariat was not mentioned in the 1969 constitution and had still not been publicly mentioned by 1973; yet it was evident that something like it was, of necessity, being slowly rebuilt. It was impossible to determine, however, even what departments operated under the Party center, to say nothing of who staffed them, how they operated, or how influential they were. What little was known suggested that it may well have been a very different body from its predecessor—and less powerful or important.

Nor has much more been known about the Party's Military Affairs Commission, the body that wielded such enormous power under Lin Piao. It is reasonable to assume that, under Yeh Chien-ying's leadership, it has continued to be a body of some significance, but very little has been publicly revealed about it, and its power may well have declined since Lin Piao's political demise.

Although it has been possible since 1972 to piece together from scattered sources substantial information about the evolution of the top bodies in the state structure, the gaps leave a wide range of questions unanswered. And the resulting picture has been similar in some respects to that we have of the Party—a situation slow to crystallize into a genuinely stable and definite pattern.

As of mid-1973, there was still no state Chairman at the top of the state structure and had been none since the ouster of Liu Shao-ch'i in 1966, although elder statesman Tung Pi-wu served as "acting Chairman" and performed a few minor ceremonial functions. The lack of a Chairman for so many years has not had any great political or operational significance, since Party Chairman Mao and Premier Chou have performed all the functions anyone in that position might have performed. Nevertheless, the failure for more than seven years to select a new Chairman (or to settle the reported differences over whether there should even be such a post) has been one of many symptoms of the leadership's inability to agree on the shape and management of a new state structure.

Another sign of continuing disagreement has been the regime's inability, as was discussed earlier, to adopt a new constitution and convene a new National People's Congress. The last time a full session of the NPC was held was in the winter of 1964–65, and the last meeting of its Standing Committee was in early 1966. Although never a very important body in decision-making terms, the NPC met almost every year until 1965 and, because of its official constitutional status as the highest authority in the government, it served as a symbolically important forum where comprehensive reports on government work were made and new national budgets, plans, and programs were unveiled. Since the last NPC was held, the regime has for the most part simply not issued comprehensive reports or broad programmatic policy statements. This has tended to reinforce other evidence indicating that, even though the general directions of policy have been shaped by Mao and Chou, important divisions have persisted within the leadership over both organization and policy, and these have made it impossible for the regime to articulate many of its goals publicly in broad policy statements—or to convene a new NPC to endorse them.

As for the state bureaucracy, as of mid-1973 no comprehensive table of organization of state institutions and leaders at the national level had been published in China since before the Cultural Revolution. The explanation in part is that the structure has continued to undergo change, and it has been extremely difficult for the leadership to agree on appointments to the top bureaucratic posts.

The broad outline of the bureaucratic structure at the national level could be delineated by mid-1973 by piecing together scattered bits of information.[66] But beyond that outline few details are known today. The State Council (consisting of China's Premier, Vice Premiers, and leading Ministers) was operating effectively again, under Chou En-lai's leadership, as the principal decision-making body at the top of the state structure. Cadres in China emphasized, undoubtedly correctly, the importance of its role. However, no announcements were yet being made of its plenary sessions, and it was not known how frequently it met or what was discussed at its sessions. (Before the Cultural Revolution, it met about once a month, and the press frequently summarized the major items on its agenda or the principal actions taken.) Nor was it known who—or even how many people—were members.

The uncertainties about the State Council's operations were underlined by the fact that the six State Council staff offices which had functioned under its aegis in the 1960s—and had exercised great power as bodies coordinating the entire state bureaucracy—apparently had been abolished, and no comparable bodies were known to have been established to replace them. Perhaps similar coordinating functions had been assumed by the Premier's own office, or by a State Council secretariat of some sort—or, as some cadres in China stated, perhaps the Party Politburo itself now did the coordinating. But there was no concrete basis for knowing the real situation.

Finally, many questions remained unanswered about the structure and functioning of the ministries and other bodies directly under the State Council—the organizations making up the bulk of the central state bureaucracy. As stated earlier, it was evident that the number of ministries had been cut by about half, largely through mergers and the regrouping of previously existing bodies, and their personnel was at one time reported to have been reduced to a small proportion of the pre-1966 level. In many instances, even by mid-1973, no one had yet been formally appointed to be permanent ministry head. The most striking case was the Ministry of National Defense. Not only had no minister been appointed to replace Lin Piao; no replacements had yet been named to succeed the subordinate service chiefs and staff officers purged along with him in 1971. In fact, as of early 1973, roughly one-third of all ministries still had no permanent minister and were being run by second-level men holding vice ministerial jobs; and roughly two-thirds of the ministers who had been announced by that time were men drawn from the military establishment rather than the state bureaucracy.[67]

In light of these facts, it was quite remarkable that, from 1970 or 1971 on, the top state agencies of government appeared to be operating with a reasonable degree of efficiency and effectiveness—to judge not only from the direct experiences of visiting foreigners dealing with those few ministries engaged in foreign relations, but also by the observable results of ministry activities at lower levels in the society. It was necessary to reserve judgment until more became known about how government agencies were operating, but they were clearly doing better than might have been expected in light of the drastic shakeup during the Cultural Revolution. How can this be explained?

One possible explanation is that a hard core of experienced and qualified bureaucrats survived the turmoil and purges of the Cultural Revolution, and it was doubtless these backbone elements who were able to restore the ministries' basic functions fairly rapidly. And although the cuts doubtless had a demoralizing effect on many cadres, conceivably some of the personnel reductions had certain positive effects, eliminating deadwood and checking tendencies toward routine bureaucratic performance. It is also possible that the ministries' staffs have steadily grown and been strengthened since the shakeup of 1969–70, and that their performance has steadily improved as this has occurred. (According to one Foreign Ministry employee, his ministry's personnel roster totaled roughly 3,000 before the Cultural Revolution, dropped to a low point of about 1,000, but by late 1972 had grown to 2,000 and was "still expanding."[68])

Another very real possibility is that the administrative reorganizations of the late 1960s were in actuality considerably less drastic and had much less impact at the bureau level in the ministries than was assumed at the time. Even before the Cultural Revolution, the regime frequently carried out fairly sweeping ministry-level reorganizations —abolishing certain ministries or creating new ones, merging some and splitting others—yet the bulk of available evidence suggests that there was significant continuity and stability at the bureau level over the years. Whatever the structure at the ministry level, the bureaus and other subministry bodies usually remained largely intact and continued to perform their essential functions. Finally, there is no doubt that both during and since the Cultural Revolution, Premier Chou has tried, with considerable success, to defend the essential integrity of the state bureaucracy against assaults and to ensure that they retained a capacity to perform the most important state functions.

It is remarkable that the institutions of government at the center in China have functioned as well as they have in recent years. But they obviously have been less effective than they could have been under more "normal" circumstances, and their new structure has yet to stabilize on a lasting basis. An atmosphere of tentativeness continues to permeate them, as it does other political institutions in China. As of mid-1973, many institutional arrangements in Peking were still almost certainly ad hoc improvisations with an uncertain future. Educational policy at a national level, to cite one example, was in the hands of a "group"—the Science and Education Group—which had absorbed three previous ministry-level organs, the Ministry of Education, the Ministry of Higher Education, and the Scientific and Technological Commission.[69] Although described by one of its ranking cadres as the "equivalent" of a ministry, the Science and Education Group was not so designated and appeared to be a temporary arrangement.

The fact that it took half a decade to fill two-thirds of China's top ministerial posts suggests that the ministries were a principal focus of political struggles. And the fact that military men outnumbered civilian bureaucrats in the new appointees to ministerial posts suggests that in the central institutions of government, as elsewhere in the system, the situation had as yet by no means returned to that existing before 1965, and that serious civil-military problems probably persisted.

The convening of the Tenth Party Congress in August 1973 was an important milestone in the post–Cultural Revolution and presuccession process of political reconstruction, but the Congress itself did not result in any dramatic new moves affecting China's institutional structure and did not even shed much new light on the changes that had occurred earlier. Clearly the principal purpose of the Congress, and its main accomplishment, was the selection—or, more accurately, the endorsement—of China's leadership for the transition from the Mao to the post-Mao era. (See Chapter 4 for details.) The new Party constitution adopted by the Congress was not a very revealing document. The clause in the 1969 constitution designating Lin Piao as Mao's successor was deleted, as expected.[70] Five men were elected as Vice Chairmen of the Party, instead of one as in 1969, and the Standing Committee's membership was expanded from five to nine. But otherwise the changes were relatively minor, and the new constitution was just as short, vague, and uninformative about the structures of the Party as the 1969 document had been. Like the constitution it replaced, it provided few details about the central Party apparatus and simply stated that "a number of necessary organs, which are compact and efficient, shall be set up" under the Central Committee.

The brevity and vagueness of the 1973 Party constitution reinforced other evidence that the situation in Peking was still an evolving one and that the leadership was not yet in a position to delineate, in any constitutional document, organizational structures that might undergo further change. Nevertheless, the fact that it was possible to hold the Congress clearly marked a new stage in the regime's effort to consolidate its institutional structures as well as its leadership as they had evolved subsequent to the Cultural Revolution and Lin Piao purge, and it now seems likely that further information about the Party's institutions will gradually be made public.

At the Party Congress, Chou En-lai announced that a new National People's Congress would be convened shortly. The convening of an

NPC should be a signal that the regime has reached a point in the reconstruction process that makes it possible to present officially a reasonably firm delineation of the new governmental structures in China and of the men who lead them. There is good reason to believe that, when it finally occurs, this will not involve many unexpected changes or real surprises. Present indications are that it will, for the most part, simply legitimate and endorse changes that have occurred in the past several years. Even if the new structures are delineated in considerable detail, however, it will not be justifiable to conclude that China's institutions have been firmly stabilized; the process of institutional adjustment and change under way since the Cultural Revolution began seems destined to continue into the post-Mao era. Looking ahead, it seems almost certain that there will be more reorganizations and further changes of personnel reflecting shifts in the political balance among competing groups in the leadership.

In the light of all that has been discussed above, it is clear that China has suffered a major institutional crisis in recent years, and the process of reestablishing a stable institutional structure has been extremely difficult, but the root of the institutional problem as of 1973 would seem to lie less in the nature of the institutions themselves than in the continuing divisions within the leadership.

It is true that China's institutional crisis in the late 1960s occurred not simply because of struggles within the top leadership, but because Mao and his closest supporters chose deliberately to shake up and try to change the basic nature of the bureaucracies; in fact, Mao's intention was to check and reverse the entire process of institutionalization. As time has gone on, however, it has seemed more and more likely that the pressures operating on the regime will result, step by step, in the restoration of a pattern of institutions generally similar to that existing before the upheaval of 1966–68. It seems improbable, moreover, that in the foreseeable future any leadership group in China will try after Mao dies to start another anti-institutional attack comparable to that which Mao instigated. This is not to imply that none of the institutional changes of recent years will leave any lasting imprint, but rather that there will probably continue to be strong pressures to restore an institutional pattern that, in broad structural terms, is not fundamentally different from that of the period before the Cultural Revolution.

It will take time, however, to reestablish in any full sense the regime's previous foundations for institutional stability and legitimacy. How long will depend on the time required for the leadership to reach a genuine consensus, restore unity, and achieve a stable pattern of relationships and balance of power among the principal institutional power centers in the post-Mao system. If and when these problems are resolved, greater institutional stability will probably follow; but until they are resolved, considerable institutional instability will probably persist.

Consequently, it is difficult to foresee precisely what will happen to China's institutional structure—as to so much else in China—until it is possible to see what the outcome of the succession is likely to be. The destabilization of institutions that resulted from the open conflict of the late 1960s has multiplied the problems facing China's leaders, but this fact, in and of itself, has not predetermined what will happen in the future. The key question for the future is whether China's most powerful leaders, in the Party, army, and state bureaucracy—and in the many subgroups within these large institutional hierarchies—will be able to subordinate their differences of outlook and conflicts of interest sufficiently to manage a relatively smooth succession and build a more cohesive leadership after Mao's death. If so, the prospects for restoring institutional stability will be relatively good. If not, one can expect continued power struggles and persistent institutional instability to go hand in hand, in the future as in the past.

II

The Changing Political
Roles of the Military

SOME of the greatest imponderables about China in the period ahead relate to the character of the military and its role in Chinese society and politics.[1] The military establishment built by the Communists is the strongest and most effective in Chinese history. It is also the most ideologically motivated and politicized. It has been subjected to conflicting pressures in the course of its development, however, and its roles in society and politics have undergone great changes in response to changing political conditions and demands. The complicated set of problems arising out of the legacy of recent events has affected both the military itself and civil-military relations, and how these problems are handled will be a major determinant of future trends in China.

Politics and military affairs have been inextricably intertwined in modern China. The People's Liberation Army (PLA) spearheaded the Communists' victory in 1949, and the Cultural Revolution emphasized the fact that after two decades of Party rule, the power of the army is still crucial in the political arena. During 1967–68, when civilian authority and institutions were seriously weakened by Mao's assaults on bureaucracy, the military was called upon to fill the vacuum. It became the dominant political force in the country, and military personnel assumed major leadership roles at every level of society. As the rebuilding of the civilian institutions of the regime has progressed in more recent years, the political roles of the military have been reduced, but the PLA continues to exercise extensive influence in civilian affairs, and overall civil-military relations are still complex and delicate. Like so much else in China, they appear to be in a state of transition, undergoing change, and afflicted by many problems.

Strains between civilian and military leaders reached a point of acute crisis in late 1971, when the central military leadership was subjected to a major purge, and important differences concerning the future of the military and its appropriate political roles still exist within the Chinese leadership as a whole, as well as within the military establishment itself. The questions still to be resolved concern not only the scope of direct military intervention in political affairs and the overall relationship between the military and civilian leaders, but also the degree of centralization and decentralization of China's armed forces, the relative importance of the various social roles performed by the PLA, and the extent to which it will be either a modernized defense force concerned primarily with national security or a politicized revolutionary army emphasizing domestic tasks and mobilizational activities.

The answers to such questions may not become clear until after the succession, and what they will be will probably depend in considerable part on the character and outcome of the succession. The kind of overall national leadership that emerges (and the influence of military men in it), the success of current efforts to rebuild strong Party and government organizations, and the degree to which strengthened civilian institutions can achieve economic growth and social stability will all affect the future character and roles of the military. The outcome will also depend on the kind of leaders who emerge within the military establishment itself and their outlook on key military and nonmilitary issues. It will also be influenced by the degree to which future Chinese military leaders are preoccupied by domestic problems and internal politics or by external pressures and foreign threats—especially those they perceive to be posed by the Soviet Union.

The Historical Context

China has long had a unique tradition of civilian bureaucratic rule, but throughout Chinese history the military has played an extremely important political role, especially in periods of domestic conflict when civilian institutions have weakened. Virtually every new dynasty during China's long imperial past came to power by military means, and military forces garrisoning the country always provided the ultimate prop for domestic political power, even when they were relatively unobtrusive. Whenever social order has broken down, power has tended to gravitate into the hands of military leaders, especially those with strong local power bases.

Following the collapse of the Ch'ing dynasty in 1911, China entered just such a period. For more than four decades, political power was monopolized by military leaders, first by the numerous local warlords who carved China up into small fiefdoms, and then by leaders of the two main revolutionary movements competing for supremacy—the Nationalists and the Communists—both of which attempted to acquire power and reintegrate China in part through military means.

From the late 1920s on, the Communists placed a high priority on the need to acquire military power, and between then and their take-over of power in 1949, they built a powerful revolutionary army. This army was fundamentally different from anything in China's past, including the Nationalists' revolutionary army. On the basis of principles evolved by Mao Tse-tung, Chu Teh, and others, politics and military affairs were intimately linked. Viewed as the military arm of the Communist Party, the army was subjected to direct and close Party control. Consisting predominantly of mobile and guerrilla units and made up largely of peasant recruits, it operated in widely scattered areas of China's rural hinterland. Its functions were not only to fight all the Communists' enemies, both foreign and domestic, but also to carry out a wide range of revolutionary political, economic, and social tasks. It was a "school" for political indoctrination, a propaganda force to win mass support, and a major instrument for unprecedented mass mobilization. It was also an important work force, heavily involved in economic activities. In addition, the army played a key role in establishing and running new revolutionary governments in local areas won by the Communists. Because local Communist military units often had to operate largely on their own in the 1930s and 1940s, they exercised considerable local autonomy and initiative, at least in a tactical sense. They were knit together into a unified force, however, by ideology and Party control. Great stress was placed on egalitarian values.

Before 1949, there was relatively little differentiation within the Communist movement between the function or roles of civilian and military leaders—especially senior leaders. The degree of emphasis on specialization and professional skills was an issue within the leadership as early as the 1930s, and some Communist leaders, including Chou En-lai, pushed for a clearer division of functions. Mao generally opposed such role differentiation, however, and a large proportion of the movement's top hierarchy as of 1949 wore several hats, serving as both military commanders or commissars and Party or government leaders. The Communists' military units constituted a special kind of Party-led revolutionary force led by politico-military leaders who concurrently performed multiple civilian as well as military functions.[2]

China's post-1949 military establishment evolved out of this background, and even today it is significantly influenced by revolutionary traditions that date to the 1930s and 1940s. Since 1949, however, it has obviously undergone great changes as it has confronted new tasks and problems. The process of transformation began slowly, even before the Communists' takeover, and greatly accelerated afterward.

Between 1945 and 1949, the Communists' regular military forces almost quadrupled in size, from roughly 1.3 million to over 5 million; and a large proportion of their guerrilla and mobile forces were gradually merged into larger units capable of fighting large-scale conventional, positional battles as well as carrying on mobile warfare. As this occurred, several regional forces took shape in various parts of the country; ultimately they coalesced into major Field Armies that played an extremely important role at the time of takeover. Increased centralization at the regional level, as well as the beginnings of military specialization and regularization, were under way even before the Communist takeover, and in 1946 all Communist forces were merged into the People's Liberation Army. As of 1949, the PLA was still essentially a politicized, revolutionary, Party army, but it had taken the first steps toward regularization and modernization.

It was the PLA that spearheaded the takeover of China during 1948–49. Step by step, and area by area, military units established their control, and then the Party and civilian cadres moved in and went to work. During the regime's initial years in power, while new Party and government institutions were gradually being built on a nationwide basis, Communist rule in most areas could be viewed in many respects as a form of military government, even though the PLA operated under effective overall Party direction.

The tasks facing the army at the start of Communist rule of China were enormous and extremely diverse. Many were essentially military: the completion of the physical takeover of the country, the consolidation of military power, area by area, once the initial takeover had been completed (a process that required continuing small-scale military action for several years against remnants of the Nationalists' forces), and the strengthening of China's defenses against potential external threats. It was in part to bolster the country's defenses against perceived threats from the United States and the Nationalists on Taiwan that Peking's leaders in 1950 signed an unprecedented military alliance with the Soviet Union, initiating a period of close—albeit relatively short-lived—military collaboration with Moscow.

Once domestic military supremacy was achieved, the major task within China in the early 1950s was political consolidation. As the PLA established the regime's control, Military and Administrative Committees, closely linked to the PLA's Field Armies (and for the most part led by military men), were set up in every major region of the country. At lower levels, the PLA took the lead in establishing Military Control Committees, also dominated by military personnel, to exercise basic local control. These Committees continued to wield great power in most areas for several years, until civilian Party structures, government bodies, and mass organizations had been established and were strong enough to take over and exercise civilian rule.

Personnel drawn from the PLA played leading and extensive roles in the new structures of civilian power. It would be an error, however, to view the military leaders who worked in the new civilian hierarchies as purely military men. The majority were Party-soldiers, concerned as much with political as with military affairs, and it was often difficult at that time to draw a clear line of distinction between them and civilian Party cadres. Gradually, in fact, many were "civilianized," and a large number ultimately left the armed forces to devote themselves entirely to civilian tasks. Others moved in the opposite direction, gradually returning to full-time military work and divesting themselves of civilian responsibilities. In short, a steady process of functional differentiation took place, and by the mid-1950s military and civilian roles were more distinct and separate than they had ever been during the struggle for power. Extremely close links continued between the Party and the army, however. Through a wide variety of control mechanisms, Party control of the military forces was maintained, and a significant overlap in key military and political positions persisted. At many levels, for example, one man often held concurrent positions as Party secretary and army commissar.

Modernization and Professionalization

The Korean war was a critical turning point in the development of the PLA. From late 1950 on, after China's intervention in the war, steadily increasing priority was given to defense considerations and to rapid military modernization. Confronted in Korea by modernized American forces with vastly superior firepower, a growing number of PLA leaders recognized the limitations of traditional Maoist military concepts in fighting external wars and accepted the need to build a more modern, professional national defense force.[3] China's ability to prevent a United States–United Nations victory in Korea gave the PLA new prestige, both at home and abroad, but the costs in terms of casualties were enormous.

During the war, the Chinese made major strides toward military modernization, with Soviet equipment and advice, and the drive toward modernization then continued into the postwar period. The main thrust of development was now toward the creation of a new kind of professional military establishment, and Soviet experience and practices were the guiding force in military affairs, as in most other fields in China, in this period. A peak in this trend occurred in 1955, when the PLA instituted a regularized system of conscription and reserves, passed new regulations for a professional officers corps, and adopted formal systems of ranks and titles modeled on those of the Soviet army. These changes resulted in a significant downgrading of politics and ideology in relation to military affairs, and reduced emphasis was placed on the Maoist concepts that had shaped the development of the Party's revolutionary armed forces before 1949.

Modernization affected the military in other ways too. As the differentiation between military and political responsibilities increased, the military establishment was subordinated to the civilian governmental structure, and ideological and political controls over the military were loosened. During 1952–54 in most local areas, civilian Party and government bodies assumed administrative control over political, economic, and social affairs and the Military Control Commissions were disbanded. The great majority of military men who stayed in civilian posts gave up their military responsibilities, and most of those who retained posts as military commanders withdrew to a large extent from political and other non-military roles. In short, some Party-soldiers became Party cadres and others became professional soldiers. At the regional level, the existing Military and Administrative Committees were converted into Administrative Committees in 1952, and then in 1954 they were abolished. In the latter year, the Field Armies were also officially disbanded. Although, as will be noted later, the ties among men who had served under particular

Field Armies continued to be politically important, a large number of the top Field Army leaders were drawn into important military or political posts at the center, and their local political power diminished. When the regime adopted a formal governmental constitution in 1954, overall civilian control of the military was strengthened, and a Ministry of National Defense, subordinate to the cabinet (State Council) was established for the first time. The Party's top decision-making bodies—in particular the Politburo and Military Affairs Commission—retained ultimate control of policy affecting the armed forces, but under the new ministry-directed structure there was a steady growth of specialized staff and other military organs, under clearer government control, and this reinforced the prevailing trend toward military professionalism.

As of 1955, therefore, the Chinese military establishment appeared to be undergoing a basic transformation. In making major strides toward modernization, it was moving away from the revolutionary concepts that had shaped its development in earlier years and was developing into a more complex, specialized, bureaucratic type of defense establishment. At the same time, the PLA retained many distinctive characteristics reflecting its revolutionary history. Even when trends toward professionalism were at their peak, it remained a highly politicized army. Although the amount of time devoted to political indoctrination declined, it was still much more than in most armies, including that in the USSR, and military personnel were still far more involved in political and economic activities than is usual in developed societies (although the military's involvement in civilian sectors was comparable to that in some other developing nations). On balance, however, the main thrust of events was gradually transforming the PLA from a revolutionary army into a modern defense force.

In the context of the mid-1950s, the accomplishments of the Chinese military establishment were impressive. It had fought a large-scale war in Korea. Despite its costly casualties and losses in that war, it was well on its way toward building a first-class conventional army and had made some progress toward developing specialized, technologically advanced service arms. It had carried out a successful and relatively smooth demobilization, unprecedented in modern China, involving a cutback of more than a third of its troops, from over five million men to under three million.[4] The regime had brought the military under more unified and centralized control than any previous modern Chinese government had.[5] It appeared to have evolved a new and workable pattern of civilian-military relations, and to have brought the military establishment under a higher degree of civilian direction than any previous regime in modern China had been able to achieve. And it had raised the prestige of the army in China to a new peak.

These trends toward regularization, modernization, and professionalization appeared to have the support of the majority of China's military leaders. But the further they developed, the more they seemed to disturb Mao and others in the leadership who shared his revolutionary vision and his belief in the crucial importance of ideology. To Mao, increased professionalism in the PLA was symptomatic of a broader process which, as he and his closest followers saw it, threatened to weaken and eventually undermine the revolutionary nature of the regime. While there was reason to have pride in the rapid and orderly transformation of the PLA from a fairly simple revolutionary army into a strong and modern conventional military establishment, Mao and some others feared that the changes would reinforce a general decline in revolutionary commitment, and consequently they regarded the trend toward professionalism as retrogressive and dangerous.

Reassertion of Revolutionary Values

By 1956 a reaction had set in. Steps were taken to reemphasize the revolutionary character of the army, and the strongest proponents of professionalism in the PLA became targets of severe political criticism. Politics, ideological indoctrination, and the nonmilitary responsibilities of the PLA were given renewed stress, and the use of army personnel on labor projects was significantly expanded. Mechanisms for ensuring Party control over the military were strengthened, and the army was again drawn into more active roles in Party-directed mass campaigns that brought them into closer contact with civilian society.

The swing of the political pendulum in late 1957 and early 1958, away from the Soviet model toward Maoist-inspired policies designed to "revolutionize" Chinese society once again, had a profound impact on the PLA, as on all sectors of Chinese society. During the Great Leap Forward, Mao's military concepts as well as his other values were clearly ascendant. One dramatic manifestation of this was a nationwide drive to expand the militia (militiamen are full-time peasants and spare-time soldiers) to make "everyone a soldier." It was claimed at the time that over 100 million persons were absorbed into the militia, although in fact only a sixth of these were militiamen in the sixteen-to-thirty age bracket who received some real military training and belonged to "basic" or "backbone" units. The majority were members of "ordinary" militia units, which could include any able-bodied person between fifteen and fifty and received almost no real military training. This drive was obviously motivated in part by a desire to organize China's work force more effectively along military lines, but defense considerations were also involved. The renewed emphasis placed on militia forces tended to downgrade the importance of China's professional army, as did the renewed stress on Maoist doctrines advocating a relatively passive "people's war" defense strategy—in which any invader of China would be "drowned" in a sea of local militia as well as conventional defense forces. In the cause of furthering egalitarianism, moreover, regular officers were "transferred downward" to spend an allotted time serving in the ranks.

The shift of emphasis away from professionalism back toward earlier Maoist revolutionary doctrines was only one facet of Chinese military policy in this period, however. China continued to increase the PLA's firepower and moved toward acquiring a nuclear capability. In an agreement signed in the fall of 1957, the Soviet Union promised assistance in this field but was unwilling to provide nuclear aid without strings. When Moscow failed to give the full backing that Peking hoped for in the offshore islands crisis of 1958, and then in mid-1959 abrogated the nuclear agreement, Peking parted company with the Russians, in military as well as in other fields. Under the slogan of "self-reliance," China proceeded on its own to develop an independent nuclear capability, allocating sizable resources to both nuclear weapons and missile delivery systems, despite Mao's continuing stress on the importance of mass militia and concepts of "people's war." In contrast, relatively low priority was given to modernization of China's "conventional forces."

The responsibilities and burdens placed on China's conventional defense establishment in this period increased rather than decreased, however, as a result of a variety of international and foreign policy developments. Renewed confrontation with the United States over the offshore islands, increasing tensions on the Sino-Indian border, and finally the Sino-Soviet split—dramatized in 1960 by the withdrawal of Soviet technicians from China—led many top Chinese military leaders to question policies that emphasized, on the one hand, poorly trained and armed militia forces and, on the other, advanced nuclear weapons (which China did not actually possess before 1964), to the relative neglect of modern conventional forces.

For other reasons, too, the early 1960s were extremely difficult years for the PLA, as they were for all sectors of China's society. While the Communists continued, as always, to give preferential treatment to members of the armed forces, the post-Leap economic depression had a serious effect on military personnel as well as civilians.[6] In particular, the hardships suffered by soldiers' relatives in China's villages had a very adverse effect on the army's morale, and dissatisfaction among military men with the regime's rural policies and general conditions in China reached major proportions. Discipline in many units sagged, and the PLA high command was clearly alarmed. In practice, if not in theory, the army began to retreat from many of the policies demanded by Mao's line. Emphasis on ideology, politics, and Party control declined in the army, the importance of the militia was deemphasized, and the nonmilitary activities of regular troops were cut back.

The Rise of Lin Piao and the Military

The Lushan Party plenum in 1959, and the purge at that time of both Minister of National Defense P'eng Teh-huai and Chief of Staff Huang K'o-ch'eng, not only brought to light the growing divisions in the leadership as a whole over broad national policy, but also constituted a serious crisis in military-civil relations. China's ousted military leaders were critical of many facets of Mao's military doctrine, his insistence that "politics" be in "command" in military affairs, and his attacks on military professionalism. And P'eng was also openly critical of Mao's entire Great Leap strategy for the nation, and was among those in the military who apparently believed that Mao's insistence on heightening rather than reducing Sino-Soviet tensions increased the risk to China's security.

Mao, however, resisted pressures to shift priorities to professional rather than revolutionary values in the military. In 1959, when Lin Piao and Lo Jui-ch'ing were appointed to replace P'eng and Huang as Minister of National Defense and Chief of Staff respectively, they were assigned the task of revitalizing the army in a political and revolutionary sense by rebuilding the Party's political apparatus within the military establishment, intensifying indoctrination of China's troops, and promoting once again Mao's basic military doctrines. Lin, who was obviously Mao's personal choice to head the PLA, rapidly assumed overall control of the military establishment and began implementing these policies. As the de facto head of the Party's Military Affairs Commission,[7] where major policies affecting the military were defined, he soon acquired great, and growing, influence.

Under Lin, army discipline and morale were rapidly restored. During 1960–61, he initiated an intensive rectification and indoctrination program glorifying the Thought of Mao that effectively repoliticized the army. The Party control system was rebuilt on the basis of revolutionary principles first defined by Mao at Kutien in 1929,[8] and various new political campaigns were pushed within the army to tighten discipline and political control. Yet Lin's policies were not by any means totally antiprofessional. Despite his emphasis on Maoist concepts and values, he also sponsored many measures to strengthen the PLA's military capabilities. The priority placed on nuclear development continued, and in 1964 China exploded its first nuclear device.

The political influence of the PLA—and of Lin himself—steadily increased during the first half of the 1960s. Lin's success in restoring army morale and in promoting Maoist revolutionary ideas within the PLA stood in marked contrast to the seeming lack of success, at least in Mao's view, of China's civilian Party leadership (under men such as Liu Shao-ch'i and Teng Hsiao-p'ing) in accomplishing similar goals in Chinese society as a whole. Mao not only turned increasingly to Lin to help recoup his own power and influence; he apparently also regarded Lin's successes in "revolutionizing" the army as one bright spot in what, from his perspective, was a generally dismal situation in China. Increasingly, he viewed the PLA as a model for Chinese society as a whole to emulate, and therefore looked upon Lin as a close political ally.[9]

Mao's disenchantment with the top civilian leaders in the Party bureaucracy and his tendency to rely increasingly on Lin and the army to promote his policies developed in parallel. By 1963 the entire country was being called upon to "learn from the PLA." Model soldiers such as Lei Feng were held up as examples for all citizens to imitate. Shortly thereafter, steps were taken to establish "political departments," modeled on those in the PLA, within the regime's principal civilian economic agencies,[10] and gradually the number of military officers in governmental posts grew. In the army itself, not only was intense indoctrination in Maoist Thought continued, but dramatic new steps—such as the abolition of ranks—were taken to reemphasize the PLA's revolutionary egalitarian character.

By 1965, on the eve of the Cultural Revolution, a close political alliance between Mao and Lin had been forged, and Lin had emerged as the principal spokesman for Mao's ideas.[11] The PLA had been thoroughly reindoctrinated and brought under relatively effective (although by no means completely effective, as will be noted below) political control. The army was held up as the embodiment of Mao's revolutionary ideals, and military personnel were gradually moving into new and expanded roles in the civilian sectors of society, roles that were increasingly competitive with those of Party cadres. The stage was thus set for the army-supported Maoist confrontation with the Party bureaucracy that occurred during the Cultural Revolution, and for the subsequent emergence of the army into dominant political roles throughout society.

The army itself was not free from serious internal problems and strains as all of this was occurring, and many units were less responsive to the center than the leadership in Peking hoped. Lin's position of dominance, backed by Mao, was for the moment unchallengeable, but, as later events were to show, many military leaders disagreed with both Lin and Mao. Some of these were replaced, but many others had strong local power bases and could not be easily removed. Debates between those favoring increased professionalism and those supporting the Mao-Lin policies continued. So too did debates over defense strategy. As the war in Vietnam escalated and the possibility of conflict with the United States appeared to increase, major differences within the leadership over the defense policies China should pursue reached a climax in 1965. Circumstantial evidence suggests that Chief of Staff Lo Jui-ch'ing disagreed with Mao and Lin over basic defense policy at this time, and soon thereafter he became one of the first major leaders purged as the Cultural Revolution got under way.[12]

It is difficult to judge to what extent the growing national political influence of the PLA during the first half of the 1960s was due to initiatives originating within the army and reflecting the political ambitions of men such as Lin, and how much it was a result of Mao's effort to push the military into more prominent political roles to serve as a counterweight to the Party. Both factors were doubtless involved, but the latter seems to have been more important. There is considerable evidence that many Chinese military leaders had mixed feelings about the PLA's increasing political involvement in civilian affairs on the national level. To some extent, therefore, the army leadership may have been drawn more deeply into politics reluctantly. By late 1965, however, Mao obviously regarded his close alliance with Lin as essential to his personal political future and looked to the PLA for crucial backing in his struggle to regain power from the leaders of the Party bureaucracy. Ultimately it was Lin and the army's propaganda apparatus that played the key role in helping Mao launch the Cultural Revolution. Without this strong military support, it is doubtful that Mao could have openly challenged the Party bureaucracy in the way that he did.

The political role of the military was still a limited one during the early stages of the Cultural Revolution, however, and in general the PLA remained in the background throughout 1966. Military support was a critical factor enabling Mao and his closest supporters to purge key opponents in the Party's Peking apparatus and the national Party hierarchy, and the army provided essential logistical and other support to the youths of the Red Guard movement when they started attacking the bureaucratic establishment in China. Nevertheless, the PLA remained relatively unobtrusive until early 1967, and a conscious effort was made to protect it from the main currents of political turmoil that were developing. On August 8, 1966, for example, a Central Committee directive on the Cultural Revolution limited Cultural Revolution activities within the armed forces and specified that they should be conducted not by the radical Cultural Revolution Group but by the army itself—specifically, by the Party's Military Affairs Commission and the PLA's General Political Department.[13]

Military Dominance during the Cultural Revolution

The situation changed fundamentally in early 1967. On January 23 of that year, a central directive declared that "all past directives concerning the army's non-involvement" in the Cultural Revolution were "null and void."[14] The PLA was ordered to intervene directly to "support and help the proletarian revolutionary leftists," using force if and when necessary to suppress Mao's opponents. This move was almost certainly dictated by necessity rather than by prior design. By this time the confused conflict resulting from Red Guard activities, and the temporary breakdown of civilian authority following Maoist-inspired mass "power seizures," had created a political vacuum, and China's cities were experiencing a dangerous level of social conflict. By early 1967, neither the Party nor the government was capable of providing national direction to society or even of restoring order. The restoration of order was urgently required, however, and the army was now the only national organizational instrument capable of doing this. Mao ordered the army to take charge.

There are many reasons to believe that there was ambivalence on the part of Mao, his civilian backers, and the army itself about this move. Mao was probably not unaware of the danger (although he may well have underestimated it) that the army, once entrenched in positions of great political influence, could become dominant in relations with the Party, government, and other elements in the regime and might then resist civilian efforts to assert control. Many military leaders unquestionably were aware that direct involvement in the political struggles sweeping China would divert the PLA from defense tasks and subject it to difficult pressures and internal strains. Nevertheless, once China's top leadership had ordered the army to join the fray, the PLA took energetic steps to establish some measure of military control over events, and military men rapidly moved into key positions of political leadership throughout the country.

The detailed story of the roles played by military units and personnel at the height of the Cultural Revolution, during 1967–68, is far too complicated to present here.[15] The instructions emanating from Peking varied tremendously over time. Whereas in January 1967 the PLA was ordered to intervene actively in political affairs, in April restraining orders instructed military units to refrain from shooting, making arbitrary arrests, or repressing leftist mass organizations. In June, instructions to the PLA again emphasized the need to establish order, suppress violence, and end all armed struggle and sabotage. Then, in midsummer 1967, following the July "Wuhan incident" in which a local commander in central China openly challenged Peking's authority,[16] "leftist" elements mounted political attacks on the PLA itself. By early fall (in August and September), these were halted, and the PLA was labeled "the pillar of the proletarian dictatorship."[17]

During 1968 there were further swings of the pendulum, as the military was alternately urged to exercise control and establish order and then to exercise self-restraint and allow leftist forces to press forward in their revolutionary struggles. Finally, however, in the late summer of 1968,[18] the army moved, with Mao's backing, to clamp down on excesses—to suppress disruptive radical Red Guard activities and establish firm military control—which most military men seemed strongly predisposed to do, in any case. Mao now emphasized the need for the "working class" rather than radical youth to exercise political leadership in China, and new "Mao Tse-tung Thought Propaganda Teams" were organized by the military and dispatched to assume supervisory roles in institutions and organizations throughout Chinese society. Although urban workers participated in these teams at the grassroots level, it was generally the army that organized them and military personnel who dominated them, so that in effect the PLA took charge. At the national level, the composition of the groups that assumed supervisory positions in ministries and comparable bodies was also overwhelmingly military.

At local levels, from early 1967 on, military units and personnel found themselves embroiled in incredibly complex factional struggles among competing political groups. Sometimes local military leaders tried to mediate local conflicts. At other times, they backed certain groups against others. In some situations, military leaders themselves were divided, and certain units backed one group while others backed their opponents. Over time, however, the main trend was for local military leaders to place primary emphasis on the restoration of order, and most of them suppressed the most militant radicals and threw their weight in favor of relatively conservative forces.

Within the military itself, the Cultural Revolution was a period of great stress and strain, and (as will be described in Chapter 4) there were widespread purges as well as shifts of personnel, both at the center and at local levels. Even the central military leadership proved to be very unstable. Lin maintained overall control, but the composition of the top military leadership underwent continuing change. Yang Ch'eng-wu, who became Acting Chief of Staff in late 1965 or early 1966, was replaced by Huang Yung-sheng in early 1968; in 1971 Huang too was purged. The army's own Cultural Revolution Group briefly played an influential leadership role in 1967 but fell into oblivion shortly thereafter. Especially hard hit in the purges affecting the military were the leaders who had held concurrent posts as Party secretaries and senior political commissars at local levels, as well as the PLA's General Political Department (GPD) and many of the political departments and commissars under it. These political officers played key roles in managing and directing political activities in the early stages of the Cultural Revolution, but when the attacks on the Party bureaucracy reached a peak, a large number of the political departments and commissars (many of whom had held concurrent Party posts and worked in close cooperation with civilian Party leaders) themselves suffered extensive purging. These purges had the effect of temporarily paralyzing the GPD, although in many places the political apparatus at lower levels survived and remained active. Military personnel serving in political roles were not the only victims, however; there was also a considerable turnover of regional and district military commanders.

The confused situation prevailing both in Peking and the provinces at the height of the Cultural Revolution meant that local military leaders, of necessity, had to assume tremendous responsibility for coping with local problems. As a result, a great deal of power gravitated into the hands of regional and district commanders. However, Peking never lost overall military control of the situation. The "Wuhan incident" in July 1967 was, in fact, the only major incident in which a local commander openly challenged the center, and he was quickly suppressed. One reason Peking was usually able to remove local commanders who were obstructionist was that the central military leadership retained basic control over key army corps—especially those whose commanders had close ties to Lin Piao—belonging to the PLA's "main forces."[19] Despite all the stresses and strains affecting the military, and all the purging of military leaders that took place, the loyalty of many of the most important of these units persisted; they continued to follow Peking's directives; and consequently the military establishment remained, throughout the Cultural Revolution, the one organizational hierarchy in China over which Peking was able to exercise effective— or at least relatively effective—central control.

It was for this reason that the PLA emerged in 1967–68 as the dominant political force throughout the country. In many respects, the army found itself in a situation similar to that of the takeover period after 1949. During 1967–68, when the civilian Party and government bureaucracies were virtually paralyzed as a result of the attacks made by the Red Guards, the PLA once again established Military Control Commissions, as it had in 1949, throughout most of the country, and exercised political control through them. The Party structure within the army remained fairly intact in this period even though the civilian

Party bureaucracy virtually ceased effective operations, and military cadres assumed leadership positions at every administrative level, and within institutions and enterprises of all kinds, exercising functions that civilian cadres had previously monopolized.

One of the functions that military personnel had to assume early in the Cultural Revolution was responsibility for ensuring local order. When the Red Guards attacked the regime's bureaucratic establishment, most Public Security organs, like the principal Party organizations, ceased effective operation, and the army had no alternative but to assume local police responsibilities. Gradually, from 1968 on, the Public Security apparatus was rebuilt under military supervision, but the process was a slow one, and public order was not fully restored until 1969–70. Military personnel also assumed extensive responsibilities during the Cultural Revolution for public indoctrination and propaganda directed at the civilian population as a whole. By late 1968, in fact, the propaganda teams organized by the PLA had spread throughout China and were one of the main instruments for enforcing ideological conformity. The military's role in running the society embraced economic affairs as well. Military representatives were stationed in many if not most major economic production units, not only in the principal industrial and commercial enterprises, but also for a time in some Communes and Brigades as well. The extent to which they attempted directly to exercise basic planning and managerial functions or simply exercised overall political control, leaving the detailed management of the economy to qualified civilians, is not wholly clear, and probably varied from place to place, but there is no doubt that they assumed basic supervisory roles in China's economic organizations, as in other kinds of institutions.

Most important, the military played a primary role in directing the initial process of rebuilding a new structure of Party and government institutions to replace those that had been largely dismantled during the early stages of the Cultural Revolution. From early 1967 on, when efforts were made to organize new Revolutionary Committees at every level and within virtually every area and institution throughout China, military personnel played key roles in establishing them, and from the start dominated their leadership, especially in the Committees at higher levels. Although representatives of mass organizations were given important roles in many of them at the beginning, military men increasingly asserted their primacy as political struggles continued through

1967 and 1968. By late 1968, when the Red Guard movement was suppressed, the dominance of military leaders in the majority of the most important Revolutionary Committees was obvious and overwhelming. Gradually thereafter, Party cadres reemerged into roles of increasing importance, but the most militant leaders of mass organizations who had come to the fore in the early stages of the Cultural Revolution virtually disappeared from the scene.

The PLA—or at least the Party leaders within the army—played a major leadership role also in the rebuilding of an independent Party structure, which began in earnest as the process of constructing Revolutionary Committees neared completion. From late 1968 on, Party "core groups," formed within the Revolutionary Committees, began the long, slow process of screening, selecting, and indoctrinating members for a reconstructed Party apparatus. Not surprisingly, military men occupying dominant positions in the Revolutionary Committees at higher levels played key roles in these core groups and in the new Party Committees that ultimately emerged. Over time, as noted already, an increasing number of former Party cadres were rehabilitated, and gradually they resumed many of the tasks they had performed before the Cultural Revolution; but in the new Party Committees, as in the most important Revolutionary Committees, military men continued to occupy very important leadership positions.

The Changing Military-Civilian Balance

Once the active phase of the Cultural Revolution had ended, steps began to be taken toward a restoration of civilian authority and civilian institutions, but not until 1971 was there a clear effort to reduce the military's political dominance. During and since 1969–71, however, former Party cadres and the Party as an institution have reemerged once again into important roles. The new Party Committees have slowly resumed leadership functions, and their key members—both civilian and military—dominate the Revolutionary Committees, which have become, in effect, bodies comparable to the government councils that existed before 1965. As this has occurred, the army's direct role in ruling the country has gradually diminished, and the number of military men assigned to supervise civilian institutions and enterprises has been slowly reduced.

The extent to which the political roles of the military have been cut back has not been easy to determine, however. Although impressionistic judgments based on brief visits to China obviously cannot be given excessive weight, they do provide some clues to the situation existing today. In eight major Chinese cities—and nearby rural areas— that I visited in late 1972 and early 1973, it was apparent that despite the recent reduction in the PLA's political roles military men still permeated much of civilian society in China (at least in key urban areas) and continued to occupy very influential political positions.

In every factory and university, as well as every province and municipality, that I visited, active military men still made up a significant portion of the membership of both the Party Committees and Revolutionary Committees. Their numbers may well have been smaller than in the recent past, but they still occupied very influential positions. Although there had been no mention in the Chinese press for some time of the Military Control Commissions established during the Cultural Revolution and it had been widely assumed that they had been disbanded, I found that the Shanghai Military Control Commission still operated (sharing a building with the Municipal Party Committee and Revolutionary Committee), and it seems reasonable to assume that others like it operated elsewhere. In all but one city that I visited, the military still exercised direct control over the police, and in Shanghai the army was still directly involved in some economic fields as well. Questioned about civil-military relations, Party leaders asserted that military personnel, like everyone else in China, must operate under Party leadership and control, but one nevertheless obtained the impression that in reality civil-military relations continued to be more complex, and less definitely crystallized, than this assertion would imply.

In every city and suburban area that I visited, moreover, ordinary rank-and-file soldiers, sailors, and airmen were ubiquitous. We were rarely, in fact, out of sight of military personnel. They were in uniform, but most were unarmed and remarkably few seemed to be engaged in military activity. In fact only a small number were doing observable work of any kind. It was difficult to explain such an obvious and enormous presence of rank-and-file military men, especially in China's major cities. Conceivably, their ubiquitousness may have reflected increased recruitment in the recent past to strengthen China's defenses. Possibly domestic political factors were the cause of it. In any case, that they permeated urban areas and were highly visible to the general populace was a political fact of considerable importance, no matter how one explained it. Even though there was little evidence of overt military-civilian tensions, the civilian population was constantly aware of a pervasive military presence.

The likely directions of future trends in military affairs and civil-military relations cannot be guessed, however, from the scanty clues available about the situation at any particular time. They will be determined by a complex interplay of forces as China wrestles with a variety of difficult problems and issues—many inherited from the past, and others that are virtually certain to emerge from new developments and pressures in the post-Mao period.

The Military and the Coming Succession

The military establishment will unquestionably play a crucial role in the post-Mao succession process, because in a fundamental sense it remains an ultimate arbiter of political power in China. In many respects the struggles of the 1960s that culminated in the Cultural Revolution can be viewed as part of an ongoing succession struggle. Mao's determination to impose his will on Party bureaucrats who opposed him and to select a new leadership to succeed him led him to turn to the military for support, designate Lin Piao as his political heir, and propel the military into a role of extraordinary political power. But Mao's attempt did not succeed, and the Cultural Revolution did not solve the succession problem. In 1971, Mao (who has never been able to tolerate the idea of other leaders acquiring power that appears to threaten his own) turned against Lin Piao, allegedly after an abortive coup attempt, and purged him as well as most of the other members of the new central military hierarchy, including Chief of Staff Huang Yung-sheng, who had acquired great power during the Cultural Revolution.

While important policy differences—including, probably, differences over policies toward the Soviet Union and the United States—may have helped to precipitate the leadership crisis of 1971, a more basic cause was the complex and still-unresolved problem of striking a reasonable balance between civilian and military leaders and institutions. In purging Lin, Mao and Chou acted in part to bring the military under greater civilian control, and in an immediate sense they were at least partially successful. They could not have purged Lin and the PLA's top staff officers, however, without drawing support from other important military leaders in China. Although it is difficult to know about the coalitions involved, one result of the purge may have been to increase the influence of certain powerful commanders, especially regional commanders such as Ch'en Hsi-lien in Manchuria and Hsu Shih-yu in central China, even though civilian Party leadership was clearly strengthened at the top. Even at the center, moreover, the purge of Lin Piao and the four other Politburo-level military leaders ousted with him did not lead to any sweeping attempt to oust military men of lesser rank from positions of great political influence. In fact, a number of steps were taken between 1971 and 1973 that were obviously designed to placate and appease other powerful military leaders. One of the most remarkable was the political rehabilitation of Ch'en Tsai-tao, the man who had openly challenged the center in the 1967 "Wuhan incident."

Although the posts held by the military leaders ousted in 1971 remained officially unfilled, the influence of certain other central military leaders (such as Li Teh-sheng, who now heads the PLA's General Political Department) has continued to rise. And the number of military men holding high government posts has increased rather than decreased. This was highlighted by the appointment during 1972 of a number of influential military leaders to top ministerial posts in the government, including the posts of Minister of Public Security and Chairman of the State Planning Commission; as a result of these appointments two-thirds of the known ministers in the central government were military men at the end of 1972.[20]

In the most critical period in the succession process in China, which still lies ahead, building a post-Mao coalition capable of effecting a smooth transition will depend in considerable part on whether it is possible to build a political alliance between key civilian Party leaders and powerful military commanders both at the center and at the local level. At the center, men such as Yeh Chien-ying, a military elder who since 1971 has served as Chou En-lai's principal aide for military affairs, are now important to Chou in managing military affairs, but Yeh's independent power may be quite limited; Chou's problem is to put together a new central military leadership that will cooperate effectively with him. At the local level, the support of such regional military leaders as Ch'en and Hsu could be a key to success; certainly their opposition could precipitate bitter conflict. The likelihood that both military and civilian leaders will subordinate differences and strive for unity will probably be increased if they continue to feel—as they do at present—that China faces a serious external threat, particularly from the Soviet Union.

If there should be an open power struggle at some point in the transitional process, direct military intervention to try to determine the choice of Mao's successor would be a strong possibility. One or more military leaders might strive to achieve top leadership positions themselves, or they might try to act as "kingmakers" and back particular civilian leaders in their struggles for power. In any of these circumstances, the balance between civilian bureaucrats and military leaders, which since 1971 has shifted at the highest level in favor of civilian leaders, could shift back in favor of the military.

Differentiation of Military and Civilian Roles

The future role of the military in China will be determined not only by the nature of the succession process but by the strength and effectiveness of China's reconstructed civilian institutions. The PLA assumed the dominant role in China during the Cultural Revolution to fill a vacuum resulting from the paralysis and ineffectiveness of civilian Party and government institutions at that time. The PLA intervention in the political situation was not motivated simply by an irresistible desire for power but was based on the recognition that the near-chaos in China's cities made firm intervention essential. It is in part because the rebuilding of the Party and government bureaucracies, especially at higher levels, has been a difficult and slow process that military personnel continue today to occupy key positions in many bodies dealing with civilian activities.

There will probably be continuing pressures to transfer functions from military to civilian personnel, especially, to begin with, at lower levels. The gradual movement in this direction evident today will probably continue so long as the major trend in the society at the grassroots level is—as it appears to be at present—toward greater economic and social stability. But there is great uncertainty about how far and how fast this process will occur. The transfer is likely to be very complicated and difficult, and significant military influence—considerably larger than that exercised by the PLA in the late 1950s and early

1960s—seems likely to persist in many forms for a fairly long time to come.

The likelihood that the regime will nevertheless be steadily "re-civilianized," even if only gradually, rests in part on the probability that there will be persistent pressures toward a clearer differentiation of military and civilian roles once again. Not only will Party and government bureaucrats probably exert such pressures; many professionally oriented officers within the military establishment itself are likely to favor a steady withdrawal of military personnel from civilian responsibilities. The diversion of large numbers of PLA personnel from military to civilian tasks during the Cultural Revolution created serious problems for the army. Not only were military functions of many sorts neglected; many men drawn from the army were ill equipped to perform the civilian tasks they had to assume.

Whatever the pressures for military personnel to return to military duties, however, one can expect that some officers, having tasted and enjoyed the fruits of political power, will be reluctant to relinquish it—more so, probably, even than in the post-takeover period of the 1950s. This is likely to be true of many local military commanders and commissars who have acquired senior leadership positions in the major political decision-making bodies of the regime—the new Revolutionary Committees and Party Committees—at subnational levels, as well as of many who now occupy powerful positions at the center. For some time, therefore, there is almost certain to be a much greater participation by military men in civilian Party and government agencies and a much greater overlap than before the Cultural Revolution period in military and civilian leadership at local levels—perhaps most of all at the provincial level. To the extent that this is true, the military establishment—or at least military men—will obviously continue to exercise, as they do today, very substantial power in directing the operation of many Party and government institutions.

One important question, however, is whether such leaders will continue to regard themselves primarily as part of the military establishment or whether they will come gradually to think of themselves primarily as civilians. While many professionally oriented officers will probably be inclined over time to divest themselves of civilian political responsibilities in order to return to their military careers, others can be expected to cling to positions that are essentially political and civilian, and many of them will probably eventually be separated, for all practical purposes, from the military establishment and in time be transformed into civilian cadres. There are some signs that this process is already under way.

As this occurs, the process may resemble in some respects what occurred in China in the early 1950s, when large numbers of military men who had assumed civilian Party and government leadership positions in the takeover period abandoned their military careers and were transformed into civilian cadres. If, as seems possible, a similar process again takes place during the next few years, the steady separation of military and civilian roles will gradually reduce the scope of direct and obvious military intervention in civilian affairs.

Even so, China is not likely to return soon to the situation prevailing immediately before the Cultural Revolution. There is a significant difference between the military men who assumed posts of political leadership in the regime's civilian institutions in 1967–68 and those who were transferred from military to civilian careers after 1949. In the earlier period, when the line between military and civilian roles was blurred and many of the Chinese Communist leaders had for years performed both military and political functions, the transfer of personnel from military to civilian roles was relatively easy to make. In contrast, many of the military men who acquired political power in the late 1960s had for years pursued careers that were more clearly and distinctively military. It is likely to be difficult for many of them to make a permanent shift from military to civilian roles and become genuinely civilian in outlook. To the extent that this is true and that such men retain distinctive military attitudes, the process of differentiating civilian and military roles is likely to be partial, at best, and the scope of the military's influence on Chinese politics will continue to be significantly greater than it was in the 1950s.

Another factor that will greatly influence the scope of direct military intervention in, and influence on, civilian life in China in the years immediately ahead will be the overall success of the regime in promoting economic development and social stability. Since the end of the Cultural Revolution, the general trend toward "normalcy" and the gradual strengthening of institutions have encouraged a steady reduction of the civilian roles of the military. So long as this trend continues, the broad political and economic roles of the military can be expected to diminish. If, however, the regime were to experience new economic setbacks and social conflicts, there would be increased pressures for military personnel to step in once again to try to cope with the problems caused by civilian failures. Even though such pressures seem to have decreased quite considerably since 1968, the Cultural Revolution set a precedent that makes it more, rather than less, likely that the military would be tempted to intervene decisively in another major domestic crisis in the future.

Problems and Tensions within the Military

The roles and influence of the military in China in the 1970s and beyond will be determined to a considerable degree by the kind of leaders who emerge within the military establishment itself and the attitudes of these leaders on the issues that have been debated by China's leadership for many years. The competition between Maoist and professional viewpoints will be of crucial importance. However, any analysis of the Chinese military establishment that concentrates solely, or even mainly, on this simple dichotomy grossly oversimplifies the complexities of the competing forces that have shaped the PLA and its roles in Chinese society in the past and will continue to do so in the future. References to *the* military establishment or *the* PLA can be very misleading since the Chinese military establishment is by no means wholly homogeneous or monolithic. It is true, in an overall sense, that since 1949 China's military forces have been more unified and subject to more effective centralized direction than any previous Chinese military forces ever were. It is also true that the military establishment has been a separate and distinct element in Chinese society, set apart from civilian institutions by virtue of the special training, attitudes, and patterns of life characteristic of military personnel. Nevertheless, despite its relative unity and distinctiveness, broad generalizations about the PLA are inevitably misleading; the interests, power, and roles of its different components vary significantly.[21]

Conflicts between Maoist and Professional Values

Since the early days of the Communist regime, as noted earlier, there have been important differences about the appropriate roles for the PLA and the character of political-military relations in China. One fundamental issue has concerned the extent to which the PLA should be a politicized Party-controlled army, focusing major attention on domestic tasks and serving as an important instrument for revolutionary mass mobilization or the extent to which it should be primarily a modernized, professionalized defense force designed above all to guarantee China's national security and support the regime's foreign policies. To use simple labels, the issue has been whether—or to what extent—Maoist or professional values should underlie major policies relating to military affairs and political-military relations.[22]

The differences of viewpoint have been extremely complicated and sometimes subtle, and virtually no leaders have adopted a purely Maoist or a purely professional viewpoint. All Chinese leaders have favored the development of a military establishment that could both guarantee China's security and support its international interests *and* play a variety of major domestic roles, both military and nonmilitary, in support of the regime's broad political, economic, and social objectives. The differences have been over emphasis. Nevertheless, the differences have had important consequences.

Whenever the Maoist viewpoint has been in the ascendancy, the top leaders have insisted upon the primacy of politics over "purely military" considerations. They have attempted to strengthen Party controls over, and within, the PLA. They have stressed the need for a strong Party committee apparatus within the military establishment, and for political control systems in which the commissars have as much —or more—authority than the military commanders. They have placed great emphasis on ideological indoctrination of both officers and men, focusing on the Thought of Mao, and have allocated large amounts of time to indoctrination and other political activities at the expense of time devoted to purely military training. In relations between officers and men, the Maoists have insisted upon measures to promote fairly extreme egalitarianism and have opposed strictly hierarchical, bureaucratic relationships. They have also opposed placing primary stress on the development of a professional officer corps and have tried to deemphasize or eliminate ranking systems. They have called for close relationships between military personnel and ordinary civilians and have favored the extensive use of army personnel in economic activities both to increase the ability of PLA units to support themselves and to aid civilian economic production. At times this has led to the use of military personnel on a very large scale as a work force. The Maoists have also favored direct military participation in and support of the Party's major mobilizational and propaganda campaigns. They have also held up individual military heroes, and the army as an institution, as models for civilian society. Repeatedly the Maoists have stressed the importance of local forces and rural militia units, and periodically they have attempted to expand the militia's size and functions.

These policies have reflected the Maoists' basic commitment to the use of the army for important revolutionary and mobilizational tasks within China. They have also, however, reflected distinctive concepts of military strategy and national defense. Denying that advanced weapons systems and modern firepower are the most crucial factors in modern defense, the Maoists have argued that China should rely to a large extent, in guaranteeing its security, on concepts of "people's war."[23] According to these concepts, what the defense of China requires above all is a highly political, fully mobilized, armed population capable of defeating any invading force by revolutionary tactics similar to those used by the Communists during the revolutionary struggles against the previous regime in the 1930s and 1940s. "Men" are more important than "weapons," they have insisted, and political mobilization is more important than technical modernization. While there is no doubt that ideological and political considerations have been fundamental in shaping Mao's concepts of "people's war," they have been influenced also by practical considerations—notably the desire to conserve scarce resources and to utilize to the full China's main resource, manpower.

Professionally oriented leaders in the PLA have differed, in varying degrees but increasingly over time, on each of these issues. They have tended to put primary stress on the need for technical modernization and other "purely military" considerations. They have resisted excessive Party controls and have attempted to strengthen the authority of the PLA's commanders at the expense of its commissars. They have attempted to cut back the time devoted to indoctrination and other political activities and to increase the time devoted to military training. They have also favored the development of a highly professional officer corps and emphasized the need for hierarchical discipline in the military establishment rather than egalitarian relationships.

In the professionals' view, the use of military personnel in civilian life, and in particular the employment of troops as a work force, should be restricted. They have focused their main attention on the development of the PLA's regular forces and have not regarded militia building as a priority objective. They have stressed the primary importance of China's modernized "main forces"—whose principal mission is national defense—rather than the locally based regional forces, which have been technically inferior and oriented to a greater degree toward domestic problems. And they have generally argued that the militia should be limited in both size and functions.

The attitudes of the professionals on all of these issues have reflected views different from Mao's about China's requirements for national defense. Never really accepting the validity of the Maoist "men over weapons" slogan, they have pressed for greater emphasis on technical modernization and professionalization of the PLA and have favored a strategy of defense that would rely on the development of a highly modernized military establishment rather than on concepts of mass mobilization. In their view, the ability of China to cope with potential threats from abroad requires the development of strong specialized forces equipped with, and capable of using effectively, the most sophisticated types of advanced weapons, both conventional and nuclear.

The character and roles of the military in the 1970s will obviously be determined to a considerable extent by the degree to which these competing Maoist and professional viewpoints influence concrete policy decisions. As in the past, there may well be some swings of the pendulum, as shifts occur both in China's top political leadership and in the leadership within the PLA itself. There are strong reasons to believe, however, that the long-term trend will be toward increased modernization, specialization, and professionalization in the military, and away from traditional Maoist concepts stressing the PLA's importance as a force for revolutionary change.

Mao himself has been the prime mover in pushing policies designed to "revolutionize" the PLA and maintain it as a mass-based "people's army." Once he passes from the scene, pressures toward increased modernization and professionalism, which have long been at work in China, seem likely to predominate eventually. Future leaders will probably not be able, even if they try—which is doubtful—to oppose such pressures in the way or to the extent that Mao has. Mao has been able to keep his concepts alive, and impose them to a degree, because of his unique position; but the pressures toward increased military professionalism have remained strong under the surface despite all of Mao's efforts to check them.

Over the years, most of the men who have risen to top command responsibilities in the PLA have sooner or later been impelled to place greater emphasis on the need for modernization and professionalism than Mao has been willing to do. China's first Minister of National Defense, P'eng Teh-huai, was firmly committed to modernization and professionalization, and his differences with Mao on this score were a major cause of his political demise. Even Lin Piao, while proclaiming Maoist doctrine, attempted to improve the PLA's capabilities as a modern fighting force, and many of his policies in the 1960s were in fact compromises between Maoist and professional goals. Despite consistent obeisance to Maoist military concepts, he was able in practice to implement many policies that steadily enhanced the PLA's "purely military" capabilities.

It is a striking fact, also, that the military leaders who have risen to top staff positions[24] in the PLA over the years—especially those who have become Chiefs of Staff—seem, invariably, to have given high priority to the need for modernization and professionalization once they have assumed leadership positions at the top of the military hierarchy. The case of Lo Jui-ch'ing provides a good illustration. Although his early career in public security affairs had been notably political, once he was elevated to the position of Chief of Staff, he became a strong supporter of the professional ethic and in practice gave priority to essentially military concerns rather than to Maoist-inspired political objectives.[25] In general, the Ministry of National Defense— and the staff officers under it—has tended to be a stronghold of professionalism; this may explain why there was such a rapid turnover in top staff positions in the PLA from the late 1950s on, as Mao tried to reassert his political views. There is good reason to believe that the PLA's senior staff officers will continue to resist tendencies to place "politics in command" of the PLA and that their views will carry increased weight after Mao's death. This likelihood will be enhanced if Chinese leaders, civilian and military, continue to believe that other major powers—especially the Soviet Union—are hostile and threatening toward China. It is significant that Chou En-lai, at critical junctures in the past, has seemed to throw his support in favor of professionalism in the military establishment as well as in the civil bureaucracies, and the recent increase in his power should reinforce trends in this direction, which in fact are probably already under way.

Central versus Local Power

One important distinction in China's military establishment, mentioned earlier in passing, is that between the "main forces" and the "regional forces." The PLA's main forces are the principal regular combat units consisting in large part of defense-oriented army corps plus the technically advanced forces in the air force, navy, and other specialized units. In contrast, the regional forces are locally based units which include garrison forces and other miscellaneous units that have a stronger orientation toward domestic problems and greater involvement in local responsibilities. The main forces, as noted previously, have been subjected to relatively close and effective central direction (although even some of them became deeply embroiled in local politics during the Cultural Revolution), and professional considerations have shaped, and probably will continue to shape, their development to a large degree. The regional forces have generally been less modernized and more deeply rooted in local situations and domestic politics. Local military leaders—at the level of the military regions in China—have exercised significantly greater discretionary power over regional forces than over main force units (although regional control has not been unlimited, and the Military Affairs Commission has issued direct commands to regional forces when it chose to do so). The role of these leaders, and the forces they control, will be very important in determining future relationships between central and local power.[26]

The primary function of regional forces in China is one that has a long-standing tradition in Chinese history: to garrison the country and serve as the ultimate guarantor of the political authority of the ruling regime. There is no doubt that a significant portion of the PLA will be assigned, in the future as in the past, to this function. What is not clear, however, is whether such forces will be effectively subjected to close central direction or will exercise significant local power under relatively loose central control.

China has periodically been plagued by the development of strong local military forces which the center has been unable to control effectively. In the immediate pre-Communist period, such forces, operating under warlord or semiwarlord leadership, in effect ran large portions of the country. Since 1949, local military leaders have never defied central leadership in the way that warlords did earlier, but many of them have nevertheless accumulated great power. In the early years of the regime, there was relatively little rotation of regional and district military leaders, and this undoubtedly contributed, more than was realized at the time, to a steady growth of localism. When Lin Piao became Minister of National Defense, the central military authorities intervened more frequently to shift local military leaders, and in the late 1960s many of them were purged during the Cultural Revolution; even so, the de facto power of local military leaders clearly increased during the confused period of public disorder in 1967–68, when substantial power gravitated from the central military authorities to local commanders as the latter exercised increased initiative to deal with complicated local problems because the situation forced them to do so.

During this period, and particularly after the Wuhan incident of 1967, some outside observers predicted that a new kind of "warlordism"—that is, some fairly extreme form of military localism—would probably emerge in China. This has not occurred. While many local Chinese military leaders were less responsive than Mao and Lin hoped, in the final analysis, the majority were basically loyal to Peking; essential central control was maintained. One important contributing factor was Peking's ability to use main force units, when necessary, to enforce its will throughout the country. Another, undoubtedly, was the fact that the technology of modern warfare now makes it very difficult for any regional commander to challenge the center, which maintains control over crucial matériel. But there were also other, more fundamental explanations. Perhaps most important was the fact that virtually none of China's local military leaders succumbed to the kind of parochial localist impulses that had been characteristic of the pre-1949 warlords. When ultimate loyalties were tested in a crisis situation, their loyalty to the center overrode local ties. No matter how strong their local roots or how much they sought to protect their local interests, their essential nationalism and commitment to national unity and to the regime's broad national goals were such that they were not prepared to challenge Peking openly or inclined to strive for extreme autonomy.

It seems highly unlikely that any trend toward extreme localist warlordism will emerge in China in the period immediately ahead, even if there is renewed internal conflict. Nevertheless, difficult questions will arise regarding the balance between central and local military leaders, the relative importance of defense-oriented main forces and locally oriented regional forces, and the pattern of relationships between them.

Currently, the dominant leadership in Peking seems determined to strengthen centralized control over local military units once again and is trying to do so through varied means, including increased transfers of local military leaders and units from one area to another. In all likelihood this trend toward centralization will continue, especially if the influence of professionally oriented leaders at the center increases. To the extent that the trend continues, it should contribute to the strengthening of the PLA's main forces and result in a reduction of the influence of regional forces.

But the shift of power back to the center may not be an easy or rapid process, and it will probably encounter significant resistance from powerful military leaders at the regional and district levels. Certain of these leaders probably now enjoy greater power than any local military leaders have since the early days of the regime, and it is logical to assume that dramatic moves to restrict or reduce their power would encounter strong opposition in some cases. Even if central leaders in Peking are determined to strengthen central control, therefore, they will probably have to compromise with the realities of decentralized power for some time to come, and local military leaders will probably continue to exercise substantial political influence not only in the regions and provinces where their power is based but also in the major Peking forums in which national policies are determined.

Commanders and Commissars[27]

Ever since the 1920s there has been a dual command structure in the Chinese military establishment, and this continues today. Following Mao's dicta that "political power grows out of the barrel of a gun" but "the Party commands the gun and the gun must never be allowed to command the Party" (the latter dictum was obviously compromised during the Cultural Revolution but was never overtly abandoned), the Chinese Communists have insisted on maintaining elaborate mechanisms for Party control over the military. At every level, from the top down to the company level, Party Committees or Branches have been organized within military units, and from the highest level down to the regiments there have been special political departments or offices, and at lower levels individual commissars, representing the Party's interests.

The relationship between the PLA's commanders, responsible for military affairs, and its commissars, responsible for political control, internal security, indoctrination, civilian-military relations, welfare, and recreation (and virtually everything else not strictly military in nature) has always been a complex one. In theory, commanders and commissars have been equals, each exercising important powers in their respective spheres. In reality, the relationship—not surprisingly—has involved many built-in tensions and problems. In view of the fact that any system of dual leadership based on a sharing of power is likely to involve frictions and a competition for power, the system has generally worked remarkably well during most of the past forty-odd years. At times, however, the frictions have been great.

As suggested earlier, the relative power and influence of the commanders and the commissars has periodically shifted over the years. When "politics" has been "in command" and the Maoist ethos emphasized, the power of the commissars has increased at the expense of the commanders, Party controls in the PLA have been strengthened, and the scope of political work of all sorts—as well as the time and effort devoted to it—has grown. More frequently than not, the commissars have been the ones who have headed the basic Party Committees and Branches in military units, and since these bodies have been the ultimate forums for resolving differences and enforcing the Party line, this has frequently given the commissars a political advantage over the commanders. On the other hand, in periods when the military high command has stressed modernization and professionalization, the influence of the commissars has declined, Party structures within the PLA have weakened, the scope of political work in military units has been cut back, and the authority of the commanders has been strengthened.

In general, Mao and the top ideologues supporting him in Peking have tended to rely on, and support, the General Political Department and the commissar system operating under its direction as a key instrument to promote Maoist military concepts within the PLA. In contrast, the civilian leaders at the top of the regular Party apparatus and the government bureaucracy have tended to share with the military commanders at all levels, from the Chief of Staff down to the officers commanding low-level units, a view of the PLA that places greater stress on its professional character.

The commissar system operating under the GPD has been a unique institution in many respects, tied to but different from both the regular professional military command and the civilian Party bureaucracy. The commissars have been a part of the army, operating within its structure, yet they have been distinct from the principal military command hierarchy. And although, when the GPD's influence has been at its peak, its political officers have constituted the core of the "Party within the army," their outlooks have differed in many ways from those of the men staffing the civilian hierarchy of the Party. While subject to both army and Party direction, they have not really been fully integrated into either, and the GPD has functioned in some respects as a separate institution, often competitive with both the regular Party apparatus and the regular military command structure.

During the early days of the Cultural Revolution, Mao relied heavily on the GPD to carry out his policies, but eventually he became disillusioned with it. After Hsiao Hua and many other GPD leaders were purged, it seemed almost to cease operating for a time. The Party within the army continued to be crucially important, however, in that it was virtually the only segment of the Party that survived intact in China during the Cultural Revolution. Under the direction of Lin and the Military Affairs Commission, Party-army men took the lead in building a new structure of civilian institutions. As the balance in commander-commissar relations shifted significantly in favor of the commanders, however, the GPD became considerably less influential.

Since the end of the Cultural Revolution, the GPD and commissar system, like other basic institutions in China, has been gradually reconstructed. It may be significant, however, that the previous career of its new head—Li Teh-sheng—was primarily as a military commander rather than as a commissar. This, as well as other evidence, suggests that the rebuilt commissar apparatus may operate under tighter control by professional military men in the future than in the past; if so, its roles and power may be reduced once again. Even the professionals in the PLA appear to favor continuation of the dual structure within the army in some form, however, and thus there is little likelihood that the commissar system as such will soon be abandoned. The extent to which the commanders have their way and the power of commissars is gradually reduced will both reflect and reinforce a trend toward increased professionalism within the PLA. It will probably be accompanied by steps to deemphasize the importance of politics in military affairs generally and to cut back the role of military personnel in mass mobilization activities affecting the civilian population. In any case, working out an acceptable relationship between the Party in the army—including both commanders and commissars—and the rebuilt civilian Party apparatus will doubtless continue to pose delicate problems for a considerable time.

The Police and Militia

The future influence of the military in civilian society in China will also be significantly affected by the degree to which the PLA continues to involve itself in local police responsibilities.[28] When Lo Jui-ch'ing became Chief of Staff in the period before the Cultural Revolution, the PLA successfully brought the principal militarized Public Security forces—which previously had operated under the direction of the Ministry of Public Security—under fairly effective direct control by the army. However, civilian police units, managed by local Public Security bureaus, remained under the Ministry's direction, and the links between these local Public Security units and the civilian Party bureaucracy at a grassroots level were extremely close. In fact, in most areas local Public Security bureaus and units were headed by top-ranking members of the local Party Committees and they operated for all practical purposes as Party organs despite their status as government agencies.

In view of the extremely close links between the civilian Party bureaucracy and the ministry-directed Public Security apparatus, it was not surprising that Public Security men generally tended to support the Party bureaucrats against the attacks made on them by radical groups during the Cultural Revolution. Nor was it surprising that, because of this, the Maoists' assaults on the Party bureaucrats were paralleled by widespread attacks on Public Security personnel.

In many areas, Public Security units were paralyzed and ceased effective operations, along with most local Party organizations, as a result of Red Guard attacks. In the resulting vacuum, many different kinds of new local security groups were formed on an ad hoc basis to restore law and order, but their effectiveness was limited. Eventually, therefore, the PLA was forced to move in and take charge of local police functions. In some areas, Military Control Commissions were established to reorganize and direct the remnants of purged old Public Security units. In others, militiamen or regular military personnel acted as policemen under PLA direction. In still others, the military authorities fostered and supported new local security groups, under varied names. In any case, the situation was such that the army was compelled to assume primary responsibility and overall control of local police activities.

Most local military leaders gave high priority to the restoration of law and order, even before the end of the Cultural Revolution, and in the period immediately after the Cultural Revolution, the Public Security structure was soon rebuilt, under military supervision and with a significant infusion of new military personnel. In most places the restoration of local law and order was accomplished by 1969–70, and it is apparent that the new apparatus is now working reasonably well again, even though relatively few details are yet known about its organization and functions or the extent to which it is being civilianized.

It remains to be seen to what extent the old close relationship between the civilian Party bureaucracy and the Public Security apparatus at the local level will be restored as the Party gains strength, or to what extent military men will continue, directly or indirectly, to supervise and participate in local civilian police activities. The future character of the Public Security system will obviously be a very significant factor affecting the extent and character of military intervention in civilian society, as well as army-Party relations at the grassroots level where the regime's apparatus of power comes into direct contact with both the Party's "basic" organization and the "masses." As time goes on, it seems likely that the Party will try very hard to reestablish close ties with and operational control over local Public Security units. Here, as in other areas in which significant adjustments in Party-army relations seem likely to occur, the process could be gradual, and the military establishment may continue for a considerable period of time to be involved to a greater extent than before the Cultural Revolution in activities affecting the civilian population. It is significant, as noted earlier, that in all but one of the major cities I visited in 1972–73 the military still exercised direct control over local Public Security organs.

Important questions also remain to be answered about the future of the militia in China and the respective roles and relationships of the Party and army in directing the militia system.[29] The army has always exercised general command over the militia, but (as in the case of the Public Security apparatus—in fact, in some cases even more so) local militia units have tended to be under the direct supervision of the local civilian Party leaders working through the People's Armed Forces departments in local governments. This pattern of overall military responsibility but local Party direction and control seems likely to persist if the broad trends affecting army-Party relations remain on their present course.

A more important question is what priority the regime is likely to give to militia activities in the period immediately ahead. In the past, as indicated earlier, the size and functions of the militia have varied greatly, as shifts have occurred in the relative influence of Maoist and professional viewpoints on overall military policies. In general, when the main thrust of policy has reflected Maoist views, the size and functions of the militia have been substantially expanded. This has generally resulted in increased "militarization" of the civilian work force and increased participation of the militia units in programs to mobilize the civilian population. The effect has often been to serve the interests of the Party rather than those of the army. When professional military men have had their way, on the other hand, their inclination has generally been to cut back the size and functions of the militia. In their view, the militia's roles should be to preserve social order at the local level and to serve as a reservoir of reserves who can rapidly be recruited into the regular military forces in case of need. To the extent that the influence of professionally oriented military leaders increases in the period ahead, the importance of the militia in relation both to defense and to domestic mobilization will probably decline. Whatever happens, the militia will doubtless continue to exist to help maintain order at the local level, and the military will continue to exert a significant influence over it and, through it, on rural society. But if the influence of Maoist military concepts declines, the role of the militia will doubtless decline too.

As all of the above suggests, the future of the military establishment in China will be influenced by trends affecting many different military or paramilitary elements: the main force regulars, the regional forces, the GPD and its commissar system, the Public Security forces and People's Armed Police, and the militia. The characteristics and interests of each of these differ, and in a fundamental sense they will remain competitors for resources, power, and influence. The future will be significantly influenced by the competition among them.

Field Army Groups and Generational Differences

Politics within the Chinese military establishment, as in most complex social institutions, is greatly influenced by group affiliations and associations of many sorts. The extent to which definable "cliques" have operated within the military leadership and exactly how these may have influenced the political process in both the military and civilian sectors of society are matters of debate. Over the years, however, evidence has mounted to support the view that the structure of loyalties within the military establishment is extremely complex and that many members of China's officer corps have been closely identified not simply with the PLA as such, but also with particular subgroups within it. The loyalties to these subgroups have greatly influenced, and will doubtless continue to influence in important ways, the competition for power in China.

The Cultural Revolution revealed that, despite the strength of basic loyalties to the PLA and the regime, political alignments and struggles in China have been significantly influenced since 1949 by personal ties within the officer corps and links between individual military and civilian leaders—more than most observers had previously been inclined to believe. The political fortunes of many officers have risen or fallen along with those of key military leaders with whom they have been closely associated throughout their careers—men such as P'eng Teh-huai, Lin Piao, Ho Lung, and others. When in the ascendancy, such leaders have placed many of their "own men" in key positions; and when they have been purged, many of their close associates and protégés have fallen from favor along with them.

On balance, however, the evidence does not indicate that personal loyalties have been as crucial in determining the power and influence of particular men as they were in the period before 1949. Many examples could be cited of officers who have been closely linked to certain leaders throughout much of their careers and yet have survived the political decline of their mentors. Although patterns of personal association appear to have been decisive in some instances, in others they clearly have not been; the overall record indicates that an officer's associates are not an infallible guide for predicting his rise or fall.

Nevertheless, affiliations and loyalties of various sorts within the military establishment have significantly affected the political process in China. Some analysts maintain, in fact, that the competition for power and influence within the Chinese leadership—whether one is concerned with the military leadership per se or with the entire top leadership, including civilian Party men—can only be fully grasped if Chinese leaders—or most of them—are seen as belonging to one of five elite subsystems.[30] These five subsystems are based on affiliations with the major Field Armies that took shape in China in the late 1940s and then dominated the major regions of the country in the early period after the takeover. According to this line of analysis, all of these Field Army systems developed as distinctive entities in the regions where they were based, and their leading officers forged lasting ties and loyalties. Even after the Field Armies as such were formally disbanded in the 1950s, their units and personnel remained, for the most part, within their original areas and the officers associated with them continued to dominate the military commands in the regions and districts that were established in these areas after the Field Armies were abolished. Most officers, and many civilian Party leaders drawn originally from the military establishment, continued to maintain a strong allegiance to one of these systems, it is argued, and their career advancement thereafter—whether within the region or outside it, within the military structure or in the civilian sectors of the regime—depended considerably on the political backing they could obtain from their associations with other men in and from their particular Field Army system.

On a national level, according to this analysis, there has been continuous competition between representatives of the five different Field Army systems, and at the same time a conscious effort to achieve unity through compromise and mutual accommodation, involving a rough balance of power in positions of both national and local power among men from all five systems. Despite the extensive purging that occurred during the Cultural Revolution, this general pattern of competition and compromise has continued essentially unchanged, it is argued, although there have been significant shifts in the relative political power of men associated with the different systems. During the Cultural Revolution, men from the former First Field Army, associated with P'eng Teh-huai and Ho Lung, lost power to a significant extent, while men from the Fourth, associated with Lin Piao, gained in influence. Then, following the 1971 purge of Lin, many of his protégés from the Fourth Field Army were demoted.

This picture may be somewhat overdrawn. Even in the regime's earlier years, the importance of Field Army ties may not have been as great as this analysis implies, especially for men involved in Party as contrasted with army careers. Moreover, neither personnel nor institutional affiliations, important as they are, provide adequate explanations for the complex patterns of alignments and conflicts involved in leadership changes since the start of the Cultural Revolution. Many other factors, including basic policy differences as well as opportunistic struggles for survival, have been of crucial importance in many cases. Nevertheless, the evidence is convincing that long-term affiliations such as these are, and will continue to be, significant factors influencing not only military politics but civilian politics as well. Future power relations among competing individuals and groups, and more broadly between central and local powers, will continue to be influenced by such ties. What is less clear, however, is that they will have a major influence on the direction of basic national policy, since it is difficult to discern significant differences in policy orientations that can be linked directly or primarily to the Field Army affiliations of particular individuals or groups.

There are other internal divisions within the PLA—aside from the Maoist-professional dichotomy already described—which could be of greater significance in influencing future policy trends than Field Army affiliations. They include divisions along generational lines, as well as functional divisions between service arms. Precisely how generational and functional ties might affect future policy is difficult to predict since we know much less than we would like to about attitudes and relative power positions in these two areas of potential conflict. Nevertheless, certain hypotheses are plausible.

One study of generational groupings[31] in the PLA argues that the dominant "military ethics" and "military style" in the Chinese Communist military establishment have changed cyclically during the past forty-odd years with significantly varying emphases at different times on Maoist or professional values, and that the attitudes now held by different groups of PLA officers on key policy issues have been shaped to a measurable degree by military or political values that were dominant in the periods in which the crucial formative experiences in their military careers occurred. One can identify, according to this thesis, several distinctive generational groups with differing basic attitudes and predilections regarding several issues: the roles the PLA should play in society; the desirable relationship between the authority of commanders and the authority of commissars; the degree to which professional or political criteria should be the main basis for advancement in military careers; the relative emphasis that should be placed on domestic garrison responsibilities or on tasks relating to foreign security threats; and the importance of modern firepower, mobility, and "active defense" (at or beyond China's borders) or of manpower, "people's war" concepts, and "passive defense" (within China).

To the extent that it is valid, this line of analysis suggests that future generational changes in China's military leadership could have significant effects on the regime's policies in regard to all of the issues discussed in this chapter. Because of the increased rate of officer turnover during the Cultural Revolution, the trend has probably been, and is likely to continue to be in the immediate future, toward reinforcement of professional considerations and deemphasis of Maoist values.

Bureaucratic Politics: The PLA's Service Arms

If the process of military modernization in China continues, as it seems likely to do, competition among the various specialized service arms in the Chinese military establishment will probably become an increasingly important factor in shaping national policies.[32] It is reasonable to believe that in China, as in all other countries with large and powerful military establishments, various service arms engage in a complex process of bureaucratic politics involving intense competition for budgetary allocations, differences over strategy and tactics, and debates over assigned responsibilities and roles. The intensity of this kind of bureaucratic infighting in the national politics of countries such as the United States and the Soviet Union, and its influence on major decisions in Washington and Moscow affecting both domestic and foreign policies in these countries, is well documented, and there is reason to believe interservice rivalry is of growing importance in China too.

The competition for influence, funds, and other resources in China not only involves the major components of the Chinese military establishment mentioned earlier in this discussion, but also—and probably especially—such specialized service arms as the air force, navy, armored forces, artillery, and nuclear and missile forces. Even though the Chinese have been more successful than most governments in concealing interservice rivalries from public view, this does not mean that they do not exist.

In broad terms, it appears that the Maoists have attempted to restrict the increases of military expenditures required for rapid technical modernization in most specialized military fields, and the emphasis given to manpower rather than firepower has probably reflected budgetary considerations as well as ideological convictions and strategic concepts. The Maoist support of nuclear and missile development would seem to have been an exception (all Chinese leaders seem to agree on the need to develop a credible deterrent), but even here bureaucratic competition for budgetary allocations may well have had, and almost certainly will have in the future, a significant influence on the outcome of debates on what priority China should give to various weapons and delivery systems, such as medium- and intermediate-range and intercontinental ballistic missiles.

Despite the Maoists' apparent predisposition to limit expenditures for technical modernization in most conventional weapons fields, there are good reasons to believe that such expenditures have steadily risen since at least the late 1960s and probably earlier, especially for such equipment as modern jet aircraft. Chinese defense policy today probably represents numerous compromises, many of them realistic and practical, but the choices will become more difficult as modernization progresses, especially when the regime confronts the problem of large-scale production of expensive modern weaponry.

The number of "machine building" ministries in China devoted to production of military matériel and headed by military men has steadily grown in recent years. As this has occurred, China has probably spawned something akin to what has been labeled elsewhere a "military-industrial complex"—a network of close ties and common interests linking certain military leaders and institutions and the most important civilian agencies and technocrats managing key sectors of the economy that serve military needs. In the absence of detailed financial and production statistics or of hard data on internal debates concerning budgetary and strategic issues, it is impossible to know how far the development of such a "military-industrial complex" has gone, how much influence it may now have on the regime's overall policies and on major decisions relating to the allocation of resources, or what the relative power of particular service arms may be. There is good reason to believe, however, that the influence of the military establishment, broadly defined in these terms, is already great in matters of national policy, and is still growing. If military men continue to occupy key posts in the central leadership, and if, as seems likely, the regime moves toward increased stress on military professionalism and technical modernization, many policy issues of major importance in China in the years ahead will focus, as they do today in countries such as the United States and the Soviet Union, on difficult military-strategic-budgetary questions.

Because China's per capita resources are much more limited than those of any other major power, and because the strategic problems of this vast but relatively weak nation confronted by several potential military adversaries are in some respects uniquely difficult, its leaders obviously face many dilemmas in making decisions on national defense issues. How much can China afford to invest in its military establishment as a whole, in light of its many pressing civilian economic needs?[33] What relative emphasis should it place on low-cost infantry units, on moderately expensive improvements in its conventional forces, or on the very expensive military equipment required to develop nuclear weapons, missiles, and other sophisticated weapons systems? In developing missiles, how many should it consider adequate to achieve a credible deterrent? Should it proceed on the assumption that medium- and intermediate-range ballistic missiles will be sufficient to guarantee China's security or that a significant intercontinental ballistic missile capability will also be necessary? How far should China go in trying to build a modern air force? In developing its air force, should it emphasize essentially defensive fighters or bombers or both? Should China try to develop a significant naval and amphibious capability, which it now lacks?

Policy questions such as these are likely to become increasingly pressing and controversial in the years ahead. As they do, China's military leaders—and especially the PLA's professionals—will probably acquire a growing voice in a wide range of decisions affecting the allocation of scarce resources in China and the shape of broad policy both at home and abroad. To a considerable extent, the outcomes of debates on these issues will probably reflect pragmatic judgments about what is best for China's defense, but they will also be determined by, and will in turn help to determine, the political influence of particular military leaders and groups representing the interests of different service arms. There will almost certainly be differences between military and civilian leaders over issues of this sort, and how the regime resolves these differences will both depend on and help to determine the overall role of the military in society and the nature of civil-military relations.

Military Issues and Priorities for the 1970s

Both external and internal pressures will shape the development of the PLA and its roles in China in the future, as in the past. Differences within the leadership over the priority that should be attached to various foreign and domestic tasks will continue, and national policy will be shaped by competing pressures, reflecting the demands of defense and security as well as those of domestic and political and economic development. Although positions will differ on specifics, no Chinese leaders can afford to neglect national security problems.

National Security Problems

Since the Communist regime was founded, its leaders have felt exposed almost continuously to serious external threats. The Korean war involved the Chinese in a major conflict on China's immediate periphery less than a year after the Communists had founded their new regime, and throughout the 1950s and early 1960s Chinese leaders believed themselves "encircled," under pressure, and vulnerable to threats from the United States at many points on China's periphery. After the Sino-Soviet alliance broke apart, fear of possible Soviet military pressures steadily grew. In Chinese eyes, the danger of war with the United States apparently reached a peak in the winter of 1965–66, and then declined when, despite escalation of the war in Vietnam, the United States carefully refrained from actions directly threatening to China. From 1968 on, however, as a result of the Soviet invasion of Czechoslovakia, Moscow's pronouncement of the Brezhnev doctrine, and heightened Sino-Soviet border tensions, China's apprehension about a direct Russian military threat steadily grew. The cooling of Sino-Soviet tensions in 1970–71 may have reduced somewhat the Chinese fears of an imminent preemptive Soviet attack, but it did not eliminate Peking's basic worries about the dangers to China posed by the huge Soviet buildup on its borders. During 1969–71, Chinese leaders also expressed increasing concern about possible Japanese remilitarization and the potential dangers to China's security. This concern was doubtless exaggerated for tactical political reasons, and has been muted since late 1971 as Peking moved toward a more conciliatory policy toward Japan; but there is every reason to believe that Japan's future military potential is still a source of concern in Peking.

In short, Chinese Communist leaders have from the outset of their rule seen themselves to be operating in an uncertain and often dangerous international environment, encircled by actively or potentially hostile forces. It is not surprising, therefore, that national security has been and continues to be a major preoccupation. Peking's decision to adopt more flexible policies toward some of its major potential adversaries, as it already has toward the United States and Japan, demonstrates a new political approach to problems of security (see Chapter 5), but the Chinese will unquestionably continue to give high priority to the need to strengthen China's modernized military defense forces.

In the light of these facts, many Maoist-inspired concepts, including those calling for a "passive," "people's war" defense strategy and the involvement of the PLA in domestic political and economic tasks, have almost certainly been viewed by many professional military leaders in China as anachronistic and an inadequate answer to the nation's real security needs. The diversion of military personnel from defense tasks to other domestic functions, the decentralization of control over large portions of the PLA, the emphasis on rural militia, and the constraints placed by the Maoists on the development and technical modernization of China's conventional forces, have obviously limited, in ways many professional leaders have opposed, Peking's policy options in solving its national security problems.

Once Mao passes from the scene it is plausible to believe that the practical importance of Maoist military doctrines may decline. It seems likely that future military leaders will press, increasingly, for greater modernization, greater centralization, and greater emphasis on the PLA's tasks as a national defense force rather than as an instrument for domestic revolution. Many of them will almost certainly favor the technical modernization of the specialized service arms of the PLA. Some will doubtless argue in favor of higher priority being given to the strengthening of major conventional elements, such as the air force, artillery, and tank corps—that is, to those elements that will increase the PLA's mobility and firepower. Nuclear and missile development will doubtless continue, with the aim of achieving a credible deterrent.

Cost considerations may impose serious limits on the development of sophisticated weapons, however, and thus difficult choices will have to be made. To the extent that the regime's major security preoccupations continue to focus on the Soviet threat rather than any presumed danger of U.S. attack, and on China's regional security problems in Asia rather than global military concerns, the development of short- and medium-range missiles may well be given higher priority, at least in the immediate future, than the goal of achieving a major intercontinental missile force. Serious debate will probably occur on the question of China's need for a significant naval and amphibious capability, and the resulting policy determination will depend in part on how the Chinese assess the policies of Japan and the United States, as well as on what policies future Chinese leaders adopt toward the Taiwan problem. Whatever strategic decisions on such questions are made, it can be expected that the debates over defense issues within the Chinese leadership will find most of the PLA's professional military leaders arguing in general for accelerating the process of modernization and for giving priority to national defense considerations instead of to domestic tasks in policies affecting the PLA.

The PLA's Domestic Roles

Yet for a long time to come, it seems highly likely that the PLA will nevertheless continue to be involved in a fairly wide range of domestic tasks, to a degree that most other modern defense establishments—including those in the United States and the USSR—are not. From the beginning of Communist rule in China, the military establishment has performed a variety of social and political functions in the society, and future Chinese leaders, whoever they are, are likely to continue to regard many of these as important. As previously described, the PLA has garrisoned the country, providing essential military backing to the regime's political authority, and it has been extensively involved, both directly and indirectly, in constabulary or police functions required for the maintenance of social order. It has also been a major channel for the recruitment of potential leaders at all levels of society. Not only have large numbers of China's top political leaders risen to power through military careers; at the grassroots level of society, demobilized soldiers, incorporated into the civilian Party apparatus, have wielded an influence disproportionate to their numbers in social and economic as well as political institutions of all sorts.[34] The PLA has played an extremely important role in training a select group in the population in both civic virtues and technical skills. In effect, it has served as a huge trade school for millions of Chinese who have subsequently returned to administrative or productive jobs in factories, communes, and other governmental and social organizations. It has also been a major instrument for ideological indoctrination and leadership training. Recruits have been selected carefully, inculcated with a respect for discipline, provided with experience in administration and organizational procedures, and imbued with a strong sense of national consciousness.

In contrast to the pre-Communist period, when soldiers were placed near the bottom of the social scale, the prestige of military personnel in China in recent years has been extremely high. The army now attracts many of the ablest young men in the country, rather than relying for its recruits on the misfits and dregs of society, as in China's past. It is in part because of the high quality of army recruits, as well as the training and experience they have received, that demobilized soldiers, on completing their military service, have assumed so many posts of leadership and responsibility in the civilian Party apparatus and other social institutions, playing major roles in activities of innumerable sorts in almost every major sector of civilian society, especially in rural China at a grassroots level.

The PLA has also, as indicated earlier, taken an active part, both directly and indirectly, in economic development programs.[35] In certain fields, such as transportation development and land reclamation, military organizations and units have borne major responsibilities for construction activity. In certain geographical areas, especially in China's border regions, the PLA has played a primary leadership role in planning and directing economic activities of all sorts, and the military establishment has itself run numerous factories and farms. In addition, military personnel have contributed large quantities of part-time labor to civilian economic projects in every region of the country. During 1959–60, for example, when this was at its peak, the military contributed more than 40 million man-days of work each year to productive economic activity.[36]

In the present stage of China's development, even post-Mao leaders who disagree with Mao's particular revolutionary vision, his stress on ideology, and many of his military doctrines are likely to see strong arguments for using the skilled and disciplined manpower available in the PLA to perform many tasks of this sort within China. Long after Mao passes from the scene, therefore, the PLA will probably continue to be a "school" for training and indoctrinating a crucial segment of China's youth (especially rural youth), a labor force that will play a significant role in China's economic development, and a constabulary that will help to preserve domestic order, as well as a national defense force responsible for guaranteeing China's security. The question is not whether it will continue to play important nonmilitary domestic roles, but rather how and to what extent.

Probabilities and Uncertainties

In light of all the above, what can be said about probable trends in the period ahead affecting the role of the military establishment in China and the character of civil-military relations? As with much in

China, so many variables are involved that any estimate of the future must be tentative. Nevertheless, on the basis of the evidence currently available, certain major directions of change seem likely.

There can be no doubt that political and military affairs will continue to be inextricably intertwined—probably more so than in any other major nation today—and that for a long time to come military institutions and military men will be heavily involved in Chinese politics and deeply engaged in many civilian sectors of Chinese society. In the period immediately ahead, however, if China does not at the time of succession suffer another breakdown of social order and paralysis of civilian institutions comparable to that which occurred during the Cultural Revolution, the overt dominance of the military in civilian life characteristic of recent years seems likely to decline gradually as civilian Party and government leadership is reasserted, in which case the situation could return to one similar to that of the 1950s rather than to the "abnormal" situation of recent years.

One should not expect, however, dramatic sudden steps to push the military establishment into a clearly subordinate and apolitical position. Leadership at key levels will probably continue for some time to consist of complicated coalitions involving both civilian and military men, with military leaders retaining a large voice in decision-making processes. However, if, as seems likely, the strengthening of civilian institutions continues to progress, and military and civilian roles in these institutions are increasingly differentiated once again, then the political roles of military men per se will probably gradually be reduced.

Within the PLA itself, the main trend in the period ahead, as has been discussed at length earlier, will probably be—as it was in the 1950s—toward increased professionalization and modernization, with greater emphasis on the national security roles of the military establishment and a gradual cutback of its domestic revolutionary and developmental tasks. The rise of younger, better-trained officers should accelerate this trend. Although powerful local military leaders will unquestionably retain great influence in Chinese politics for a long time to come—a fact that will reflect a considerable diffusion and decentralization of power that will impose important constraints on the central leadership—their influence will probably be cut back gradually as the leadership in Peking attempts to assert increased central control. The imperatives of modernization, requiring increased planning and coordination of both military and military-industrial elements, will probably reinforce trends toward centralization. Within the PLA's structure, military commanders seem likely to improve their position relative to that of the commissars, and the PLA's main forces will probably gain power and influence at the expense of the regional forces. Local militia forces will continue to exist, mainly to perform security functions in rural areas, but their importance seems likely to decline, and the present level of PLA involvement in both militia and public security affairs may diminish as the influence of Party and government organizations increases once again.

Complex bureaucratic politics and competition for influence within the military establishment will continue to be a major factor affecting both the distribution of power in China and the process of policy making at both the national and local levels. However, as younger, more professionally oriented military leaders come increasingly to the fore, especially at the center, the issues will probably change. In particular, the conflicts between Maoist and professional viewpoints, which have been crucial in recent years, will probably decline in importance as professional attitudes become more and more dominant. In contrast, interservice rivalries concerning budgetary allocations and reflecting differences over defense strategy and assigned military roles will probably become increasingly important.

In broad terms, the transformation of the PLA from a revolutionary army into a modern national defense force, which was begun in the 1950s but interrupted by Mao's reassertion of his particular revolutionary vision from the late 1950s on, seems highly likely to gain force and accelerate once again. The transformation could still take considerable time, however, and the PLA will probably continue for the foreseeable future to be more politicized, more influenced by revolutionary values, and more broadly involved in developmental roles in society—both economic and political—than the defense establishment of any other major power.

Whether this estimate—projecting a gradual transformation of the PLA from a military force still strongly influenced by ideology and revolutionary traditions and still performing extremely broad and diverse domestic political and economic roles into a modern defense establishment concerned primarily with its national security responsibilities—proves to be correct will depend fundamentally, however, on the degree of internal stability in China, on the extent to which Chinese leaders continue to believe the country faces major external threats and pressures, and, perhaps above all, on whether or not there is a relatively orderly process of succession at the time of Mao's death.

The results of the Tenth Party Congress in August 1973 suggested that, in the two years since the Lin Piao affair, Chou En-lai (backed by Mao) had made progress toward establishing a new relationship between China's civilian and military leaders and that he had apparently been able to create a new and delicate political balance in the complicated coalition building involved in selecting China's top leadership. The role of the military in the new Party Standing Committee, Politburo, and Central Committee selected at that time will be discussed further in Chapter 4. Suffice it to say here that, apart from purging many military leaders who had been closest to Lin, Chou seems to have been able to establish a modus vivendi with key military leaders both at the center and at the regional level, and such leaders were granted important roles in all the Party's reconstructed leadership groups. At the same time, however, the representation of military men in both the Politburo and Central Committee was reduced—significantly though not drastically. These developments appeared to enhance the prospects for a gradual return to a more "normal" civil-military relationship and for a relatively smooth succession, thereby increasing the likelihood that trends in the period ahead will be in the directions suggested above.

If the succession should precipitate a period of violent domestic struggle, however, the course of events and direction of trends could be quite different. Under such circumstances, the arena for politics in China might become rapidly militarized to an extreme degree once again, as it was during the Cultural Revolution, and military leaders might again assume clearly dominant political positions. This does not necessarily mean that the PLA's Maoist revolutionary traditions would be reasserted in the same way that they were in the 1960s. With Mao gone, a reassertion of PLA primacy might be much more in the nature of a crude assertion of military power, without the ideological and political restraints that existed when the PLA acted as Mao's major ally during the late 1960s. Without Mao, overt military rule conceivably could follow a pattern similar to that which has emerged in recent years in many non-Communist Asian nations following the failure of civilian leadership. Even though this does not, at present, seem to be the likely outcome, in part because of the nature of the PLA's and the Chinese Communist Party's traditions, it is a possibility that cannot be excluded if there should be an open struggle for power and a breakdown of civilian institutions.

III

Strategies for Economic Development

ANOTHER primary determinant of the general course of China's development in the period ahead will be the degree of success or failure the regime achieves in solving the nation's economic problems and sustaining economic growth.[1] The problems it faces are diverse. Some are similar to those confronting all Communist states with "socialist" economies. Others are comparable to problems faced by many if not most developing nations. But some are clearly unique, resulting from China's distinctive history, society, and culture and its immense size and complexity. The regime's economic performance will not only have a direct and immediate impact on the welfare of China's population; it will also significantly affect China's prospects for internal political stability and its capacity to play a major role in world affairs.

Economic development has been one of the most important goals of virtually all Chinese political leaders in the twentieth century, and the Communists' commitment to this objective has been stronger than that of any previous Chinese rulers. The progress made since 1949 in fostering modernization has been impressive in many respects. The structure of the Chinese economy has been transformed, and a significant process of growth has been initiated. The economy has been socialized, major strides have been made toward industrialization, and China has begun to build the foundations of modern national power.

The course of China's economic development since 1949 has not, however, been a smooth or uninterrupted process, and important questions can be raised about the future. Competing pressures are at work, and complex conflicts of interests exist. In the early years after Communist takeover, the Chinese leadership seemed to share a deep consensus on the "correct" strategy to foster development, but this consensus gradually eroded as the developmental process unfolded. There have been many shifts in the regime's economic policies over the past two decades, some of them fairly drastic, resulting in an uneven process of development. Periods of rapid growth have alternated with serious economic setbacks and crises caused by policy failures as well as the intrinsic difficulty of solving China's problems.

As in most societies—in fact, more so than in most—economic problems have been inextricably intertwined with political and social issues in modern China. In many respects, the essence of day-to-day politics has focused on economic questions—especially those concerning the allocation of resources and output. In China, as elsewhere, the question "who gets what" has involved fundamental issues relating to political and social as well as economic values, motivation, and power. Economic problems have been the focus of some of the most important policy debates over the years, and they were among the critical causes of the split in the leadership in the 1960s.

Disputes over economic policies have been of several different kinds. Some have focused on means rather than ends. Given certain shared goals—including the goal of general economic growth—leaders have differed on what policies would be most effective, in the Chinese context, to achieve them. Others have involved differences on priorities among different goals. Despite consensus on many ultimate goals, Chinese leaders have differed significantly on short-run and intermediate objectives, in particular on the priority to be given to the maximization of economic growth or to the pursuit of other ideological, political, and social objectives.

The Major Economic Periods: Shifting Strategies

It is not possible, in a brief space, to analyze or even to enumerate fully the many disputes that have occurred within the Chinese leadership on economic issues. In part because of revelations made during the Cultural Revolution, it is now known that these differences have concerned a wide range of questions, some of them relatively narrow and specific and others broad in their implications.[2]

A list of even the most important economic questions that have concerned the leadership at one time or another must be a fairly long one.

How rapidly should the structure of the economy be changed? Should collectivization and socialization be accomplished by a step-by-step process or by sudden and dramatic moves? Should agricultural mechanization precede or follow collectivization? What forms should collectivization take? How soon should steps be taken to move beyond Soviet-style collectivization toward large-scale rural Communes that introduce "communist" features of distribution? Should full "communism" be regarded as a short-term objective or a fairly distant goal?

What mix of economic and noneconomic incentives would most effectively promote both the regime's economic aims and its noneconomic goals? More broadly, what relative emphasis should be given to "politics" and to economics? How fast a rate of industrial development and overall economic growth is feasible and desirable for a country like China? How much of the nation's output should be allocated to consumption or to savings and investment instead of consumption? What relative emphasis should be given to industry, agriculture, and other economic sectors? How heavy a burden can and should be placed on the agricultural sector to obtain the resources necessary to support industrialization? Is large-scale urbanization desirable, or should it be curtailed? How can the problems of unemployment and underemployment best be met? In industrializing the economy, should the primary emphasis be on large-scale or small- and medium-scale enterprises? Should new industries be concentrated in old industrial centers, in large new centers, or dispersed throughout the country?

To what extent is centralized economic planning desirable and possible in a country as vast and diverse as China, and what is the most reasonable balance between economic centralization and decentralization? To what extent should the state authorities attempt to plan and control the economy directly or allow market forces to operate? What kind of enterprise management is desirable? What kind of personnel should manage the economy at all levels? Should the regime rely primarily on "experts," advanced techniques, and regularized bureaucratic management, or on Party cadres, simple technologies, and mass mobilization techniques? Should China attempt to be essentially autarkic, "self-reliant," and self-sufficient, or should it involve itself fairly extensively in international economic relationships?

This list does not begin to exhaust the economic questions that have preoccupied—and in many instances divided—China's leaders, but it gives some idea of the scope for differences that has existed. Until the late 1950s and to some extent even thereafter, most differences within the Chinese leadership over economic policy were not based on "either-or" positions; they were matters of degree. A significant trend toward polarization took place over time, however, and ultimately Peking's leaders were divided by very different outlooks on questions relating to developmental strategy. As this occurred, differences concerning specific problems tended to be subsumed under, or linked to, broad differences on overall approaches.

During the Cultural Revolution, China's dominant leadership attempted to relate all past differences on concrete economic policies, as well as policies in other fields, to a fundamental conflict between "two lines," one associated with Mao and the other with Liu Shao-ch'i. Although this distorted the character of past controversies, it did contain an important element of truth. Many of China's leaders, though lacking clear, immutable concepts of development strategy, have nevertheless been strongly predisposed to try to develop a coherent strategy of development, based on a clear definition of priorities and goals and integrated policies, instead of dealing with particular policy issues on an ad hoc basis. Disputes over strategy became very divisive in the 1960s.

One can identify at least four, and possibly six, distinct economic periods in post-1949 China, in which aims, policies, and overall strategy have differed significantly.[3] The precise dating is arguable, since the transition from one stage to another has not always been clear-cut, but the distinctiveness of each of these major phases is undeniable. These periods have been: the initial period of rehabilitation and recovery, 1949–52; the first Five-Year Plan, 1953–57; the Great Leap Forward, 1958–60; the post-Leap readjustment and recovery, 1961–65; the Cultural Revolution, 1966–69; and the period since the end of the Cultural Revolution. The last three of these phases, since 1961, can in some respects be viewed as a continuum, since there have been significant continuities as well as changes. It is true that economic conditions in China during 1961–65, 1966–69, and from 1970 to the present have differed in important respects, which would seem to justify viewing them as separate periods, and it appeared that the stress placed on Maoist values during the Cultural Revolution heralded the introduction of a new development strategy. In fact, many of the regime's present economic policies can clearly be traced back to the early 1960s, and the evolution of Peking's policies since 1961 has involved fewer dramatic changes than those in earlier years.

Nevertheless, the regime has pursued a distinctive mix of policies with different outcomes in each of these six periods. The degree to which there was a consensus within the leadership about the specific policy changes from one period to the next is subject to argument. In general, however, it seems valid to say that in the regime's early years conflicts over economic strategy and policy were usually latent rather than manifest, and many were relatively minor; that significant differences then developed over the pace of collectivization in the mid-1950s; and that from the late 1950s on debates over economic issues became increasingly serious and reflected a widening gap in basic outlook concerning overall strategy for China's development.

A brief summary of the salient characteristics of policies in each of these periods will clarify past changes in overall development strategy in China, as background for analysis of present and future problems and policy options. The initial discussion will focus on *policy;* economic *performance* in various periods, in quantitative terms, will be discussed later in the chapter.

Reconstruction and the First Plan Period[4]

During its initial period in power, the regime's primary goals were relatively modest: to restore pre-1949 peak levels of production in both industry and agriculture, to begin establishing state control over the economy, and to carry out a social revolution in the countryside through land reform in preparation for later collectivization. Although land reform and many other state-directed programs began to modify the structure of the Chinese economy, there were no dramatic moves at this stage toward either collectivization or socialization, and primary emphasis was placed, of necessity, on economic recovery rather than on rapid expansion of production. In general, the regime achieved its initial goals in an impressive fashion and in a relatively short period of time. Between 1949 and 1952, inflation was brought under reasonable control. Fiscal and monetary stability was restored. Production in many fields rose to pre-1949 peaks, although total recovery of production to pre-1949 levels was not achieved until some time later. Through political organization and various nationwide mass campaigns—including the so-called Five Anti-Campaign, which brought the business class under effective control, and the land reform campaign, which redistributed ownership of China's farmland—the basis was laid for the regime's later socialization policy and development program.

China then embarked, during its first Five-Year Plan, on a new and extremely ambitious program of rapid development, and in the same period it proceeded to socialize and collectivize the economy. The Chinese Communists had come to power already committed to a particular socialist approach to development, based on the Soviet model and experience, and this commitment shaped their overall economic strategy throughout this period. Peking looked to Moscow for both advice and aid. In their approach to socialization and collectivization, however, the Chinese modified the pattern followed earlier by the Russians. They attempted, at the start, to pursue a more gradual step-by-step process. Then at midpoint in the plan, Mao decided, against the better judgment of many other Chinese leaders, to abandon gradualism and to move rapidly toward both socialization and collectivization; the result was accelerated institutional change.

One basic objective during the first Plan period was to maximize the rate of growth, especially industrial growth. Egalitarian social values were not ignored, but the requirements of growth were given higher priority. The regime attempted to institute a highly centralized system of economic planning, in which central state planners would exercise maximum controls over the economy as a whole, whenever possible through direct physical controls rather than simply indirect fiscal or market controls. A large bureaucracy of central economic agencies was rapidly built up. Rationing and central allocation of grain and other key commodities were introduced, and the regime attempted to increase savings and investment and to keep the lid on consumption. In its investment policies, Peking gave clear priority to industry over agriculture and to heavy capital goods industries over light consumer goods industries. Economic inputs into agriculture by the state were relatively small. The regime obviously hoped that the peasants themselves, through the collectives, would increase their investments—as in fact they did to some extent—and that collectivization would spur increased agricultural output; but the stress was on industrialization rather than on agricultural development and on increased investment rather than increased consumption. Relatively little attention was given by Peking's planners to maximizing labor utilization, and, in part because many of the new industries built were capital-intensive ones, unemployment became a real problem, especially in the cities.

In general, the regime's thinking during the first Plan focused on regularized bureaucratic management of the economy by experts and professionals, rather than on mass mobilization techniques. Mass mobilization of labor was carried out, especially in the countryside, to build certain public works, but the regime's principal hopes for growth focused on the development of urban industries. Industrial management policies were modeled on Soviet practices, stressing the key role of highly qualified enterprise managers. Chinese planners accepted the need for important material incentives and significant income differentials to stimulate hard work and efficiency, and many measures adopted resembled Stakhanovite approaches in the Soviet Union. The growth of foreign trade, while not spectacular, was substantial, since the regime formulated its plans on the basis of commitments made by the Soviet Union to provide essential capital goods (through sales, however, not gifts) plus important financial and technical assistance.

On balance, the first Five-Year Plan was highly successful. It initiated a very significant process of industrialization and resulted in an impressive overall rate of growth, probably averaging roughly 7 percent a year. By the end of the Plan period, however, it was probably clear to most, if not all, key leaders in Peking that Soviet experience could not be transplanted into Chinese society without major modifications. It had become apparent that China's growth rate would almost certainly slow down if the policies of 1953–57 were continued in a second Plan period. Moreover, Mao and some others in the leadership had become increasingly disturbed by many of the political and social consequences of attempting to model China's basic developmental strategy on that of the Soviet Union.

That it would be either impractical or undesirable for China simply to follow past policies without change was becoming evident in several areas of the economy by 1957. Agricultural output was lagging seriously behind expectations and needs, and the rate of growth was certain to slow down unless something was done to change this. Population growth continued unchecked, and this made the problem of sustaining real per capita growth increasingly difficult. Moreover, increased urbanization and urban unemployment had created many new problems. Because the emphasis in the first Plan had been on large-scale capital-intensive industries, the problem of how to achieve full employment and take full advantage of China's huge pool of labor remained unsolved. China was also faced with a serious international payments problem. Soviet development loans to China had been almost completely used up by 1957, and no further long-term credits seemed to be in prospect; moreover, China was now saddled with the burden of repaying past Soviet loans. Peking's leaders were driven to the conclusion that China would have to rely primarily on its own resources, which would make the problem of capital formation more difficult, particularly the acquisition of advanced capital goods for modern industries. China's planning system, moreover, clearly was not working well. Too much was being attempted by the central economic agencies. Mao was disturbed also by the fact that China's huge cumbersome economic bureaucracy was acquiring great power and by the fact that, as the professionals and experts who manned it acquired increasing influence, there was a decrease in emphasis on revolutionary values and on the involvement of the masses. Overall, the prospect was for a declining growth rate and, even more important, as Mao saw it, increased bureaucratization, specialization, and professionalization that would weaken the regime's commitment to egalitarian revolutionary goals.

The Great Leap Forward

The Great Leap Forward was Mao's answer to these problems.[5] During the Leap, China in effect abandoned the Soviet model and adopted a new developmental strategy, designed both to accelerate growth and to promote Mao's revolutionary political and social values. "Politics" was placed "in command." The aim was to "walk on two legs"—to speed up growth in agriculture and industry, and in large-scale and small-scale industry, using both modern capital-intensive and indigenous labor-intensive methods. Every attempt was made to maximize the use of all China's vast labor resources, including not only unemployed and underemployed men but women as well. The labor force was organized on semimilitary lines and mobilized to work for very long hours. Planning and economic management were substantially decentralized from the top down to local authorities—especially to Party authorities at the provincial level. This was in part a result of a virtual breakdown of the central planning and statistical apparatus, but it also represented a deliberate effort to decentralize decision making, to encourage local initiative. The importance of technical experts, specialists, and professionals was deemphasized; they were subordinated to Party apparatus men and "the masses."

Radical institutional change, especially in the countryside, was another key feature of the Great Leap strategy. New rural Communes were rapidly organized throughout the country. They were designed to maximize the mobilization of local labor and other resources and encourage local self-reliance and self-sufficiency. Prime stress was placed on egalitarian values, and the regime attempted to substitute ideological and political incentives for material incentives. It also tried to reduce consumption in order to increase savings and investment. In its foreign economic relations, Peking not only shifted its trade from the Communist nations to the West; it also put increasing emphasis on the need for China to be "self-reliant."

The Great Leap was innovative and audacious. It was an attempt to devise radically new solutions for real and important problems. But, on balance, it proved to be a serious failure. Instead of producing an economic breakthrough, it resulted in a crisis of massive proportions. Many of the new experiments simply did not work, and the economy was badly disorganized. Central planning broke down, and the Communes could not be operated effectively as initially conceived. The nation's transportation system was disrupted. To compound these problems, China experienced three years of bad weather beginning in 1959. The result was the Communist equivalent of a major economic depression. First agricultural and then industrial production declined precipitously. The population suffered severe hardships, and there was widespread malnutrition and a serious deterioration of health conditions. In broad economic terms, the result was not just economic stagnation but significant retrogression.

Although the natural disasters during 1959–61 exacerbated the problems, the basic causes of the failure of the Great Leap were policy errors. While there was an understandable rationale behind many of the specific policies associated with the Leap, the regime tried to do too much too fast and incorrectly estimated economic realities as well as the tolerance of the Chinese population. As a consequence the strategy was simply unworkable. Untested agricultural innovations such as deep plowing and close planting, applied indiscriminately without regard to local conditions, failed. With the breakdown of central and regional planning and statistical services, labor and other resources were poorly allocated and used wastefully. Many of the small local industries established at that time—most notably the backyard steel furnaces—did not work. The reduction in economic incentives had a seriously adverse impact on peasants' and workers' motivation. The population was overorganized and worked to the point of exhaustion. And the new Communes simply could not operate as planned because local leaders lacked the capacity to manage them efficiently, and the peasants did not work as effectively in such huge units as they had in the smaller collectives.

All of these factors forced the regime to retreat, step by step, from the extremes of the initial Great Leap policies. From late 1958 on, and especially during 1959–60, many of the Leap policies were abandoned, while others were drastically modified. In the process, Mao withdrew into the background, and other men—especially the Party's top bureaucratic leaders and economic planners and administrators—took charge. They set China on a new economic course.

"Readjustment" and Recovery from the Leap[6]

The new developmental strategy that emerged in the early 1960s was significantly different from both that of the first Plan and that of the Leap period. The immediate emphasis was on neither Soviet-style rapid growth nor Maoist concepts of radical egalitarianism, but on basic problems of survival. What took shape in this period of "readjustment" and recovery was an intermediate strategy involving compromises between the policies of the first Plan and those of the Great Leap. The approach was now essentially pragmatic and experimental. In some respects, it appeared more ad hoc than planned and lacked the kind of broad, coherent underlying philosophy or rationale that had characterized the policies of the two earlier periods. As the new policies evolved, however, it became evident that they did reflect certain important guiding principles and goals; most important, steps were taken to restore incentives, to give priority to agriculture, and to emphasize national self-reliance.

Early in the process of retreat from the Leap, the regime took major steps to restore incentives, in both agriculture and industry. It also abandoned the most radical institutional innovations of the Leap. In effect, the original Commune idea was set aside, and local responsibility for both production and distribution was decentralized to the Production Teams; as a result, the organization of agriculture returned to a pattern very similar to that of the pre-Leap collectives. Functional specialists and experts came to the fore once again, and renewed attention was focused on efficiency and technical improvements. Profitability was given new importance in the assessment of an enterprise's performance, market forces were allowed somewhat greater scope than before, and egalitarian considerations were given less immediate importance. Efforts to mobilize labor on a mass scale declined, and many of the small labor-intensive industries built during the Leap were closed down.

Perhaps most important of all, top priority was given, for the first time since the Communists came to power, to efforts to spur agricultural growth. Not only were private plots reestablished and free markets reopened, but modern industrial inputs into agriculture—including chemical fertilizers—were steadily increased. Foreign trade was now largely with the West, and China's largest imports consisted of food and support commodities for agriculture, such as fertilizers, rather than industrial capital goods. Emphasis on self-reliance continued and increased, although practical considerations now predominated over ideological ones in reinforcing this trend. No overall expansion of large-scale industry was undertaken, but serious efforts were made to expand specific industries, especially those related to defense and agriculture.

Economics, not politics, was now in command. Immediate problems took precedence over long-term developmental goals. The focus was on recovery rather than rapid growth. The principal criteria for evaluating any policy were pragmatic ones. Would it work? Would it spur recovery? Would it increase efficiency and output?

The policies of the early 1960s did work, and by 1965–66 China had recovered remarkably from the post-Leap crisis. There was good reason to believe that these policies could sustain a respectable rate of growth, although not one as high as in the 1953–57 period. The emphasis on economics over politics was not universally accepted, however, for it compromised the kind of revolutionary values embodied in Maoist thought. The new policies did not answer, therefore, some of the most basic questions preoccupying China's top leaders, in particular Mao himself. The search for a more effective strategy of development continued, as did debates over specific policies, and over what China should do to achieve both revolutionary change and rapid growth in the long run.

The Cultural Revolution and Subsequent Trends[7]

As the process of economic recovery took place during 1962–65, so too did the polarization within the leadership. A dichotomy between political and economic policies emerged. In the field of politics, Mao pushed steadily, from 1962 on, for "radicalization," while in the field of economics the regime's bureaucratic leaders, planners, and administrators continued to support the relatively pragmatic nonrevolutionary approach that had put China on the road to recovery. This dichotomy contributed greatly to the growing tensions that laid the stage for the Cultural Revolution.

Finally, when the Cultural Revolution began, politics took command once again. However, in contrast to the late 1950s, despite the radical policies that Mao pushed, there was no attempt to undertake a new Great Leap Forward, no sweeping attempt to reorganize China's economic institutions once again, and no wholesale scrapping of the economic policies of the preceding period. The urban industrial sector suffered a significant setback during 1967–68, as a result of the political conflicts of the period, but the agricultural sector was not seriously affected, and the adverse impact of political developments on the economy as a whole proved to be comparatively minor and relatively short-lived. Nevertheless, the leadership's new emphasis on Maoist values and concepts did have some significant effects on economic strategy, and the mix of policies that has emerged since the Cultural Revolution— a mix that continues to undergo change and has not yet crystallized into any immutable shape—has been different in several respects from anything in the past.

It is no simple matter, however, to distinguish between rhetoric and reality in assessing China's economic policies in the period since the Cultural Revolution. On the basis of Peking's rhetoric alone, one might conclude that the Chinese have defined a dramatically new economic strategy. The regime's declaratory policies emphasize Maoist egalitarian values, "redness" rather than "expertness," nonmaterial incentives, decentralization, and local as well as national self-reliance. They also give priority to agriculture and rural areas and stress the development of small-scale industries, maximum utilization of labor, population control, and mass participation in economic management and decision making. In the eyes of some observers, this adds up to a new "Maoist model" of development.

In practice, however, the regime's approach to economic problems since the Cultural Revolution appears to have been much more practical, and ad hoc, than its declaratory policies might seem to imply. The main thrust of policy has seemed to be increasingly pragmatic and flexible, in ways more reminiscent of the early 1960s than of the Great Leap period. Although information on the structure, operation, and performance of the Chinese economy is still scarce, the bulk of information available suggests that the economic system as a whole is very similar today to what it was a decade ago, with relatively few basic changes in fundamental institutions or operational principles, and that current economic priorities and policies are comparable in many respects to those that first emerged in the early 1960s. Within the framework of these priorities and policies, the economy is again functioning reasonably well and is experiencing a moderate rate of growth comparable to that of the period immediately before the Cultural Revolution.

Basic Problems and Issues

While the changes in overall strategy resulting from the reemphasis on Maoist values and goals in the late 1960s appear to be considerably less far-reaching in practice than one might assume from reading the official Chinese press, some significant innovations were introduced during the Cultural Revolution. Some of these reflect the predispositions of ideologues rather than technical specialists, but many of the innovations appear to be fairly practical and sensible responses to the existing conditions of Chinese society and the problems now facing the Chinese economy. A few raise important questions about the future, however, since they could well create new problems if pushed to extremes.

In analyzing China's economic problems and prospects in the period ahead, I have been compelled, like all specialists on China today, to base my analysis mainly on the information that can be gleaned from official Chinese statements and publications. But my judgments are also based on data and insights obtained on the trip I made to China in 1972–73, during which I visited a variety of Communes, factories, and other economic institutions and interviewed numerous officials—both in Peking and at provincial and lower levels—on diverse economic matters. The fragmentary data and impressions that I gathered left many large questions unanswered, but they did provide insights into the realities of the present situation that the regime's rhetoric and the published data do not.

What are the most distinctive features of China's still-evolving economic policies as the People's Republic begins its second quarter-century? To what extent are these policies being implemented, with what effects? Do they appear to represent "rational" and realistic approaches to China's problems? To what extent can they provide answers to problems that the regime's previous policies did not? What problems and costs could they involve? Are current policies likely to be effective over the long run, and on what factors will their future success or failure probably hinge? Are Maoist elements likely to be significant after Mao dies? What pressures for change can be expected in the future, and toward what ends? If current policies are pursued for some time, what are the results likely to be, politically and socially as well as economically?

Economic Egalitarianism: Theory and Reality

One of the most distinctive aspects of Maoist thought, as applied to economic policies, has been the tremendous stress placed on egalitarian values.[8] Almost all Chinese Communist leaders have emphasized the goal of distributing output in such a way that the economic basis for class differences will be minimized. Mao, in particular, has energetically opposed all manifestations of "elitism." The regime has been committed to ensure that everyone is guaranteed minimum levels of consumption and that no one will be allowed to achieve an economic—or social—status that sets him apart from the masses. To close the gap between physical and intellectual work, it has insisted that everyone should engage in manual labor. To narrow the gap between the rural and urban population, it has tried to ensure that as many urbanites as possible are exposed to life and work in the countryside. The most important key to development, Mao has often proclaimed, is dedicated hard work by everyone, rather than the special knowledge or skills monopolized by a few; "experts" must learn that they cannot expect special status, should not regard themselves as superior to the masses, and must not ignore ideas that originate with ordinary workers and peasants.

The Maoist goal has been to transform the incentive structure of the economy and society—to develop new ideological, political, and moral incentives, and new kinds of social and psychological rewards that will substitute for material incentives.[9] In recent years even the most ardent Maoists have recognized that China is not yet ready for a "communist" system of distribution; during the early days of the commune program, in 1958, they learned at considerable cost that if economic incentives are cut back too drastically the results can be disastrous. They concede, therefore, that at China's present stage of development, income should be based on the amount and quality of work done—but only up to a certain point. Beyond that, everyone should be prepared to labor for the collective good of the nation and society as a whole. In short, political and social consciousness and nationalism, rather than economic self-interest, should be the principal fuel for the engine of development in China.

It is not easy to assess the effects of the regime's stress on egalitarian values. As indicated in Chapter 1, some of the subtle effects may be significant. Under the slogan "serve the people," the regime has doubt-less been able to encourage a greater spirit of public service. And the relentless attacks on elitism have probably inhibited and checked ten-dencies for special groups to regard themselves as superior to "the masses." Many visitors to China have been impressed by visible effects from all of this on general patterns of behavior and relations. People at various levels in the society now appear to have more contacts and, frequently, easier relationships with those at other levels than was often true in the past.

Yet one also soon discovers in China that many old patterns of thought and behavior persist. To a remarkable degree, in fact, the Chi-nese one encounters today still show deep-rooted traditional predis-positions to think in terms of hierarchy and status and to fit into the social roles prescribed for them. The egalitarian values promoted by the regime have modified some old patterns, but they have certainly not "transformed" them. Compared to the situation in China in the pre-Communist period, the extremes of wealth and poverty appear to have been eliminated, and therefore the range of income differentials has been greatly narrowed. But the differences in income that still exist are significant, and material incentives continue to be very im-portant, in fact crucial, to the operation of the system.

One of the most striking economic and social accomplishments of the regime has been the apparent elimination of the worst poverty and the raising of living standards of the lowest strata of society to an acceptable minimum—at least in the areas that a foreign traveler can visit. One does not see the kind of grinding poverty, the miserable beggars, or the shantytown slums that were encountered fairly fre-quently in the past. The mass of ordinary Chinese one sees in major cities and nearby rural areas appear to be reasonably healthy, well fed, and well clothed. This has been an achievement of no mean propor-tions.

To put this accomplishment in perspective, however, it should be recognized that the minimal subsistence standard guaranteed for everyone is very low—in fact Spartan—and it has been achieved in part by a leveling downward of living standards for many. In the cities, not only has all great wealth been eliminated; the living standards of city residents who belonged to the middle strata of urban society before 1949 have clearly declined. Per capita national income may have risen, according to one estimate, by almost 50 percent—from about $100 to $150 in U.S. dollars—in the twenty years since 1952, but only a limited amount of this has gone toward improving living standards.[10]

What the regime has done is set a viable minimal living standard for the population as a whole, which it has been able to sustain at least for the last decade, since the end of the harsh depression following the Great Leap. It has accomplished this through a number of crucial measures. It has rationed basic grain and cotton clothing and cloth and maintained their prices at a level both low and stable. It has subsidized rents at an extremely low, even nominal, level. And it has not only subsidized greatly expanded education and simple health care, but has kept fees for both of these basic services very low. Beyond these basics, although the prices for most other consumer goods and services are startlingly high, they have been kept remarkably stable.

The setting of a minimal floor under living standards has not meant, however, the disappearance of significant income differentials; in strictly economic terms, therefore, egalitarianism is far less evident than the regime's rhetoric would seem to imply. In fact, the variations in income are surprising; incomes at the top of the highly differentiated wage and salary scales are as much as fifteen or twenty times, or more, those at the bottom.[11] A few figures in Chinese yuan obtained in 1972–73 will illustrate this. (The official yuan–dollar rate in early 1973 was 2.22 yuan to $1.00, and the following yuan figures can therefore be translated to dollars very roughly at a rate of two to one, without undue distortion of values. As will be illustrated, however, the real value of the currencies in terms of different kinds of goods varies greatly.) The lowest-paid urban Chinese—young apprentices in economic enterprises —receive 18 or 19 yuan a month. Industrial workers fall in eight wage grades that range from slightly over 30 yuan to a little more than 100 yuan a month. "Average" factory workers in grades 4 and 5 receive about 60 yuan a month, but it is not clear whether this category is used by the Chinese to denote "median" or "average." State and Party cadres are today classified, as they were before the Cultural Revolution, according to twenty-four regular grades (plus several supplementary grades below them). Those in the lowest regular grades—from 24 to 18—receive somewhere between 40 and 90 yuan a month; the salaries of grades 17 to 13 range from roughly 100 to almost 160 yuan; the highest grades (a relatively small number of cadres from grade 12 up) obtain salaries that reportedly rise to about 400 yuan for grade 6, and are higher above that. There are numerous grades of teachers and professors, with large differentials. In Kiangsu Province, primary school teachers "average" 40 yuan a month, middle school teachers 50 yuan, and all teaching personnel in higher education 75 yuan. At Futan University in Shanghai, the salaries of twelve grades of university teaching personnel range from 60 yuan for the lowest to 301 yuan for the highest; professors (associate and full) range from 157 to 301 yuan.

These figures do not mean very much, in and of themselves. The key question is what such salaries can buy. The answer would seem to be that those at the lowest wage levels can pay for the essentials of living, but for very little else; "average" workers' families (especially if a family has two breadwinners, as many now do) can, by saving and careful budgeting, buy a limited number of consumer goods beyond basic essentials. Probably only those in the higher income brackets really have sufficient surplus to purchase any significant amount of the consumer goods that the fairly well-stocked department stores carry.

Although the budget items for food, clothing, rent, education, and health care in urban areas must vary considerably from family to family, a plausible estimate of average monthly costs (based on estimates that Chinese cadres made to me in early 1973) for an "average" family of five (which conceivably might earn 100 to 120 yuan a month from two incomes) could well be something like 60 to 75 yuan for food (up to 15 yuan per person for fairly simple fare), 5 to 15 yuan for rent and utilities, and 1 to 2 yuan for educational and health fees—leaving perhaps 30 yuan, or somewhat more, a month for cloth (or clothing) and other consumer goods.

What can this buy? Not a great deal. What is notable about the prices of almost all consumer goods other than the most basic necessities (apart from the fact that they have been quite stable, which is not unimportant) is how remarkably high they are. A few examples, obtained in 1972–73 from price tags in department stores in Peking, Anshan, and Shanghai, are indicative: the cheapest men's shoes, 4.10 to 4.65 yuan; ordinary leather street shoes, 9.80 yuan up; a simple pair of cotton pants, 6.20 to 7.40 yuan; a pair of padded winter pants (essential in North China), 10.50 yuan; a wool blanket, 22.50 to 51.00 yuan; a thermos jug (which every Chinese family needs for hot water or tea), 4.50 to 6.79 yuan; an enamel washbasin (the only means of washing for most Chinese), 2.65 to 3.04 yuan; a fountain pen, 2.15 to 14.08 yuan; a locally made watch, 100.00 to 110.00 yuan; the smaller transistor radios, 18.10 to 52.00 yuan; the cheapest cameras, 120.00 to 198.00 yuan; an inexpensive bicycle (essential transport for most people), 138.00 yuan; an expensive bicycle, 172.00 yuan.

Even though one of the regime's stated long-range goals is to narrow the gap between urban and rural living standards in China, and in some areas this process has doubtless gradually begun, the gap is still a large one. Large differentials persist not only between urban and rural residents, but also among peasants themselves. Individual peasant incomes vary greatly from Commune to Commune and depend also on the performance of the particular Production Team to which a peasant belongs, the number of work points an individual can earn within his Team, and the supplementary income that a family can earn from cultivation of its private plot and "sideline" activity. Even in a showplace Commune visited in early 1973, per capita incomes from collective work averaged 120 to 130 yuan a year—close to half of which had to go for the grain ration allocated to each individual by his or her Production Team. In most Communes in China, peasant incomes are doubtless lower. The regime's efforts in the countryside, as in the cities, appear to have established and maintained a minimal floor on rural living standards, reduced if not eradicated the worst cases of rural poverty, and increased the sense of security of the peasants when confronted with natural and other disasters. But income differentials have not been eliminated and the situation is certainly not one in which extreme egalitarian values have been realized.

The explanation lies in the nature of Chinese society, and the leadership's realism in responding to existing problems. Despite its commitment to egalitarian goals and to the creation of "new socialist men," the regime in practice has recognized in recent years that normative ideological appeals, while they may supplement material incentives, cannot substitute for them. There has been neither a cutback in recent years in material incentives, nor any serious attempt to narrow income differentials in the name of egalitarianism. In fact, there have been some steps since the Cultural Revolution to increase material incentives, though to a very limited degree and within the framework of the basic system that has been maintained without drastic change for more than a decade. In 1972, for example, some attempts were made to promote workers at the lowest levels of the wage scale as a spur to greater work efforts, and recently there have been some increases in incentives for peasants, often in the form of improved prices for agricultural products.

The Maoist ethic continues to act as a brake on large increases in material incentives and income differentials. To a greater extent than in the past, also, incentives have tended to be associated with collective rather than individual effort, especially in the countryside but to a lesser extent in the cities as well. Recent moves to stress local initiative in economic matters and to encourage expanded rural services increase material incentives for the rural population, but in a way that operates to some extent to reinforce collective rather than individual motivation. Nevertheless, the desire of the Chinese people for individual material incentives obviously remains strong, and the regime's current policies take account, in a fairly realistic fashion, of this fact of life. If the main trend of economic policy continues, as in the recent past, toward an increasingly pragmatic approach to problems, there may be further steps to increase material incentives and income differentials may grow even though Maoist values will doubtless continue to set limits on this trend and to affect the degree to which the incentives are associated with collective or individual efforts.

As the development process unfolds and output rises, demands from various groups in the population for better living standards and increased consumption are likely to grow. Whether—and how—the regime responds to such pressures will clearly have a significant impact on the economy's performance. If it is not responsive, the effects on China's developmental process could be adverse. Yet like other countries at a similar stage of development, especially Communist countries, China will face serious dilemmas, since large increases in material incentives would not only compromise high-priority social values but would also involve a diversion of resources from investment to consumption, which could slow the process of growth.

If future leaders were to try to swing policy back in a more radical direction and translate Maoist egalitarian values into a system of incentives that actually cut back material rewards and reduced income differentials significantly, the results would probably be as damaging as they were when this approach was last attempted during the Great Leap. Such a shift does not, however, appear likely in the immediate future.

Decentralization and Local Initiative

Another important feature of China's developmental strategy since the Cultural Revolution has been the regime's stress on decentralization and local initiative and responsibility. During the past two decades, the problem of striking a rational balance between centralization and decentralization has been a continuing one, and the pendulum has swung back and forth.

In the regime's early years, there was a substantial degree of economic decentralization, especially at the regional level. Then, during the first Five-Year Plan period, the trend was toward fairly extreme centralization. The pendulum swung back toward decentralization in 1956–57, and during the Great Leap this was carried to extremes. In the post-Leap period, this trend was gradually reversed, but the economy remained more decentralized than it had been in the first Plan period. During the Cultural Revolution the disruption of the central planning agencies and economic ministries strongly reinforced, in a de facto sense, pressures toward decentralization of economic responsibilities. Since the end of the Cultural Revolution, with the restoration of central planning, there has been a steady trend toward centralization again in many spheres, even as the regime has stressed the desirability of fostering local initiative and responsibility, extolling the positive virtues of decentralization.

While these broad generalizations are valid, they obscure as much as they reveal because the issues relating to centralization and decentralization are extremely complex in China.[12] Either phenomenon can occur, and in fact has occurred, in varying forms as well as varying degrees in different periods, and at times decentralizing and centralizing trends affecting different levels or sectors of the economy have taken place simultaneously. Moves in either direction, moreover, involve a complicated mix of potential benefits and costs.

The heart of the issue of centralization versus decentralization is how and where and to whom to allocate economic powers, responsibilities, and benefits. A key question is whether to give higher levels of administrative authority extensive power in order to facilitate control, planning, and coordination, or to increase the powers of lower-level authorities in order to stimulate local incentives and initiatives and permit greater adaptation of policy to local conditions. If power is to be decentralized, decisions must be made on how much and what kinds of authority to transfer from the central authorities to various lower levels and whether to give greater authority to local political-administrative units or to basic-level production units. These decisions involve difficult questions regarding who should exercise the powers allocated to lower levels—government economic bureaucrats and experts, professional managers, Party cadres who are political generalists, military personnel (who during and since the Cultural Revolution have exercised important supervisory roles relating to many economic activities), or representatives of the "masses" and mass organizations. The history of alternating trends toward centralization and decentralization in China is far too complicated to analyze here in detail, but a few comments about these trends are necessary in order to place the problem in context.

In the early days of Communist rule, a substantial amount of authority for economic matters rested with the Military and Administrative Committees in the major regions into which China was then divided. This situation changed fundamentally in the mid-1950s, when the regime moved toward organizing China as a Soviet-type "command economy" emphasizing central planning; the powers assumed at that time by Peking's central planning agencies and economic ministries were extensive. This situation did not last long, however. Before the end of the first Plan, the Chinese leaders recognized that the huge and diffuse nature of the Chinese economy, as well as their own lack of the skills and knowledge required for extensive central planning, made it imperative to reduce the responsibilities of central agencies, and redistribute decision-making powers.

During the Great Leap, when the influence of the Party's political generalists at all levels increased substantially at the expense of the regime's economic specialists and experts, the economic powers of Party leaders at provincial and local levels increased greatly and the central ministries' functions were significantly cut back. As the Leap developed, local leaders took charge of setting their own production targets—constantly raising them—and there was really no effective central direction or coordination. In effect, central planning was virtually abandoned. Mao and other political leaders in Peking nonetheless continued to be the main source of the most important policy impulses during the Great Leap period. It was the decisions they made that stimulated the principal developments of the period—including not only the entire Leap effort and establishment of the Communes, but also the implementation of specific innovations such as deep plowing and close planting.

When the Leap resulted in serious setbacks in the early 1960s, the regime's attempts to restore economic order and promote national recovery included the restoration of some, although by no means all, of the previous powers of central planning agencies and economic ministries in Peking. This shift back toward greater centralization focused more on financial controls than on direct physical and administrative controls, and the bulk of the industries that had been transferred to local control after 1957 remained under the administrative supervision of lower-level authorities.

These comments on the evolution of the decentralization issue must be qualified, for they are made from the perspective of one looking from the top down. If one examines the oscillating trends toward centralization or decentralization from the bottom up, the picture is different. In the 1950s, especially during the first Five-Year Plan, local production units, both agricultural and industrial, were steadily grouped into larger units—bigger industrial units, cooperatives, and agricultural collectives—and were gradually subjected to increasing direction and control from above.[13] During the Great Leap, even though the overall national trend resulted in decentralization of authority from agencies in Peking to lower-level authorities, the establishment of the Communes represented a major centralization trend at the bottom levels in the agricultural sector of the economy. The reverse occurred during the post-Leap period. Although the trend at the national level was toward a somewhat greater degree of centralization, economic authority in the countryside was decentralized first from the Communes to the Production Brigades and finally to the basic-level Production Teams, in order to provide more incentives to the peasantry. There was even talk of, and some experiments with, radical decentralization of decision-making authority down to the level of the individual family.[14] In the industrial sector, there were experimental moves to give greater authority to individual enterprises, organized under national "trusts," which would have made them more independent of local political authorities but also subject to a greater degree of supervision by central ministries.

In short, no simple generalizations about centralization or decentralization trends can take adequate account of the complex mix of policies at different periods. The search for a workable balance in the allocation of economic powers among various levels and groups in China has been continuous, and no "final" solution is yet in sight. Although policy since the Cultural Revolution has emphasized the need for decentralization, the reconstruction of the national system of economic planning has, in fact, resulted in a steady trend toward greater central controls. In describing how the planning system works today, Chinese Communist cadres make it very clear that central authorities again exercise effective and extensive overall control over the economy. One obtains the impression from cadres in basic production enterprises such as factories and Communes that even though major annual targets are supposed to be set through a process that begins with proposals "from the bottom," in reality the crucial decisions about the most important targets are handed down "from the top." This does not mean that nothing significant has resulted from the regime's stress on decentralization. It does mean, however, that the effects of decentralization have been considerably less than some observers have assumed from Peking's rhetoric.

Economic cadres at all levels in China are willing today to outline the present planning system, as they understand it from their varied vantage points, but their descriptions leave unanswered as many questions as they answer, and there must be considerable guesswork in any analysis of how the system actually operates. Even so, some generalizations can be set forth with a degree of confidence.

At the center the most important economic policy decisions are obviously being made today, as in the past, by a handful of top leaders belonging to the Politburo and other leadership groups. After being badly shaken up during the Cultural Revolution, the State Planning Commission appears to be back in effective operation and making many key decisions concerning output and other targets, not only for lower-level, especially provincial, administrative units but also, at least in some instances, for large enterprises. It has absorbed the State Economic Commission, and therefore is now responsible for annual as well as longer-term plans. The Commission's annual plans are the most important plans in national decision making at present. Even though a fourth Five-Year Plan was initiated in 1971, no details about it have yet been published, and it is difficult to obtain very many data that reflect planning beyond a one-year period. One suspects that longer-range planning has relatively limited significance at present. There is little doubt, however, that the Planning Commission is now a very powerful body and that planners at lower levels regard it as the organization that will ultimately set—or at least must approve—the most important production targets that will directly or indirectly affect their operation.

However, there are fewer economic ministries in the national bureaucracy as it has been gradually reorganized and reconstructed following the disruptions of 1966–68. Some industrial ministries still exercise direct control over a limited number of large-scale enterprises, especially in defense or defense-related industries, but the majority have been administratively decentralized to the provinces or lower levels. The ministries' role in planning for such enterprises is now clearly smaller than when the ministries administered them directly; some large and important enterprises are under "dual" central and local control, however, and the ministries' role in planning that affects them is larger. In agriculture, the Ministry of Agriculture sets key overall production targets, divided among the provinces, and the Ministry of Commerce sets targets for 260 "category two" commodities. ("Category one" commodities, including grain and cotton cloth, are subject to direct control and planning by the State Planning Commission.)

Overall, however, the ministries' roles, and power, now seem to be less important than in certain periods in the past. They are clearly less powerful than they were during the first Five-Year Plan period. Whether their roles are significantly different from what they were in the period before the Cultural Revolution period is difficult to judge.

Below the national level, planning authorities at lower levels—especially in the provinces but to a lesser extent at levels below them—now seem to play more significant roles than previously, but it is not wholly clear how much real power these lower-level planners now have. Cadres at all levels stress that current Chinese economic policy is based on "two initiatives"—central and local—and that local initiative is extremely important. Provincial cadres themselves assert that, as a result of decentralization, they now have greater "administrative" control over production units within their territorial jurisdiction than before, and that they have more leeway than previously in "balancing" plans of subordinate units (i.e., coordinating and adjusting their plans and making decisions regarding the resources required to meet them). A major stress is now placed, moreover, on diversifying the economy and developing "comprehensive" economic systems within provinces, and to a lesser extent subprovincial areas; this has required granting the planners in these areas new responsibilities and powers. Provincial planners also bear the responsibility of deciding how to divide province-wide targets set by national planners among subordinate administrative areas and enterprises. And in commerce, planners at the provincial level and below are responsible for planning regarding all "third category commodities"—which are actually more numerous, though less vital, than commodities in categories one and two.

It is still difficult, however, to judge how much real power has been decentralized to the provincial level or below. More day-to-day "administrative" functions are performed by local planners than before, and these local planners clearly have the power to make more planning decisions than in the past, but it is nevertheless evident that the most important economic decisions (especially investment decisions) are still made at the center. All decisions made at lower levels must be within the framework of general plans and targets set at higher levels, ultimately at the center, and all important local decisions must obtain central approval. In sum, under a loosened planning system, central planners now do somewhat less, and local planners do somewhat more, than at certain periods in the past; this downward shift of responsibilities makes considerable sense and helps the system operate; but it is nevertheless evident that many of the most important economic decisions are still ultimately made in Peking.

At the very lowest levels of the economy, in the Communes and at the Street Committee level in the cities, the emphasis on decentralization and local initiative is important in the sense that local units are now strongly encouraged to mobilize labor and resources to build new small-scale enterprises, and the planning system obviously allows them the necessary leeway to do so. (The program to promote such enterprises will be discussed below.) Yet they too must operate within the limits set by decisions made at higher levels.

Do present Chinese policies achieve a sensible and efficient balance between centralization and decentralization? Until more information is available about the way the system actually operates, it will be difficult to make any real judgment on this. It appears that the leaders recognize—as they have, really, since the late 1950s—that the extreme centralization of power in the central planning agencies and ministries characteristic of the first Plan period is not feasible or desirable, and that a looser system is therefore required under existing conditions in China.

One cannot say, however, that the present allocation of authority to various levels is necessarily an optimal one. It remains to be seen whether present policies will permit the growth of dangerous economic localism, particularly at the provincial level. At what point, if such growth occurs, might the central leadership conclude that it poses a potential threat to the existing internal balance of power, politically as well as economically? The regime has strongly emphasized the desirability of achieving a higher degree of regional and local self-reliance and self-sufficiency, stressing the need to develop local "industrial systems." Mao is quoted as saying: "Various localities should endeavor to build up independent industrial systems. Where conditions permit, coordination zones [a term apparently referring to supraprovincial regions, with what organizational structure is unclear], and then provinces should establish relatively independent but varied industrial systems."[15] Revolutionary Committees "at all levels" (including counties and Communes) have also been urged to do what they can to "make full use of local resources and rely on their own efforts" to establish "local industrial systems."

To the extent that local "balancing" in the planning process and the stress on building "comprehensive" economic systems, especially at the provincial level, determine major economic decisions, one can question also whether it will be possible to make national planning decisions that will take full and rational account of comparative advantages in different regions of the country. The more decision making on resource allocation takes place at a provincial level, the more danger there will be that the system will work to the advantage of economically advaced areas and penalize more backward areas.

Except for key small local industries, which do appear now to have considerable autonomy, a question that can be raised about most industrial enterprises in China today is not whether decentralization has given them too much authority, but whether they are subject to so much control from above and have so little real leeway for important decision making at the enterprise level that the system has a significantly adverse effect on their efficiency. One obtains the impression—admittedly from limited evidence—that most factories of great size really have relatively little autonomy and that greater local authority, competition, and exposure to market forces at the enterprise level might have favorable effects on the operation of many enterprises. In time there may be pressures to move in this direction in China, as there have been in some other Communist countries.

The current balance between centralization and decentralization does appear to be a workable one. Central planning has been restored, yet there have been some potentially significant decentralizing moves. The present balance appears to avoid many of the disadvantages of the extreme centralization of the first Plan period and of the extreme decentralization of the Great Leap. Nevertheless, one can question whether the balance is in any sense either ideal or permanent. The search for an optimal balance—one that can increase efficiency, ensure a desirable allocation of resources, and spur local initiative while maintaining overall central control—will require constant experimentation and adjustment over an extended period. It is plausible to expect that competing pressures and further oscillation of policy between the poles of centralization and decentralization will be the pattern in the future as in the past.

Encouragement of Small-Scale Industry

While there are few overall national statistics from which to estimate the scale and results of the recent program to develop small and medium-sized industries, there is little doubt, judging from first-hand observation as well as the fragmentary data available from official Chinese sources, that decentralized small and medium-sized industries of many sorts have mushroomed in many parts of the country, in rural as well as urban areas. By the fall of 1971, the regime claimed that more than half of China's counties had built plants for the repair or manufacture of small machinery (generators and small irrigation pumps are particularly important items), factories producing chemical fertilizers, cement, and iron and steel, and small local coal pits.[16] Priority has also been given to the construction of local power plants, and considerable attention has been given to the building of small factories processing agricultural commodities. In January 1972 it was claimed that 60 percent of national chemical fertilizer production in 1971 and 40 percent of cement production that year came from small plants.[17] Local smelting capacity was said to have increased 2.5 times in 1970, compared with 1969, and pig iron output 2.8 times.[18] In one province alone—Shansi—over 18,000 factories and mines were said to have been built in recent years by the special districts, counties, Communes, and Brigades as well as by the province itself, most of them probably very small-scale enterprises.[19]

Like many aspects of current policy, the stress placed on construction of small and medium-sized industries dispersed throughout the country, in rural as well as urban areas, is not entirely new. It really began, under the slogan "walking on two legs," during the Great Leap. The idea at that time was to build large *and* small industrial enterprises, as well as industries using both advanced modern technology and relatively simple indigenous methods. The development of smaller industries was to be in addition to, rather than instead of, large modern plants.

In some respects, the central authorities are still committed to the expansion of large-scale as well as small industry. A question that is difficult to answer, however, is whether, or to what extent, the emphasis on dispersed small industries has slowed the pace of development of large-scale modern industries. While it is possible to build some dispersed local industries with material and human resources that might not otherwise be utilized, a program of great magnitude could involve a diversion of resources that might otherwise be used for the development of large-scale projects. In a country such as China, where both capital and skilled personnel are in such short supply, diverting large resources to small and medium-sized industries could detract from the pool of resources available for building large-scale enterprises.

One important contrast between China's present policies and those of the Great Leap period, however, has been that the small and medium-sized plants recently built appear to be more rationally planned and of higher quality than those built earlier.[20] As noted earlier, the small industry program of 1958–60 was, in many respects, a failure; many of the enterprises that received the greatest publicity at the time were unsuccessful. The "backyard iron and steel" plants were soon abandoned as impractical after resulting in a significant waste of effort and resources. Some other small and medium-scale plants established during that period survived, but many of these too were inefficient and wasteful, and a sizable proportion of them were closed down during the post-Leap depression. Subsequently, the Maoists were highly critical of Liu Shao-ch'i and other leaders said to be responsible for this retrenchment, but only rarely did they contend that these industries were in fact "profitable"; rather they condemned the idea that "profitability" should be used as a basic criterion to judge them.[21]

Stimulation of local initiative and mobilization of local resources to meet local needs are the prime goals of recent efforts to build local industry, and there is considerable evidence that the program has in fact stimulated increased inventiveness and ingenuity on the part of both local authorities and local managers and workers. Most of the financing for these industries has had to come from the local areas themselves. Although some of this capital might otherwise have been mobilized by the central authorities for investment in large-scale industry, some has been capital that would otherwise not have been effectively mobilized at all. Special emphasis has been placed on factories that can meet local needs—especially the needs of agriculture—and in many areas this has increased the availability of simple producer goods as well as some consumer goods. Local authorities have been urged to open up new local sources of raw materials, and the resource base for industry has thus been broadened. In many instances, labor has been used as a substitute for capital, since most of the new local industries have required relatively little capital, and the workers employed have often been persons who might otherwise have been either unemployed or semiemployed.

One can argue, therefore, that all of this has made possible fuller utilization of the country's limited capital and labor resources, and mobilized resources that would not otherwise have been mobilized. Because the primary focus has been on local production for local markets, the strain placed on the country's limited transportation facilities has probably been somewhat reduced. Moreover, the new industries have clearly trained many new skilled workers and helped to increase and disperse modern skills. One can also argue that the strain on central planners has been eased.

Nationally, the small industry program and stress on local self-sufficiency have probably reduced the need for large-scale transfers of resources between major regions, or from rural areas to a few major cities, with a consequent reduction of many of the problems that generally accompany rapid large-scale urbanization. At the same time, the development of low-level skills has probably been accelerated and spread throughout the entire country more rapidly than would otherwise be possible. One can argue that "modernization" of a sort is likely to occur more rapidly even if development of the most advanced levels of science and technology is less rapid than might otherwise have been the case. Because of the limited quantities of both capital and high-level skills required in the smaller industries, it is possible to build and put them in operation fairly rapidly; in this respect the payoff for labor and capital invested may be quicker in many instances than if the same resources had been allocated to large industries that require many years to build.

There is another side of the picture, however, and a number of questions can be raised about the possible problems, costs, and liabilities if such a program is carried "too far." Because small and medium-sized factories generally must forgo the economies of scale possible in more efficient, large-scale modern industries, many may prove to be both inefficient and costly. Moreover, the extent to which they really absorb large amounts of previously unutilized labor is not wholly clear: some evidence suggests that the scale of employment in many of them may not yet be very large. Some will probably be too inefficient to be viable in the long run.

Yet on balance, the program probably does make good economic sense. Many of these plants remind one of those that played an important role in Japan's industrial development in its early stages. To the extent that the new small and medium-sized plants put to work unused resources, increase employment, meet local needs, and reduce the strain on China's transport system, they can add significantly to the economy —if they develop reasonable standards of efficiency. In urban areas, those that are directly linked to larger enterprises, as many are, have a particularly good chance to survive and meet basic criteria for economic rationality under existing conditions in China. Plants of this sort cannot substitute for large-scale modern factories, and there is no reason to believe, despite the regime's publicity about them, that China's leaders are seriously attempting to make them do so. The goal is obviously still to "walk on two legs."

However, if the small industry program were pushed to extremes, without regard for efficiency or cost, it could be a liability in China's efforts to spur overall development. Such a trend would only become likely if the present leadership's generally pragmatic approach to problems were set aside by ideologues committed to policies of the sort that characterized the Great Leap. Since this does not seem likely in the immediate future, the balance sheet will probably show positive gains, and the contribution to China's economy made by small and medium-sized industries will probably outweigh in importance the liability of those among them that are too costly or wasteful to make good economic sense. There may well be economic pressures in time to close down some of the less viable projects. It is also possible, however, that noneconomic arguments in their favor could prevail. This may become an important economic and political issue in the future in debates about the kind of nation that China is to be and the overall development strategy it should follow.

Priority to Agriculture and a Rural Bias[22]

More important than any of the features of China's developmental strategy discussed earlier in this chapter is the priority given in recent years to the development of agriculture and to rural areas. In some respects, China has been pursuing an "agriculture first" policy and stressing overall rural development. Not only have inputs into agriculture been significantly increased; the regime has also carried out a fairly massive transfer of personnel and resources from urban to rural areas and has given greatly increased priority to the development of rural education, health, and other services in the countryside.

All developing nations face a serious dilemma in determining a feasible and desirable balance between industrial and agricultural growth and between rural and urban development. The tendency in many has been to place the highest priority on industrial and urban development, just as China did during the 1950s. The Stalinist model called for a fairly extreme concentration of resources and efforts on the urban industrial sector, particularly on the development of industries producing capital goods. The idea was to extract as much as was feasible from the agricultural sector and to restrict state investments in the rural economy in order to invest and reinvest as much as possible and as rapidly as possible in "capital construction" of modern large-scale industry. During 1953–57, state investment in capital construction (that is, government expenditures for fixed capital investments) totaled over $20 billion (exceeding the planned figure of over $18 billion), averaging $4 billion a year. Total "economic construction expenditures," plus supporting educational and other outlays, totaled over $32 billion.[23] Of the planned investments in capital construction, 58.2 percent was allocated to industry (88.8 percent of which was earmarked for heavy industry and 11.2 percent for light industry); 19.2 percent to transportation and communications; 15 percent to education, health, culture, municipal utilities, banking, trade, and so on. Only 7.6 percent of state investments was allocated to agriculture, forestry, and water conservancy. Although state investments in the agricultural sector were supplemented by some self-investment by rural collectives, these mainly involved traditional inputs that had less effect in modernizing farming or increasing output than more modern inputs, and the overall result of the policy emphasis was a relatively slow rate of increase in farm output. Agricultural development barely kept ahead of population growth, and the lag in farm output was a fundamental cause for the dilemmas faced by the regime as the first Plan drew to a close.

Chinese leaders hoped in the 1950s that institutional changes affecting agriculture—first the collectives and then the Communes—plus local self-investment by the collectives would go a long way toward solving China's agricultural problems, but it was clear by the end of the 1950s that this was not the case. The major agricultural crisis of the post-Leap period not only forced the regime to modify the Communes and use a large percentage of available foreign exchange to import food; it also impelled Peking to change its priorities in a fundamental way. This shift of basic priorities which began in the early 1960s resulted in the new policy according first priority to agriculture, second priority to light industries serving agriculture or producing consumer goods, and only third priority to civilian industries producing capital goods. (Defense-related industries, however, continued to receive special treatment and high priority.)

Because of the lack of detailed figures on Chinese investment since the start of the 1960s it has not been possible to determine the precise ratio of investments in different fields. It is clear, however, that the regime has steadily increased its investments in agriculture both directly and indirectly ever since the early 1960s and that this has been a major factor—together with the good weather that generally prevailed from 1962 through 1971—in the steady, if still gradual, rise in farm output.

If anything, it would appear that the stress on agricultural modernization has been even greater since the Cultural Revolution than in the 1960s. For example, the use of chemical fertilizers, both domestic and imported, has steadily risen. (U.S. government analysts estimate that the total use of chemical fertilizers rose from 540 thousand tons of nitrogen in 1962 to 2.5 million tons in 1970. Roughly 60 percent of this still had to be imported in 1970.[24]) The use of small electric-powered pumps for irrigation has spread widely. (The consumption of electricity by Chinese agriculture rose, according to U.S. government analysts, from 1.5 billion kilowatt-hours in 1962 to 5.5 billion in 1971.[25])

The production of improved small tools for agriculture has also increased substantially, as new local industries have been built to produce them. Despite the regime's determination to accelerate overall agricultural mechanization, however, the use of tractors and other large-scale agricultural machinery is still extremely limited. It is estimated that in 1971 China produced 28,000 conventional tractors and 22,000 "garden type" tractors.[26] Great emphasis has been placed on the construction, by Communes and other units, of water conservancy projects of all sorts, and evidence of reforestation efforts can be seen by the visitor to China in many places. Local agrotechnical organizations which can develop and promote improved seeds and techniques are also encouraged. Despite some seed improvements, however, China has yet to introduce new high yield varieties on a large scale, and therefore has not yet achieved "miracle" increases.[27]

This focus on agriculture has made very good economic sense, even though the actual degree of success achieved should not be exaggerated. The rate of agricultural growth—with the grain output increase averaging somewhat over 2 percent a year over the past two decades—has remained fairly modest and lags considerably behind the pace China needs for rapid development. What is important is that the increased inputs into agriculture have done much more than stave off disaster; they have been a crucial element in the Chinese economy's recovery from its nadir in the early 1960s and in the renewal of growth in recent years.

China's recent policy has also included unique "Maoist" features. Some of these have been both more dramatic as innovations and more questionable in terms of their possible long-term effects than the increase in rural investment and technical improvements. One of the most dramatic steps taken by the regime has been the massive transfer of urban residents to rural areas. The *hsia hsiang* ("transfer to the countryside") program since the Cultural Revolution has been very different, in scale as well as purpose, from the efforts to *hsia fang* ("transfer downward") personnel that took place in China in previous years. Estimates vary on the number of Chinese urbanites "transferred downward" from cities to the countryside since 1968, but some place the total between ten and twenty million.[28] Whatever the correct number, it is clearly huge. Leading cadres in Shanghai told me that since 1968 900,000 persons—mainly educated youth—have been sent to the countryside and remote provinces from that city alone.[29] A significant proportion of those transferred, moreover, have been told to regard the move to the countryside as permanent rather than temporary. Many different kinds of people have been involved. At the start, prime emphasis was placed on sending radical Red Guard members and potentially dissident intellectuals out of the cities to the rural areas. Later some urban workers were included. Most recently, the bulk has consisted of educated young people, especially recent graduates of junior and senior middle schools.

The motivations for this large-scale transfer of population have undoubtedly been mixed. In broad philosophical terms, it has represented a conscious effort of the kind that Mao has long believed necessary to break down the barriers and bridge the gap between urban and rural society. In the cases of many young radicals sent to the countryside, the aim was a political and punitive one; the regime wished to get them out of the cities and stop their agitation and factional struggles. Many others were selected because it was thought that compelling them to live and work in primitive circumstances in China's villages would "remold" their thinking and "revolutionize" their outlook.

But there has also been an important economic rationale for the decision to transfer such a large number of urban residents—including persons with considerable education and training—to the countryside. The program has constituted an effective, though drastic, attack on the continuing problem of urban unemployment and underemployment, significantly reducing the number of people who have had to be fed, housed, and provided with jobs in China's cities. Moreover, the transfer of large numbers of trained, educated, and skilled personnel from urban to rural areas has strengthened the regime's capacity to innovate in the countryside. The knowledge and skills of those "transferred downward" have been regarded as important assets for improving Commune management, developing local industries, expanding rural education and health services, and generally promoting "modernization" in the countryside.

Education and health policies during and since the Cultural Revolution have complemented the economic priorities. In keeping with Mao's determination to "reform" Chinese education and make it serve the common man,[30] prime stress has been placed on simplified, shortened courses of education for the masses rather than on higher-level training designed primarily to produce specialists and experts, and special priority has been given to the development of low-level education in rural areas. Local authorities have been encouraged to develop and expand, to the extent possible with their own resources, mass education in rural areas.

In the field of medicine, similar priorities have applied. In China, as in most developing nations, medical personnel have tended in the past to concentrate in urban areas. In recent years, as the regime's primary focus of interest has shifted from the development of medicine and health in urban areas to the expansion of health services in China's rural areas, thousands of doctors and nurses have been sent to the villages, not only to practice there themselves, but also to train large numbers of paramedical "barefoot doctors."[31] Every local area has been urged to develop self-sufficient local "cooperative health services," mostly, as in the case of education, by relying on local resources. The result has been a significant expansion and improvement of simple medical care in the Chinese countryside, but also, inevitably, a weakening of the base for high quality medical training and care in the cities.

In these and other ways, the regime has weighted its policies in favor of rural China. The potential payoff from this rural bias, in terms of improved utilization of rural resources, better management of local programs, increased development of rural industry, and the expansion of education and health services, as well as increased agricultural growth, theoretically could be significant. Yet there is little doubt that it could create serious problems and involve some significant costs.

The massive transfer of urban residents, while in theory "voluntary," has obviously involved subtle coercion on a large scale, and there is considerable evidence of problems in absorbing these people into rural society and of pressures from those sent out to return to the cities. It is difficult to assess the extent of tensions created by disaffection among those sent to the countryside, as well as those in rural areas who must accept these "outsiders." But it would be surprising if there were not serious problems of adjustment on both sides. It is possible to argue that in time such tensions will be reduced if improved conditions in the countryside make living easier for the rusticated urbanites and convince the peasants that the expertise brought by the "outsiders" clearly helps to improve their lot. But if these positive results are slow in evolving, tensions in some areas could steadily grow, conceivably becoming explosive.

On balance, it is not yet self-evident that the rapid, large-scale, and arbitrary transfer of skills and other resources from urban to rural areas is necessarily an efficient use of China's very scarce developmental assets, or the optimal way to achieve maximum acceleration of overall national development and growth. Even if the regime's rural programs do result in improved rural conditions, pressures for a reversal, or at least a modification, of the bias in favor of rural areas could well increase in time if the rate of overall growth in GNP remains relatively slow.

Labor: Utilizing China's Most Abundant Resource

China's overall economic strategy in recent years has emphasized the need for maximum utilization of China's most abundant resource, labor.[32] The regime's leaders have attempted not only to substitute labor for capital but to achieve full employment, or something close to it. Policies aimed at these goals have been many-faceted, including the mass mobilization of labor at local levels, especially in the countryside, to construct water conservancy projects and other public works. While the use of mass labor has had a long tradition in China, dating back at least to the period when the Ch'in dynasty created the Chinese Empire in the third century B.C., the Communists have been able to organize the population at a grassroots level more effectively than any past Chinese rulers and to carry out labor-intensive public works projects on a scale unprecedented in Chinese history. The scale of this type of activity has varied at different periods since 1949. It reached its peak during the early phases of the Great Leap, and declined thereafter. Recently, it has again become important, but the regime has carefully avoided the extremes of 1958 when a large part of the population was organized into labor groups along military lines and was severely overworked.

The newest element in this policy of maximum labor utilization, as mentioned earlier in this discussion, is the large-scale transfer of persons from urban areas, where unemployment had become a serious problem, to rural areas, where they have been set to work either in administrative jobs, services, local industry, or agriculture. Increased irrigation, double-cropping, and use of fertilizers have probably increased the need for labor in agriculture in many situations. And China's economic planners hope that the development of decentralized small and medium-sized labor-intensive industries will absorb considerable amounts of additional manpower in both the countryside and the cities.

As in so many other areas of Chinese economic policy, there has been little statistical basis for reaching firm conclusions about the results. It appears, however, that the regime has come closer to achieving full employment in recent years than China has ever been able to do in the past, and that the accomplishment in this area exceeds that of most other developing nations.

In China today, a visitor does not see evidence of significant unemployment. Everyone appears to be at work, and there is no doubt that the regime's determination to provide employment for virtually the entire population—including large numbers of women—has reduced unemployment to a minimum. The regime's drastic frontal attack on the unemployment problem, involving not only remarkably effective organization of the entire labor force but also sizable transfers of people, represents in many respects a notable achievement.

To understand fully the Chinese employment picture in relation to that of other nations, two points need to be made. First, the overall political and social context has been crucial. The regime's ability to organize China's huge labor force has rested on tight political controls, enabling the authorities to assign and transfer labor as the state sees fit, disregarding individual preferences when it seems necessary from the state's point of view, in a manner that regimes in more pluralistic or democratic societies could not even seriously consider.

At the same time, however, there is ample evidence of a great deal of disguised underemployment and, in many situations, relatively inefficient use of labor. A visitor to China sees many examples of obvious labor redundancy, in which several persons are employed in tasks that probably a single person—or at least significantly fewer persons—could perform.[33] Factory managers report that they seldom fire anyone for ineffective performance, and schools rarely flunk out students. The emphasis in many if not most places appears to be mainly on keeping people at work, rather than increasing efficiency and maximizing labor productivity.

As a consequence, while most people one sees in China seem to be working conscientiously, they appear at times to lack the dynamic, competitive pressure to work that characterizes the people in many other areas in Northeast Asia. There is no doubt that the Chinese today are "hard-working," as they have always been; the country's culture continues to place great stress on the work ethic. In factories and many other enterprises and institutions, "emulation campaigns" are used with considerable effectiveness—at least during periods in which such campaigns are a major focus of attention—to introduce a competitive spirit to spur harder work and increased productivity. Where there is deliberate overstaffing and labor redundancy, however, such campaigns cannot eliminate the fact of real underemployment. In the major factories I visited in late 1972 and early 1973, the emulation programs that were being conducted at that time seemed to me to be relatively low key. The major emphasis throughout the society, as best as one could judge it then, seemed to be on full employment and security of employment rather than on competitive efforts to increase labor productivity and reduce labor costs.

There is obviously much that can be said for this emphasis, in terms of the regime's basic social as well as economic goals. Eliminating overt unemployment and increasing the population's sense of economic security undoubtedly contribute to general stability, and the costs of underemployment may well be less, in many instances, than the costs of unemployment. But underemployment involves costs too, and the need for improved labor productivity and reduced labor costs may pose new and difficult policy issues as China's development progresses.

"Redness" versus "Expertness"

As discussed in earlier chapters, believers in the Maoist ethos in China have, during certain periods, put extreme emphasis on the importance of "redness," or ideological dedication and purity, rather than "expertness," or technical skills. They have always, it is true, asserted that everyone should be both "red" and "expert," but in practice they have tended to denigrate expertness when stressing "redness." This was the case, for example, during the Great Leap period, and in the regime's rhetoric during the Cultural Revolution the need to be "red" was a major theme in the attacks on China's bureaucratic and intellectual leaders.

How much has this affected the regime's concrete policies, and what sort of economic price has it involved? There is no simple answer, but there is reason to believe that the wastage of skills in recent years as a result of some of the regime's more radical policies has been significant. The emphasis on egalitarianism, labor-intensive projects, and decentralized enterprises using simple technologies, while helping to mobilize the "masses," have also tended to prevent full and effective use of many skilled persons in tasks for which they have been trained. The transfer of educated personnel from the cities to the countryside has involved, for many, a substitution of relatively simple tasks for more complicated ones they are capable of performing. Most important, many of the regime's policies have reflected, in explicit and concrete ways, strong biases against intellectuals, specialists, and technical experts in general.[34] The Maoist ethos calls for the creation of omnicompetent revolutionary citizens who through sheer will and hard work can perform miracles. Experts have been viewed with considerable suspicion and subjected to strong political pressures and intense reindoctrination efforts.

The substantial gap between rhetoric and practice makes it difficult, however, to judge the effects of recent policy. Even at the height of the Cultural Revolution, many technical specialists continued to put their skills to effective use while the Party line made them targets of attack. Those working in priority fields and advanced industries (including those related to defense) were clearly protected from the political storms of the period. Since the Cultural Revolution, moreover, available evidence suggests that technical specialists in many places have made a fairly rapid comeback. How much they are still subjected to onerous political controls and continuing political pressures is hard to judge, but one obtains the impression in enterprises one can now visit in China that their special skills are being utilized, and probably fairly effectively.

Nevertheless, the denigration of specialization and of technical expertise in the name of ideology and egalitarian values has doubtless had some important practical consequences involving a significant, though unmeasurable, price. Even though the talents of many of China's technical experts are now being effectively used, some are still performing tasks that do not fully utilize their highly specialized knowledge. Specialists are still urged to apply themselves to "practical" problems in their fields of expertise rather than to "theoretical" problems. Most of them have been required, at various periods in the recent past, to devote large amounts of time and energy to "politics" and "ideology." This emphasis may have helped, as Mao has hoped, to overcome the past tendency of many intellectuals and technocrats—in China as in numerous other countries—to operate in a world of their own, to avoid getting their hands dirty, and to devote their attention primarily to theoretically interesting questions rather than to the mundane and practical day-to-day problems of their society. At the same time, it has undoubtedly diverted many highly qualified people from activities that could utilize their knowledge most effectively. It has probably slowed the progress of important "theoretical" work that, while perhaps not having as immediate or visible a payoff as work on immediate "practical" problems, could be crucial to China's long-run development.[35]

One price that China has paid can be seen in the impact of ideology and politics on higher education in China, as a result of the Cultural Revolution and its aftermath. Virtually no normal traditional educational activity was carried on at most Chinese universities from 1966 until they began a short while ago to recruit new university students, class by class—a few in 1970, and more in 1971 and 1972. By the time the first members of the current crop of university students graduate in 1973 or 1974 (at the end of a shortened three-year course), seven to eight years will have passed in which no normal graduating class will have emerged from China's major universities. (Some holdover students "graduated" during the Cultural Revolution, but they had done no regular class work since 1966 and in reality never completed a "normal" course of studies.) Even now, ideology and politics continue to dominate the atmosphere at the universities, for the Cultural Revolution was succeeded by a new movement, the "educational revolution." The purpose of the educational revolution is to carry out a radical restructuring of higher education, eliminating all traces of elitism (the alleged tendency to produce "experts" who are "spiritual aristocrats"), purging the universities of all "revisionist tendencies," and enshrining Maoist values as the ultimate repository of truth. It is apparent to any visitor that decision-making power in China's universities today rests in the hands of political cadres (many of them in their thirties or forties), not educators. In the background, the role of the military—exercised through Mao Tse-tung Thought Propaganda teams—continues to be very significant.

The attempt to "transform" the universities has had varied and far-reaching consequences.[36] Almost all members of their teaching staffs have had to undergo intensive reindoctrination, combined with physical labor, and have been compelled to recant past errors of ideological judgment; for most older professors, this has been the third or fourth time they have had to do this since 1949. (To a remarkable degree the full and associate professors in China's major universities even today are men trained before 1949; in Futan University in Shanghai, for example, more than 120 out of a total of 151 fall into this category.) All university texts and teaching materials are now undergoing revision. As of 1973, in fact, there are no regular texts in use, apart from the classics of Marxism-Leninism-Maoism. Other written matter now being used consists of provisional mimeographed materials still in the process of being discussed and approved by students, workers, and peasants, as well as teachers.

The length of study in universities has been drastically cut, on an "experimental basis"—in most institutions from five to three years. The time devoted to traditional classroom work has been curtailed, and everyone is required to spend a substantial portion of time in practical work, in factories, Communes, or elsewhere. A major effort is being made to consolidate, reorganize, and simplify courses, with the stress on practical work experience rather than "theoretical study," and on broad subject areas rather than "narrow specialization." Teaching methods are also undergoing change, with increased emphasis on self-study, discussion, and "practice." For a time, almost all examinations were eliminated. The character of university student bodies has also changed greatly. The students enrolled in 1971 were almost entirely workers, peasants, and soldiers who had had several years of practical work experience; some had previously graduated from middle school, but many had not. There were no formal entrance examinations; admittance was based largely on the recommendations made by an applicant's organizational unit.

All of these changes appear to have created an atmosphere of considerable confusion and uncertainty about the future. Almost nothing has crystallized in final form; everything is still regarded as experimental. In fact, although the "educational revolution" is still in full swing, a cautious retreat from the extremes of two years ago has already begun. It has evidently become clear to some Chinese leaders that if the universities are to recover their traditional capacity to train competent people, especially in the crucial fields of science and technology now being emphasized, steps will have to be taken to restore higher standards and more regularized methods.

As a result of the retreat, applicants now are required to take entrance examinations as well as tests in their basic courses. The time allocated to classroom work and lectures is being gradually increased. The importance of "theory" as well as "practice" is receiving increased recognition, and there is pressure to lengthen the time of study. (At Tsinghua University, for example, most students must now spend three and a half years to get a degree, one-term refresher courses having been added to bring new students up to acceptable minimum standards.) The universities have also begun to admit some students directly from middle schools and to set certain basic admission standards in departments where "specialized vocational requirements" make it necessary. In Peking University, all students accepted into the physics department now are middle school graduates.

The retreat is clearly dictated by the necessity of restoring the standards required for quality education. But with the politically inspired "educational revolution" still under way, it is a difficult and delicate process that might take a good many years to complete. China's "leftists" are openly critical of recent trends.

The final result is difficult to foresee. Some Maoist values—including the stress on practicality and the determination to combat educational elitism—will probably leave a lasting imprint. But one suspects that the imperatives inherent in the society's need for competent university graduates will push the universities gradually back toward methods and standards similar to those that prevailed before 1966, even though this will require compromising purist Maoist values. In the meantime, China has paid a very significant price for a decade of confusion and abnormality in higher education. And the regime has yet to work out a viable relationship among its political leaders, ideologues, and intellectuals (including its technical experts) that will enable the society to make full use of its limited reservoir of skilled personnel.

Some would argue that, whatever the price paid as a result of recent policies, the economic and social cost has been counterbalanced by the positive effects of the regime's attempts to stimulate everyone—from expert to peasant—to experiment, innovate, and focus attention on the solution of immediate practical problems. This, it is argued by some, has not only encouraged imaginative local solutions for local problems, thereby accelerating basic processes of change and development; it may also have helped to transform underlying patterns of mass thinking and behavior in ways that will give a stronger impetus to, and provide sounder foundations for, broadly based "modernization" than alternative policies would. Recent policies, these observers assert, have fostered in China a "scientific and technological revolution" at a grassroots level, rather than just in China's major urban centers.[37] There may be some truth in this line of reasoning, but it is too early to determine how China's "masses" will be affected in the long run by the regime's attempt to encourage innovative problem solving, on the one hand, and its demand for total ideological orthodoxy and conformity, on the other. Particularly at the height of the Cultural Revolution, Mao was virtually deified, and his "thought" was propagated as sacred and un-challengeable. This encouraged attitudes that in many respects are the antithesis of those usually associated with the scientific approach and modernization.[38]

One suspects that the conflicting demands made on the population will prove to be incompatible in the long run and that either the force of political dogma will be gradually eroded or the emergence of a gen-uinely scientific, problem-solving approach to development will be impeded. To the extent that one can judge from trends in the most recent period, it appears that the stress on "redness" has been declining and recognition of the crucial role of experts has been steadily growing. While the "red-expert" battle may continue to be intense in the uni-versities for some time, the general thrust of China's policies toward increasing pragmatism appears to be moving the pendulum gradually in favor of "expertness" in much of the society.

Limiting Population Growth[39]

Birth control measures have been another extremely important fea-ture of China's recent development policies. Peking's leaders recognize that China's success in achieving economic development in the years ahead will depend not only on how effectively it is able to increase agricultural and industrial production but also, directly and crucially, on the extent to which it can limit population growth.

During some earlier periods, the regime tended to argue—on the basis of classical Marxist as well as Maoist concepts—that China had no real population problem. Steps were taken to encourage birth control in the mid-1950s, before the Great Leap, and in the early 1960s, after the Great Leap's failure, but in the first years of Communist rule, and then later during the Great Leap, Peking's leaders argued on the basis of Maoist concepts that the more people China had the better.

It has been apparent for some time, however, that even Mao has changed his mind on the matter of China's population explosion. Re-cently, the regime has been energetically promoting, without apparent dissent or opposition, the use of contraceptives, late marriages, steriliza-tion, and many other measures designed to slow down the rate of China's population growth. There are no reliable public statistics on China's population today but there can be no doubt that it is eminently rational for the regime to push birth control.

The first census conducted by the regime in the early 1950s indicated that China's annual rate of population growth at that time was over 2 percent. This may have dropped slightly during the early 1960s as a result of the widespread malnutrition and the adverse effects on public health of the post-Leap depression, but it may well have risen again subsequently as a result of improved economic conditions and expanding medical and health care. There is evidence that a second national census of some kind was conducted in 1964, and posters appearing in Shanghai in late 1972 indicated that a third might then be under way, but officials disclaim knowledge of it, and no results of any of either of these efforts have been made public. The statement by Li Hsien-nien quoted below (page 166) suggests that even China's top bureaucrats do not feel confident that they know the facts about China's population. All judgments on the rate of China's population growth are based, therefore, on inadequate data.

Some observers believe that the rate may now have dropped below 2 percent, but the basis for such judgments is fragmentary and impressionistic. In many parts of the country, Chinese cadres are willing to provide figures on local birth and death rates, but the impression I received in late 1972 was that these statistics were of questionable reliability. Some figures seemed to be targets rather than achievements, and even when the figures for one locality seemed reasonable it was difficult to know how much one could generalize from them about a broader area.

Estimates made by population specialists outside of China suggest that the regime's birth control efforts are only beginning to take effect. Some estimates indicate that the country's net annual rate of population increase may still be close to 2 percent, others that it may be slightly over 2 percent.[40] Because China has such a huge population, either figure would mean that the country is still experiencing an increase of 15 million or more people a year. Obviously, such a large increase requires considerable growth in output simply to prevent economic retrogression.

The demonstrated skill of the Chinese Communists in organization and indoctrination and their ability to manipulate strong social pressures to promote their priority programs gives China a chance of greater success in fostering birth control than most developing nations have had. To the extent that the regime is able to ensure a significant degree of economic security for the bulk of its people, improve the status of women (and involve them in activities outside the home), and induce the population to regard collective production units rather than individual families as the primary basis for personal security, the regime's efforts to enforce birth control should produce results. The evidence so far, however, suggests that while progress has been made it has probably been relatively gradual.

It seems likely that the birthrate will drop in the period ahead, but more in urban than in rural areas. Since the overwhelming majority of China's population is still rooted in agricultural villages and since the regime is currently trying to retard urbanization (which elsewhere has helped to slow population growth), it may prove extremely difficult to achieve dramatic or sudden results in limiting national population growth in the years immediately ahead. This is obviously not to suggest that the attempt to curb population growth is unsound or unimportant. It does mean that even if birth control efforts are promoted to an unprecedented extent, China's population could continue in the immediate future to grow at a rate of 15 to 20 million people a year, or even more, and this could represent one of the most baffling conundrums about China's long-run economic and political future.

One highly qualified U.S. government specialist on China's population has analyzed the problem in a way that highlights its potential seriousness. He estimates that, under pessimistic assumptions, the net rate of population growth could remain fairly constant, in which case China's total population could theoretically reach 1.33 billion by 1990. He also calculates that, even under relatively optimistic assumptions in which rigorous birth control efforts begin to take effect, the net growth rate might only drop to 1.6 percent a year by 1990; and even if this occurs, because of the particular patterns of likely population growth China's population could theoretically still reach 1.30 billion by 1990, a figure only slightly lower than that projected under more pessimistic assumptions.[41]

It should be noted that the above projections are based on estimates that may overestimate the present population and underestimate the possible decline in fertility and growth rates in the future. Some other specialists on Chinese population problems project somewhat lower figures in the latter part of this century. Even these more optimistic analysts see no alternative to continuing population growth for many years, however; one, for example, who believes a change in fertility patterns in China is occurring, nevertheless concludes: "Regardless of how the population responds to fertility decline, therefore, China's population will certainly reach the one billion mark before it can complete its demographic transition."[42]

To date the Peking regime has been able to increase output at a rate exceeding that of population growth, which in and of itself is an achievement of great importance. To keep barely ahead of population growth is not enough, however, and the degree of success in limiting population growth will determine the per capita rate at which China's economy will be able to grow. Economic development in China will continue, therefore, to involve a race between production and population growth for the foreseeable future.

National Self-Reliance

Underlying China's entire developmental approach in recent years has been its commitment to "self-reliance." One might argue that the Chinese Communists have always attempted to be as self-reliant as possible, but this goal became especially important after the Sino-Soviet break in 1960 and by the time of the Cultural Revolution was an overriding priority.

As indicated earlier, China's leaders began to realize, even before the end of the first Plan period, that the Soviet model did not provide automatic answers to China's most pressing problems. When Soviet aid was cut off in 1960, they felt badly "burned." The basic question thereafter was not whether China would be able to obtain foreign assistance but whether it wanted any. Following the withdrawal of Russian technicians in 1960 and the ending of all long-term Soviet aid to China, the Chinese concluded that their only alternative was to pursue go-it-alone policies. The Great Leap Forward was therefore based essentially on a do-it-yourself bootstrap approach.

The split between Moscow and Peking, coming as it did when China was entering a severe depression, had extremely adverse effects on the Chinese economy. It greatly exacerbated the immediate difficulties China already faced as a result of its own policy mistakes as well as large-scale natural disasters, and the effects, lasting for several years, seriously impeded the progress of industrialization. The Chinese attempted on their own to complete as many as possible of the planned "Soviet aid projects," but nearly a third of the most important ones scheduled for completion by 1967 had to be dropped or were left uncompleted.[43] This was a major factor contributing to the decline of China's industrial output in the early 1960s. It also led China to shift a majority of its foreign trade in the 1960s from Communist to non-Communist nations.[44] China was forced to adopt a policy of self-reliance; because of the general foreign policy China was then pursuing (see Chapter 5), its leaders did not have the options that some other countries—such as India, for example—had in looking to foreign nations for financial and technical assistance.

Instead of bemoaning their fate, Chinese leaders accepted the situation and went to great lengths to try to make necessity a virtue. For the most part since then, they have relied almost totally on China's own financial and technical resources and have taken great pride in doing so. Not only have they paid off all of China's foreign debts, which were mainly to the Soviet Union; they have actually been a net exporter of capital. They have conducted foreign trade essentially on a pay-as-you-go basis, limiting it accordingly. Self-reliance has been a major factor, moreover, impelling them to devise policies capable of being implemented without foreign assistance—policies maximizing the utilization of China's domestic resources and skills. This has reinforced the other pressures impelling them to stress projects that are labor-intensive rather than capital-intensive and that rely whenever possible on relatively simple rather than complex technologies.

It is true that the Chinese continued to import capital goods after 1960 and to borrow advanced technology. In the mid-1960s, they purchased a number of "complete plants" from Japan and Western Europe that provided "turnkey" models for building other plants in China. The scale of this effort was limited, however, in part by the necessity for earmarking much of China's foreign exchange for the purchase of needed grain and fertilizers and in part by design. If China had actively sought larger and longer-term credits from the Japanese or others, it might have been able to obtain them. However, it deliberately chose not to become thus indebted. And during the Cultural Revolution, China turned more determinedly inward, economically as well as politically. As a result, the Chinese economy was probably more autarkic than that of any comparable large nation.

The painful experience with the Soviet Union seems to have convinced Peking's leaders that any economic dependency on foreign nations should be avoided, since this might make China vulnerable to dangerous pressures from abroad. The main public arguments in support of autarkic policies have not focused on the necessity for self-reliance, however, or even on the dangers of dependence, but rather on the positive virtues of economic independence. Nations, like individuals, can only "learn from doing," they have argued, asserting that a country such as China should be able more effectively to develop its own skills, mobilize its own resources, and pursue policies suited to the nation's needs over the long run by pursuing a do-it-yourself approach rather than by soliciting help from abroad.

This emphasis on self-reliance has reinforced domestic policies stressing maximum mobilization and utilization of China's own skills and human resources. The Chinese economy has been, in fact as well as in theory, remarkably "independent" in recent years, and this has been a source of genuine pride. This pride, and the strongly nationalistic impulses associated with it, may have been an asset in some respects, helping to stimulate inventiveness and hard work in the search for indigenous solutions to China's economic problems.

However, China's emphasis on self-reliance has involved significant costs. To achieve rapid growth, a developing country must mobilize adequate capital and acquire the scientific and technical knowledge to use it. Many developing nations have relied to a considerable extent, especially during the early stages of growth, on the importation of both capital goods and scientific and technical knowledge from abroad. One can argue that heavy dependence on foreign economic relations is a mixed blessing, but there is no question that a developing nation can benefit greatly from foreign trade and that the pace of its development can often be accelerated with the help of foreign credits or loans. As growth occurs, moreover, the pressure to participate more actively in the world economy generally increases rather than decreases. A go-it-alone strategy is likely to slow the pace of development in China, particularly in large-scale industry, and to place intense pressure on domestic resources.

Realistically speaking, could a Communist-governed China seriously consider the option of obtaining greater financial and technical assistance from abroad that would help to accelerate its rate of development? The answer is doubtless yes. Direct foreign investment will probably not be a practical possibility unless the regime's policies undergo fundamental change. But if the Chinese were to decide to promote exports more actively, import more capital goods and technical know-how from abroad, and solicit foreign credits and loans, China's rate of growth could almost certainly increase, especially in the modern industrial sectors of the economy. Even if these measures were taken, its foreign trade might never be very large as a proportion of GNP. But in recent years China's foreign trade has been among the smallest in the world in per capita terms.[45] (In absolute terms, it is smaller than that of Taiwan, which has roughly 2 percent of China's population.)

Since 1972, Chinese leaders have been cautiously reconsidering and adjusting their policies toward the international community, gradually expanding foreign trade, and even accepting foreign credits to help finance trade.[46] One compelling reason is probably the belief that if China wishes to accelerate its development of modern industry, it must not only step up its own investments in major plant construction but also import the most up-to-date foreign technology, including new complete plants from abroad.

Although the evidence is not conclusive, there are reasons to believe that much of the increase in industrial output since the Cultural Revolution has come from fuller utilization of plants built in the 1950s and 1960s. The Chinese are cl early concerned about their t echnological lag in important fields, so much so that they began in 1972, for the first time in many years, to indicate a strong interest in importing foreign technology on a sizable scale and in accepting medium-term "extended payment" foreign credits to finance the importation of complete plants from abroad. By late 1973 it appeared that China's foreign trade for the year would approach $7 billion, and Peking had already purchased several hundred million dollars' worth of commodities under extended payment agreements.

It would be premature to conclude that the Chinese have abandoned their belief in the concept of self-reliance. Nevertheless, recent trends are significant. They suggest that China is moving cautiously to increase its involvement in the international economy.

The question is how far they may be willing to go in this direction. Today China still remains highly autarkic in basic respects. To go much further (which would require greater emphasis than in the past on the development of the country's export capacity, or the acceptance of larger credits or loans from abroad, or both) would necessitate significant compromises of values that China's top leadership has rated very highly in recent years. This issue could be a major subject of debate in China in the period ahead, and how it is decided will have a major impact on the pace and direction of Chinese development.

China's Performance in Quantitative Terms

The discussion so far has described the evolution of China's economic strategies and policies since the Communists came to power, and analyzed some of the pros and cons of those now being pursued. To evaluate economic performance since 1949 in quantitative terms is more difficult, for there have been less statistical data about China's economy than about that of any other major nation.[47] In only one period, lasting a relatively few years in the 1950s, did the Chinese Communists authorities publish fairly comprehensive national economic statistics. During the Great Leap, the Chinese statistical system broke down. Although it was gradually reconstructed in the recovery period, Peking issued virtually no overall national production or growth statistics from 1960 until 1970, and even now—or at least up to mid-1973—no comprehensive statistical data are yet being published. A few important production figures have been released in recent years, but that is all. For the period since 1960, therefore, estimates of Chinese production and growth must of necessity be based to a large extent on informed guesswork.

There are good reasons to doubt that even the top leaders in Peking have possessed reliable statistics for many of the key indicators of China's development since the start of the 1960s. One extraordinarily candid and revealing statement indicating that this has been the case was made by one of China's top economic specialists in November 1971. In an interview with an Arab newsman, Vice Premier Li Hsiennien, discussing China's population problem, said: "We have been racing against time to cope with the enormous increase in population. Some people estimate the population of China at 800 million and some at 750 million. Unfortunately, there are no accurate statistics in this connection. Nevertheless, the officials at the supply and grain department are saying confidently, 'The number is 800 million people.' Officials outside the grain department say the population is '750 million only' while the Ministry of Commerce affirms that 'the number is 830 million.' However, the planning department insists that the number is 'less than 750 million.' The Ministry of Commerce insists on the bigger number in order to be able to provide goods in large quantities. The planning men reduce the figure in order to strike a balance in the plans of the various state departments."[48]

Li Hsien-nien may have overdrawn the situation somewhat, but his statement is probably an accurate reflection of the basic situation. If the estimates of China's population made by top members of the Peking regime vary so much, it is hardly surprising that analysts outside of China must be extremely tentative in making estimates of the country's economic performance. But unless and until Peking releases more information on the Chinese economy, the careful estimates made by some well-qualified economists in the West and Japan provide the best data available on China's economic performance.

Gross National Product

One carefully constructed set of estimates, based on research by U.S. government analysts, is summarized in Table 1. (It should be noted that these are necessarily estimates and must be viewed with a certain skepticism, but they can be regarded as indicating reasonable orders of magnitude.) As the estimates show, China's GNP probably rose from about $36 billion in 1949 to about $128 billion in 1971, but the rate of growth has varied greatly in different periods. In the initial period of recovery and rehabilitation, 1949–52, it rose $23 billion, or roughly 64 percent, in three years, averaging close to 20 percent a year. This figure is not really comparable, however, to those for subsequent periods, since it was to a large extent the result of the rehabilitation of previously existing production facilities and did not represent real expansion. The most important period of rapid substantial growth occurred during the first Plan period, 1953–57. In those five years GNP rose by $23 billion, an increase of over 39 percent, averaging roughly 7 percent a year.

During the Great Leap years, there was a rapid rise in 1958, which dropped off slightly in 1959 and 1960. Over the three-year period 1958–60, the overall increase in GNP, compared to 1957, was only about $7 billion, or roughly 8 percent, averaging less than 3 percent a year. The period of retreat and readjustment, from 1961 through 1965, began with a large drop in GNP, followed by a gradually accelerating process of recovery marked by substantial increases in GNP during 1964 and 1965. For the five-year period as a whole, however, the rise in GNP was only $8 billion, or roughly 9 percent, an average of under 2 percent a year. Ups and downs characterized the succeeding Cultural Revolution period, with—apparently—drops in both 1967 and 1968, followed by rapid recovery in 1969. For the four-year period from the end of 1965 to the end of 1969, the overall GNP increase of $12 billion raised the total by about 12 percent, averaging roughly 3 percent a year.

TABLE 1. *Estimated Economic Performance of China, 1949–71*

Money in 1970 U.S. dollars

Period and year	GNP (billions of dollars)	Population, midyear (millions)	GNP per capita (dollars)	Industrial production (1957 = 100)	Agricultural production (1957 = 100)	Steel output (millions of metric tons)	Grain output (millions of metric tons)	Foreign trade Volume (billions of dollars)	Foreign trade Percentage with Communist countries
Rehabilitation									
1949	36	538	67	25	54	0.16	108	0.83	[a]
1950	43	547	79	31	64	0.61	125	1.21	29
1951	50	558	90	42	71	0.90	135	1.90	51
1952	59	570	104	51	83	1.35	154	1.89	70
First Five-Year Plan									
1953	63	583	108	64	83	1.77	157	2.30	68
1954	66	596	110	73	84	2.22	160	2.35	74
1955	72	611	117	74	94	2.85	175	3.04	74
1956	78	626	124	91	97	4.46	182	3.12	66
1957	82	642	128	100	100	5.35	185	3.06	64
Great Leap Forward									
1958	95	658	144	131	108	8.0	200	3.76	63
1959	92	674	137	166	86	10.0	165	4.29	69
1960	89	689	130	161–163	83	13.0	160	3.99	66
Readjustment and recovery									
1961	72	701	103	107–110	78	8.0	160	3.02	56
1962	79	710	112	108–113	90	8.0	175–180	2.68	53
1963	82	721	114	119–125	90	9.0	175–180	2.77	45
1964	90	735	122	133–142	96	10.0	180–185	3.22	34
1965	97	751	129	148–161	101	11.0	190–195	3.88	30

Cultural Revolution

1966	105	766	137	165–181	106	13.0	195–200	4.24	26
1967	101	783	129	134–149	115	10.0	210–215	3.90	21
1968	100	800	125	144–163	106	12.0	195–200	3.76	22
1969	109	818	134	170–194	109	15.0	200–205	3.86	20

Resumption of regular planning

1970	122	836	146	199–230	116	18.0	215–220	4.22	20
1971 [b]	128	855	150	223–258	115	21.0	215–220	4.50	21

Source: Arthur G. Ashbrook, Jr., "China: Economic Policy and Economic Results, 1949–71," in *People's Republic of China: An Economic Assessment*, A Compendium of Papers Submitted to the Joint Economic Committee, 92 Cong. 2 sess. (1972), p. 5. Hereafter cited as *An Economic Assessment*.
a. Negligible.
b. Preliminary

Since the Cultural Revolution, the rate of growth has increased, but not at a steady pace. During the two-year period 1970–71, the increase is estimated to have been $19 billion, representing an increase of about 17 percent for the two years; but the 1970 rate of about 12 percent probably dropped in 1971 to roughly 5 percent.

In the light of these ups and downs, it is clear that the growth rate one decides to use for China depends very much on the years employed for calculations. If one uses 1957, the final year of the first Plan period, as a base year, the subsequent rate of growth can be said to have averaged roughly 3 percent a year—or perhaps a little more. However, if the rate of growth is measured from the start of the first Plan period, 1952, to the present, the average rate becomes almost 4 percent a year in overall terms, or roughly 2 percent in per capita terms.[49]

These are not unimpressive figures. They are higher than those for pre-1949 China. They are also slightly higher than the rate of growth achieved by India during the same period. But if China's rate of growth is compared with those of other developing nations, it is apparent that China's performance over the twenty-four years since 1949, although respectable, has not placed it at the forefront of the developing nations. Its growth rate has exceeded that of many developing nations, but has been lower than that of many others, and while its growth rate was well above the average of all developing nations in the 1950s, it was somewhat below the average in the 1960s. U.S. government estimates indicate that for the decade 1961–70 the average GNP growth rate for all developing nations as a group (calculated in 1970 U.S. dollars) was 4.7 percent in absolute terms and 2.2 percent in per capita terms.[50] China's performance did not quite reach that level.

It is noteworthy that China's overall growth rate has been substantially lower than that achieved in recent years in many countries or areas around China, including Korea, Taiwan, Hong Kong, and Singapore, as well as Japan. One can argue with considerable validity that a continental-size economy could not hope to duplicate the performance of the small nations on China's periphery even under the best of circumstances. One can also argue that comparisons between China and Japan in the recent period are not valid, since the Japanese situation in recent years has very special, in fact almost unique. It is perhaps more relevant that China's growth since 1949 has been comparable to that of Japan in its early development period.

Industrial Growth

By far the most rapid growth in China since 1949 has occurred in the industrial sector, and this has been truly outstanding though uneven. A great deal of it took place in the 1950s, not the 1960s.

The Communists started with a relatively small inherited industrial base, concentrated in Manchuria, Shanghai, and a few other major centers. Since 1949, the industries in Manchuria and Shanghai have been greatly expanded, and important new industrial development has occurred in dozens of cities scattered throughout China—Wuhan, Tientsin, Paotow, Peking, Taiyuan, Chengchow, Loyang, Sian, Lanchow, Canton, and many others. Various estimates of Chinese industrial growth differ on particulars, but the overall picture is one of impressive gains in industrial capacity and output. From the start of the first Five-Year Plan until the end of the 1950s, the industrial growth rate was very rapid. According to one estimate, for example, using the level of modern industrial output in 1952 as a base figure of 100, the index of output had risen to 371.4 by 1959.[51] This was a higher rate than the Soviet Union achieved during its first Plan period, and much higher than—perhaps about double—the rate achieved in India during the 1950s. During the entire first Plan period, industrial production seems to have grown at an average rate of between 14 and 19 percent a year, and the average annual rate for the regime's first decade as a whole was even higher, probably above 20 percent.[52]

Estimates are more difficult to make for the 1960s, because the shortage of statistical data increases the margin for possible error. On the basis of the data that are available, it appears that industrial production, after reaching a peak in 1960, dropped fairly precipitously in the years immediately following, before making a recovery by the mid-1960s. Using 1959 as a base year (index = 100), one set of estimates indicates that the gross value of industrial output rose to 104 in 1960 and then dropped to 69 in 1961 and 60 in 1962, before slowly rising again to 66 in 1963, 74 in 1964, and 81 in 1965.[53] By 1966, output was approaching past peaks, but then the disorder associated with the Cultural Revolution caused further setbacks in 1967–68, probably by around 15 to 20 percent.[54]

According to some other estimates, total overall industrial output may have risen modestly during the 1960s, mainly in the final years of the decade, but the average annual rate of increase for the decade was perhaps only about a quarter of the rate of the 1950s. If, however, one compares the rate during the period 1957–68 with that of the first Five-Year Plan period, the rate in the period since 1957 may be about half that during the first Plan.[55] During the regime's entire first two decades, from 1949 to 1969, the average annual rate of increase in industrial output may have been about 10 percent. For the period from 1957 to the present, the average rate has been about 8 percent, as compared with roughly 20 percent in the 1950s alone.[56] Since 1969, fairly rapid industrial growth has resumed once again, and during 1970 and 1971 the rate of increase may have been 10 percent, or more, a year in overall terms. The current rate is thus comparable to the average for the entire period since 1949, but is still only half the rate achieved during the 1950s.

A similar overall picture emerges if one examines the growth in selected industries. Table 2 summarizes estimates made by U.S. government analysts of Chinese production in certain key industries from 1949 to 1970.

The trends in industrial output are highlighted most clearly if the output of selected industries is compared not only between key periods since 1949 but also with pre-1949 peak years (see Table 3).

Several distinct patterns are revealed by these figures. One, obviously, is that overall industrial growth has been extremely impressive if one compares output figures for 1970 with those for 1949 or, perhaps more appropriately, with the peaks of the pre-1949 period. Compared with pre-1949 peak levels, electric power output had increased about tenfold by 1970, steel output roughly twentyfold, coal output approximately fivefold, crude oil output about sixtyfold, cement output almost sixfold, machine tool output close to tenfold, chemical fertilizer output roughly thirty-fivefold, and cotton cloth output between two- and threefold.

Except in certain special fields, however, such as crude oil and fertilizers, a very large percentage of the growth in key industries occurred in the 1950s; the expansion in the 1960s was more limited. In coal and cotton cloth, for example, the 1970 levels of output were roughly the same as those of a decade earlier. And whereas by 1960 the output of electric power, steel, cement, and machine tools was many times that of the pre-1949 peaks (almost eight times in power, about fourteen times in steel, approximately five times in cement, and roughly seven times in machine tools), the increase in output in these industries between 1960 and 1970 was relatively modest (roughly in the range of 20 to 40 percent). Crude oil and chemical fertilizer production was given special priority, however, so it steadily rose, even during the 1960s.

The above picture may be changing, however. If the fairly rapid rate of increase in output that has occurred in some key industries since 1969 is sustained, industrial expansion in the years immediately ahead could be more impressive than in the 1960s. To sustain a rapid rate, however, China will have to find a way to step up its investments in new plant construction in the period ahead.

Agricultural Growth

The pattern of growth in agriculture since 1949 has been less impressive than that in industry. In contrast to industry, agricultural output lagged seriously in the 1950s, and this was a crucial factor leading to Mao's radical Great Leap and Commune experiments in the late 1950s, and then to the regime's crucial decision to shift priority from industry to agriculture in the 1960s. During the first Five-Year Plan, the rise in the gross value of agricultural production was probably around 25 percent, which was far below what the regime hoped for and probably considerably below expectations. It kept ahead of population growth, but only by a small margin.[57] Agriculture accounted for only 12 percent or so of China's total economic growth in that period. As in the Soviet Union, as well as in other developing countries such as India, agricultural output simply failed to keep pace in China during the early years of planned development.

Table 4 summarizes two sets of estimates for China's output of grain since 1949. As the table shows, the adjusted estimates made by U.S. government analysts are lower for the period since 1957 than those from official Chinese sources. There is considerable room for debate about the relative validity of the two sets of figures, but in the discussion below, the Chinese figures—except those concerning the Great Leap period—will be used.

As the figures indicate, China's grain output recovered fairly rapidly in the initial period after Communist takeover, from the low point of 1949, rising from 108 million metric tons in 1949 to 154 million metric tons in 1952. During the first Plan period (1953–57), output rose each year, reaching 185 million tons in 1957, but the rate was much slower. There was a surge forward in 1958, but what actual output that year

TABLE 2. *Estimated Production of Selected Industrial Commodities in China, 1949–70*

Year	Electric power (millions of kilowatt-hours)	Coal (thousands of metric tons)	Crude oil (thousands of metric tons)	Crude steel (thousands of metric tons)	Chemical fertilizer[a] (thousands of metric tons)	Cement[b] (thousands of metric tons)	Timber (thousands of cubic meters)	Machine tools (units)	Paper (thousands of metric tons)	Cotton cloth (millions of linear meters)	Sugar (thousands of metric tons)
1949	4,308	32,430	121	158	27	661	5,760	1,582	228	1,889	199
1950	4,550	42,920	200	606	70	1,410	6,640	3,312	380	2,522	242
1951	5,750	53,090	305	896	137	2,490	7,640	5,853	492	3,058	300
1952	7,261	66,490	436	1,349	194	2,861	11,200	13,734	603	3,829	451
1953	9,195	69,680	622	1,774	263	3,877	17,530	20,502	667	4,685	638
1954	11,001	83,660	789	2,225	343	4,600	22,210	15,901	842	5,230	693
1955	12,278	98,300	966	2,853	426	4,503	20,930	13,708	839	4,361	717
1956	16,593	110,360	1,163	4,465	663	6,393	20,840	25,928	998	5,770	807
1957	19,340	130,732	1,458	5,350	803	6,860	27,870	28,297	1,221	5,050	864
1958	28,000	230,000	2,300	8,000	1,400	9,300	35,000	30,000	1,600	5,700	900
1959	42,000	300,000	3,700	10,000	1,900	11,000	41,000	33,000	1,700	7,500	1,100
1960	47,000	280,000	4,600	13,000	2,500	9,000	33,000	38,000	1,700	5,800	920
1961	31,000	170,000	4,500	8,000	1,400	6,000	27,000	30,000	1,000	4,000	700
1962	30,000	180,000	5,000	8,000	2,100	5,500	29,000	25,000	1,000	4,200	480
1963	33,000	190,000	5,500	9,000	2,900	7,300	32,000	35,000	1,100	4,500	540
1964	36,000	200,000	6,900	10,000	3,500	8,700	34,000	38,000	1,500	4,900	1,100
1965	42,000	220,000	8,000	11,000	4,500	11,000	36,000	44,000	1,700	5,400	1,500

1966	47,000	240,000	10,000	13,000	5,500	12,000	38,000	48,000	1,800	6,000	1,600
1967	41,000	190,000	10,000	10,000	4,000	10,000	30,000	40,000	1,700	4,800	1,700
1968	44,000	200,000	11,000	12,000	4,800	11,000	32,000	40,000	1,700	4,800	1,800
1969	50,000	250,000	14,000	15,000	5,800	12,000	35,000	45,000	1,800	6,500	1,600
1970[c]	60,000	300,000	18,000	18,000	7,400	13,000	40,000	50,000	2,000	7,500	1,700

Source: Robert Michael Field, "Chinese Industrial Development: 1949–70," in *An Economic Assessment*, p. 83.

a. Production is measured in standard units of fixed nutrient content. For nitrogen fertilizer, the standard is 20 percent nitrogen; for phosphorus fertilizer, 18.7 percent phosphoric acid; and for potassium fertilizer, 40 percent oxide.

b. Large-scale plants only.

c. Some of the figures cited in the table for 1970 are lower than official Chinese figures. For example, Premier Chou stated, in an interview with Edgar Snow ("Talks with Chou En-lai: The Open Door," *The New Republic*, March 27, 1971, p. 20), that 1970 chemical fertilizer output was approximately 14 million tons, cotton cloth output 8.5 billion meters, and crude oil output more than 20 million tons. A New China News Agency article at the start of 1972 stated that steel output in 1971 reached 21 million tons, and it reported percentage figures indicating substantial rises in other major industries (*Peking Review*, Jan. 14, 1972, p. 7). In early 1973 Peking announced that steel production in 1972 reached 23 million tons (*Peking Review*, Jan. 12, 1973, p. 9).

The large discrepancy between the U.S. and Chinese fertilizer figures for 1970 can be explained by the fact that the U.S. government analysts attempted to convert the estimates into figures indicating fixed nutrient content. The discrepancies in the figures for cotton cloth and crude oil are smaller. Although the official Chinese claims may be correct, for purposes of comparability the figures in Table 2 have been used as the basis for calculations in the discussion starting on page 172.

TABLE 3. *Production of Selected Industrial Commodities in China during Key Periods*

Commodity	Highest pre-1949 annual output	1949	1952	1957	1959–60[a]	1961–62[b]	1966	1967–68[c]	1970
Electric power (billions of kilowatt-hours)	6.0	4.3	7.3	19.3	47.0	30.0	47.0	41.0	60.0
Crude steel (millions of metric tons)	0.9	0.2	1.4	5.4	13.0	8.0	13.0	10.0	18.0
Coal (millions of metric tons)	62.0	32.4	66.5	130.7	300.0	170.0	240.0	190.0	300.0
Cement (millions of metric tons)	2.3	0.7	2.9	6.9	11.0	5.5	12.0	10.0	13.0
Machine tools (thousands)	5.4	1.6	13.7	28.3	38.0	25.0	48.0	40.0	50.0
Chemical fertilizers (millions of metric tons)	0.2	0.03	0.2	0.8	2.5	1.4	5.5	4.0	7.4
Cotton cloth (billions of linear meters)	2.8	1.9	3.8	5.1	7.5	4.0	6.0	4.8	7.5
Crude oil (millions of metric tons)	0.3	0.1	0.4	1.5	4.6	4.5	10.0	11.0	18.0

Source: Most of the data are from Field, "Chinese Industrial Development," p. 83; the pre-1949 peak figures are from U.S. Central Intelligence Agency, *People's Republic of China Atlas* (1971), p. 69.
a. Whichever year was highest. This was during the Great Leap Forward.
b. Whichever year was lowest. This was during the readjustment period.
c. Whichever year was lowest. This was during the Cultural Revolution.

TABLE 4. *Two Sets of Estimates of China's Grain Output, 1949–71*[a]

Millions of metric tons

Year	U.S. estimate	Estimates from Chinese sources
1949	(108)	108
1950	(125)	125
1951	(135)	135
1952	(154)	154
1953	(157)	157
1954	(160)	160
1955	(175)	175
1956	(182)	182
1957	(185)	185
1958	200	250
1959	165	270
1960	160	150
1961	160	162
1962	175–180	174
1963	175–180	183
1964	180–185	200
1965	190–195	200
1966	195–200	n.a.
1967	210–215	230
1968	195–200	n.a.
1969	200–205	n.a.
1970	215–220	240
1971	215–220[b]	246

Source: Alva Lewis Erisman, "China: Agricultural Development, 1949–71," in *An Economic Assessment*, p. 121.

n.a. Not available.

a. The grain series in column one consists of estimates made by a U.S. government analyst, Erisman, for the years 1958–71. (For 1949–57 Erisman uses the official Chinese figures, which he believes to be internally consistent and reasonably accurate; these are shown in parentheses in column one.)

The grain series in column two is compiled from official Chinese sources. "Grain," as defined by the Chinese, consists of any staple foodstuff (primary source of calories) and normally includes: (1) rice, wheat, and other small grains; (2) coarse grains such as corn, millet, and kaoliang (Chinese sorghum); (3) tubers (white and sweet potatoes, yams, and cassava) at a ratio of four units of tubers to one of grain; and (4) lentils, such as field peas and various types of beans. Rice, small grains, and coarse grains are reported on an un-milled basis. The definition of "grain" varies, however, from period to period and province to province. For example, chestnuts are considered a grain in some areas of Southwest China whereas in Central China a portion of the sweet potato crop is reported as an industrial crop. At various times, soybeans have been reported by Hopeh and the provinces of Northeast China as a grain crop and by the provinces of Central China as partly a grain and partly an industrial crop.

b. Preliminary.

was is debatable; estimates vary from 200 million tons to 250 million tons. In the subsequent depression years, output dropped precipitously, to lows in the range of 150 million to 160 million tons in 1960–61. It was not until 1964 that the figure approached the 1957 level. Thereafter, recovery was steady as output rose above the 200-million-ton mark sometime between 1964 and 1966 and then continued upward to claimed levels of 240 million in 1970 and 246 million in 1971. An uninterrupted series of good crop years, with relatively favorable weather, was partly responsible for the steady rise from 1966 through 1971; but another basic, and perhaps even more important, explanation was the significant increase in modern industrial inputs into agriculture in accordance with the regime's shift to an "agriculture first" policy in the early 1960s.

The tabulated figures indicate that China's grain output increased by roughly 20 percent from 1952 to 1957, roughly 8 percent from 1957 through 1965, and perhaps 23 percent from 1965 to 1971. In the entire period, from 1952 through 1971, the increase was about 60 percent.

The growth of China's agricultural output has kept ahead of population growth since 1949 but only by a slim margin. Since 1952, the annual increase in grain output has probably averaged between 2 and 3 percent, while the annual increase in population may have been around 2 percent. The importance of the accomplishment in raising food output at a rate more rapid than the rate of population growth should not be underestimated, but China must sustain a higher rate of agricultural growth or reduce the rate of population growth in order to achieve a higher rate of overall growth.

In this connection, it is important to note that in the nine years after 1962 the rate of growth in grain output steadily increased, averaging more than 3 percent a year. If a breakthrough in agriculture can be achieved by increasing modern inputs, the question then will be whether it can be sustained. Maintenance of the upward trend will depend not only on the regime's policies—in particular its willingness to keep up a significant level of investment in the modernization of agriculture, provide adequate incentives to peasants, and avoid disruptive institutional changes—but also on the vagaries of the weather.

In 1972, bad weather resulted in a 4 percent drop in grain output to 240 (or less) million tons.[58] This doubtless meant, of course, a drop of 6 or more percent in relation to planned output. There is little doubt that this will adversely affect China's prospects in the immediate future, probably causing a slowdown in China's planned economic growth, including industrial growth, in 1973. Temporary setbacks of this sort are not likely to halt the steady, albeit gradual, rise in China's agricultural output, however, so long as the regime continues its policies of the recent past.

Future Prospects

Looking back over the entire two-plus decades since the Communist takeover of China, one is impressed by a number of very important accomplishments. The regime has apparently gone far toward eliminating the most extreme poverty. While living standards remain low, the nation's output has been distributed more equitably than previously, in such a way that minimal standards have been assured to most Chinese. Full employment, or something remarkably close to it, seems to have been achieved during the past few years. The regime has been able to maintain fairly stable prices and avoid debilitating inflation.

Many basic social services, including education and health care, have been expanded, especially in the countryside. As far as is known, the Chinese government bears no burden of long-term debt, foreign or domestic. China's foreign trade, while still limited, is roughly in balance. The country has been able to invest large sums of money in building China's defense forces, and it has been a sizable contributor of foreign aid to other developing nations.[59] In overall growth terms, the 4 percent average rate of annual increase in GNP, while lower than that of some other developing nations, is obviously not unimpressive, and the rate of industrial growth averaging close to 10 percent annually is very impressive indeed. While the growth rate in agriculture for the entire period since 1949 is much less impressive, it has, as described earlier, kept ahead of population growth, and the increase in recent years has been significant.

It is clear, however, that one cannot speak of a "Chinese model" of development. At various periods in the past quarter-century, Peking has experimented with quite different strategies, and none has provided "final answers" to China's problems. The Soviet-based strategy of the first Plan produced remarkable results in the field of modern industry, but compromised Mao's egalitarian values, failed to solve China's agricultural problems, and proved to be unsustainable. The Great Leap strategy stimulated a dramatic effort to accelerate growth in all fields by radically new "Maoist" methods, but it proved to be unrealistic and very costly and led to serious failures. Instead of achieving an economic breakthrough, China suffered a serious depression that created major economic and political crises, and several years of development were lost. The post-Leap policies of the 1960s, based on relatively realistic and pragmatic approaches to the urgent immediate problems of recovery, pulled the economy up from its 1960–61 nadir and set the country on the road to development once again. But economic pragmatism clashed directly with many of Mao's social and political values and helped to provoke the Maoist reaction that culminated in the Cultural Revolution, when ideology again took over and derailed the developmental process temporarily.

Development strategy since the Cultural Revolution contains a new mix of elements, and the Chinese economy today is definitely on the upswing again. Because nature was not kind in 1972, the year 1973 may be disappointing, but the setback is likely to be temporary. If the performance achieved during 1970–71 could be sustained in the years ahead, China's industrial output would probably continue to grow by perhaps 10 percent a year, its agriculture by 2.5 to 3 percent, and its GNP by perhaps 4 to 5 percent. But in light of the shifting patterns of the past, it still seems wise to reserve judgment on whether China has hit upon a set of economic policies and an overall strategy that will guarantee sustained growth in the long run.

While Maoist values continue to have a significant impact on economic policy and are responsible for many of the innovations and special emphases in recent years, the key factor in the regime's success in stimulating growth since 1969 has been the increasing pragmatism and flexibility of its policies. The respectable economic performance has occurred because, in a fundamental sense, the regime has retained generally practical and sensible priorities and approaches that first emerged in the 1960s and has avoided Maoist extremes such as those that characterized the Great Leap period.

What are the prospects for continuation of the current strategy in the period ahead? This is not a simple question to answer. Policies since the Cultural Revolution have not remained static, and they are almost certain to continue to evolve as compromises are made between impulses that in the past have been described as being either Maoist or non-Maoist. But the trend has been steadily in the direction of increased pragmatism.

The Tenth Party Congress in August 1973 implicitly endorsed the main thrust of the economic policies evolved by Premier Chou since the end of the Cultural Revolution. There was evidence, in the major reports at the Congress and the Party constitution it adopted, of continuing pressure from the "left," and proper obeisance was made to Maoist principles and slogans. But the few hints concerning concrete economic policies that emerged from the meeting did not point to any major policy shifts.

In his political report,[60] Chou underlined the need to combat "revisionism," continue the "struggle between two lines," oppose "Rightist Opportunist errors," and prevent a "capitalist restoration." He also reiterated numerous Maoist slogans concerning economic policy that have become standard elements in the regime's rhetoric: "carry out the general line of going all out, aiming high, and achieving greater, faster, better, and more economical results in building socialism"; "take agriculture as the foundation and industry as the leading factor"; "walk on two legs"; "rely on the masses"; be "self-reliant"; and "learn from Taching and Tachai." Of greater practical significance, however, was the fact that he also emphasized that "planning and coordination must be strengthened, rational rules and regulations improved, and both central and local initiative further brought into full play." While asserting that China's "industry, agriculture, transportation, finance, and trade are doing well," he declared that "we are always lagging behind the needs of the objective situation." "Economically, ours is still a poor and developing country," he observed, stressing that in the period ahead the "Party organizations should pay close attention to questions of economic policy, concern themselves with the well-being of the masses, do a good job of investigation and study, and strive effectively to fulfill or overfulfill the state plans for developing the national economy." This sounded like a prescription for continued pragmatism. There was no suggestion that China was considering any new "leap" or a return to other radical policies in its approach to economic problems.

Although it seems likely that present trends will continue in the period immediately ahead, one cannot rule out the possibility that stronger pressures from either the "left" or the "right" could result in significant policy shifts. Pressures from the left could result, for example, in demands for greater emphasis on collectivism (including steps to return toward the initial Commune idea) and a reduction of material incentives (such as those provided by rural private plots or urban wage differentials). Pressures from the right would probably militate in favor of greater material incentives and even more flexibility and pragmatism in policy making. However, drastic swings in policy in one direction or another, while imaginable, seem less likely than in earlier years.

What are the probabilities in the near future? There will probably not be any drastic changes in overall strategy unless the present balance of forces within the leadership is radically altered. Yet, even if the general framework of current policy continues, there may be pressures for further experimentation, adaptation, and change. One source of pressure could be impatience with China's relatively modest rate of growth. Military leaders and others might press to accelerate the growth of sophisticated defense-related industries. And the kinds of problems, discussed earlier, that some current policies create may generate pressures for change. Factors such as these could impel the leadership to place even less emphasis than at present on Mao's egalitarian social and political values and more on the requirements for rapid development of large-scale modern industry.

As development progresses, moreover, pressures for increased consumption—and for greater material incentives—may increase. Specialists and experts in China will probably argue for more technocratic approaches, and many urbanites seem likely to press for a return toward a more urban-oriented strategy. In sum, many of the more traditional "imperatives of modernization," which Mao has attempted to counterbalance by stressing egalitarian and other revolutionary social values, could create new pressures toward greater centralization, faster urban development, increased priority to modern science and technology, and more rapid growth in the advanced industries, as well as more comprehensive economic planning, greater emphasis on regularized administration, and increased material incentives. This is not to suggest that, even if such pressures grow, China's leaders are likely to eliminate all of the most distinctive aspects of the current Chinese approach, but they may be impelled to consider modifying them significantly.

China's development strategy will almost certainly continue to be distinctive in many respects in comparison with that of most other developing countries—for example, in terms of the importance attached to noneconomic political and social values, to labor mobilization, and to rural development. But to the extent that they are moved by the desire to speed up overall growth, Chinese leaders may well, over time, become less ideological in their approach to economic policy and more preoccupied with the problems of devising pragmatic ways to increase agricultural and industrial output.

If the leadership avoids extremes and there are no major setbacks resulting from natural disasters or political developments, a number of important factors will almost certainly work in favor of continued growth. Improved agricultural performance will be of critical importance, and China's growing industrial base will improve prospects for obtaining the capital and equipment required for further development. As China's GNP grows, so too, in all probability, will the level of national investment—certainly in absolute terms and perhaps as a proportion of GNP.

Any attempt to project a precise rate of growth must be based on guesswork. But something close to the present 4 to 5 percent rate is a very plausible estimate for the period immediately ahead, and that could increase gradually. There will almost certainly continue to be ups and downs, however, and the range could be between 2 and 6 percent a year, although one cannot exclude rates that are temporarily lower or higher than these. Whether the rate is likely to be nearer the high or the low level of such a range will depend on many factors, including the success achieved in maintaining and improving incentives, the regime's ability to increase its investment level, the way in which resources are allocated between civilian and military needs, and China's willingness to modify its current emphasis on extreme self-reliance and to become more involved in the world economy through trade and perhaps even increased credits from abroad.[61] The regime's success or lack of it in checking population growth will obviously be of crucial importance.

If the above projections are valid, China's growth rate during the rest of the 1970s will continue to be respectable but not dramatic or spectacular; it will be lower than China's rate in the mid-1950s, and also below the current rate in many other rapidly developing nations, although sufficient to sustain a process of steady, but gradual, modernization. There is little prospect that China will become an economic superpower in the foreseeable future. In fact, the economic gap between China and countries such as Japan (to say nothing of the United States or the Soviet Union) will probably continue for some time to widen rather than to narrow. Nevertheless, the projected rate of growth, if achieved, should be sufficient to support steady modernization. It should increase the prospects for political and social stability in China. And it will clearly permit the regime to continue to invest sizable resources in developing China's military power and international influence. (Chinese leaders have already demonstrated that, even with a relatively small national economic base and per capita GNP, they are able to allocate resources in such a way that China's foundation for national power has steadily grown.) However, competing pressures on the country's limited resources will continue to pose many hard policy choices for the regime.

But this estimate of future economic trends rests on the assumptions that there will be no major setbacks resulting from natural disasters or political developments and that future Chinese leaders will avoid extremes in their policies. It is precisely such possibilities that create continuing uncertainties about China's economic prospects in the years ahead. Weather also continues to be one of the great imponderables for Chinese planners; although the regime is now able to cope with natural disasters more effectively than it was in earlier years, any prolonged period of droughts or floods could result in very serious economic setbacks. Politics and in particular the approaching succession also raise uncertainties about economics as well as leadership and military affairs. If, after Mao dies, there were to be an open struggle for power leading to widespread political disorder, the process of development could suffer a major setback. Or if, at some point, the balance of forces were to swing in favor of leftist leaders committed to radical or extreme Maoist revolutionary policies of the kind embodied in the Great Leap Forward, a new political-economic disaster of major proportions could not be ruled out. Political trends do not now appear to be moving in this direction, but a swing to the left must be considered to be at least within the realm of possibility.

IV

Problems of Future Leadership

THE DISCUSSION in previous chapters has focused on a range of basic ideological, institutional, military, and economic problems that remain unresolved or only partially resolved as China prepares to make the transition to the post-Mao era. How future leaders cope with these problems will go far toward determining the character of China's post-Mao regime and the direction of its future policies. Underlying all other questions about China's future, however, is the question of what kind of leadership the country will have after Mao dies.[1] What sort of succession will China experience and what will its outcome be? And who will then hold the reins of power? What will the new structure of authority be like?

The Cultural Revolution shattered the previous unity of China's leadership. The purges of 1966–68 affected every institutional sector of the regime and every geographic region of the country. Then in 1971 Lin Piao and a large proportion of the senior military hierarchy were ousted. These purges were all the more traumatic in their effects because for three decades before the Cultural Revolution the Chinese Communist Party had maintained a far greater unity than most revolutionary groups. The Cultural Revolution had a profound impact not simply on the individuals affected, but also on the entire structure of leadership and nature of authority in China.

Ever since these purges, those of China's leaders who survived politically have been attempting to rebuild the country's leadership structure and prepare for the coming succession. The process has been a difficult one, marked by continuing struggles, but under the leadership of Mao and Premier Chou En-lai, significant progress has been made in the two years since Lin's death. The results of their complex efforts at coalition building can be seen in the membership of the new Party

Politburo and Central Committee announced at the Tenth Party Congress in August 1973.

When the 1,249 delegates to the Tenth Congress convened in Peking, the succession problem was almost certainly uppermost in their minds. The leadership bodies they endorsed represented, in effect, a new coalition, which they doubtless hoped would be able to guide China through the succession into the post-Mao period. Even though the Tenth Congress was an important milestone in the process of repairing the political damage left by the Cultural Revolution and preparing for the succession, great uncertainties about the future remained unresolved. The transition to the post-Mao era will undoubtedly be difficult, and the search for genuine stability will not be over until a new leadership can be consolidated after Mao's death.

A comprehensive analysis of China's elite would require an examination of many levels of leadership, perhaps even of the entire composition of the twenty to thirty million Chinese who are Party members and cadres in all the varied institutions in China today. No such ambitious dissection of the elite will be made in this discussion. Instead, the focus will be on "the top elite," the relatively small number of men who have dominated the highest organs of national power, especially at the center. A restricted analysis of this sort is less than wholly satisfactory, since leadership problems in China cannot be fully understood without an examination of trends affecting the entire elite. It is defensible, however, since China operates under a centralized authoritarian system where the main direction of policy and the overall course of development have been, and will be in the future, determined above all by the relatively few leaders who dominate the top political and military organs that exercise ultimate power.

Mao Tse-tung and the Succession Problem

Mao Tse-tung has occupied the dominant position in the Chinese Communist Party and regime for more than thirty-five years,[2] and his role has been a complicated—and changing—one. The personal impact that Mao has had on the Party, on Chinese society, and on the overall course of events in China in recent decades has been extraordinary; at crucial turning points he has often imposed his own will on the entire leadership and nation. He has not been able, however, to rule simply by personal fiat. There have been very real limitations on his power and influence, since he has had to deal with extremely complex forces and to work with and through many complex groups.

The emergence of Mao to a position of primacy in the Party is generally dated to the Party's Tsunyi Conference in 1935.[3] There is considerable basis for the use of this date; the Chinese Communists themselves regard the 1935 conference as a crucial turning point, marking Mao's rise to the top. Mao continued to face opposition after 1935, however, briefly from Chang Kuo-t'ao and then from Wang Ming and the "Returned Students" group as well as others. Gradually, in the late 1930s and early 1940s, he was able to achieve a firm basis for personal power and leadership, partly by skillfully allying himself with other key leaders (including Liu Shao-ch'i). It was the Seventh Party Congress in 1945 that gave a clear stamp of approval to Mao's leadership, his "Thought," and his policies.[4]

Mao's rise to the top position in the Party—ultimately to the post of Chairman—was due to more than his skills in political maneuver and infighting within the Party, although he possessed such skills to a remarkable degree. He stood out in the early years as a man of vision, who during the struggle for power analyzed the major problems and forces at work in his country in terms that struck a responsive chord in a great many Chinese. Chance, luck, and changing circumstances resulting from the Communists' prolonged revolutionary struggle clearly contributed to Mao's rise and the decline of his rivals, but, above all, he demonstrated impressive skill—even genius—at formulating and articulating what proved to be successful principles of strategy and tactics for the revolutionary armed struggle in China.

It was predictable and logical that Mao should be chosen to fill the highest post in the state apparatus as well as in the Party when the Communists established their new national regime in 1949. He became, in everyone's eyes, "Chairman Mao"—chairman of the Party and of the government. However, his actual leadership of China during the ensuing quarter-century cannot be characterized by simple or glib generalizations; his role in fact has varied substantially over time.

From 1949 to 1954, as head of the Central People's Government Council which was in charge of running the state apparatus, Mao chaired the government's top body responsible for both policy making and administration,[5] and his voice was unquestionably the dominant one in determining policy. The unity of the senior leadership under

Mao in this early period of the regime was impressive; apart from a brief threat posed by Kao Kang and Jao Shu-shih in 1953–54, he faced no serious overt challenges.[6] This was in part due to his personal qualities, the general respect accorded him for his role in the Communists' rise to power, and his skill as a political tactician. In this early stage of the regime's revolutionary and developmental policies, moreover, there was, by and large, a fairly impressive consensus among China's top leadership on how to deal with the country's most pressing problems. Although important differences occurred within the leadership, even then, over specific policy and power matters, a strong thread of agreement existed on immediate goals and the main lines of policy. When there were differences, Mao's views generally prevailed, but the occasions before the mid-1950s when Mao had to overcome strong opposition were relatively few.

In a sense, Mao in this period probably operated as, and was regarded as, first among equals. All of the top leadership placed a high premium on the need to preserve unity, and they were able to maintain a monolithic public facade. Unity was reinforced, moreover, by the notable successes that the regime achieved in its early years. Until the mid-1950s, no really fundamental cleavages on policy had yet emerged, and the regime had not yet suffered any major setbacks to shake the confidence of other leaders in Mao.

Gradually, however, this situation began to change, for many reasons that have been discussed in Chapter 1. But the analysis would not be complete without a close look at the way in which Mao's personal leadership style and idiosyncrasies affected the situation, since his role was crucial. Mao apparently was never inclined, even in the pre-1949 period, to act as an executive, a bureaucratic manager, or a day-to-day administrator.[7] These roles he tended to assign or leave to others. He preferred to concentrate attention on broad questions relating to power and ideology, and to overall goals, strategy, and general policy. He obviously gave a great deal of thought to organizational problems, and he frequently prescribed how policies should be implemented. His ideas on these matters had an enormous impact on the ways in which the regime went about the task of pursuing its goals, but he apparently was not inclined to try to maintain a firm personal grip on the day-to-day operation of China's bureaucracies. Mao, in short, assumed the role of the regime's principal ideological leader, political philosopher, and ultimate authority on broad policy, but he tended to stay aloof from the routine problems of implementation.

As a result, other leaders inevitably had to assume the main responsibilities for running day-to-day affairs, managing China's growing bureaucracies, and actually carrying out the Party's policies. Gradually these men accumulated great bureaucratic power. Not surprisingly, many of them acquired outlooks, perspectives, and priorities that increasingly reflected their special responsibilities and concerns, and consequently they differed from Mao in their thinking on many questions. They also acquired organizational power bases of their own.

As members of China's top elite, the men directly under Mao were expected to act as political generalists, concerning themselves with broad policy questions and overall national goals. Gradually, however, many of them also became bureaucratic specialists (in a leadership, rather than a technical, sense), concerned primarily with the particular fields of activity they directed—in the Party apparatus, state agencies, or the military—and the bureaucracies they directly managed. Because they were of necessity forced to confront China's social and political realities in a direct and immediate fashion and constantly had to deal with pressures that filtered up from below through the bureaucracies, both from lower level cadres and from the general population, their tendency was to view issues less in terms of broad theoretical considerations and more in terms of concrete problems, obstacles, and opportunities.

As the organizational structures of the regime became more complex and as the leadership undertook more ambitious tasks and confronted increasingly difficult problems, Mao's ability to control and manage the bureaucracies in any direct sense waned. Differences on policy gradually increased,[8] and eventually they brought Mao into conflict with many—in fact the majority—of the regime's top bureaucratic leaders. In a huge bureaucratic state headed by a charismatic revolutionary leader, there are built-in tendencies for such conflict to develop. In China, if one also considers Mao's personal predispositions and style, it was probably inevitable.

By the end of the 1950s, the widening gap between Mao and the powerful leaders running the country's bureaucracies under his aegis was reflected in a decision—apparently Mao's own—to divide China's top leadership into two groups, a "first line" and a "second line."[9] The former apparently consisted of China's highest bureaucratic leaders: men such as Liu Shao-ch'i, Teng Hsiao-p'ing, and P'eng Chen, who ran the Party on a day-to-day basis, and probably others, such as Chou En-lai, who directed the machinery of government. The second line, which included Mao, ostensibly preoccupied itself with broad policy questions. Exactly when this differentiation occurred is debatable. Judging from the fragmentary and conflicting evidence available, it might have taken place, at the earliest, soon after the succession struggle in the Soviet Union following Stalin's death (1953); perhaps, however, it occurred later, at the time of the Chinese Communists' Eighth Party Congress (1956), or, at the latest, when Mao formally retired from the chairmanship of the government (1959).

Mao apparently believed that this division of function would enable him to play the kind of role he preferred, and that it would also help to lay the basis for an eventual smooth transfer of power to his successors. It also reflected the growing influence of key bureaucratic leaders and the decline of Mao's capacity to use the bureaucracies for his own purposes. Despite this gap, significant open challenges to Mao's position of primacy in the Party or attempts to oust him were rare. Only two power struggles resulting in purges of men of Politburo rank occurred between 1949 and 1966. In the first of these, in the mid-1950s, Kao Kang (and Jao Shu-shih) attempted to achieve a position of power second only to Mao's but apparently did not challenge Mao himself. (Some evidence suggests, however, that Mao may have been seriously ill at the time, in which case Kao Kang may have been maneuvering to succeed him.)[10] Five years later, in 1959, P'eng Teh-huai openly criticized Mao's policies, but again there is no convincing evidence that he attempted to usurp Mao's top leadership position.[11]

Although, as these incidents illustrate, Mao's personal prestige made him almost invulnerable to head-on confrontations, his control over the organizational structures in China weakened gradually and subtly. Over time, the number of top bureaucratic leaders who doubted his judgments and disagreed with at least some of his policy prescriptions increased. Open defiance of Mao was avoided, but their differences with him in many instances were substantial and obvious. Resistance to his policies grew—especially during and after periods when Mao recommended dramatic policy innovations and initiated radical mobilizational policies, many of which resulted in serious economic setbacks or failures. Some of the more powerful bureaucratic leaders simply tried to go their own way as much as they could, especially in the early 1960s, and at times the policies that emerged in the process of actual implementation were quite different from those that Mao had favored. While the tendency of the bureaucratic leadership was to stress the need for realism in facing immediate problems, Mao was prone to launch radical "drives" to achieve long-term goals. The gap between these conflicting tendencies was particularly wide in the period immediately after the Great Leap.

Yet Mao apparently never lost his capability—at least not for more than very brief periods—to make the major policy decisions, initiate dramatic policy innovations, and inject his views into the policy process in ways that launched the regime on new courses that were to have a tremendous impact on both the regime itself and society as a whole. In the oscillating pattern that has characterized the evolution of policy in China since 1949—a pattern in which periods of radical revolutionary forward surges have alternated with periods of retreat and relatively moderate "consolidation" policies[12]—personal initiatives by Mao have invariably launched the more radical or innovative periods, overriding the doubts and objections of more cautious or conservative leaders.[13]

One can point to a few Maoist policy initiatives that might be labeled "moderate," but the overwhelming majority of them were "radical," in the context of the Chinese political situation. Among the most notable of these were the decisions to launch a big push toward rapid collectivization in 1955, to loosen political controls in the Hundred Flowers Campaign of 1957, to initiate the Great Leap Forward and Communes in 1958, to launch a major Socialist Education Campaign in 1962, and to start the Cultural Revolution in 1965. There was almost certainly high level opposition to—or at least doubt about—every one of these Maoist moves; but when Mao was determined to push a major new policy through, he was generally able to do so. He was skillful in mobilizing the necessary backing (sometimes drawing support from regional and provincial leaders to overcome resistance at the center); and when he made endorsement of his policies a test of political loyalty, few of China's other top leaders were inclined to challenge him directly.

By the 1960s many of China's top bureaucrats were convinced that the erratic, audacious, even reckless character of Mao's radical initiatives had been responsible for some of China's most costly failures and setbacks.[14] Ultimately, tensions within the top leadership intensified, until they finally exploded in the Cultural Revolution, which represented a clear break between Mao and the majority of key leaders who ran China's bureaucracies, especially the Party bureaucracy. More important for the long run, it had a profound impact on the basic structure in China, altering the roles of "The Leader" and the Party.

Before the Cultural Revolution, the Communist Party as an institution had been unchallenged, and unchallengeable, as the ultimate source of legitimate political authority in China. Theoretically, its legitimacy rested on its claim to be the "vanguard" of the masses—reflecting their true interests. The Chinese Communists have consistently given lip service to the idea of "proletarian dictatorship," but they have also based their claims to legitimacy on the assertion that they reflect the broad interests of "the people." In actuality, authority was institutionalized in the Party organization; all other institutions, and all individuals, derived their authority from the Party. Mao was no exception. The Party was not regarded as Mao's personal instrument. He was regarded as China's foremost leader because he was head of the Party, and his authority basically derived from that of the Party, and not from any other legitimizing source or from his own personal attributes.

Ultimate Party authority was supposed to be vested in its highest collective leadership organs—the Politburo Standing Committee, the Politburo, and the Central Committee—not in the Chairman or any other individual. There was no "führer" principle, or mystique about "The Leader," that might justify an individual's monopolizing the exercise of authority. This was the theory, and it had considerable validity in the early years of the regime. Although by then Mao had acquired a special position as the highest symbol of the Party's authority, neither he nor anyone else claimed that as an individual he held authority superior to that of the Party or that he held a position superordinate to the Party.

In practice, however, the idea of collective leadership at the top was significantly qualified, even in earlier years, by the fact that Mao clearly did hold a special position and was the object of deliberate efforts to glorify him—efforts that started well before 1949. By the early 1940s the seeds of a cult of Mao had been planted, and the "Thought of Mao Tse-tung" was enshrined along with Marxism-Leninism as an essential part of the ideological foundation of the Party's policies in the Party constitution of 1945.[15] From that time on, Mao was consistently portrayed as a leader with special qualities and special insights into the problems of revolution in China, and he was never successfully challenged as the ultimate arbiter of ideological orthodoxy within the Chinese Communist movement.

The degree of emphasis on the cult of Mao varied significantly over time, however. In the immediate takeover period after 1949, Party policy forbade such actions as the naming of streets after Mao. Glorification of Mao increased during the first half of the 1950s, but then this trend was reversed. When a new Party constitution was adopted in 1956, soon after destalinization had occurred in the Soviet Union, all references to the "Thought of Mao Tse-tung" were eliminated.[16] In part this may have resulted from a decision approved by Mao himself to stress collective rather than individual leadership; however, it may also have reflected shifts in power relations within the leadership and a deliberate effort, pushed by leaders other than Mao, to deemphasize the Mao cult.

The Mao cult again came to the fore during the Great Leap period of the late 1950s. Then it was muted again in the post-Leap years of the early 1960s. The efforts made at that time to publicize Liu Shao-ch'i's earlier writings, and the oblique criticisms of Mao contained in the writings of some Chinese intellectuals, may have helped to convince Mao that his ideological influence and authority were being weakened, if not challenged.

From 1962 on, when Mao again asserted himself and assumed a more active political role, emphasis on his cult steadily increased once more. This reached a climax with the launching of the Cultural Revolution, when Mao was virtually deified as the foremost Marxist-Leninist in the contemporary world and the true inheritor of the mantles of Marx, Engels, Lenin, and Stalin. The process leading to this climax began in the army, under Lin Piao's direction. Even before the Cultural Revolution started, a major effort was under way throughout Chinese society as a whole to propagate Mao's Thought and to glorify him as a charismatic individual. There is no doubt that Mao himself approved of this, believing that the cult would bolster his influence and help to perpetuate his revolutionary values.[17]

The lengths to which the deification of Mao was carried during the Cultural Revolution were extraordinary, far surpassing even the efforts in Russia to glorify Stalin in the 1940s. Mao's name was invoked to justify every action. Everyone in China wore badges with Mao's image. Statues and busts of Mao sprouted throughout the country. And the "little red book" with selected quotations from Mao's writings, compiled by the army, became a political talisman which even the highest Chinese leaders felt compelled to study and display.

In effect, Mao, and leaders acting in his name, now asserted that legitimate authority was vested in him alone—that is, in Mao as an individual, not in the Party or any other institution. In power terms, he built his own political base outside the Party, and finally attacked and partially dismantled the Party's apparatus. This greatly weakened, at least temporarily, the Party's institutional claim to monopolize ultimate authority.

While it was Mao's Thought, reputed to be a unique revelation of revolutionary truth, that was ostensibly glorified, the fact was that Mao himself was sanctified as a person said to possess magical qualities that made him infallible. Profession of loyalty to Mao, at least in a verbal sense, became the prerequisite for political survival in China.

This development altered in a very fundamental way the basic structure of legitimate political authority in China.[18] "The Leader," charismatic and infallible, replaced the Party as the primary legitimizing source of all authority. While his unique role was still ascribed to the wellsprings of legitimacy—the will of the "masses" and the ideological "truths" contained in Mao's Thought—and his real power was now dependent on the army's support, the ultimate source for authority was now vested in him as an individual rather than in any institution. As one writer has put it, political authority came to depend on the link between an "infallible Mao" and the "infallible masses," but "infallible Mao" was the key.[19] The Party's top bureaucratic leaders were pilloried as being apostate.

The deification of Mao, and the resulting individualization of authority in his own person, were important factors explaining Mao's ability to defeat his opponents during the Cultural Revolution. But the attack on the institutionalized authority of the Party seriously weakened the underlying structure of authority in China. Although the army, acting in Mao's name, moved in to fill the power vacuum created by the Party's paralysis, lines and sources of authority were terribly confused. Thousands of Red Guard and Revolutionary Rebel groups, all claiming to be the true supporters of Mao and thus representative of legitimate authority, competed fiercely for political survival and power.

This deification of Mao during the Cultural Revolution raises a number of important questions about Chinese politics. Is there a built-in tendency in China for authority to gravitate toward a single supreme charismatic leader? How compelling in twentieth century China is the tradition-rooted predisposition to concentrate ultimate authority in one man—in a modern equivalent of the pre-1911 emperors? When a political culture places such great stress on centralization and hierarchy, as China's still does despite Mao's stress on egalitarian values,[20] are there irresistible pressures to concentrate authority in a single leader? In a system in which ultimate power is monopolized by a small elite, are there inherent tendencies toward instability, if collective leadership is attempted, that make it likely that one man will eventually emerge supreme? When authority gravitates into the hands of a single individual in such a society, is some sort of leadership cult inevitable?

There are, of course, no certain answers to these questions, but it is clearly relevent that for millennia ultimate authority in China has generally gravitated into the hands of one man. In pre-1911 imperial China, it was the emperor. In the Republican period, both Sun Yat-sen and Chiang Kai-shek sought a monopoly of both power and authority, and each assumed special political roles and titles. Now it is "The Chairman" who is supreme. It is also relevant to note that, in authoritarian or totalitarian regimes of many different sorts, collective leadership has frequently tended over time to become unstable, eventually breaking down and being replaced by one-man dictatorship.

In authoritarian societies (and especially in China because of its particular political traditions and culture) it is clearly not easy to achieve and maintain political stability under a collective leadership in which ultimate authority is shared. Especially in times of crisis, there are strong pressures in such regimes militating in favor of one-man rule—which may, or may not, lead to greater stability.

One should be cautious, however, about jumping to the conclusion that collective leadership must fail. Under certain conditions, necessity dictates that leadership be collective, and in some circumstances such leadership can succeed. In earlier years, the Chinese Communist leadership apparently was collectivist in some respects, and successfully so. In recent years, the pattern of Russian leadership appears to have involved a collective sharing of power, and Moscow's leaders have been reasonably successful in the pursuit of at least some of the Soviet Union's national goals.

As will be discussed below, the emergence of a new coalition leadership of a collectivist sort in China seems likely in the immediate future, since the alternative would probably be destructive open conflict within the elite. Over the long run, however, there will probably be a dialectical and cyclical interaction between conflicting pressures toward a collective sharing of power, on the one hand, and one-man rule, on the other.

The manner in which Mao has asserted his personal power in recent years will make the post-Mao transition more difficult than it might have been if the structure of authority had not become so highly individualized. While individualized charismatic leadership can have an enormous impact on a society, it tends to be more fragile in fundamental respects than institutionalized authority. It is really impossible for a charismatic leader to pass supreme leadership intact to a single successor; by definition, charisma is associated with individual attributes. It would almost certainly have been easier to pass on the authority of "The Chairman" in China if Mao's authority had remained strongly rooted in the Party. It will be difficult—in fact, probably impossible—for any individual in the immediate post-Mao period to try to assume the kind of personalized supreme role that Mao has played in recent years. In this sense, no one can really succeed Mao, and when he dies the basic structure of authority in China will inevitably change.

In the post-Mao period, the leaders who emerge as key figures will doubtless try to legitimitize their positions by claiming to be Mao's true successors, but there will be no automaticity about the acceptance of such claims. Almost certainly the reconstructed Party will attempt to reassert its former position as the main institutional source of authority, and in fact it is already trying to do so. But it may take some years, at best, for it to reestablish its former position.

It is ironic that present uncertainties about the succession in China are so great, because Mao—more than most historical leaders in comparable positions—has attempted to plan the succession and ensure a smooth transition after his death. He first began to concern himself with the problem many years ago—at least by the early 1950s and possibly earlier. His initial choice of an individual to inherit his power was obviously Liu Shao-ch'i. Even though he never went so far as to designate Liu in any formal way as his chosen political heir, he began grooming him for this role many years ago—perhaps as early as the 1940s—and supported his rise to the second-ranking position in the Party.[21] After Stalin's death, he took further steps that were designed to prepare Liu to be his successor.

Subsequent events illustrate the intrinsic difficulties any authoritarian leader faces in trying to groom a specific successor. Once a protégé is elevated to a position just below the summit of supreme power, he is likely to become a highly influential figure in his own right, with his own sources of power and his own independent views, and he may gradually seem to be less an ally than a potential threat. This appears to be precisely what happened in the relationship between Mao and Liu. By the time of the Cultural Revolution, Mao concluded that Liu was not a fit successor, and that he had to be purged.

Although, or perhaps because, this initial effort to prearrange the succession failed, Mao was more determined than ever to make a personal choice of his political heir. The next man he turned to was Lin Piao. After replacing P'eng Teh-huai as Minister of National Defense in 1959, Lin was not only China's foremost military leader, but also the most energetic propagator of Mao's Thought and promoter of the Mao cult. His personal loyalty to Mao was demonstrated on repeated occasions. Mao apparently concluded that Lin, more than any other individual, could be trusted to perpetuate Mao's values, and that he had the power, through his control of the military, to manage the post-Mao succession effectively. One cannot be sure when Mao began to groom Lin to replace Liu as his successor, but from the late 1950s on, he backed Lin's steady rise in the hierarchy and looked to him increasingly for support. By 1965 Lin had emerged as the leading spokesman for Mao, and in August 1966, when the Eleventh Central Committee plenum designated him as the only Party Vice Chairman (whereas formerly there had been five), it was obvious that he was the new chosen heir. Finally, the regime took the extraordinary—in fact unprecedented—step of inserting a clause in the new 1969 Party constitution specifically naming Lin as Mao's successor.[22]

From the start, it seemed doubtful to many observers that Lin could really be expected to succeed Mao in the sense of inheriting his full authority. Despite Mao's patronage and a strong power base of his own, Lin was never able to achieve unchallenged predominance, even within the military. He played a crucial role in the confused struggles within the leadership during and after the Cultural Revolution, but he was only one of several leaders who shared power and competed for influence in the constantly changing situation. Moreover, unlike Mao, he had no stature as an ideologist; in fact, despite his strong support for the Mao cult and Mao's Thought, he seemed to have relatively little personal interest in ideological questions. Finally, he lacked the personal qualities and style of operation that had made Mao unique.[23]

Generally shunning the limelight, he remained a fairly shadowy figure to the Chinese public. In dealing with other powerful leaders, both military and civilian, Lin had to rely to a considerable degree on political maneuvering, persuasion, and a conscious balancing of influence and interests. Even after his designation as the heir-apparent, he could not count on automatic deference or compliance.

Another major factor casting doubt on Lin's chances of actually succeeding Mao in any real sense was his physical condition. Periodically, at least since World War II and perhaps earlier, he had suffered serious health problems. At certain periods in the past, in fact, he had been completely incapacitated. No one could be sure that he would outlive or outlast Mao.

For all these reasons, it was widely believed, even when he was designated as Mao's heir in 1969, that although he might succeed Mao in a formalistic sense he was unlikely to inherit Mao's full power or prestige. There was even doubt, despite his staunch verbal support of Maoism, that he would necessarily promote Maoist policies and values. Lin's own personal policy priorities as a military leader almost certainly differed substantially from Mao's; professional and bureaucratic concerns, as well as military and power considerations, probably influenced his outlook more than they did Mao's.

In the early fall of 1971, only two years after Lin's designation as successor, a new and dramatic round of purging occurred at the highest levels in China, which eliminated from the leadership not only Lin but many other top Chinese military leaders as well. Lin was accused of having attempted to oust Mao through a coup,[24] and Peking asserted that he was killed in a plane crash while trying to flee to the Soviet Union. Whether or not this was true, it was apparent that Lin had not only been purged but had also died, and Chou En-lai rapidly emerged as China's most prominent leader other than Mao himself. Once again the succession issue was very much in doubt.

Between the fall of 1971 and the fall of 1973 it became increasingly clear that Mao now pinned his hopes above all on Chou as the man to guide China through the succession period, and the Tenth Party Congress underlined this fact. But not only was Chou not designated by Mao as his successor in the new Party constitution adopted by the Congress; there was no indication that Chou himself wished to achieve the personal dominance that such a designation would imply. Instead, he apparently viewed his role as that of a conciliator, compromiser, and coalition builder for the transition ahead. After two abortive attemps to choose a single individual as his successor, Mao appeared to have abandoned the attempt, and the fate of both Liu Shao-ch'i and Lin Piao did not encourage others to aspire to the position of designated successor.

In light of all the above developments the correct answer to the question "who can succeed Mao?" is doubtless "no one." Although the leaders who survive Mao will have to try to reach some kind of consensus on who should fill Mao's formal positions—above all, who will become the Party Chairman—no individual, including Chou En-lai, will be able to inherit his unique prestige and personal authority as leader of the revolution, and no one is likely soon to achieve a position of primacy in any way comparable to the one Mao has enjoyed. Aside from the fact that no man on the horizon has the stature and ability to reassert effective one-man rule, the leadership as a whole shows no indication that it will soon be prepared to submit again to the will of any one individual.

What seems probable, therefore, is that in the period immediately following Mao's death China's leadership will, of necessity, have to be coalitional and collective.[25] If Chou En-lai survives Mao and does not suffer the fate of those before him who have risen to the top, he will play a pivotal role in the coalition that probably will govern China in the transitional period. But a variety of other leaders, representing different power centers and institutional interests in the Party, military, and state apparatus, will seek to share power and authority, and both Chou and they will be compelled to work out a new basis for collaboration.

It is impossible to predict with confidence precisely who will belong to any post-Mao collective leadership, but the Party's top bodies chosen by the Tenth Congress (discussed in detail later in this chapter) provide some good clues. There will almost certainly be further changes before any post-Mao leadership stabilizes, but the Standing Committee, Politburo, and Central Committee chosen in late 1973 will probably provide the core of the leadership in the immediate post-Mao era unless there is another major political upheaval in China before Mao's death. Somewhere in the lists of these new bodies are doubtless the names of the men who will try to lead China not only after Mao but after Chou as well.

Although one cannot exclude the possibility that power and authority may eventually gravitate into the hands of a single leader—perhaps someone who is not well known at present—this does not seem likely to happen soon unless there is open strife leading to a military takeover. Any leader who attempts to achieve personal dominance in China in the immediate post-Mao period will probably provoke bitter opposition. Mao's death seems likely, therefore, to mark the end—at least for some time—of highly personalized, charismatic, one-man rule.

The search for a new and stable pattern of legitimized authority in China may take considerable time. The resulting structure of authority will of necessity be different from both the individualistic leadership prevailing in Mao's final years and the relatively homogeneous and consensual leadership of the regime's early years. Authority and power will probably be more diffuse, and one of the regime's major challenges will be to accommodate competing and conflicting interests. In a very real sense, China will experience a succession "crisis." Some further power struggles and purges, if not inevitable, are at least highly possible, and there is little basis for predicting accurately what the outcome may be. Much will depend on unpredictable human reactions, and on individual decisions made in the future by leaders who will represent different interests and power centers.

One can conceive of a transition process in which a handful of skillful leaders, led by men such as Chou En-lai, determined to preserve China's unity, and willing to put national interests above parochial or personal concerns, may be able to work out compromises that will consolidate a viable leadership coalition involving a genuine sharing of power and accommodation of conflicting interests. The result, in that case, could be a relatively smooth transition to a new pattern of collective leadership.

On the other hand, one can also envisage a breakdown of the delicate balance Chou sought to achieve at the Tenth Congress and a resulting situation in which contending leaders, fearful about their own political survival and preoccupied with parochial interests, attempted to expand their own power at the expense of others. If such a situation escalated into open conflict and involved major splits in the Chinese military leadership, the result could be serious internecine struggle for a substantial period of time.

Which outcome is most likely to occur? No one can say with certainty. It would be remarkable if the succession period proved to be completely painless and smooth. Yet it is conceivable that the Chinese leaders now coming to the fore will be able to agree on a new basis for cooperation that will facilitate a reasonably orderly transition to some new form of collective leadership. They will doubtless try to do so, since the alternative to a workable coalition is not likely to be an immediate restoration of effective one-man leadership under some new charismatic leader, but rather growing conflict that could throw the country once again into turmoil.

Success will require great skill, however, in balancing diverse interests, not only among military, state, and Party leaders, but also between central and local leaders. If Chou En-lai is still alive and in a key position when Mao dies, chances of success will be relatively favorable; of all China's leaders during the past twenty-odd years, he has distinguished himself for his talent for compromise and restraint, and for his ability to lead without asserting personal dominance.[26] It should be noted, however, that Chou, who was born in 1898, is only five years younger than Mao, and the very fact that he is the second-ranking leader in China today means that he faces some of the same hazards encountered by Liu Shao-ch'i and Lin Piao.

Assuming that collective leadership is consolidated, what can one say in general terms about how this may affect the policies China is likely to pursue at home and abroad? Much will obviously depend not only on the type of leaders, but on specific individuals who emerge into key roles. The policy options that will be at least theoretically open to the Chinese will continue to be varied, whatever kind of leadership the country has.

It seems probable, however, that policy making in a regime governed by a delicate coalition would be significantly different from what it has been in the past, under Mao. Mao was both inclined and able to initiate bold and dramatic policy shifts that overrode all the doubts and opposition of other leaders. In a collective leadership, drastic policy shifts of this sort would be much less likely. Because the viability of a coalition leadership group would depend on its ability to make compromises preserving minimal consensus, the tendency would be to eschew policies either too "radical" or too "conservative." The built-in pressures would be toward "centrism," with the bias probably favoring relatively cautious policies. In theory, one could argue that post-Mao leaders might be tempted to adopt highly nationalistic, radical policies to mobilize support. What seems more likely, however, is that, in order to survive, a collective leadership would be impelled to balance and accommodate diverse interests, and to evolve relatively pragmatic, "realistic," and instrumental approaches to policy making. Ambitious grand strategies of the kind characteristic of Mao may therefore give way to relatively flexible ad hoc approaches to problems. Although ideologues may continue to exert some leverage on policy, their influence will probably wane as the influence of military and civilian bureaucrats and "experts" of many kinds increases.

Any coalitional type of leadership is subject to a variety of potential weaknesses. Such leadership groups are often indecisive and vacillating, unimaginative and pedestrian, or fragile and unstable. But this is not inevitable. Under favorable circumstances, unity based on a process of mutual accommodation can have advantages over unity imposed by a powerful charismatic leader. A leadership group that must search for viable compromises among varied groups in order to survive may be more sensitive to diverse interests, and more responsive to many kinds of social pressures from below, than a supreme leader who is determined to mold society to fit his personal vision. And if such a leadership group approaches problems with relative realism, even if it is less dynamic than a personalized, charismatic, revolutionary leadership might be, it may avoid many of the excesses and costly failures that can be the result of one-man rule.

The fact that no one can really succeed Mao in any full sense might therefore have some political advantages as well as some obvious disadvantages for China. Even though the departure of Mao will unquestionably create many uncertainties and instabilities, if an effective new collective leadership coalesces, it could evolve policies that are less visionary but conceivably more effective than many Mao has promoted.

Rebuilding the Top Elite

The far-reaching impact of recent political struggles in China becomes evident when one examines the extent to which the unity of the top elite that had monopolized policy formulation and execution was shattered during the Cultural Revolution.

The term "top elite" is hardly a precise or scientific one. It might be defined in any of several ways. One could argue that, at a minimum, the roster should include not only the members of the highest national-level decision-making bodies in the Party, government, and army, and perhaps the most important mass organizations as well, but also men occupying other high-level national posts under them (for example, Party department heads, heads of ministries and equivalent bodies, and military department and service arm commanders and commissars and their principal deputies) as well as the principal regional and provincial leaders (Party, government, and military) and their deputies. Even this list would constitute only a minuscule fraction of the twenty to thirty million people who in a very broad sense might be regarded as belonging to China's political elite; yet to analyze such a group in any detail would require a book.

The primary focus of this discussion, therefore, will be restricted to those occupying positions in the very highest Chinese decision-making bodies in the Party, government, and army—a group totaling perhaps 200 to 300 persons. Because an extensive pattern of "interlocking directorates" has prevailed for many years in the Chinese leadership structure, top Party leaders have occupied key positions in all important sectors of the regime—for example, as leading commanders and commissars in the military establishment, heads of ministries in the government, and leaders in various regional and provincial bodies. (There are others who hold key positions of this sort, and wield great power and influence in many instances, but they will be arbitrarily excluded from this analysis if they do not belong to the highest Party bodies.)[27]

The general characteristics of three concentric circles, or layers, of top leaders will be examined. First, a small "inner circle" of supreme leaders who, under Mao, have exercised ultimate collective decision-making power in China (through the Party Secretariat before 1956 and the Politburo Standing Committee after 1956). Second, a somewhat larger group, consisting of roughly one to two dozen leaders of Politburo rank, involved in many of the most important policy deliberations in China. For the most part, the group at this level has been the Politburo, but at certain times other groups, notably "Mao's Proletarian Headquarters" or the "Cultural Revolution Group," seem to have played comparable roles. Third, the Central Committee as a whole, which, although its function has generally been to endorse and implement rather than initiate major policies, has nevertheless constituted, in effect, a roster of those Chinese leaders occupying both national and local positions who have been officially recognized as members of the top elite. An examination of the changing composition of each of these three groups, and the salient characteristics of their members, throws important light on the changing nature of the top leadership in China and highlights a number of problems that China faces in the future.

The Inner Circle

The processes of policy making in Communist China have always been shrouded in considerable secrecy; consequently one must be tentative in making judgments about the roles played by particular bodies and individuals. Nevertheless, it is clear that in the highly centralized hierarchy of authority existing since 1949, ultimate power has always been constitutionally vested in a handful of top leaders—roughly half a dozen men. Although we know relatively little about how this highest leadership group has functioned, there is no doubt that in practice as well as in theory many of the most important policy decisions have been made at this level.

In the early days of the regime, the supreme group, as defined in the 1945 Party constitution, was the Party Secretariat, consisting of five men: Mao, Liu Shao-ch'i, Chou En-lai, Chu Teh, and Ch'en Yun. These men had risen to the summit of leadership during the struggle for power, and one can assume that in these early days they were all close to, and compatible with, Mao. All five were men of great ability who had occupied varied political positions, and they were all, in some respects at least, broad-gauged political generalists. Even within this small group, however, particular men clearly came to represent, over the years, a variety of specialized concerns and interests. Mao was the Party's leading interpreter of ideology and the foremost articulator of broad strategies; he was, in short, the dominant political generalist. Liu was the Party organization man par excellence and played a very special role in managing and directing the Party apparatus. Chou, from 1949 on, bore primary responsibility for the operations of the entire state bureaucracy, directing foreign policy as well as domestic programs. Chu Teh, the oldest member of the group, appears to have been less active and influential than the others even by 1949; but he nevertheless played a significant role in the early days as the principal representative and spokesman for the Chinese military establishment within the top circle. Ch'en Yun's general stature was not as high as that of the other four, but his inclusion was significant;

he emerged very early as the leading Chinese Communist figure who focused his attention primarily on economic affairs, and his position in the Secretariat symbolized the high priority placed by the leadership after 1949 on economic development. This was an impressive body of men by any standards. They included men with varied expertise and interests who were representative of different key elements and sectors in the regime. What is most striking about this original inner circle is that it remained essentially intact and, with only minor change, functioned as the supreme policy-making group in China for a decade and a half after 1949.

When a new Party constitution was adopted in 1956, a new Politburo Standing Committee replaced the old Secretariat as the supreme policy-making group. It consisted at the start of six men—the Chairman of the Party, four Vice Chairmen, and the General Secretary. The first five of these were the same men who had constituted the earlier Secretariat; the sixth was the General Secretary (tsung shu chi) of the Party, Teng Hsiao-p'ing.[28] The Secretariat now became the highest administrative organ in the Party, operating under the top policy-making bodies but exerting some influence on policy in the process of implementation.

From 1956 until the Cultural Revolution, there was only one formal change in the Politburo Standing Committee—the addition of Lin Piao (who had been elected a Politburo member only in 1955) as the fifth Vice Chairman in 1958. This addition was, however, extremely significant. Chu Teh was by now fairly inactive, and Lin therefore became the highest-ranking spokesman for the military establishment in the Party's top inner circle. He was elevated to this position over the head of P'eng Teh-huai, who was not only a Politburo member but had been Minister of National Defense since the ministry was first established in 1954. More than most observers realized at the time, Lin's elevation to a Party position above that of P'eng probably reflected major shifts that had already occurred in the relationships in the top leadership. A year later, in 1959, P'eng was purged for his opposition to Mao, and Lin replaced him as Minister of National Defense. The close alliance between Mao and Lin, which by the mid-1960s had become one of the crucial facts of political life in China, began to be forged in this period.

Although the essential continuity of this top inner circle for such a long period of time was one of the most notable features of China's post-1949 leadership, surface appearances were probably misleading to some extent. Evidence now available suggests that relationships within this key group must have changed gradually, leading ultimately to a situation in which policy differences and personal rivalries made it impossible for the top leadership to preserve unity and act effectively in concert. It was the breakdown of consensus at the summit that led to the shattering conflict that split the regime and society as a whole in the Cultural Revolution.

Any attempt to assess changing relationships within the inner circle must, of necessity, be speculative in part. But on the basis of what is now known, it is reasonable to believe that between the mid-1950s and the mid-1960s relationships within the group began to change significantly. In the mid-1950s, the most important trend was the steady rise in the power and influence of Liu Shao-ch'i and Teng Hsiao-p'ing, who worked in close collaboration and exercised a high degree of control over the operation of the vast Party apparatus. In some respects the increase in their influence was inevitably at the expense of Mao's. The most notable development in the late 1950s was the rapid rise in Lin Piao's influence, with Mao's strong personal backing. It is impossible to know the full facts about how and when the polarization between Mao and Lin, on the one hand, and Liu and Teng, on the other, developed, but there is ample evidence that from 1959 on, after the Great Leap Forward and the subsequent Party leadership crisis at Lushan, differences steadily increased until they finally exploded in the Cultural Revolution.

Throughout this period Chou En-lai played a unique, skillful, and highly influential role. This role was essentially "centrist." However, when basic political loyalties were at issue, he invariably backed Mao rather than Mao's opponents. The other two Standing Committee members were less important. Chu Teh gradually became inactive—a respected Party elder but one lacking any great power or influence. Ch'en Yun's position seems to have been the most precarious of any in this top group, and his star periodically rose and fell fairly dramatically. Closely linked to Chou in directing state economic affairs, he was highly influential in economic policy making until the Great Leap Forward. Then, in the late 1950s, he went into virtual eclipse, almost certainly because of Mao's displeasure with Ch'en's opposition to, or doubts about, the Great Leap policies. His star rose once more in the early 1960s when Liu and Teng propelled him back into a key role in economic policy making again. When the struggle between Mao and Lin and Liu and Teng reached its climax, Ch'en's position was uncertain and ambiguous. He survived the Cultural Revolution, probably because of his ties to Chou, but by the late 1960s he appeared to have relatively little power or influence.

There is no way of knowing how the Standing Committee really functioned or what specifically occurred as these trends and shifts in power and relationship developed. There seems little doubt, however, that as differences among its members grew its effectiveness as a decision-making body was gradually reduced. Finally, when unity at this level collapsed at the time of the Cultural Revolution, Mao tried to reconstruct a new inner circle to replace the old one. It seems likely that the Standing Committee as such simply did not operate in any real sense for a considerable time. Key decisions were probably made by Mao himself and his immediate entourage, and by a variety of other groups led by Mao's closest supporters. Some of these, such as the Party's Military Affairs Committee, were in theory clearly subordinate to the Politburo Standing Committee, but during the Cultural Revolution they appeared to operate to a considerable extent on their own— under Mao's overall direction. A new Cultural Revolution Group, led by Ch'en Po-ta, was ostensibly an organ of the Central Committee, but it almost certainly operated directly under Mao. Another group that emerged during the Cultural Revolution was the so-called Group of Fourteen, or "Mao's Proletarian Headquarters."[29] This was an ad hoc transitional leadership group composed of those included in Mao's new inner circle. Whether it actually functioned, and if so, to what extent, as an organized decision-making group is unclear.

Finally, after three years of confusion and struggle, a new Politburo Standing Committee emerged from the Ninth Party Congress in April 1969. The sweeping changes that had occurred in Mao's top inner circle were now formalized. The new Committee had five members. Three were holdovers from the previous group, and they constituted the core of the new Committee: Mao, Lin Piao, and Chou En-lai. However, four of the predecessor group had been purged or demoted: Liu Shao-ch'i, Chu Teh, Ch'en Yun, and Teng Hsiao-p'ing. In their place were two newcomers, Ch'en Po-ta and K'ang Sheng, whose spectacular rise to the summit was due, above all, to their close personal association with and loyalty to Mao, or his wife, or both.

This new Standing Committee was less broadly representative of the leadership as a whole, or of the major institutional and functional components of the political system, than the one it succeeded. Although Ch'en and K'ang had been Politburo members for many years, they had ranked relatively low in the hierarchy and did not control any of the major institutional bases of power in China. Both lacked the solid bases of power of their predecessors. This made it seem unlikely, from the start, that the new Standing Committee could be as strong or as effective as the previous one. It actually began to fall apart almost as soon as it was created. Ch'en Po-ta was purged in 1970. K'ang Sheng became ill and inactive. And then in 1971 Lin Piao was killed.

According to the official story later publicized by Peking, Lin Piao's designation in 1969 as the only Vice Chairman of the Party and Mao's chosen successor was more a reflection of his own overweening ambition than of Mao's will, and Peking charged that he and Ch'en Po-ta had been coconspirators from the start in a plan to oust and replace Mao. Peking's account of the deteriorating relationship between Lin and his backers, on the one hand, and Mao and Chou and their supporters, on the other, indicates that tensions began to develop as early as the time of the Ninth Party Congress in 1969, and had reached serious proportions by 1970. Thereafter, according to the official story, Lin plotted to assassinate Mao and seize power; when the coup attempt was aborted, he tried to flee China and was killed when his plane crashed in Mongolia.[30]

The causes of this dramatic power struggle will doubtless be debated for a long time to come. There have been hints and allegations concerning important policy conflicts, including differences over policy toward the Soviet Union and the United States, and these may have some validity. Probably the basic causes, however, were rooted in the problems of achieving an acceptable military-civilian balance in China and questions concerning the succession.

Whatever the causes, the results were traumatic. The first attempt since the Cultural Revolution to restore cohesion at the top of China's leadership had failed. This meant, in effect, that China now had no functioning, stable "inner circle" at the top. Mao and Chou were the only politically active survivors of this group.

During 1971–73, many of the top-level decisions in China probably had to be made in a relatively ad hoc fashion, by Mao and Chou working informally with their closest personal supporters and advisers, but it was apparent that increased stability in the leadership would require restoration of the Standing Committee or some institutionalized inner circle with ultimate decision-making authority.

Finally a new top leadership was unveiled, immediately after the Tenth Party Congress; the newly elected Central Committee announced at that time the membership of the Party's new Standing Committee (and Politburo). The Standing Committee was now a nine-man body. Under Mao, who remained as Chairman, there were five Vice Chairmen—Chou En-lai, Wang Hung-wen, K'ang Sheng, Yeh Chien-ying, and Li Teh-sheng—and three other members—Chu Teh, Chang Ch'un-ch'iao, and Tung Pi-wu. Since Mao and Chou obviously hope that this group will play a key role in restoring stability and cohesion to China's leadership and carry China through the succession period, its membership merits careful analysis.

Apart from Mao himself, five men unquestionably constitute its active core. Chou, who is clearly the senior Vice Chairman, occupies a pivotal position. The other four include two military men—Yeh Chien-ying and Li Teh-sheng—and two rapidly rising leaders from the Party apparatus—Chang Ch'un-ch'iao and Wang Hung-wen.

Yeh Chien-ying (who, at seventy-five, is the same age as Chou En-lai) is an old-time military leader who has been Chou's top military adviser and probably, in effect, de facto Minister of National Defense as well as acting head of the Party's Military Affairs Commission. Li Teh-sheng, in his early sixties, is a commander who rose to the top during the Cultural Revolution and thereafter became head of the General Political Department of the People's Liberation Army (PLA) and commander of the forces in Peking.

Chang Ch'un-ch'iao and Wang Hung-wen are both Party apparatus leaders who emerged to prominence in Shanghai during the Cultural Revolution. The career of Chang, who is about sixty, had mainly been in propaganda work before he catapulted to the top in Shanghai in 1966. Thereafter, both as head of the Shanghai Revolutionary Committee and as a leading member of the Cultural Revolution Group in Peking, Chang steadily rose in national stature. Just before the Tenth Congress there was some evidence that Chang may actually have taken over the functions of Secretary-General of the Party even though he was not publicly designated as such. The fact that he was designated Secretary-General of the Presidium of the Tenth Congress gave credence to this possibility—even though the Presidium itself existed only for the duration of the Congress.

The greatest single surprise of the Congress was the spectacular rise of Wang Hung-wen to the third-ranking position in the Party. Still in his mid-thirties, Wang is much younger than anyone else in China's top "inner circle." Although as a deputy head of the Shanghai Revolutionary Committee under Chang he had helped to run China's largest city, he had not played any significant role at the center until 1972. Presumably, his dramatic promotion was supported by both Chou En-lai and Chang Ch'un-ch'iao as well as by Mao Tse-tung. The fact that he became a Party Vice Chairman while Chang did not made his sudden rise particularly striking.

The other three Standing Committee members—Chu Teh and Tung Pi-wu, who are both eighty-seven, and K'ang Sheng, who is seventy-four and incapacitated—are symbolic links with the past, rather than leaders who can be expected to play active roles in the future.

One of the most notable features of the new Standing Committee is the delicate balance between top military leaders and rising Party bureaucrats. Another is that three of the members are newcomers at the top whose stars rose during the Cultural Revolution. These three—Li Teh-sheng, Chang Ch'un-ch'iao, and Wang Hung-wen—are now well positioned for high leadership posts not only after Mao dies but perhaps after Chou as well passes from the scene.

There are some notable absences. No leader drawn from the top layer in the state bureaucracy, apart from Chou En-lai himself, is included; particularly conspicuous is the absence of Li Hsien-nien, who appears to have been Chou's closest associate in running the state bureaucracy and China's economy since the end of the Cultural Revolution. Neither of China's two most powerful regional military leaders, Ch'en Hsi-lien and Hsu Shih-yu, was selected for the Standing Committee, although both are Politburo members. While consistent with the past practice of including only men stationed in Peking on the Standing Committee, their exclusion is nonetheless significant. Perhaps most important of all is the absence of the two surviving leaders who, more than any others, symbolized the most extreme "radicalism" of the Cultural Revolution period—Mao's wife, Chiang Ch'ing, and her young protégé, Yao Wen-yuan—even though both retained their Politburo membership and in Party rankings were listed just below those on the Standing Committee.

Where should the new members of the Standing Committee be placed on the left-right political spectrum in China today? Some observers are inclined to believe that, because Chang Ch'un-ch'iao, Wang Hung-wen, Li Teh-sheng, and the aging K'ang Sheng all came to the fore during the Cultural Revolution in association with the left, their inclusion on the Standing Committee signifies a tipping of the political balance toward the left. It seems quite possible, though, that Chang, Wang, and Li may all have moved closer to Chou En-lai and therefore toward a generally centrist position since the end of the Cultural Revolution.

Within the limits imposed by Mao's insistence that most of China's top officials be men with whom he has special links, Chou En-lai appears to have attempted to create a delicate balance in the new leadership, with the main weight in the center. It is a leadership in which both China's military hierarchy and its political leftists are well represented, but the power and influence of both of these groups appear to have been "contained." Whether or not a stable balance within the Standing Committee has in fact been created—and this remains to be seen—will be one crucial factor shaping China's future course. However, to understand more fully the nature of the changing political balance in China, it is necessary to look beyond the Standing Committee and analyze the memberships of the full Politburo and Central Committee.

The Politburo

The changes that have occurred in recent years in the Politburo have been as dramatic and as far-reaching in their implications as those in the top inner circle. When the Chinese political leadership was operating at peak effectiveness in the period before the Cultural Revolution, the Politburo was an extremely important policy-formulating body. Because it was larger and more broadly representative than the small Standing Committee, most major policy decisions required Politburo support to become effectively operative. And because it was not excessively large—varying in size from roughly a dozen to slightly over two dozen persons—the Politburo was a more suitable forum for real debate and discussion of policy questions than the much larger and relatively unwieldy Central Committee.

The history of the Politburo since 1949 has in general paralleled that of the Standing Committee. In its early years, especially in the 1950s, it was an impressive body composed of proven leaders, all of whom had had long Party experience and most of whom derived their power from strong institutional foundations. It was, moreover, fairly broadly representative of the diverse institutional and other interests of the regime's bureaucracies. Until the Cultural Revolution, the core group of Politburo-level leaders had shown a degree of stability and continuity comparable to that of the Standing Committee's membership. It could be argued that the low turnover in top leadership bodies was in some respects a weakness, because so little new talent had a chance to reach the top, but on balance the continuity of leadership was nevertheless a major source of political strength. From the late 1950s on, however, the consensus of this group, like that of the top leadership as a whole, gradually weakened, and then, during the Cultural Revolution, it was shattered. When a new Politburo was established in 1969, it was a very different kind of body.

The best way to highlight the changes that have occurred is to analyze in detail the membership in the Politburo since 1949. Although this requires mention of sizable numbers of persons whose names may be unfamiliar to nonspecialists in Chinese affairs, the far-reaching character of the changes is much clearer if described in terms of specifics rather than broad generalities. In any case, it is important for Westerners who would acquire more than a superficial understanding of Chinese affairs to have some knowledge of at least the top two dozen or so Politburo-level leaders in China and not just the handful of Chinese leaders whose names appear regularly in the Western press.

There are some differences of opinion as to who constituted the Politburo at the time of the Party's 1949 takeover.[31] No official listings were published at that time, although the Politburo had been elected four years earlier, at the Party's 1945 Seventh Congress. There is fairly broad agreement, however, that at least eleven men were definitely members in 1949—the five, discussed above, who made up the early Secretariat (Mao, Liu, Chou, Chu, and Ch'en), and six others of long and varied Party experience who had occupied key organizational leadership positions during the struggle for power.

Two of the six were already, relatively speaking, Party "elders": Tung Pi-wu and Lin Po-ch'u (Lin Tsu-han). Born in the 1880s, both men had held many organizational positions of major importance in the 1930s and 1940s. The other four were all able men who also had made outstanding records during the struggle for power. Jen Pi-shih had held many influential posts, among them the position of head of the political department of the Eighth Route Army. P'eng Chen was a key leader in North China in the 1940s, and had served as a political commissar as well as in other roles. (Some sources speculate that P'eng Chen did not join the Politburo until after 1949, but Soviet sources, probably rightly, date his membership to 1945.[32]) Chang Wen-t'ien, one of the so-called Returned Students Group trained in the Soviet Union, had briefly held the top leadership post in the Party in the mid-1930s —that of General Secretary—and among the many subsequent positions of importance he held was that of head of the Party's organization department. P'eng Teh-huai, who had already established a reputation as one of the Communists' foremost military commanders, was probably a member at this time, although the evidence is not indisputable; some observers believe that he did not join the Politburo until the 1950s. (Some analysts believe that Kao Kang and K'ang Sheng were also Politburo members at this time, but it seems more likely that they were chosen later, Kao Kang possibly in 1952 and K'ang Sheng perhaps in 1954.[33])

Essentially, this core group at the Politburo level remained intact for the next two decades. Throughout the final struggle for power and the regime's initial years in power—from 1945 until the late 1950s— there were remarkably few important changes. In the first half of the 1950s several new members were added (probably four, although possibly five, if P'eng Teh-huai is included), but one of those was soon purged. The four men added were Kao Kang, K'ang Sheng, Lin Piao, and Teng Hsiao-p'ing. Kao had been a key leader in the Yenan area before Mao arrived in the 1930s, and after 1949 he was the dominant leader in Manchuria and the first chairman of China's State Planning Commission. His period at the top was extremely short. He was purged in 1954–55, allegedly for having tried to achieve a position second only to Mao's; significantly, no other Politburo member was seriously affected by this development (although Jao Shu-shih, the other major leader purged along with Kao, was close to achieving Politburo status). K'ang Sheng, onetime director of the Party's organization department, was a rather shadowy figure—both then and later— who played a key role in Party intelligence and security work. Lin Piao, as noted already, was, like P'eng Teh-huai, one of the Communists' outstanding military commanders. Teng Hsiao-p'ing, after a period as foremost leader in Southwest China, had taken charge of the Party Secretariat (in the post of Secretary-General) in the mid-1950s. At the time of the 1956 Party Congress, the Politburo membership of thirteen included all of the surviving original 1945 members minus Kao and Jen Pi-shih, who had died, plus the four rising lights mentioned above.

When the Eighth Party Congress met in 1956, the size of the Politburo was roughly doubled. The new group, now totaling twenty-three (seventeen full or regular members and six alternates), contained every one of the surviving members of the previous Politburo, plus ten new members. In short, the entire original core group of the top leadership was confirmed in power, though Chang Wen-t'ien and K'ang Sheng dropped to alternate member status.

The new members strengthened the Politburo as a representative leadership group. In effect, the Politburo coopted into its membership the key men who had achieved roles of supreme importance in the regime's various institutional hierarchies during the previous decade. All of the six new full members elected in 1956—Lo Jung-huan, Ch'en Yi, Li Fu-ch'un, Liu Po-ch'eng, Ho Lung, and Li Hsien-nien—had been prominent military or military-political leaders at one time, and most had exercised major regional power immediately after 1949 before being brought to Peking in the centralization moves of the early 1950s. By the middle and later 1950s, however, a number of these men had been thoroughly "civilianized" and now played very important roles in government affairs. Ch'en Yi was en route to becoming China's Minister of Foreign Affairs, in which position he would play a role second only to Chou En-lai's in shaping Peking's foreign policy from the late 1950s until the Cultural Revolution. Li Fu-ch'un and Li Hsien-nien had already emerged as top leaders in economic planning and financial affairs. Lo Jung-huan, Liu Po-ch'eng, and Ho Lung continued to be active military leaders and were members of the Party's powerful Military Affairs Commission.

The four new alternate members—Ulanfu, Lu Ting-yi, Ch'en Po-ta, and Po Yi-po—participated actively in Politburo discussions, but without voting rights, and further broadened the Politburo's representation of special interests and policy fields. Ulanfu, the principal leader in Inner Mongolia, had a unique role in relation to minority group affairs. Lu Ting-yi was the senior Party leader dealing with propaganda and cultural and educational affairs, and Ch'en Po-ta was one of his principal deputies as well as an intimate associate of Mao's. (Ch'en had once been a private secretary to Mao and a speech writer for him.) Po Yi-po, like Li Fu-ch'un and Li Hsien-nien, had become a senior leader in economic affairs and was in charge of formulating short-term annual economic plans.

A further moderate expansion of Politburo membership occurred in 1958, when three new full members—K'o Ch'ing-shih, Li Ching-ch'uan, and T'an Chen-lin—were added. The first two of these were powerful regional leaders, in East and Southwest China respectively, and both continued to maintain their primary power bases outside Peking. T'an had by this time replaced Teng Tzu-hui as the Party's top rural specialist (apart from Mao himself) and was concerned primarily with policy regarding agriculture and collectivization.

At the start of the Great Leap Forward, therefore, the Politburo had twenty-six members (twenty full members and six alternates) and it was an impressive as well as powerful group. The continuity of the original core group—nine were still in the Politburo—was striking, and testified to the strength of the basic consensus that still united China's top leadership. Moreover, the seventeen new men who had been added since 1949 had made the Politburo more broadly representative of the most important interest groups, policy areas, and power centers in the regime's bureaucracies.

Analyzing the 1958 membership in terms of special interests, one can differentiate its members into several mjaor categories, according to their fields of responsibility and institutional or regional bases of power. Mao still occupied a unique position as the supreme generalist, but most of the others were increasingly identifiable with particular functional fields or specific institutional bases. Liu Shao-ch'i, Teng Hsiao-p'ing, and P'eng Chen bore primary responsibility for organizational affairs in the Party. Liu, as second-ranking Party leader, head of the National People's Congress Standing Committee, and soon-to-be state chairman, had very broad responsibilities, and P'eng, as Party chief in Peking, had a strong local base of power; but both men had their strongest roots in the national Party apparatus. K'ang Sheng's primary roots were also in the Party, but he did not belong to the dominant Liu-Teng-P'eng group. Later events suggest that he had a particularly close personal relationship with Mao and that he probably exercised a significant influence in the field of political security. Lu Ting-yi and Ch'en Po-ta were both specialists in ideology, propaganda, and cultural and educational affairs. Lu's primary power base was in the Party apparatus. Ch'en's position, however, depended heavily on his close personal association with Mao.

Six Politburo members were active military leaders: Chu Teh, P'eng Teh-huai, Lin Piao, Lo Jung-huan, Liu Po-ch'eng, and Ho Lung. P'eng and Lin Piao overshadowed the others in real power and influence; as later events were to indicate, they were in a basic sense competitors for supreme leadership in the military field. Some of the others too, especially Liu Po-ch'eng and Ho Lung, were influential as representatives of China's pre-1949 "old guard" military commanders, and even though they no longer held key operational posts in the military chain of command, they continued as members of the Party's Military Affairs Commission to be directly involved in policy making.

A striking fact about the Politburo in the late 1950s was that the largest new functional category of members consisted of leaders actively responsible for running governmental economic affairs. This reflected the high priority now placed by the regime on economic matters. In addition to Premier Chou En-lai, these were Ch'en Yun, Li Fu-ch'un, Li Hsien-nien, Po Yi-po, and T'an Chen-lin, who together dominated the fields of planning, industrial development, finance, and agriculture. All but T'an were key members of the state bureaucracy. Like the majority of China's leaders, these men had emerged from a military-political background, but they had successfully adapted themselves to new kinds of responsibilities and tasks in the civilian sector. Two members—Ch'en Yi and Chang Wen-t'ien—were by now specialists in foreign policy problems and worked primarily in governmental rather than Party posts. Party "elders" Lin Po-ch'u and Tung Pi-wu were less easily categorized, or identifiable with particular fields, although Tung was to some extent a specialist in "political-legal" affairs and in problems of discipline and "control" within the Party.

Although the Politburo remained intact in formal terms until the Cultural Revolution (except for three members who died: Lin Po-ch'u in 1960, Lo Jung-huan in 1963, and K'o Ch'ing-shih in 1965), it had become a far less cohesive or effective leadership body even before 1966 than it had been in the 1950s. In retrospect, it seems clear that the 1959 Lushan Central Committee plenum was a major turning point that set in motion trends that gradually weakened and finally destroyed the consensus of this Politburo group, and of the leadership as a whole. Even though only two Politburo members were purged in 1959— P'eng Teh-huai and Chang Wen-t'ien (and they continued for some years to be listed as Politburo members)—the effects of the inner-Party conflict that the Lushan meeting produced were much greater than appeared on the surface, and from then on steady polarization occurred. During the first half of the 1960s, policy debates at the Politburo level intensified, and competing leaders increasingly tried to use this forum for their own purposes. As consensus weakened, there was also a growing tendency to try to bypass the Politburo on some issues—to discuss policy issues in a variety of ad hoc Party work conferences,[34] some apparently dominated by Mao and others by Liu and Teng.

When the Cultural Revolution finally erupted into open power struggle, Mao at first attempted to carry out a selective and limited purge at the level of the Politburo. The first Politburo-level victims were P'eng Chen and Lu Ting-yi in early 1966. (Other major victims at this stage were Lo Jui-ch'ing and Yang Shang-k'un, who, though not Politburo members, were nevertheless powerful leaders belonging to the top elite.) This, however, was only the beginning. Later in the year, at the Eleventh Central Committee plenum, a more substantial restructuring of the leadership took place, and the rank positions of many Politburo leaders were altered. No official Politburo list was revealed at the time, but subsequent protocol listings indicated very significant changes. Most important, Lin Piao replaced Liu Shao-ch'i as the second-ranking Politburo member; Liu dropped precipitously in the rankings, to eighth place; T'ao Chu, a newcomer at the top, had a meteoric rise, to fourth place; and Ch'en Po-ta and K'ang Sheng also rose spectacularly, to fifth and seventh places, respectively.

The total Politburo apparently now consisted of twenty-five men. Four members of the earlier Politburo were dropped entirely at this stage: P'eng Teh-huai and Chang Wen-t'ien, both of whom had actually been purged years earlier, plus P'eng Chen and Lu Ting-yi. And six new members were added: T'ao Chu, Hsu Hsiang-ch'ien, Nieh Jung-chen, Yeh Chien-ying, Li Hsueh-feng, and Hsieh Fu-chih.

In the months that followed, the Politburo underwent further sweeping purges and was radically transformed. It is not necessary to summarize here the details of how and when, between 1966 and 1969, particular changes occurred. The overall scope of the changes is evident, however, when the new Politburo that finally emerged from the Cultural Revolution in 1969 is analyzed.

When the previous structure of leadership at the top in China broke down at the peak of the Cultural Revolution, the Politburo appears to have become inoperative. The Central Committee's Secretariat, the principal body responsible for day-to-day administrative supervision of the Party apparatus, also went into virtually total eclipse. A number of other groups and organizations tried to carry out Mao's policies and directives, in effect temporarily replacing both the Politburo and Secretariat as well as the Party departments under the Secretariat. The resulting situation was one in which power was much more diffused and decision making much more confused and unstable than at any point in the past.

The Chinese press frequently referred at the height of the Cultural Revolution—in 1968 particularly—to "Mao's Proletarian Headquarters," an ad hoc group of fourteen persons. Only five of its members—Mao, Lin Piao, Chou En-lai, Ch'en Po-ta, and K'ang Sheng—were pre-1966 Politburo members. The others had catapulted into positions at the summit as Mao (and his wife and other close associates) turned for support, in the heat of the confused struggle then going on, to the army and to "leftists" they considered to be completely loyal in a personal sense. The new top group included Chiang Ch'ing (Mao's wife, who suddenly rose from obscurity to a position of extraordinary importance), Chang Ch'un-ch'iao, a key leader from Shanghai who had supported Mao and his wife in launching the Cultural Revolution; and Yao Wen-yuan, a young and radical Maoist propagandist from Shanghai closely linked to Chiang Ch'ing and Chang Ch'un-ch'iao. Also included were Hsieh Fu-chih, the man who had succeeded Lo Jui-ch'ing as Public Security chief; Huang Yung-sheng, China's new military Chief of Staff; Wu Fa-hsien, the head of the air force, regarded then as "leftist" and pro-Mao; Yeh Ch'un, Lin Piao's wife; Wang Tung-hsing, Mao's one-time bodyguard who had become a Vice Minister of Public Security and a key figure in political security work as head of the Central Committee Staff Office; and Wen Yu-ch'eng, the new commander of the Peking garrison, one of the most sensitive and important military units in China. Although little is known about whether, and if so how, these people operated as a group, they probably served as a kind of "kitchen cabinet" under Mao. When a new Politburo was ultimately formed in 1969, all but one of them (Wen) were made members.

On public occasions, this core group of fourteen was sometimes joined by ten others. Some observers believed that, together, these twenty-four persons were the closest equivalent to a Politburo in this period. Seven of the ten additional men were pre-1965 Politburo members: Tung Pi-wu, Liu Po-ch'eng, Chu Teh, Ch'en Yun, Li Fu-ch'un,

Ch'en Yi, and Li Hsien-nien. The other three—Hsu Hsiang-ch'ien, Nieh Jung-chen, and Yeh Chien-ying—were all senior, old-time military leaders to whom Mao turned during the Cultural Revolution. Of these ten, however, only half were ultimately chosen for the 1969 Politburo.

While these ad hoc groups were important, primary operational leadership of the Cultural Revolution appeared to gravitate into the hands of several other organizations, each of which exercised power through various channels. Apart from Mao and his wife, Chiang Ch'ing, four men obviously played very special roles in these—the four who were later to be designated members of the new Politburo Standing Committee in 1969.

Most important was Lin Piao. As Mao's closest "comrade in arms" and chosen heir, as well as the dominant military figure in China, Lin— and the Military Affairs Commission (MAC) that he headed—played a crucial role in running the country and in carrying out Mao's policies. The MAC was undoubtedly one of the most important decision-making bodies in China during this period, in a broad political as well as strictly military sense; in practice, it took over many of the Party's previous functions and issued many central directives through the local Military Control Commissions that it established throughout most of the country.

A second body that wielded great power and influence during 1967–68 was the Cultural Revolution Group, established in early 1966. Ch'en Po-ta headed it, and Mao's wife was his first deputy. It, too, established its own channels of communication to local levels and attempted (with only limited success) to manage and guide the confused struggles and purging that were occurring at all levels; later, it attempted to bring its considerable influence to bear in rebuilding a new institutional structure. This group was the principal center of radical "leftist" Maoist impulses during the Cultural Revolution.

Chou En-lai operated, as always, primarily from his base in the state bureaucracy, but his influence was much broader and tremendously important. Loyal to Mao throughout, he nevertheless exercised a restraining hand, frequently checking the most extreme "leftists." More than anyone else, he kept the Chinese government operating during the period of greatest chaos.

K'ang Sheng's role is less clear, but there is reason to believe that for a time he headed a special political security group, probably directly under Mao's supervision, that wielded major influence—although exactly how, or through what channels, is difficult to determine. Publicly, he was known to be an adviser to the Cultural Revolution Group.

Throughout this period there was great instability at the top. Leaders rose spectacularly and then fell abruptly. One of the most notable examples was the former top regional leader in South China, T'ao Chu, who catapulted to the top in 1966, not only replacing Lu Ting-yi as the regime's propaganda chief, but for a while ranking directly behind Mao, Lin, and Chou in the leadership. He may even have acted as de facto General Secretary of the Party. By 1967, he had been purged. There were some equally striking cases involving military men. For example, Yang Ch'eng-wu rose to be Acting Chief of Staff from late 1965 to early 1968, and then quickly fell into oblivion, and Hsu Hsiang-ch'ien played a major role in carrying forward the Cultural Revolution for some months and then disappeared from the top leadership group. Of the nineteen persons who had been leading members of the Cultural Revolution Group in 1966–67, only three (Chiang Ch'ing, Chang Ch'un-ch'iao, and Yao Wen-yuan) still retained positions of major prominence and power five years later.

The extent of the purging at the top levels of China's leadership became clear when the Ninth Politburo was formally constituted and announced in 1969. This new group, with twenty-five members (twenty-one regulars and four alternates), was roughly the same size as the Eighth Politburo, but its composition revealed that China now had a very new—and in some respects a new kind of—ruling group.

Of the twenty-three men who had been members of the Politburo just before the Cultural Revolution, only nine (fewer than half) had survived, and only three of the fourteen missing retained even Central Committee membership.[35] In short, a large majority of the twenty to thirty men who had exercised supreme power during most of the first two decades of Communist rule were now shunted aside. Of the nine survivors, two, Chu Teh and Tung Pi-wu, were aging and their functions largely ceremonial. Only five had belonged to the small group of "giants" in the Party who had dominated the regime in the days immediately before the Cultural Revolution. Two (Ch'en Po-ta and K'ang Sheng) were men who previously had been among the lowest ranking Politburo members.

Almost all of the men who had previously run the Party's own organizational apparatus were now gone. So too were a majority of those, with the notable exception of Li Hsien-nien, who had held predominant positions under Chou in the state bureaucracy dealing with civilian affairs. (A number of others retained Central Committee status, however.) This sweeping and traumatic purge was wholly unprecedented in the Chinese Communists' history.

The 1969 Politburo was a very different group in fundamental respects from the Politburo of earlier years. The Politburo previously had consisted almost entirely of men who had risen in power and status gradually, over a long period of time, through generally accepted channels and by fairly well-established means; most had been elevated to the Politburo because of proven leadership qualities generally recognized within the Party. The new Politburo emerged suddenly from a chaotic situation of violent struggle. Many of its members rose in a meteoric fashion largely because of their personal ties or ideological affinities to Mao. Others reached the top rung because they were agile, in an opportunistic sense, and jumped the right way at the right time as the Cultural Revolution unfolded. A majority were men whose control of the military instruments of power in China was such that Mao and his inner circle obviously believed it necessary to grant them top leadership posts once the PLA had been called on to fill the vacuum created by the weakening of the Party.

The old Politburo had appeared to enjoy—at least in the early days —a fairly broad consensus, based on years of shared experience and cooperation in pursuing common goals. The new Politburo was a much more heterogeneous group. It was a mixture of old-timers and newcomers, of "conservatives" and "radicals," of military leaders and civilians, who lacked the kind of common bonds that had been forged in the earlier group during years of close cooperation in the revolution. Another significant difference was that most members of the old Politburo had been men whose primary responsibilities were national (even though many had arrived at Politburo status via regional power bases). The 1969 Politburo contained a large number of members whose primary roots continued to be local. The old Politburo had been, by the late 1950s at least, fairly broadly representative of the most important functional fields of policy and administration, as well as the most important subgroups of the leadership in the Party apparatus, military establishment, and state bureaucracy. The new Politburo lacked this balance, and was much less broadly representative in a bureaucratic sense; some sectors were heavily overrepresented while others were notably underrepresented.

Although the twenty-five members of the 1969 Politburo might be categorized in several different ways, the following breakdown high-lights some of the group's principal characteristics.[36] As indicated earlier, the most striking feature of the new group was the dominance of military personnel, reflecting the basic shift in the balance between military and civilian power described in Chapter 2. Eleven members of the new Politburo were active military men. The careers of three other members had been primarily in the field of political security. Of the military men, five were leaders in the central organs of the national military establishment. They included Lin Piao, China's senior military commander; Huang Yung-sheng, Chief of Staff; Ch'iu Hui-tso, the PLA's logistics chief; Wu Fa-hsien, the air force commander; and Li Tso-p'eng, the top commissar in the navy. All the major service arms were thus represented. Three were powerful regional or local com-manders. Two of these—Ch'en Hsi-lien, headquartered in Manchuria (Shenyang), and Hsu Shih-yu, in the lower Yangtze valley (Nanking) —were particularly important. The third, Li Teh-sheng, was in some respects a surprising choice, since he had been a relatively low-ranking leader commanding the Anhwei provincial military district; by 1970–71, however, he had jumped to a key national position as new head of the PLA's General Political Department.

Three other military men on the Politburo—Liu Po-ch'eng, Yeh Chien-ying, and Chu Teh—were survivors of the older generation of military leaders; the first two continued to play important roles in the Military Affairs Commission, but Chu Teh's position as an aging sym-bol of the past was honorific.[37] Three men had political security (in-cluding public security) backgrounds: K'ang Sheng, Hsieh Fu-chih, and Wang Tung-hsing. K'ang's influential but shadowy role has already been noted. Hsieh was head of the Ministry of Public Security, and Wang Tung-hsing, Director of the Central Committee Staff Office, was a public security official of second rank who jumped to the top because of his ties with Mao. Perhaps one should add Yeh Chun, Lin Piao's wife, to this military group, raising the total to twelve, since she cannot be fitted easily into any other category. And it should be noted that Chang Ch'un-ch'iao's power was based not only on his role as head of the Shanghai Revolutionary Committee but also on his posi-tion as first political commissar of the Nanking military region.

The other notable new grouping consisted of the cluster of "leftists," closely associated with Mao, who had played a crucial role during the Cultural Revolution as prime initiators or supporters of radical Maoist policies. Chiang Ch'ing, Mao's wife, had a very special position in this group. Ch'en Po-ta was officially its highest ranking leader but shared power with K'ang Sheng, whose rise has been described. Other powerful "leftist" newcomers included the two men from Shanghai: Chang Ch'un-ch'iao, top leader in the Shanghai area, and Yao Wen-yuan, the Shanghai propagandist who was the youngest man of Politburo rank. All five had played leading roles in the Cultural Revolution Group.

Another striking feature of the new Politburo was the almost total absence of the leaders who previously had managed the Party apparatus and the very small representation of men whose primary careers had been in the state bureaucracy. Not a single one of the old Party apparatus leaders was included in the new Politburo and, apart from Chou En-lai, the only leading government bureaucrat from the years before the Cultural Revolution was Li Hsien-nien. (Perhaps Party elder Tung Pi-wu could also be included in this category, although he had never been a leading government bureaucrat in the sense that Chou and Li had been, and his role in recent years had been primarily ceremonial.)

The other two Politburo members, who do not fall into any of the above groupings, were primarily local civilian political leaders: Li Hsueh-feng (in Hopei province) and Chi Teng-k'uei (a relatively unknown local leader from Honan province). Although there were now two women in the Politburo for the first time in history, neither had been an outstanding leader in Party affairs previously, and both attained their positions primarily because they were married to Mao and Lin, China's two dominant leaders.

The high percentage of Politburo members operating from regional and local bases of power reflected the very significant decentralization of power that had occurred during the Cultural Revolution. In fact, of the total of twenty-five members, between a quarter and a third were military or civilian leaders who continued to maintain strong local positions. In general, personal ascriptive ties were now more important than ever before. Many of the new Politburo members—including virtually all of the "radical" leaders who had run the Cultural Revolution Group—had jumped to the top primarily because of their links to Mao and his immediate entourage, and their political survival was linked to Mao personally.

Because the "ideological" spread within the new Politburo was much wider than at any time in the past, there was clearly less basis for consensus than previously. All members of the new Politburo, it is true, were persons who had professed loyalty to Mao, but in reality the Politburo included a diversity of individuals whose perspectives and priorities varied and who pushed in different directions as they tried to influence policy.

For all of these reasons, it appeared unlikely from the start that the 1969 Politburo would be a stable, effective group or that it would have long tenure. It reflected the situation at a particular time in early 1969, but the political situation was then—and has continued to be—a constantly changing one. It was virtually certain, therefore, that major changes would occur eventually—after the death of Mao if not before. In fact, the changes started long before the succession process began. By late 1971, major changes had already taken place. Ch'en Po-ta, one of the most prominent "leftists," was purged in 1970. Then Hsieh Fu-chih and Li Hsueh-feng disappeared from the scene. Finally, during the Lin Piao affair in 1971 came the purging of Lin, his wife, and four other leading military men on the Politburo, Huang Yung-sheng, Ch'iu Hui-tso, Wu Fa-hsien, and Li Tso-p'eng.

The task facing Mao and Chou in late 1971 was to rebuild the severely weakened Politburo by pulling together the divided elements that had survived the purges of 1970–71, replacing those who had been ousted, adding some new members, and attempting to strike a new balance among the diverse and competing interests operating at the top levels of China's leadership.

When the membership of a reorganized Politburo was announced in August 1973 after the Tenth Party Congress, it was apparent that progress had been made toward this goal. The new Politburo represented a new and delicate balance. It by no means resolved, however, all the existing doubts as to whether—or at least to what extent—China again possessed a firmly based, balanced, and stable top leadership group that would be able to prepare for and manage an orderly succession.

With twenty-five members—twenty-one regular members and four nonvoting alternates—the Tenth Politburo is identical in size to the Ninth.[38] Included are all nine members of the Standing Committee, already discussed, and sixteen others. Of the twenty-one regular members sixteen are survivors of the 1969 Politburo (although three of these had only been alternates rather than regulars then). Nine of the total of twenty-five are newcomers to the Politburo, replacing those purged or deceased since 1969.

The carryover of members from the previous Politburo is slightly larger than had been expected by some observers. All of those dropped were persons known to have been ousted (or who had died) well before the Tenth Congress—mainly in connection with the intertwined Ch'en Po-ta and Lin Piao affairs; there were no new purges at the last minute. The fact that some observers have been impressed that *only* one-third of the Politburo has changed in four years is indicative of a general recognition of the degree of instability that continues at the top of the Chinese leadership. While less extensive than the changes that occurred in 1969, just after the Cultural Revolution, the 1973 Politburo changes have been far more extensive than any in the entire 1949–66 period.

The nine who have been purged or dropped since 1969 include the "leftist" leader Ch'en Po-ta; Lin Piao, his wife, and the four other central military leaders purged with him (the Chief of Staff, head of the air force, navy commissar, and logistics chief); Li Hsueh-feng, the Party leader who had emerged to the top in Peking and Hopei during the Cultural Revolution; and Hsieh Fu-chih, the Public Security Chief who had recently died.

As a group, the nine newcomers on the Politburo are not persons who had achieved national stature previously. In addition to Wang Hung-wen, whose meteoric rise was discussed earlier, they include four provincial-level Party apparatus leaders, from Peking municipality, Kwangsi, Hunan, and Sinkiang; one junior deputy commander of the navy; and for the first time in Politburo history, three representatives of the "masses"—a model peasant and two model workers. (The latter include Ch'en Yung-kuei, the well-publicized peasant head of the Tachai Brigade, and one man and one woman drawn from among model workers.) Apart from Wang and some of the provincial leaders, most of these are not persons of great stature.

If one assumes, as seems justifiable, that the three representatives of the "masses" and the four aging or ill Party elders who survived from the Ninth Politburo—Chu Teh, Tung Pi-wu, K'ang Sheng, and Liu Po-ch'eng—are not likely to play very important or very active roles in the period ahead, the core of the Politburo leadership now consists of eighteen persons, sixteen of whom are regular Politburo members and two of whom are alternates.

The most notable change, perhaps, has been the reduction in military representation, reflecting a significant shift in the military-civilian balance. With Yeh Chien-ying and Li Teh-sheng on the Politburo Standing Committee, the military establishment has maintained a strong position at that level. The full Politburo also still includes the two most powerful regional military leaders in China, Ch'en Hsi-lien from Manchuria, and Hsu Shih-yu from the Nanking Military Region. And, as noted earlier, one relatively minor naval leader, Su Chen-hua, has been added. In overall terms, however, the cutback of military men on the Politburo has been from eleven (if one includes Chu Teh and Liu Po-ch'eng) in the Ninth Politburo to seven in the Tenth, and only five of these are active military leaders.

Unquestionably, central military leaders, such as Yeh and Li, and regional military leaders, such as Ch'en and Hsu, will play important roles—perhaps crucial ones—in the period ahead, but the membership of the new Politburo as a whole indicates that Mao and Chou have attempted, with some success, to correct the imbalance that characterized the Ninth Politburo and have definitely cut back the political role of the military in the top leadership.

The representatives of China's military professionals who occupied the top staff positions in the PLA and headed its major service arms have been hard hit by the cutback in military membership, and this could be a cause of serious dissatisfaction. If, as was suggested in Chapter 2, the trend in China in the years ahead is toward increased stress on professionalism in the PLA, pressures may grow for the addition of new Politburo members from among staff officers and service arm chiefs.

The new Politburo membership also appears to reflect some reduction in the influence of China's radical leftists, although, as was noted earlier, this is not certain. The conclusion that the influence of the leftists has declined is based in considerable part on the facts that their titular leader during the Cultural Revolution, Ch'en Po-ta, has been purged and that neither Chiang Ch'ing nor Yao Wen-yuan, or others associated with them, such as Wang Tung-hsing, have achieved Standing Committee status. It is also, however, based on the judgment that Chang Ch'un-ch'iao and Wang Hung-wen, who were at one time closely associated with the leftists, have subsequently moved toward more centrist positions. Whether or not this judgment is correct is a crucial question for the future. Even so, there is a much broader ideological spectrum in the Politburo than there was in the period before the Cultural Revolution period, and China's leading leftists still have important representation at the top.

The apparent reduction in the influence of the military and China's leftists has been paralleled by a very significant increase in the representation of Party apparatus leaders, not only central leaders but, even more important, provincial-level Party leaders. In addition to Wang Hung-wen and Chang Ch'un-ch'iao, who still have important ties in Shanghai even though they are rising stars in the central Party apparatus, the new Politburo includes five other important provincial-level Party leaders. One is Chi Teng-k'uei, a Honan Party Secretary who remains a shadowy figure after four years on the Politburo. The others are newcomers at the top. They include Wu Teh, an old Party bureaucrat who steadily rose in Kirin and Peking and is now Party First Secretary and Chairman of the Peking Revolutionary Committee and First Political Commissar of the Peking garrison; Hua Kuo-feng, a Party leader in Hunan, who is now provincial Party First Secretary, Acting Chairman of the Revolutionary Committee, and First Political Commissar of the Canton Military Region; Wei Kuo-ch'ing, Party boss for many years in Kwangsi, who was a "conservative" during the Cultural Revolution but nevertheless emerged to head both the provincial Party Committee and Revolutionary Committee and became the First Political Commissar of the military district; and Saifudin (an alternate Politburo member), the recently chosen Party First Secretary, Chairman of the Revolutionary Committee and First Political Commissar of the region of Sinkiang. (The fact that both Wei and Saifudin are members of minority groups is probably no accident, but rather reflects a deliberate step to give such groups top-level representation once more.)

The inclusion of so many men whose primary responsibilities are at the local level rather than at the center is remarkable. (In a sense, one can say that eight of the nine new Politburo members were drawn up from the provincial level rather than from the central bureaucracy.) At the Politburo level, the representation of regional and provincial Party and military leaders is now greater in the Tenth Politburo than it was in the Ninth, which is a significant reflection of continuing problems of central-local relations and the difficulties involved in trying to strike a balance between Peking and the regions and provinces.

One of the most important areas in which there has not been change in the new Politburo is in the representation of China's state bureaucracy. In the Tenth Politburo, as in the Ninth, only Li Hsien-nien, apart from Chou En-lai himself, has his primary roots in the state bureaucracy. If one classifies Hsieh Fu-chih, who was in the Ninth and is not in the Tenth Central Committee, as primarily a state bureaucrat (as some would), then there has actually been a drop. One would have expected Chou En-lai to have tried to strengthen the representation of this group, not only because he himself has operated primarily from a base in the state bureaucracy but also because added representation from this quarter would probably increase support for the generally centrist, pragmatic policies he has been pursuing. The failure to add to this group means that the 1973 Politburo, like its predecessor, is relatively weak in terms of representation of China's bureaucratic specialists in economic affairs and other specialized fields.

Why Chou could not—or at least did not—expand the representation from the state bureaucracy in the Politburo cannot be easily answered. The lack of such representation could prove to be a significant weakness not only in the Politburo as a leadership group but in Chou En-lai's own political position. It is reasonable to assume that many leaders occupying senior positions in the state bureaucracy are far from satisfied with the government's representation in the highest leadership ranks, and that there will be pressures from them in the future, and probably efforts by Chou himself, to try to rectify this Other underrepresented leadership groups in China will probably also press for changes in the Politburo over time.

The critical question is whether the new coalition under Chou, which the Tenth Politburo reflects, rests on alliances and compromises that are solidly enough based to carry China through the succession period without another far-reaching breakdown of leadership unity resulting in an overt, violent struggle for power after Mao dies. The balancing of varied groups reflected in the formation of the new Politburo makes it seem more possible now than at any time since the Cultural Revolution that the foundations for a viable post-Mao collective leadership may have been laid. But in view of all the changes that have occurred since the start of the Cultural Revolution, the complicated mix in the present leadership, and the inevitable uncertainties inherent in a succession period such as that which will follow Mao's death, the possibility of continued leadership instability and open struggles cannot be excluded.

The Central Committee

The far-reaching nature of recent changes in Communist China's leadership is also reflected in the membership of the Party's Central Committee as it has evolved over the years. The Central Committee has from the start of Communist rule been the largest group of recognized members of the top political elite in China.[39] Its role in decision making has been limited, however. Although at times major policy debates have occurred during its plenary meetings, generally it has endorsed decisions previously made by the Politburo or its Standing Committee. Its relatively large size, the infrequency of its meetings, and the dispersion of its members throughout the country have imposed unavoidable limits on its actual policy-making role. It has, nevertheless, been a body of great power and influence, and its membership has included most of those leaders who have dominated and managed virtually every sector of the regime and every major region of the country.

In more pluralistic societies, it is often difficult to identify the top political elite with any precision. In China, the roster of Central Committee members has provided, in practice as well as in theory, a reasonably accurate guide to the men who have monopolized power throughout society and have borne the primary responsibility for implementing Party policies. This is true despite the fact that at any given time a leader whose power and influence have been rising might not yet have achieved Central Committee status, while another may have retained Central Committee membership after he has become a "has been."

The Seventh Central Committee, elected in 1945, constituted the basis of Communist China's leadership for almost two decades, from the time of Communist takeover in 1949 until the Cultural Revolution. It was a remarkably tightly knit group, consisting at the start of seventy-seven persons (forty-four full members and thirty-three alternates), almost all of whom had joined the Party in the 1920s. "Old school ties" of many sorts linked them—including participation in the Nanchang and Autumn Harvest uprisings, the Kiangsi Soviet, the Long March, and the protracted struggles of the 1930s and 1940s against both the Japanese and the Kuomintang. Roughly 80 percent of the Seventh Central Committee's full members had belonged to the Central Executive Committees of the Kiangsi Soviet in the early 1930s.[40]

A majority of these leaders came from middle and upper class family backgrounds,[41] as did the Kuomintang leaders whom they defeated, but they had been gradually "proletarianized" (or perhaps one should say "ruralized") during long years of revolutionary struggle. Many had strong rural rather than urban family roots, and almost all had worked in the countryside during the 1930s and 1940s.

They were a relatively well-educated group, as virtually all top leadership groups in China have been. A majority had received some sort of postsecondary education or training in military academies, teacher training institutions, or universities. A majority had had some educational training or experience abroad, mostly in the Soviet Union but also in Japan, France, and elsewhere. Partly because of this, many were fairly cosmopolitan in outlook. Few, however, were really "intellectuals." (One scholar has labeled many of them as men having the backgrounds of "petty intellectuals."[42]) Above all, they were political activists, professional revolutionaries who had spent their formative years in a wide variety of revolutionary activities. A great many had become revolutionaries while they were still students, and only a few had had significant careers of any length before joining the Party. Over time, however, many of them developed in their work for the Party certain areas of specialization and professional concern. Although most leaders held both military and civilian-political jobs before 1949, many tended gradually to become identified with certain lines of work —which included different types of military command responsibilities and various civilian Party and administrative jobs. The Seventh Central Committee had a large number of military members, but they did not constitute a majority; even though the Committee was elected while the Party's armies still were fighting to achieve power, over three-fifths of the Committee's members were identified primarily with civilian (especially Party) careers and responsibilities.

Most of the men elected to the Seventh Central Committee were very young when they joined the Party and were still relatively young when they reached high leadership positions. By 1949, however, the average age of the entire Central Committee was slightly over fifty. In geographical terms, the majority came from a relatively few areas. This was partly a result of the accidents of history, but it also reflected the importance of personal ties. Roughly a quarter came from Mao's own province of Hunan, and over half came from the three provinces of Hunan, Hupeh, and Szechuan. A large majority were from central interior provinces, and most other regions of the country were underrepresented. This was particularly true, for example, of North China. Even though the North had been the main recruitment ground for new Party members just before 1949, only about a tenth of the top leaders came from this region.

The remarkable cohesion of this group was strikingly demonstrated in 1956 and again in 1958. The Eighth Party Congress of 1956 selected a new Central Committee consisting of 170 members (97 full members and 73 alternates), which was roughly double the size of the 1945 group. The continuity between the old group and the new one was almost total. On the eve of the Eighth Congress, the Seventh Central Committee still had 68 of its original 77 members. Only 2, Kao Kang and Jao Shu-chih, had definitely been purged in the seven years since 1949, 5 had died, and 2 minor figures had simply disappeared from sight. Sixty-seven of the 68 survivors were reelected to membership in the new Central Committee; only one man—a very minor figure—fell by the wayside. This extraordinary demonstration of continuity and stability among the Party's highest leaders was perhaps unique in the history of major revolutionary groups.

In 1956, 103 new members were added, roughly one-third as full members and two-thirds as alternates. Still another expansion took place in 1958 at the second session of the Eighth Congress, when 25 additional alternate members were added. These new members had been cast in essentially the same mold as the men they joined.

The increase in the Central Committee's size in the late 1950s was a logical move that substantially strengthened the Central Committee as a leadership group. The Party's size and responsibilities had increased enormously since its takeover of power. As a result, many new men had risen throughout the country to positions of great power and influence in all the growing organizational hierarchies of the regime, including the Party, state, military forces, and mass organizations. Co-opting these rising leaders into the Central Committee accorded them a status that accurately reflected their power. The representative character of the Central Committee was thus broadened, and its membership now included the dominant figures in virtually every important sector of the regime's bureaucracies.

Perhaps the most striking single feature about all the changes in 1956–58 was the fact that so little fundamental change was involved.[43] As stated above, the core of the new Central Committee included all but one of the surviving members of the Seventh Central Committee. The general characteristics of the membership remained essentially the same even though the size of the Central Committee was more than doubled. There were a few signs of gradual change, however. Even though the Party membership of all of the new Central Committee members predated 1938 and the great majority of members still consisted of men who had joined the revolution in its early years, there were now many who had joined the Party in the early 1930s rather than in the 1920s. The Committee's membership still consisted predominantly of men from middle and upper class families, many of whom had strong links to rural areas, and the new members, like the older ones, were essentially professional revolutionaries, most of whom had not had significant previous careers; however, the new members had a somewhat broader range of backgrounds than was true of the members of the previous Committee.

As a group, the new Central Committee was still relatively well educated, although the new members had less training or experience abroad than the original core group had. While the Central Committee's geographical representation was still not well balanced and the predominance of members from central interior provinces continued, there was a rise in the number of men who came from the North. The overall average age of the entire Central Committee now approached the mid-fifties, but the age spread had broadened and there were men in their forties as well as men in their sixties or older. Another trend was the increase in the proportion of Central Committee members whose careers had been essentially in civilian spheres of activity—especially in Party organizations but also in the state apparatus—rather than in the military. And whereas two-thirds of all Central Committee members in 1949–50 were men whose principal work was in the regions and provinces (only one-third or so worked mainly at national headquarters at that time), this ratio was now reversed, and the main work of two-thirds of the Central Committee members was now in Peking.

On balance, the leadership appeared to be coping fairly successfully with the problem of maintaining cohesiveness at the top while slowly changing to adapt to new conditions, especially by coopting new and slightly younger men who strengthened the bureaucratic and regional representativeness of the group and broadened its base of skills and experience. If this process had continued throughout the 1960s and 1970s and if the top leadership had not been subjected to the strains that developed from the late 1950s on, the leadership might well have been able to cope successfully with the changing demands and pressures confronting the regime without traumatic upheavals.

Instead, the shattering of the unity of China's top leadership in the Cultural Revolution decimated the Central Committee along with other key Party and state bodies. The Central Committee that emerged from the Cultural Revolution was very different from the group it replaced. The Ninth Central Committee[44] chosen in April 1969 consisted of 279 members, 170 of whom were full members and 109 alternates. Born in the midst of the bitter power struggles of the previous three years, its composition reflected the radical changes in power relations that had occurred throughout China. Even though all of its members had been able to pass, in a superficial sense at least, the essential test of loyalty to Mao, many members achieved membership in the Central Committee primarily because they had come out on top in local power struggles. No longer was it possible to say that the membership of the Committee was broadly representative of all important sectors of the top elite in China, that its members constituted a cohesive group that could work effectively together, or that its members were likely to retain top leadership posts for any extended period of time.

Little was known about many of the new members. Almost a quarter of them were "representatives of the masses" with no real constituencies, no real power, and no important political influence. They appear to have been placed on the Committee mainly for symbolic reasons. Most of them were the kind of "model" citizens the Chinese Communists have traditionally selected for well-publicized but powerless positions in various united front bodies and people's congresses. Mao doubtless wanted such people on the Central Committee in 1969 to symbolize his antibureaucratic "mass line" policies, but this inevitably raised a question as to whether Mao and his closest supporters now regarded the Central Committee as less important in policy-making terms than in the past.

A high proportion of the new members were essentially local leaders, especially local military leaders, who had not previously achieved any important national reputation or stature and about whom very little was known. In many cases, Mao and his closest supporters obviously chose a particular individual mainly because he had been the victor in a local power struggle. It was unclear, however, how many of them had actually consolidated firm control in the local areas where they operated. It was even less certain that all were genuinely committed to support Mao's values or that they would be able to operate successfully on the national stage.

The Ninth Central Committee might be compared to a still photograph of a dramatically moving scene. It reflected the power situation at one brief moment in a time of great instability. The overall turnover of personnel was spectacular. Only one-third of the living members of the previous Central Committee were reelected, while two-thirds were dropped. The purge was most devastating in its effect on the members who had been elevated to Central Committee status in 1956–58; more than three-fourths of these were ousted. The living survivors of the group that had been elected to full membership in 1945 fared better, retaining two-thirds of their seats; however, two-thirds of the 1945 alternates were purged. Although a significant core group of the highest ranking Party "old-timers" thus continued to be Central Committee members, roughly 80 percent of the Ninth Committee's total membership—226 of the total of 279—had no previous Central Committee experience.

Of the 279 members on the new Committee, about 45 percent (estimates vary from over 110 members to almost 130) were active military men.[45] Some of these were political commissars in the armed forces but a majority were active commanders of regular military units. This was a higher proportion than in the takeover period two decades earlier when military men had played such crucially important roles. The new military membership included not only strong representation of central military leaders drawn from all the major service branches, but also numerous local military leaders.

In contrast, only a quarter, or perhaps slightly more, of the Committee's total membership were men whose careers had been primarily in civilian Party and government posts—about 40 in government and 30 to 40 in the Party. For the first time in many years, a majority of the top ministerial-level government institutions in China had no one on their staffs enjoying Central Committee rank.

Another striking feature of the new Central Committee was the high proportion of members (approximately two-thirds) who were primarily local leaders without previous experience in important national roles. More than 120 of the total membership (over 40 percent) were individuals who had achieved local leadership positions in the Provincial Revolutionary Committees established throughout China during 1967–68. (A majority of these were from the military, and all the chairmen of the Revolutionary Committees were included.) This evidence of decentralization and diffusion of power indicated a dramatic reversal of the trend of the 1950s. The proportion of Central Committee members whose roots were strongest at the local rather than at the national level was as high, or possibly even higher, than in the period immediately after the Communists had achieved power.

Other changes of lesser importance differentiated the profile of the Ninth from the Eighth Central Committee. There were still no signs of dramatic generational change, but the age of some of the new members, especially among the military, was slightly below the average age of members of the previous Central Committee. The average now ranged from the high fifties for full members to the low fifties for alternates, but the overall average was still fairly high—roughly in the mid-fifties.

The northerners added to the old Central Committee in the 1950s had a low survival rate in the 1966–69 purges, and the dominance of representatives from central interior regions continued. The average educational level dropped somewhat, and a significantly lower percentage of the new membership had had any educational experience abroad.

Broadly speaking, the new Central Committee was much more heterogeneous than its predecessor group. Its membership, like that of the new Politburo, was a product of complex bargaining among those who had emerged in positions of power during the struggles of the Cultural Revolution. As in the Politburo, personal factors (especially personal ties with Mao, Lin, and their closest supporters) were obviously more important in establishing eligibility for membership than in the past. The rapid rise of so many individuals lacking strong institutional bases of power could only be explained in these terms.

The "ideological" spectrum (within the overall parameters of Marxism-Leninism) represented in the new Central Committee was wider than ever before. In particular, the gap in outlook between the radical ideologues and law-and-order-oriented local commanders was substantial. However, the membership was less representative than in the past of the varied institutional sectors of the regime, the different specialized areas of the regime's policy concerns, and the major civilian subgroups within the Chinese elite. Relatively few of the regime's specialists in such varied fields as economic policy, foreign affairs, youth work, labor problems, education, and cultural affairs were included. While many second-level leaders in these fields continued to play crucial roles in operating the regime's bureaucracies and implementing its policies, only a limited number of them were given Central Committee status.

From the outset, the prognosis for the 1969 Central Committee, like that for the 1969 Politburo and Standing Committee, was not very promising. The struggles for power that began during the Cultural Revolution did not end in 1969, and by mid-1971 significant local leadership changes had already occurred in more than a third of China's provinces. As a result, almost half of the local leaders who in 1969 had achieved Central Committee status failed to emerge as leaders of the new Provincial Party Committees established during 1970–71. Meanwhile, in Peking, another major purge at the highest levels in the summer and fall of 1971 shook the central leadership to its foundations once again. And the shock waves produced by this political earthquake at the center continued for some time to be felt in leadership groups at lower levels of the regime. Between the Lin Piao affair in 1971 and the convening of the Tenth Party Congress in 1973, the Central Committee had to be rebuilt again.

The membership of the Tenth Central Committee, announced in August 1973, revealed a variety of changes, some of great importance.[46] Even though it is not possible until more information is available to make as detailed analyses of the new body as of its predecessors, enough data are available to discern some of its principal characteristics and the principal directions of recent trends.

The overall size of the Central Committee rose slightly once again, as it had at previous Congresses. The Tenth started with a total of 319 members (one died almost immediately after the Congress)—195 regulars and 124 nonvoting alternates (as against a total of 279 in the Ninth). This enlargement in itself is not very significant, since it resulted mainly from a rise in the number of representatives of the "masses." But some of the other changes are much more important.

One major trend, not unexpectedly, has been a large turnover in the Committee's membership. Roughly two-thirds of the members of the Tenth Central Committee were members of the Ninth, it is true, but a third of them are new since 1969, replacing those dropped since the Ninth Congress. Even though this turnover is less than appeared likely as late as 1972, in part because of an acceleration in the process of rehabilitating old cadres since then, it still represents a major cleaning out of disgraced Party leaders and a large infusion of new blood.

Of the total membership of the Tenth Central Committee (excluding about twenty-five whose backgrounds are not known in detail) there are now approximately a hundred cadres from the Party and state bureaucracies, roughly eighty with backgrounds primarily as active military leaders, seven inactive Party elders, and approximately a hundred worker-peasant representatives. This rough breakdown indicates some very significant shifts in the balance of major groups in China's leadership since 1969.

The most important single change reflected in the new Central Committee, as in the new Politburo as well, has been the cutback in military representation. It is true that most of the officers now known to be occupying key military positions in China, including those in top positions at the center as well as all but one top regional military leader (the latter did better, actually, than those at the center), are now on the new Central Committee. But overall, as a percentage of the entire Central Committee's membership, active military leaders have dropped from between 40 to 50 percent in 1969 to a little more than 30 percent at present. Moreover, about three-quarters of those ousted from the Central Committee since 1969 have been military men.

Paralleling the cutback in military representation has been a significant increase in the membership of civilian cadres. Three groups have benefited: Party apparatus officials in Peking to a certain extent, cadres from the state bureaucracy to an even greater extent, and Party cadres at the provincial level most of all.

All of the men who are currently Party first secretaries in the provinces and approximately half of all provincial-level cadres, civilian and military, who now have the rank of Secretary are included. All but one of the Commanders and First Political Commissars of China's military regions are also included. It is also noteworthy that about ten high-ranking old Party leaders who were purged during the Cultural Revolution have reappeared on the Tenth Central Committee, including former Party General Secretary Teng Hsiao-p'ing and former Politburo members Li Ching-ch'uan, T'an Chen-lin, and Ulanfu. The rehabilitated cadres now on the Central Committee also include a number of former provincial Party first secretaries.

Perhaps the most striking of all the increases in the representation of major groups on the Central Committee, however, has been the increased number of cadres from the state bureaucracy. At the Central Committee level, even if not in the Politburo, the leaders of the state bureaucracy have clearly begun to make a comeback. Particularly noteworthy is the rise in the number of members from the Foreign Ministry, leaders who have been particularly closely associated with Chou.

In general, the trend has obviously been toward a gradual broadening of the base of the Central Committee and a gradual increase in the number of bureaucratic specialists in varied fields who are included in it—although the number is still smaller than before the Cultural Revolution.

The balance between leaders whose primary roots are at the provincial level and those working in Peking has not fundamentally changed, however, since 1969. (Even if "mass representatives" are excluded from one's calculations, the balance today is still in favor of provincial leaders with perhaps 55 percent having primarily local roots.) This situation parallels that in the Politburo noted earlier and highlights the unresolved problems involved in balancing central and local power in China.

Several other trends are worth noting. A number of former members regarded essentially as leftists have been dropped, although a few new ones have been added. Representatives of the "masses" have been increased since 1969, from approximately eighty persons to more than a hundred; their increase accounts for most of the overall rise in Central Committee membership. At least some of these are not simply symbolic figures but are in effect representatives of the rebuilt mass organizations. There has apparently been a conscious effort to broaden such representation, as well as representation of other special groups such as the national minorities.

It is difficult, until additional information becomes available, to describe with any precision recent trends in regard to the social characteristics of the Central Committee's membership. It seems likely, however, that some of the trends discernible earlier are continuing. There has certainly been some drop in the average age level of the total Central Committee, despite the continuing predominance of old cadres. Not only are a significant number of the representatives of the "masses" noticeably younger than most Central Committee members in the past; so too are some of the new representatives of provincial cadres. Perhaps these are signs of the beginning, but only the beginning, of a process of real generational change that will ultimately involve a transfer of power to post-"liberation" cadres. (In late 1973 a provincial radio broadcast, in Hupeh, asserted that 82 percent of nearly 300,000 new Party members recruited into the Party in the province since the Ninth Party Congress were under thirty-five years of age—and 20 percent were women.[47])

In sum, the nature of the new Central Committee, like that of the other new Party leadership groups, suggests that some progress has been made in adjusting power relations, compromising conflicting interests, and correcting some of the most glaring imbalances of the recent past, but that many tensions and sources of instability doubtless persist. Achievement of anything like the cohesion and stability that characterized the Central Committee before the Cultural Revolution seems unlikely until a new leadership can be built and consolidated after the succession.

Broader Effects of the Leadership Purge

As was indicated at the start, the focus of analysis in this chapter has been on the "top elite" in China, defined arbitrarily to include only those Chinese leaders who have achieved Central Committee status. While a comprehensive examination of the effects of the recent purges on the leadership in specific functional areas of activity in China is not possible in the space available, a few general comments are warranted on the extent of the purging of high-level personnel in a few specific fields, in order to illustrate the far-reaching effects of the Cultural Revolution on the Chinese leadership as a whole.

Among the major targets of the Cultural Revolution were the key organization men who had previously dominated the Party apparatus at central, regional, and provincial levels. A large majority of them were purged during 1967–69. For example, of the thirteen men who had made up the Party Secretariat in the early 1960s (ten regular members and three alternates), nine were ousted from the Party's top leadership during the Cultural Revolution. These were Teng Hsiao-p'ing, P'eng Chen, Wang Chia-hsiang, T'an Chen-lin, Lo Jui-ch'ing, Lu Ting-yi, Liu Lan-t'ao, Yang Shang-k'un, and Hu Ch'iao-mu. As of 1969, only four had survived politically—Li Hsueh-feng, Li Fu-ch'un, Li Hsien-nien, and K'ang Sheng—and since then Li Hsueh-feng has disappeared. In fact, the Party Secretariat as such stopped operating during the Cultural Revolution. The rosters of the Party departments under it were also decimated during 1966–69. Hard data are lacking to determine precisely who survived and who was ousted, but some clues can be found in post-1969 Chinese press reports identifying various "responsible persons" working for one or another of the "Party Departments." The great majority of the names mentioned have been new ones.

Most of the heads of the major regional Party bureaus were ousted during the Cultural Revolution, including T'ao Chu in the central south, Sung Jen-ch'iung in the northeast, and Li Ching-ch'uan in the southwest. So too were the majority of leading Party secretaries in the provinces. In fact, of the 28 men who in 1966 served as provincial first secretaries, only 8 remained in leading provincial leadership posts in 1969.[48] Of 247 persons at the provincial level who had held the rank of Party secretary (either first secretary, second secretary, secretary, or alternate secretary), 186—over three-fourths of the total—had apparently lost their jobs, and were presumably purged. A few of these are being rehabilitated, but not the majority.

The purging of top-level leaders in the government was almost as extensive. Of the 350-plus men who in 1965 had been governmental ministers or vice ministers (or had held equivalent rank in central government commissions) at least half had been purged by the end of the Cultural Revolution.[49] There were still some old faces, including important vice ministers, but more than half of all ministers and vice ministers were subjected to political attack during the Cultural Revolution. Some of these began gradually to reappear after the Cultural Revolution, and by 1973 it was evident that a significant number would be rehabilitated. It was equally clear, however, that many had been permanently ousted.

There were also far-reaching changes affecting leading personnel in many specific functional fields, including culture and education, political and legal affairs, and economic policy making. The available data on the disruption of China's top economic elite provide a good concrete example.[50] One detailed study indicates that, as of January 1966, there were 316 known leaders holding 337 top positions (of assistant minister rank or higher) in central government economic agencies in Peking. By 1969 one-third of these were believed to have been purged and only one-fourth were presumed to have survived in leadership positions; the fate of the others was uncertain, although many of them had probably also been purged. Of the highest-ranking 75 leaders in the economic field (men with Central Committee status), about 70 percent had apparently been ousted. Of the others, many if not most of whom could be regarded primarily as bureaucratic specialists rather than major political leaders in the bureaucracies, the percentage ousted was lower but nevertheless still high—perhaps between 30 and 40 percent.

Even the military, which emerged as the dominant political force in China during the Cultural Revolution, was itself subjected to extensive purging. Despite the fact that Lin Piao as Minister of National Defense had already presided over a general shakeup of the military leadership during the first half of the 1960s (involving a high turnover of commanders and commissars at the military district level), another sweeping purge occurred once the Cultural Revolution was under way.[51] During 1966–67, nearly one-third of the top military leaders in China were replaced. Roughly half of the highest military leaders in Peking— leading members of the Military Affairs Commission, the Ministry of National Defense, the General Staff, the General Political Department, and the service arms and specialties—were affected. In addition, approximately 40 percent of the top military figures (commanders and commissars and their deputies) in China's military regions and districts were apparently ousted. Especially hard hit were the commissars because of their very close links to the Party apparatus, but the turnover among commanders was very high. Finally, in 1971, the death of Lin Piao and the purge of his top military hierarchy in Peking, followed by purges at lower levels, had repercussions that are still being felt.

In sum, a sizable portion of China's experts in almost every specialized field came under attack during the Cultural Revolution, and many were permanently purged. However, as Chou En-lai has attempted —since 1969 and especially since 1971—to repair China's bureaucracies as well as consolidate a new leadership, an increasing number of those victimized in earlier years, including some top-level leaders, have made a comeback. The rehabilitation of "second-level" leaders has been even more extensive. How far this rehabilitation of old cadres will ultimately go remains to be seen. There is no doubt, however, that even if it is extensive, the majority of the top leaders who guided China's fate in the 1950s and 1960s are not likely to recover their past power. A new group of bureaucratic specialists—many of them somewhat younger than those purged and most of them little known to the public at home or abroad—seems to be emerging. The task of welding them into a unified and effective leadership will obviously take time, however, since all who survived the Cultural Revolution have been affected in subtle ways by the legacy of tensions, conflicts, and uncertainties resulting from that upheaval.

The succession is clearly the foremost domestic concern in the minds of China's political elite today. When I visited China in 1972–73, Party cadres everywhere were prepared to discuss the succession, and they acknowledged that it would be a major milestone in Chinese Communist history and another crucial test in the "struggle between two lines." Most of them predicted that a new and stable collective leadership—doubtless with Chou En-lai in a key position, if he is still on the scene—would emerge and that such a leadership would be able to define and adhere to a "correct line" in the future. One sensed, however, a basic uncertainty about the process of succession, who would finally emerge at the top, and what the "correct line" would be after Mao goes.

Even if one accepts that the Tenth Party Congress in August 1973 was a convocation to prepare for the succession and to choose leaders who would be able to manage it, it is reasonable to believe that the members of China's new Politburo may have almost as many unanswered questions as ordinary cadres have about what will happen when Mao dies.

The Uncertain Future

The one certainty about the future is that China still faces a major task in rebuilding and consolidating a new leadership and that the all-important problem of succession will—in the relatively near future—add greatly to the complexity of the task. As emphasized earlier, the chances for a relatively smooth transition and the creation of a leadership that balances the conflicting interests of the varied centers of power in China will doubtless be enhanced if Chou En-lai remains in a position to manage the succession process at the time of Mao's death. At present, with Mao's blessing, Chou is clearly in charge and is shaping China's policies both at home and abroad. The top leadership still appears, however, to be in the process of sorting out relationships among the Party, government, and army, and these relationships are still uncertain.

To create a workable collective leadership that can survive after Mao goes, Chou will have to continue his efforts to compromise with, and at the same time restrain, both the "radicals" and the military. With the help and cooperation of others, he will have to broaden further the regime's top leadership groups, making them more representative of China's diverse bureaucratic interests than at present. This will probably require bringing to the top an increasing number of younger second-level leaders who have not in the past participated in decision making at the highest levels and are therefore little known to the public in China, to say nothing of the outside world. Although the prospects for building a viable new leadership may be reasonably good as long as Chou is on the scene, success is by no means certain. And without Chou to manage the succession process, the outcome becomes more problematic.

The chances for a smooth transition may be greatest if, in the period immediately ahead, Mao fades into the background and relinquishes his power while still alive, allowing Chou, while he remains vigorous and is in an accepted position of leadership, to continue his efforts to consolidate the basis for the post-Mao collective leadership. Even if Mao dies in the near future, the chances that the transition can be successfully managed without a breakdown of the coalition now evolving may be reasonably good if Chou is able to exercise his skillful leadership for a significant period thereafter.

But there is no guarantee that Chou, who is seventy-five, will have enough time to consolidate a new situation—or even, for that matter, that he will outlive eighty-year-old Mao. If both Mao and Chou die, a crucial question will then be whether those who replace them will somehow be able to reach the compromises necessary to form a viable new collective leadership and avoid open conflict. At this time, several men younger than Chou seem to be political frontrunners who might play critical roles in such a situation. They include Party leaders Chang Ch'un-ch'iao and Wang Hung-wen and PLA leaders Li Teh-sheng, Ch'en Hsi-lien, and Hsu Shih-yu. Perhaps Wang Tung-hsing and Hua Kuo-feng should also be included in this list, which might well change, of course, before such a situation arose. These are all able men, but it is not clear what their relationships are or whether they would be willing and able to continue the complex process of political reconstruction and consolidation that Chou has been attempting. Chou has been trying to work out acceptable compromises, build new coalitions, search for a delicate political balance, and establish a strengthened consensus. There is no doubt that such an approach will still be desperately needed, not only after Mao, but after Chou as well.

If Chou does not survive Mao—and possibly even if he does—one cannot exclude the possibility that the succession will precipitate an open struggle for power. At worst, this could lead to renewed social and political disorder of the kind that wracked China during the Cultural Revolution. If such a struggle began—or if it seemed in prospect —the possibility would increase that some military leader or leaders, perhaps one or more of those now on the Politburo or perhaps others less well known, would attempt to reassert the PLA's political primacy. The prospect then would probably be for more overt military rule and a substantial delay in the creation of a more broadly based civilian-led leadership.

These alternatives by no means exhaust the conceivable developments in the period immediately after Mao's death. They are sufficient,
however, to underline the fact that China is approaching a new period
in its history, unlike any the Chinese Communists have experienced in
the past. China faces, in fact, not a single succession problem, but at
least two, since the men who first succeed Mao will probably be members of the Party's "takeover generation" who themselves will pass
from the scene before long. Within the decade of the 1970s, therefore,
it is certain that China will have to grapple not only with the problem
of replacing the supreme leader who has dominated the Communist regime since its inception but also with the broad problem of generational
change at the top. Whatever the results, there will doubtless be a fairly
long period of transition before a new post-Mao, and post-takeover
generation, leadership can be firmly established and stabilized.

V

China and the World

THE INTERPLAY of the domestic forces discussed in previous chapters will clearly be the primary determinant of the nature of the Chinese Communist regime and the broad thrust of its policies in the period ahead. But the key question for other nations is how China will interact with the outside world. What will China's priority foreign policy objectives be and how are they likely to be pursued? What impact is China likely to have on the international community, and how should other countries view and respond to Chinese activities on the world stage? If it is assumed that China is now—and will be for some years—in a period of transition, what effect is this likely to have on external relations?

While domestic political developments will have a major impact on Peking's foreign policy, China's relations with the outside world will also be shaped by developments beyond its borders and by the responses of the Peking leadership to these developments. What perceptions have the Chinese had—and are they likely to have in the future—of the international environment and its relationship to China's interests? What specific goals, both long run and short run, will shape concrete and specific foreign policy decisions? To what extent will ideological considerations and "revolutionary interests" influence China's foreign policy behavior, or will it largely be shaped by more conventional "national interests"? Are defensive considerations or expansionist aims likely to be more important policy determinants? To what extent is foreign policy likely to reflect Chinese initiatives or to be reactive to forces and developments abroad? Is China, on balance, likely to be inward-looking or outward-looking?

And what can be said about China's probable capabilities—military, political, and economic—to pursue the goals it sets? What Chinese foreign policy strategies and tactics—and style—can be foreseen in the period ahead? Will Peking be inclined to use military force in pursuing its foreign policy aims or will it rely on nonmilitary means? To what extent will foreign policy be constrained by domestic factors? And are differences within the Chinese leadership likely to have a major influence on foreign policy?

Chinese Foreign Policy, 1949–73

China's foreign policies, like its domestic policies, have undergone many changes in direction and emphasis during the past twenty-three years and therefore cannot be characterized with simple generalizations. At different times since 1949, Peking's leaders have had sharply differing perceptions of the opportunities and the dangers confronting them, have shifted national priorities and goals, and have pursued varying strategies and tactics.[1] Despite all the changes, however, there have been significant continuities, and it is important to understand both the elements of change and the elements of continuity.

The Immediate Post-Takeover Period

When the Chinese Communists first established their new regime, their principal goals were to complete their revolution, end all vestiges of Western imperialist and colonialist influence in China, reunify the country, and reestablish centralized control over all areas considered to be Chinese territory. In the flush of victory, both nationalistic sentiment and ideological fervor were at a high pitch, and Peking's leaders were in no mood to be compromising. They proceeded to establish military control over areas such as Hainan and Tibet, and prepared to invade Taiwan. Within China, they applied gradual but effective pressures to eliminate Western personnel and influences.

The image of the international community propagated by the Chinese Communist leadership in 1949—shared at the time with leaders in Moscow and, for that matter, in Washington as well—reflected the cold war views of the time. The world was portrayed in essentially black-and-white, bipolar terms. The crucial fact of international life was believed to be an intense struggle between two blocs or "camps"—a revolutionary "socialist camp" headed by the Soviet Union and a counterrevolutionary "imperialist camp" headed by the United States.[2] The

Chinese, like the Russians and Americans, regarded the arena for this struggle as worldwide. Neutrality was said to be impossible. There was no possibility, Mao declared in 1949, of pursuing a "third road";[3] all nations and forces must of necessity be linked to or associated with one side or the other.

Several conclusions followed naturally from this set of premises. The Chinese decided that in such a bipolar world their interests required close alignment with the Soviet Union and the Communist bloc. Ideology was obviously a major factor influencing this conclusion, but Peking's security concerns were also involved. The new Chinese regime considered the United States to be China's prime adversary and the main threat to its interests. Several years earlier, when they were still struggling for power, Chinese Communist leaders had intimated to American officials that they might be prepared to adopt a more flexible posture, less hostile to the United States, and perhaps less clearly aligned with the USSR.[4] Some flexibility may have lasted until 1949,[5] but now, in view of the direct support provided by the United States to the Nationalists during the final years of China's civil war and in the cold war climate of worldwide conflict between the Communist and non-Communist blocs, Peking adopted an overtly antagonistic posture toward the United States.

Despite signs that the United States was gradually disengaging from China during 1948–49, Chinese leaders in early 1950 signed a thirty-year military alliance with the Soviet Union, directed against both the United States and Japan.[6] This was the most important single foreign policy decision made by Peking in the period immediately after 1949, and it established the basic framework for Chinese foreign policy throughout the 1950s. Never before had any Chinese government joined a well-defined bloc or signed a close military alliance with a major foreign power. The Communists' decision to do so in 1950 proved to be a mixed blessing. While the alliance reinforced China's defense capabilities, in a period when it was relatively weak and was concerned about a potential U.S. threat, the close alliance with Moscow limited Peking's freedom of action in various ways. Over time, moreover, it proved to be disappointing to the Chinese in other fundamental respects. Before many years had passed, clashes between Moscow and Peking over both ideology and national interests led to open Sino-Soviet competition and conflict, with the result that for all practical purposes the alliance lapsed. In the early 1950s, however, there was no reason for Peking's leaders to anticipate this course of events, and they deliberately chose to make the Sino-Soviet alliance the keystone of China's foreign policy.

At the time of their takeover, the Chinese Communists also made a point of identifying their interests closely with Communist-led insurrectionaries throughout the world, most particularly with those who were mounting efforts in 1948–49 to seize power throughout much of Asia. Peking openly proclaimed its support for these revolutionary struggles abroad, and gave strong moral support to Communist movements in many countries.[7] In short, the revolutionary component in its foreign policy was overt and intense in this period. This was not surprising. As revolutionaries who had just won power in China, Peking's leaders had a self-image that dictated a posture of open support for fellow revolutionaries elsewhere. Self-confidence born of their own success impelled them to hold up their experience as a model for others to emulate.

The revolutionary militancy of the Chinese Communists was largely expressed, however, in rhetoric rather than concrete action. Even though Peking did give support—in the form of matériel and training—to the Communists in neighboring Indochina, and proffered advice to others, it did not back revolutions outside China's borders with its own combat forces. The task of consolidating power at home was Peking's primary concern, and while the Chinese fervently hoped that revolutionaries elsewhere would succeed, they were not inclined or prepared to help them directly with Chinese troops. In sum, Chinese support for revolutions abroad was largely in the form of moral exhortation.

The Korean War: A New Situation

The outbreak of the Korean war and the decisions relating to this war made in both Washington and Peking created a very new situation for China, and for East Asia as a whole.[8] In mid-1950, following the North Korean attack on South Korea, the United States decided to send American troops to support South Korea. At the same time Washington intervened again in the Chinese civil war, sending the U.S. fleet to "neutralize" the Taiwan Strait. Later, ignoring Chinese warnings, the United States ordered its troops to cross the 38th parallel in Korea to pursue the war northward. Peking responded by deciding to intervene in Korea itself, at which point the war became essentially a U.S.–Chinese conflict. From late 1950 until mid-1953, when both sides finally accepted the fact of stalemate and signed a truce, the Korean war was for China—as well as for the United States—a foreign policy concern to which all others were subordinated.

In retrospect it seems clear that both the United States and China made serious miscalculations during the early months of the Korean war, with consequences that were to shape their respective policies for years to come. Both reacted in ways they believed to be defensive against threats they perceived to come from the other side. Washington tended to generalize the very real and immediate threat posed by the North Korean attack in Korea into a challenge posed by the entire Communist bloc to the entire "free world." In the Chinese case, U.S. intervention in Taiwan and Korea revived images of past threats to China's territorial integrity and security posed in earlier years by Japan.

Available evidence suggests that, while Peking from the outset gave moral support to the North Koreans in their attack on the South, it was the Soviet Union rather than China that was initially involved in direct military support of the attack; apparently the Chinese did not envisage or plan for Chinese military intervention.[9] Peking's decision to intervene was probably influenced by several factors. When American troops crossed the 38th parallel, Peking probably concluded that the United States posed a direct threat to China's security, in particular to Manchuria. Chinese leaders may also have believed that, even if no attacks were launched against Chinese territory, defeat of the North Korean regime would eliminate an important buffer area on China's critical northeastern flank and create a security threat for the future. It is probable, also, that the Soviet Union pressed for Chinese intervention to prevent a North Korean defeat, and that Peking concluded that its new alliance with Moscow required China to assist in a struggle that obviously had broad implications for the entire conflict between the Communist and non-Communist worlds. In any case, whatever the specific reasons, Peking decided to send its own troops to Korea in the fall of 1950, even though this involved high military risks. These risks included the possibility of U.S. nuclear attack, although the Chinese doubtless hoped that their alliance with Moscow would help to deter such an attack, as in fact it did.[10]

The Korean war significantly enhanced the prestige of the new Communist regime in China. The recognition that Chinese troops prevented the United States and United Nations forces from defeating North Korea impressed upon the world the fact that China was no longer a helpless giant, but rather a dynamic and highly mobilized nation determined to defend its vital interests and assert its place in the world. The war also, however, involved sizable political as well as military costs for Peking. One was a significant delay in China's entry into the international community and the postponement by several years of normal state-to-state relations between China and the majority of the non-Communist nations of the world.

In the period between the establishment of China's new regime and the start of the Korean war, Peking had established diplomatic relations with all of the other Communist nations except Yugoslavia, but it was deliberately cautious and slow about formalizing relations with non-Communist governments. Although fourteen non-Communist nations recognized Peking during 1949–50, the Chinese had established diplomatic relations with only six of them before the start of the Korean war, and with only two more by the end of the war.[11] The Chinese leaders obviously placed a relatively low priority in this period on the importance of state-to-state relations with non-Communist states. In any case, Washington's opposition to recognizing the Communist regime and American pressure on allies to follow the U.S. lead in this policy made it difficult for Peking to expand its relations.

The war created new fears and hostilities in many non-Communist nations that continued long after the war was over, and the image of China as an expansionist aggressive power was a major factor inducing numerous nations to postpone recognition of Peking for many years. Most important, the legacy of mutual hostility between the United States and China left by the war led Washington to use its influence for roughly a decade and a half thereafter to do all it could to try to isolate China and exclude it from the international community, thus creating serious barriers to Peking's subsequent efforts to achieve worldwide recognition and expand its influence by conventional political means.

Post-Korea Trends

Even before the Korean war had ended, Peking was beginning to modify its assessment of the world situation and to adjust its foreign policy strategy and tactics. Whereas from 1949 to 1952 China's foreign policy interests had focused almost exclusively on other Communist nations and parties and closely associated insurrectionary and revolutionary forces, in late 1952, under the slogan of "peaceful coexistence," the cultivation of nonofficial relations with many different kinds of groups abroad was begun. Both Moscow and Peking now recognized the desirability of adopting a more flexible and somewhat less doctrinaire approach to the world—one aimed at creating a broad united front of "people's" forces directed against the "imperialists." It was at this time that Peking initiated an active program of "people's diplomacy."[12]

Soon after the end of the war, it went further and began to show a new interest in expanding state-to-state relations with non-Communist nations, searching for opportunities to broaden China's formal diplomatic ties. Between 1954 and the end of 1958, Peking established relations with thirteen more non-Communist nations, and with Yugoslavia. Three were non-Communist Western European states (including the United Kingdom), but the rest were nations—mostly small—in the developing world.

Chinese policy in the period immediately after the Korean war was still predicated on the assumption that it was essential to maintain extremely close ties with the Soviet Union and other Communist bloc nations, and to coordinate policies among the Communist states in competing against the United States and the "imperialist camp." But by now the Chinese had begun to acquire a somewhat more sophisticated view of the world in general, and gradually recognized that the leaders of most "neutralist" nations could not be viewed simply as "running dogs" of the United States. Accordingly, Peking's leaders decided that to expand Chinese—and Communist bloc—influence and weaken the position of the United States, a major aim of Chinese policy should be to cultivate and woo the neutralist nations, in order to draw them into a broad anti-imperialist, anticolonial united front.[13] This policy soon began to pay limited dividends, despite the fact that adamant U.S. opposition slowed the process of expanding China's international ties. Peking's main diplomatic successes in the middle and late 1950s were in South Asia, the Middle East, and North Africa, areas where in fact China's concrete interests were comparatively limited and its capacity to play a major political and economic role was not great.

Thus, even though China began to shift in the 1952–54 period from a fairly narrow doctrinaire policy based on the concept of a bipolar world toward a more flexible policy aimed at creation of a broader united front to align neutralists with the Communist camp, Peking continued to feel threatened and on the defensive. However, its persistent use of militant rhetoric appeared threatening to many of its neighbors as well as to much of the rest of the world, and suspicion about China's intentions was heightened by Peking's continued use of limited military pressures and probes in pursuit of some of its priority goals in areas immediately adjacent to China.

Two serious international crises involving China occurred in the period immediately after the Korean war. Each intensified fears of Chinese intentions, even though in neither case did Peking intervene militarily to try to achieve its maximum goals. One of these was the Indochina crisis of 1954.[14] Although the Chinese were not the initiators of this crisis, Peking's large-scale material support of the Vietnamese Communists and Western anxiety about the possibility of direct Chinese military intervention led to the Geneva Conference on Indochina in the summer of 1954. At that conference, where for the first time since 1949 Chinese Communist representatives participated actively in a major international meeting, Peking ultimately threw its weight in favor of a compromise settlement which divided Vietnam at the 17th parallel. The Chinese, like the Vietnamese Communists, doubtless assumed that this agreement would be a prelude to a fairly rapid Communist political takeover in Vietnam; nevertheless the Chinese position at the conference indicated that Peking placed highest priority on the need to forestall the danger of another large-scale conflict involving the major powers and on the desirability of ensuring the survival of a buffer area adjacent to China, rather than on the need to ensure an immediate Communist takeover of all Indochina.

The second crisis in this period, which *was* initiated by Peking, focused on the small Nationalist-controlled offshore islands in the Taiwan area near the China coast.[15] Recovery of control over Taiwan was one of Peking's fundamental national aims, but the presence of the U.S. Seventh Fleet now blocked the possibility of direct attack. Peking undertook to see if Taiwan's U.S. protectors could be dislodged by means short of invasion. Within three months of the signing of the Indochina agreement at Geneva, Peking launched a large-scale bombardment of Quemoy, creating a situation of great tension and raising the specter of possible war. In retrospect it seems clear that Peking was not prepared to launch a full-scale invasion of the islands in the face of strong U.S. as well as Nationalist opposition. Its primary objective was to test whether, by means of limited and controlled military pressures and threats, it could create tensions that might ultimately split the United States from the Nationalists and lead to a withdrawal of the American military presence from the Taiwan area. When Peking concluded that its pressures were not achieving this goal but instead were creating a new danger of major conflict, it backed away from direct confrontation, allowed the crisis to subside, and turned to political tactics to pursue its goals in relation to Taiwan. Peking's military probe in this case did, however, reinforce the image already accepted in many non-Communist nations—and in particular the United States—of China as a militant expansionist power, with effects that were both far-reaching and long-lasting.

The net effect of these developments and of the response of the non-Communist nations to them was to intensify the level of hostility in U.S.–China relations, increase the fear of China among the leaders of many of its immediate neighbors, and stimulate greater efforts by the United States to induce other non-Communist nations to participate in a structure of military bases and alliances on China's periphery designed to "contain" what was perceived to be a dangerous threat of Chinese expansionism. In 1954, the United States not only signed a mutual defense treaty with the Nationalist regime on Taiwan, further strengthening the ties between Washington and Taipei, but also took the lead in creating the Southeast Asia Treaty Organization which, together with U.S. treaties already signed between 1951 and 1953 with Australia, New Zealand, Japan, the Philippines, and South Korea, completed a network of alliances and bases that partially "surrounded" China.[16] Initially the treaties with the Philippines, Australia, and New Zealand were made with Japan in mind, but by the mid-1950s their primary significance was in relation to China.

From Peking's viewpoint, these American initiatives—as well as the cold war rhetoric of Secretary of State John Foster Dulles and other U.S. policy makers in the 1950s—reinforced fears of external pressures, encirclement, and even possible attack by the United States. Peking's security concerns still focused almost exclusively on the United States at this time, and its leaders were acutely aware of China's vulnerability to U.S. military action. Even though the Sino-Soviet alliance provided an important counterbalance to the United States and a deterrent against nuclear attack, the Chinese probably felt genuinely threatened—a fact that reinforced their determination to build up their independent military strength.

The Bandung Period

From their position of comparative military weakness and relative political isolation, Peking's leaders increasingly recognized in the 1950s the need to take new political initiatives designed to broaden China's relations with non-Communist as well as Communist nations. Their goal was to break out of isolation and to create a united front that would have substantial Third World support. They also hoped to weaken gradually the international position of the United States, particularly in Asia.

In 1954–55, therefore, Peking adopted a new foreign policy strategy which deemphasized China's revolutionary objectives and stressed the theme of "peaceful coexistence." Peking now proclaimed its desire to develop normalized state-to-state relations with a wide variety of non-Communist nations, and it adopted many new policies that were notable for their flexibility, relative moderation, and stress on conciliation.

The first important manifestation of this new approach was the signing, in 1954, of a Sino-Indian agreement on Tibet, in which Peking and New Delhi cosponsored the so-called five principles of peaceful coexistence. Then, in April 1955, Premier Chou En-lai attended the Bandung Conference of Asian and African states in Indonesia and attempted to assume the role of peacemaker, conciliator, and spokesman for the Asian-African world.[17] He also proposed negotiations with the United States on "relaxing tension in the Taiwan area" and tried to reassure Asian nations worried about their Chinese minorities that China would not attempt to manipulate the overseas Chinese to subvert the non-Communist governments under which they lived.

During what has come to be known as the "Bandung period," which lasted until 1957–58, Peking worked hard to establish its respectability and responsibility as a major power and to underline its desire for peaceful, friendly relations with non-Communist nations. "Revolution cannot be exported," the Chinese Premier proclaimed.[18] Going beyond mere tolerance for the neutralist nations, Peking in effect became a sponsor of neutralism. In particular, great importance was placed on the need for cooperation between China and India, which under Prime Minister Nehru was perhaps the most influential leader and symbol of the neutralist and anticolonial nations. Peking's efforts after Bandung to expand its state-to-state foreign relations produced gradual and limited, but nevertheless significant, results. Efforts to promote foreign trade were part of the new policy, and China also began in this period its first programs of foreign aid to non-Communist nations, and its program of "people's diplomacy" was greatly expanded.

One can only speculate about how China's international relations might have developed if Peking had pursued its Bandung strategy for an extended period. It seems likely that Peking's policy makers could have made steady progress in obtaining general acceptance of China by the international community and could have increased Chinese influence abroad substantially, primarily by conventional political and economic means. In fact, however, the Bandung period proved to be brief.

Militancy Revived

By late 1957 Peking had abandoned its relatively flexible and moderate posture of 1954–57 and was moving toward a much more militant and revolutionary stance once again. Proclaiming that the "East Wind Prevails over the West Wind," Mao called in November 1957 for greater militancy on the part of the entire Communist world toward the "imperialists" and in particular toward the United States.[19] The causes of this major shift in strategy are still a subject of debate. However, it is clear that several important factors were involved.

In a basic sense, the shift reflected changes in the Chinese domestic political and economic situation. It paralleled the change within China from the relatively pragmatic policies of the first Five-Year Plan to a more revolutionary period of economic and social policy. The Bandung period and China's first Five-Year Plan were mutually reinforcing; both at home and abroad the Chinese leaders gave priority concern to concrete immediate goals and deemphasized long-range ideological and revolutionary aims. The increased militancy of Chinese foreign policy beginning in late 1957 coincided with Mao's abandonment of the Soviet model for Chinese development and his decision to push new domestic policies that were to be a prelude to the radical Great Leap Forward and Commune Program of 1958. Both Peking's "East Wind" policy abroad and its "Great Leap" policies at home were manifestations of Mao's reassertion of his distinctive revolutionary values and visions.

China's 1957 foreign policy shift also reflected a new assessment by Mao of the overall international situation and the prevailing balance of world forces. Mao put forward his "East Wind" slogan when he was in Moscow to attend a Soviet-convened conference of Communist states and parties, on the occasion of the fortieth anniversary of the Bolshevik Revolution, shortly after the Russians had launched their first satellite and intercontinental ballistic missile. He took the position that these Soviet space and missile accomplishments marked a new "turning point" in the "world situation," and apparently concluded that the world balance had been significantly altered, psychologically if not militarily, in favor of the Communists.[20] Although Moscow did not fully accept this assessment, Mao nevertheless argued that all Communist nations and parties should take advantage of the altered balance to press much harder against the "imperialist camp" to achieve their goals. By this time he had already begun to have doubts about Moscow's leadership of the Communist bloc and world movement, as a result of Khrushchev's destalinization program and the ensuing crises in Eastern Europe in 1956, and he urged the Soviet Union not only to reassert revolutionary discipline and orthodoxy within the Communist bloc but also to adopt a more militant "forward policy" toward the West.

A third and more subtle factor influencing the Chinese decision to adopt a new "hard line" in 1957 may have been simple impatience. Although China's international image had improved, its political influence had expanded, and its acceptance by the world community had increased during the Bandung period, the process was far too slow from Peking's point of view. The United States continued its hard-line policy of "isolation and pressure" against China, rejecting in 1955 several conciliatory Chinese gestures and initiatives, including proposals for trade, exchanges of journalists, and a meeting of foreign ministers. In large part because of American opposition, the majority of non-Communist nations still held back from recognizing the Peking regime, and the Chinese Communists were still excluded from the United Nations and other international bodies. Although the U.S.–Chinese ambassadorial talks started in 1955 still continued, Peking had not made any significant progress in weakening the ties between Washington and the Nationalists. In fact, as Peking saw it, the United States was moving steadily toward a "two Chinas" policy, and the prospect of "liberating" Taiwan appeared to be more distant than ever.

Whatever the explanation for the 1957 shift, it had profound effects. From late 1957 on, Peking demonstrated in one situation after another a renewed commitment to militant revolutionary values. In the spring of 1958, it launched a major propaganda attack on "revisionism" within the Communist world, focusing its criticism on Yugoslavia and pressing the Soviet Union to take a harder line against all "liberalizing" tendencies in Communist nations and parties. In the summer of the same year, when the United States intervened in the Middle East during a crisis involving Lebanon and Iraq, Peking urged Moscow to take strong action, and there was even talk in Peking of sending Chinese "volunteers" to the Middle East; although this gesture had little practical significance, it nevertheless symbolized Peking's new posture. In Vietnam and Laos, in the ensuing period, China gave moral and material support to active insurrection.

In none of these situations, however, did Peking intervene with its own combat forces, and the verbal militancy was not indiscriminate. China continued to woo such countries as Cambodia, for example; and when the situation in Laos reached a critical stage, Peking ultimately threw its weight in favor of the compromise political settlement effected at the Geneva Conference of 1962.[21] Nevertheless, the broad thrust of the new Chinese strategy from late 1957 on made it appear that Peking was again prepared to use threats and pressures to promote its revolutionary goals. Not surprisingly, Peking's new stance tarnished China's Bandung image and intensified fears in many quarters about Chinese intentions.

Although Peking's new hard-line strategy obviously affected China's relationship with smaller powers, the more important result was that the new policies ultimately placed Peking at odds with all four major nations whose interests impinged most directly on China—not only the United States but also Japan, India, and, most serious of all, the Soviet Union. By 1960 China found itself more isolated, in terms of big power relationships, than ever before.

In early 1958, Peking decided to exert direct and intense pressures on the government of Prime Minister Nobusuke Kishi of Japan, to try to influence the outcome of the upcoming Japanese elections and to induce Tokyo to loosen its ties with the United States and adopt a more compliant policy toward China. In perhaps the most blatant attempt that Peking has made to use economic policy as an instrument of political pressure, all trade relations with the Japanese were severed and Peking called for major changes in Japan's leadership and policies. Although the immediate results were clearly counterproductive, Peking kept up the pressure in a continuing effort to stimulate new tensions in

American-Japanese relations. It was not until after the U.S.–Japan security treaty had been renewed in 1960—and after the Sino-Soviet split, which necessitated a basic reevaluation of China's trade and overall policies, had come into the open—that Peking abandoned its policy of economic and political pressure on Tokyo and began to repair Sino-Japanese relations.

In the fall of 1958, in the midst of the Great Leap Forward, Peking launched its second major military probe against the offshore islands.[22] As in 1954–55, the Chinese Communists apparently did not intend to undertake a major military operation but rather to strain relations between Washington and Taipei and thus weaken U.S. support for the Nationalist regime; but once again the tactic of limited threats and pressures failed to achieve this objective. At the height of this crisis, the danger of war was even greater than four years earlier, and in the end Peking backed down and reverted to negotiations and political tactics. The net effect was to reinforce the American image of a hostile and dangerous China—and to postpone any real possibility of reducing tension in the Taiwan area or improving relations between China and the United States.

The Sino-Indian crisis of 1959 was the next important episode in Chinese foreign policy in this period.[23] Its immediate causes were rooted in the problems Peking was encountering in maintaining political control in Tibet—an area of Chinese colonial rule over which all Chinese leaders, including the Nationalists, have claimed sovereignty, but where the local population has consistently resented and resisted Chinese control. Tibetan disaffection, which had steadily grown for some years, exploded in 1959 in open revolt. When Peking suppressed the uprising with a heavy hand, the Dalai Lama and thousands of other Tibetans fled to India, where the Indian government granted them sanctuary. Bitter mutual recriminations ensued between China and India, with Peking claiming that the Indians had instigated the revolt and New Delhi openly criticizing China's actions and charging publicly that China had for some years been violating the Indian border. Whatever the perceptions and motives underlying Peking's tactics in this crisis, it marked the beginning of the end of Peking's policy of cooperation with India in wooing the Third World, which had been a basic element of Chinese foreign policy since 1954.

Border tensions between China and India steadily grew after the Tibetan revolt, reaching a climax in the short Sino-Indian "border war" of 1962. Blame for this conflict cannot be assigned exclusively to either side. Both countries had an arguable basis for their particular territorial claims, and neither was willing to consider compromises acceptable to the other. Chinese military action, moreover, may have been initiated partially in response to Indian military pressures northward.[24] Nevertheless, Peking's attack was a calculated exercise of intense military pressure, which was doubtless designed to, and in fact did, humiliate India and strengthen Peking's political hand. Even though China's forces generally did not penetrate beyond the territories claimed by Peking, the attack highlighted India's weakness and vulnerability.

Between 1959 and 1962, Peking shifted to an overtly hostile political and diplomatic posture toward New Delhi, maintaining pressure on the Indians while cultivating all of India's neighbors. Thereafter, support of Pakistan against India became an increasingly important component of China's foreign policy. Peking not only granted the Pakistanis substantial military and economic aid; in 1965, and again in 1971, China gave strong moral and political support to the Pakistani position in Indian-Pakistani conflicts over Kashmir and Bangladesh. In neither case, however, did China directly intervene, nor was it able in either case to determine the ultimate military outcome.

The Sino-Soviet Dispute

While growing tension in areas to the east and south of China in the late 1950s were important to Peking, Chinese leaders increasingly were compelled to turn their attention to the north and west. By far the most important development in China's foreign relations in the late 1950s was the widening rift between Peking and Moscow.[25] Whereas Peking's foreign policy in the 1950s had been premised on the concept of a worldwide struggle between the Soviet-led socialist camp and the American-led imperialist camp and had as its keystone the Sino-Soviet alliance, by 1960 the Communist bloc was deeply divided, and the future of the Peking-Moscow alliance was problematic. This new situation fundamentally changed China's international position and greatly altered the basic framework for Peking's perceptions of the world. Major changes in China's foreign policy strategies and tactics were obviously required.

In tracing the origins of the Sino-Soviet dispute, it can be argued that the causes must be sought in deep-rooted historical, geopolitical, and cultural differences between the two countries and in ideological and policy differences between the Chinese and Soviet Communist parties that long predated any overt signs of conflict in the post-1949 period. There is some validity to this view. The historical record of Sino-Russian relations for centuries has been replete with recurrent conflict, mutual suspicion, and friction; and from the 1920s on, there were serious differences on many occasions between Chinese and Soviet Communist party leaders. In the first half of the 1950s, however, the Chinese Communists seemed confident that close cooperation with the Russians was both possible and desirable, and committed themselves to strengthen the alliance in every way possible. During the Stalinist period, and especially during the Korean war, there were some strains in the Sino-Soviet relationship, but Peking subordinated any doubts and dissatisfactions it may have had. In the immediate post-Stalin period, when both Moscow and Peking took steps to cement their relationship, the alliance reached its peak of intimacy.

The Chinese now date the start of their dispute with the Russians to 1956, and from their perspective this dating has considerable logic. Khrushchev's dramatic destalinization moves that year, taken without prior consultation with Peking, raised serious doubts in the Chinese leaders' minds about the Soviet Union's policies and capacity for leadership of the Communist world. During the ensuing crises in Poland and Hungary, these doubts increased, and the Chinese began for the first time to articulate their own independent views about basic issues affecting the Communist bloc and movement as a whole; for the first time, Peking intervened directly in the politics of Eastern Europe. At the Moscow meeting of Communist states and parties in 1957, it became clear that the Chinese and Russians now held divergent views on many broad ideological, political, and strategic issues. Thereafter, differences between Peking and Moscow over such issues developed gradually but steadily until finally in 1960 Peking took the initiative in launching a bitter polemical attack against Soviet "revisionism."[26] Moscow responded not merely with its own propaganda counterattack but by withdrawing all of its technicians and ending all assistance to China.

The arguments in the Sino-Soviet debate as it evolved in this period focused on such broad ideological and strategic issues as the present character of imperialism, the inevitability or noninevitability of war, the nature of "peaceful coexistence," the feasibility and desirability of using violent revolutionary methods, the possibility of disarmament and détente with the West, and many others. On all of these issues,

Peking took the more militant revolutionary position and accused Moscow of departing from Marxist-Leninist orthodoxy. The ideological element in the dispute was obviously important and reflected a widening gap between Khrushchev's and Mao's perceptions of the world and their basic policy predispositions both at home and abroad. Underlying the polemical arguments, however, were a growing number of specific policy differences and clashes of national interest that had relatively little to do with ideology. These conflicts of interest, above all, led to the ultimate breakup of the Sino-Soviet alliance.

Overall policy toward the United States and the West was one of the crucial issues on which Soviet and Chinese views steadily diverged. Khrushchev, as leader of a major nuclear power, became increasingly convinced that Soviet policy must be adjusted to the realities of a nuclear world and that he must undertake the quest for some kind of limited détente with the United States to prevent nuclear war. In contrast, Mao, as a dedicated revolutionary and as head of a nonnuclear nation still relatively weak in military terms, refused to acknowledge openly that nuclear weapons had fundamentally changed the world situation, although he was obviously aware of the disaster nuclear war could bring. He feared that any Moscow-Washington détente could only occur at the expense of China's interests. Fearing a weakening of the forces for revolutionary change in the world, he pressed for increased militancy against the West rather than détente.

In more specific terms, the Chinese learned, during several crises involving crucial Chinese interests between 1957 and 1959, that Moscow was unwilling to give full support to Peking and in fact was now prepared to oppose certain major Chinese policies. One of these cases was the second offshore islands crisis in 1958.[27] Moscow failed to give the strong, active support the Chinese hoped for, and made it clear that, while it was willing to extend a defensive nuclear umbrella over China to deter a major U.S. attack, it was *not* willing to give positive support to any attempt by Peking to "liberate" Taiwan. Moscow's unwillingness to back Peking in crises involving Chinese territorial claims was also made evident in the Sino-Indian border crises of 1959 and 1962; in the latter case, in fact, Moscow's behavior indicated that it sympathized more with non-Communist India than with Communist China. The Chinese were already disturbed by the substantial aid the Russians had been giving India since the mid-1950s; and now Peking found itself in open competition with Moscow throughout South Asia. By the

1960s, the Russians were giving increasing military as well as political support to the Indians while the Chinese strengthened their backing of the military rulers in Pakistan.

Another extremely important clash of Chinese and Russian interests in this period (although it was not publicized at the time) concerned nuclear weapons. From Peking's perspective, this may well have been the straw that broke the camel's back in Sino-Soviet relations. In late 1957, the Chinese and Russians had signed a secret agreement in which, according to later Chinese claims, Moscow pledged to assist Peking in developing a Chinese nuclear capability.[28] Precisely what differences emerged over the implementation of this agreement in the ensuing year and a half is not known, but Moscow ultimately was unwilling to provide the nuclear assistance Peking desired on terms acceptable to the Chinese. The scanty evidence available suggests that the USSR probably insisted on conditions and controls that Peking believed would compromise China's national integrity. In any case, according to the Chinese, the agreement was "torn up" by the Russians in 1959, and from 1960 on Peking was compelled to pursue a go-it-alone policy in developing an independent nuclear capability.

The limits of Soviet support to China were demonstrated in a variety of other ways in the late 1950s. Although Moscow gave some crucial short-term trading credits to China in 1959, all long-term Soviet economic development loans to Peking were exhausted by 1957, and it became apparent to the Chinese that the Russians were not willing to provide such support for China's second plan. This was particularly galling in view of the increasing amounts of aid Moscow was now undertaking to provide to such non-Communist countries as India. And when Mao abandoned the Soviet model of economic development and launched China on the Great Leap Forward in 1958, Khrushchev's undisguised contempt for the Communes and Mao's other economic and social experiments obviously angered the Chinese.

Eruption of the Sino-Soviet dispute into open ideological debate in 1960 climaxed these developments, marking the end of all pretense of close Sino-Soviet cooperation and the beginning of a period of steadily escalating conflict. Not only did the polemics intensify, but Peking and Moscow began to compete actively for support in other Communist nations and parties, and throughout the Third World as well. The fact that each side regarded the other as ideologically heretical intensified the passions resulting from the schism, but the clash increasingly found expression in differences over national interests and concrete policies. When the Russians decided in 1963 to conclude a limited nuclear test ban with the United States—an agreement Peking viewed as aimed specifically against China—a "point of no return" had been reached in the Sino-Soviet dispute. During 1963 and 1964, the Chinese made a sweeping ideological and political attack on the Soviet leadership, climaxed with a denunciation of "Khrushchev's phoney communism." From Peking's point of view, China and the Soviet Union were now bitter adversaries rather than allies.[29]

The Sino-Soviet conflict basically altered China's perception of and approach to the outside world. Peking now accused the two superpowers of "colluding as well as contending" and of cooperating to establish a superpower duopoly to dominate the international community and ride roughshod over the interests of China and the rest of the world. China now saw itself confronted with threatening adversaries on both its eastern and western flanks. In this new situation, China's priority foreign policy task, in the view of Peking's leaders, was to cope with the threats they believed were posed by both of the superpowers, and to compete against both "social imperialism" (i.e., the Soviet Union) and capitalist "imperialism" on a worldwide basis.

There is ample evidence that during the 1960s China's conflict with the Soviet Union became such an obsession in the minds of many of China's leaders—and particularly in Mao's mind—that the perceived threat posed by Moscow, real or presumed, gradually came to overshadow in Chinese thinking the threat presumed to be posed by the United States.

In the first half of the 1960s, although there were some Sino-Soviet border frictions, as in Sinkiang in 1962, Mao's concern centered primarily on the subversive influence that he feared the Soviet example could have—in fact, was already having, he felt—in China. This was the period when Mao became convinced that the revolution in China was gradually being eroded and undermined, and when he concluded that an all-out counterattack against "revisionist" thinking was required both at home and abroad.[30]

In the second half of the 1960s, Peking's concern focused increasingly on the danger of a direct Soviet military threat. The intensity of Chinese anti-Soviet rhetoric and hints that the Chinese were reviving claims to large portions of Soviet territory had meanwhile aroused reciprocal fears in the Soviet Union, and Moscow began a large military buildup around China's borders. This buildup reinforced Peking's apprehensions. Then the Russian invasion of Czechoslovakia in 1968 and Moscow's proclamation of the "Brezhnev Doctrine," asserting the Russians' right to intervene to suppress counterrevolutionary trends in other socialist states, heightened Peking's alarm. Shortly thereafter, in 1969, a series of bitter military clashes exploded on the Sino-Soviet border and brought the two countries close to war.[31] By the end of that year, the danger of war had diminished and negotiations on border issues had begun, but the adversary relationship continued, with a high level of fear and suspicion persisting on both sides.

Secondary Effects of the Sino-Soviet Split

The Sino-Soviet split set the basic framework for China's foreign policy in the early 1960s. Peking's opposition to the United States continued, but gradually its principal concern shifted to the Soviet Union. The split reinforced the Chinese tendency, evident from the late 1950s on, to put ever-increasing stress upon the need for complete "independence" and "self-reliance." Since Peking was now at odds with all the major powers whose interests impinged most directly on its own, the policy of self-reliance was, in some respects, a matter of making a virtue of necessity (see Chapter 3). But there was more to it than that. The policy also reflected a deep conviction on Peking's part, born of disillusionment with its alliance with Moscow, that China must henceforth avoid dependence on any other major power. This did not mean that Peking had lost interest in the outside world. On the contrary, it stepped up its activities in many areas during the first half of the 1960s, competing directly with both the United States and the Soviet Union, and to a lesser extent with India as well, in an energetic attempt to expand China's influence on a global basis.

By 1960, Chinese leaders recognized that if they did not modify the posture of revolutionary militancy that Mao had called for in 1957, they probably could not achieve their aims—particularly without Soviet support. Peking therefore initiated a variety of new policies, which represented a new mix of revolutionary and nationalistic aims and were characterized by considerable flexibility and pragmatism. In part because China was now committed to compete against the Soviet Union on a global basis, and in part because Mao was determined to make Peking rather than Moscow the principal center of inspiration for worldwide revolution,[32] China maintained a fairly high level of revolutionary rhetoric. Peking held itself up as the principal interpreter of orthodox Marxism-Leninism, continued to call for intensified revolutionary struggle and a broad united front directed against Soviet "social imperialism" and U.S. "imperialism," and attempted to mobilize under Chinese leadership all nations or groups dissatisfied with the existing international status quo. In practice, however, Peking now tended to view the enemies of its enemies as potential friends, with relatively little regard for ideology, and to do whatever seemed possible to promote the interests and influence of China as a major power.

Both Peking and Moscow attempted to assert their primacy throughout the Communist bloc and world movement, which, as a result of both the Eastern European crises of 1956 and the Sino-Soviet split, was now characterized by growing polycentrism. Sino-Soviet competition strengthened trends toward more "independent" policies in several Eastern European Communist countries. Broadly speaking, however, the Chinese were handicapped in this competition by the fairly extreme ideological positions Peking put forward. China's closest link with a ruling Communist party in this period was with its tiny Eastern European ally, Albania, which turned to China for support because it too was at odds with Moscow. China's main backing from other Communist parties came from a few small splinter parties that endorsed Mao's distinctive views. Although the Chinese achieved only limited success in increasing their own influence in other Communist states and parties in the 1960s, the Sino-Soviet competition resulted in a temporary weakening of Moscow's control.

Increased Activity in the Third World

Unable to achieve a position of primacy in the Communist world, Peking turned its attention to other areas and stepped up its efforts to expand China's diplomatic ties and influence in the Third World.[33] Some limited successes had been achieved in the Middle East by the late 1950s. In the early 1960s, the Chinese began to focus special attention on Africa,[34] where a large number of new nations had just achieved independence. From 1959 to 1964, Peking established diplomatic relations with nineteen additional countries, fifteen of which were in Africa. It also initiated a number of programs of economic aid to African nations.

The principal Chinese appeal to the underdeveloped world in general, and to the new African states in particular, was the call for a broad anti-imperialist, anticolonial, national liberation movement against the major powers (and in the case of Africa, against the white-ruled nations of southern Africa as well). Peking viewed Africa as a region where, as Chou En-lai indiscreetly put it while touring the continent in 1964, "revolutionary prospects are excellent,"[35] and it threw its support behind a variety of revolutionary movements in the region. Many African leaders, jealous of their newly acquired independence, were inclined to be suspicious of the intentions of Peking as of all major powers, however, and they found such statements alarming. As Peking's activities in the region grew, so too did frictions between China and several governments with which it had only recently established relations; four of these broke diplomatic ties with Peking for various reasons during 1965–66.

The Chinese also began to show increased interest in Latin America in the early 1960s,[36] although there its efforts achieved less success than in Africa. The establishment of formal relations with Cuba in 1960, immediately after Fidel Castro's rise to power, gave Peking its first diplomatic toehold in the region. Before long, however, it became clear that Mao's revolutionary line differed significantly from Castro's as well as Moscow's, and in the competition among the three, China made only limited headway. By the mid-1960s, in fact, Sino-Cuban relations were seriously strained. Moscow's ability to outbid Peking in material support was not unimportant in the Cuban situation, but the key factor was doubtless Castro's nationalism, which involved him in some disputes with the Russians as well as the Chinese. Elsewhere in Latin America, Peking's stress on revolution and on the Maoist model inhibited governments in power from recognizing Peking, and except for a few splinter Communist parties, the major revolutionary movements in the region looked elsewhere for their primary inspiration and support. In sum, although the Chinese established new contacts in Latin America and emerged as a definite factor influencing the development of ideological and political forces in the region, its impact was still very limited.

In South Asia,[37] Peking continued the hostile policies it had adopted toward India during 1959–62, but it pursued generally conciliatory policies toward all the other nations in the region. The keystone of China's new South Asia policy was Pakistan, to which Peking gave strong political support and increasing amounts of economic aid. A complex competition for power and influence emerged, with Peking supporting Pakistan against India and Moscow supporting India against Pakistan. Elsewhere in the region Peking attempted to woo all of India's immediate neighbors, and between 1960 and 1963 it concluded important border settlements or friendship agreements not only with Pakistan but also with Afghanistan, Nepal, Burma, and Ceylon. The Chinese hoped this strategy would isolate India diplomatically, weaken its influence, exert pressure on New Delhi to agree to a compromise settlement of the Sino-Indian border dispute, and check the growth of Soviet influence in the region. While Peking did not succeed in the last two of these aims, it did have some success in the first two. It was not until after India had successfully supported the Bangladesh revolt against Pakistan in 1971 that New Delhi emerged, with renewed self-confidence and increased Soviet backing, in a clearly dominant position in South Asia. China's room for maneuver in the region declined thereafter, although Peking has continued to give various kinds of support to the Pakistanis.

In other Asian areas close to China, Peking's policies were extremely varied in the early 1960s. In the states of Indochina, it gave increasingly strong backing to the government of North Vietnam and to the Vietcong in their conflict with South Vietnam as the fighting there intensified, and it continued to support the Pathet Lao as they stepped up their revolutionary activities in Laos. It also continued to endorse several other "revolutionary struggles" throughout the region.

However, the Chinese now found it expedient to adopt a conciliatory stance and to develop cooperative relations with a range of non-Communist nations and groups in Southeast Asia. A major effort was made to promote good relations with neutralist Cambodia and Burma,[38] and Peking's ties with the Sihanouk regime in Cambodia became increasingly close. China's hopes for developing a united front of anti-imperialist forces in the region now centered, however, on Indonesia. Encouraged by the steady growth of the Peking-oriented Communist Party of Indonesia, China doubtless hoped that Indonesia would soon fall under Communist rule, but Peking's short-run policy concentrated on the goal of forging a close tie with President Sukarno, who for his own reasons was more than willing to collaborate with China. Sukarno adopted a strongly anti-imperialist and pro-Chinese stand, withdrew Indonesia from the United Nations, and exerted strong hostile pressures on Malaysia. He also attempted to take the lead in developing wider cooperation among what he called the "newly emerging forces" in the underdeveloped world. Peking decided that it was in China's interest to support and cooperate with Sukarno in many of these efforts. At one point it hinted at the possibility of trying to mobilize the underdeveloped nations of the world to establish a new international body, competitive with the United Nations. This was obviously a trial balloon, however, and it never really got off the ground.

New Flexibility toward the Developed Nations

The increasing flexibility of China's policies in this period was demonstrated most of all, perhaps, by its efforts to expand trade and political contacts with a number of important capitalist countries, notably Japan, several Western European nations, and the principal grain-producing members of the Commonwealth. Practical economic considerations were obviously a major factor impelling Peking to move in this direction. Following the emergence of the Sino-Soviet dispute, the Chinese decided to shift their foreign trade from the Communist bloc to other areas, in part because the economic crisis after the Great Leap necessitated large-scale imports of food products from abroad. The result was a rapid and fundamental shift in both the direction and composition of China's foreign trade. Whereas in the 1950s more than three-quarters of China's trade had been with the Soviet Union and Eastern Europe and less than one-quarter was with non-Communist nations, this ratio was now reversed. And whereas China's imports previously had consisted largely of industrial equipment and raw materials, now Peking had to use the largest portion of its foreign exchange to purchase grain from abroad. Japan and Western Europe became the main suppliers of the kind of industrial goods China formerly imported from Communist nations, and Canada and Australia were now the main sources of its food imports. Economics took precedence over politics in these important developments and trends. In fact, many of China's largest trading partners now—including Japan, Germany, Canada, and for a time Australia—were nations that did not officially recognize Peking.

Despite the crucial importance of economic factors impelling China to develop more active policies toward the developed nations, political considerations were also involved. Peking's leaders now viewed the world in more pluralistic terms than in the past and decided that there could be political as well as economic advantages for China in expanding ties—and especially trade—with many capitalist nations. The rationale for this new policy was articulated early in 1964 when Peking stated that the "intermediate zone"[39] of the world now included two zones, a first intermediate zone consisting of the underdeveloped nations of Asia, Africa, and Latin America, and a second intermediate zone consisting of the capitalist countries in Western Europe and elsewhere (other than the United States). This was not the first time this intermediate zone concept had been put forward; however, the new formulation differed from that put forward in the 1950s. Peking now argued that because the interests of the second intermediate zone diverged in many ways from those of the two superpowers, there existed —or should exist—a basis for cooperation between the nations in both zones (with China playing a leading role) in opposing domination by the superpowers. In some respects, this position may well have been a rationalization of China's desire to expand its ties with such nations for economic and other practical reasons; but it also appeared to reflect an increased recognition in Peking that polycentrist trends were altering relationships in the West as well as in the Communist world. In concrete terms, China placed highest priority on the establishment of formal diplomatic relations with France, which under President Charles de Gaulle was clearly working against many U.S. policies, and in 1964 Peking and Paris agreed to exchange ambassadors. This was the first new diplomatic link to be established between China and a Western European nation since 1954.

By late 1964 and early 1965, Peking's more flexible foreign policies appeared to be achieving some successes. The degree of success obviously varied from area to area, but it was apparent that China was expanding its international ties on a broad basis. The 1965 UN General Assembly vote on seating Peking was 47 to 47 with 20 abstentions; Peking was not seated only because the American-sponsored "important question" resolution made it necessary to obtain a two-thirds vote to seat Peking and expel Taiwan.[40] Despite its continued exclusion from the UN China gradually assumed a more influential global role, and its entry into the "nuclear club" with the explosion of its first nuclear device in late 1964 significantly bolstered its international prestige.

The Retreat to Isolation

Then in 1965 and 1966, Peking experienced a series of major setbacks abroad that undercut important elements in its foreign policy, while at home, during the winter of 1965–66, it entered a period of intense domestic political conflict and turmoil that forced Chinese leaders to turn their attention almost entirely inward. In the fall of 1965 Marshal Lin Piao, in "Long Live the Victory of People's War"— a major exegesis of Maoist thinking on strategy and tactics—made a ringing declaration of Peking's faith in revolutionary struggle, in which he called for the "countryside of the world" (the underdeveloped areas) to unite against the "cities of the world" (the developed nations). This was less an operational blueprint for Chinese policy, however, than an exercise in revolutionary rhetoric.[41] The statement stressed the need for all revolutionaries to be self-reliant and not to expect others to fight their battles for them, and it proved to be a prelude to China's turning inward rather than to a more activist foreign policy.

The foreign policy reverses encountered during 1965–66 were of varied sorts. In Indonesia and Ghana, two countries that Peking had regarded as being of special importance to its strategy in the Third World, military coups brought to power new leaders who were openly hostile to Peking. In Indonesia, the local Communist Party attempted to seize power in 1965 and failed. Although the degree of Peking's complicity in the coup is not wholly clear, it chose to back the rebels openly as soon as the revolt was under way.[42] The results—the crushing of the coup, the ouster of Sukarno, and the violent suppression of the Indonesian Communist Party—seriously weakened the fundamental basis of Peking's policy toward Indonesia, and in a broader sense toward many other underdeveloped nations.

Another setback with even more far-reaching effects on China's policy toward the Third World was the collapse in 1965 of Peking's efforts to help organize a second Asian-African conference in Algiers.[43] The Chinese attached great importance to this meeting, as a move to broaden and strengthen a Third World united front against the superpowers. But Peking alienated many Asian and African leaders in the preparatory meetings by its rigidity in opposing Soviet participation and insisting on an overt condemnation of U.S. policies, and by attempting to shape the conference to fit its own preconceptions. These tactics helped to torpedo the meeting before it was held.

Perhaps most important of all, the escalation of U.S. intervention in Vietnam in 1965 posed new dangers, from Peking's perspective, in a crucial area on China's immediate borders. This development—apparently unexpected by Chinese leaders—heightened Peking's fear of major war during 1965–66 and precipitated a debate within China over alternative defense strategies including whether Peking's security interests required greater cooperation with Moscow.[44] In the end the Maoist view prevailed, with the result that no steps to improve Sino-Soviet relations were taken.

All of these external developments contributed in some degree to China's dramatic inward turn, but the principal causes of Peking's extreme isolationism during the next two years were domestic rather than foreign. From 1966 through 1968, when the Cultural Revolution was in full swing, China's Foreign Ministry, like the rest of the bureaucratic establishment, was virtually paralyzed, and Chinese leaders were almost totally preoccupied with internal political struggles.[45] For all practical purposes, Peking abandoned normal state-to-state foreign relations for a two-year period. The Chinese continued to give major support to the Communists in Indochina and gave substantial aid to a few non-Communist countries such as Pakistan, Tanzania, and Zambia, but every Chinese ambassador abroad except one (in the United Arab Republic) was called home for political screening and reindoctrination. The Chinese in effect retreated into a shell.

During the Cultural Revolution, China's approach to the outside world was primarily a reflection of ideological and political priorities at home rather than the expression of any coherent foreign policy strategy. The obsession with ideology and the virtual deification of Mao within China led to a posture of extreme revolutionary militancy toward the outside world. Verbal support was proclaimed for revolutionaries everywhere, but in fact Peking gave them relatively little tangible aid. Local Chinese, inspired by Red Guard fanaticism, instigated political crises in several areas on China's immediate periphery, including Burma, Macao, and Hong Kong, creating serious tension in China's relations with the areas involved. But these outbursts were essentially a spilling over beyond China's borders of the struggles at home, rather than a manifestation of deliberate Chinese foreign policy decisions. Certainly Peking did not attempt to exploit them to the extent that would have been possible.[46] In Peking itself, Red Guard units, incited by radical leftist leaders, ignored the rules of traditional diplomatic practices and attacked several foreign embassies.

The damage the Cultural Revolution inflicted on Peking's international image and on China's relations with many countries in the Communist bloc, the Third World, and the West was substantial. In fact, the image China projected to much of the world during the Cultural

Revolution was that of a nation seized by irrational extremism, exhibiting an intense xenophobic isolationism, and almost totally uninterested in normal relations with the outside world.

Post-Cultural Revolution Flexibility and Pragmatism

In retrospect it is clear that, to a surprising degree, the damage to China's interests was limited and temporary. Within three years, China's image had radically changed once again; Peking had adopted a new foreign policy approach, and the world showed a greater willingness than at any point since the Communist takeover to accept China into the international community.

The explanation for this rapid and remarkable turnabout must be sought in the attitudes of other countries as well as in the policies adopted by Peking after the Cultural Revolution. By the start of the 1970s, the international community in general believed that the time had come to try to deal with China by incorporating this vast nation as much as possible into normal patterns of international relations rather than by continuing to exclude it. When Peking began to look outward again, therefore, it found a receptive world. The speed with which the turnabout took place was due in large part to the flexible new policies pursued by Peking. Once again, as in the Bandung period of the mid-1950s, China adopted a relatively pragmatic and moderate approach to the world, concentrating its efforts primarily on the tasks of promoting China's immediate national interests and expanding "normalized" state-to-state relations rather than pursuing long-term revolutionary goals.

China's emergence from isolation began in late 1968 and early 1969, in a gradual and step-by-step fashion. There was no sign that Peking had adopted any new "grand strategy." All the evidence suggested, in fact, that Chinese leaders were for the most part simply responding to the necessities created by the problems confronting China at home and abroad, and cautiously feeling their way. The initial signs that Peking was interested once more in repairing and expanding its normal state-to-state relations with foreign nations were small ones. The Chinese first began to treat resident foreign diplomats in Peking with civility again, and then, one by one, Chinese ambassadorial vacancies abroad were filled. The men who were now emerging to take charge of China's foreign relations were professional diplomats, close to Premier Chou En-lai, and not the ideologues who had dominated the scene during the Cultural Revolution. As they began reestablishing relation-

ships in foreign capitals, they acted, for the most part, wit
skill and restraint, muting the revolutionary rhetoric o
period.

During 1970 and 1971, China's new foreign policies ......
shape, and soon Peking was operating more actively and flexibly on
the world stage than ever before. A major thrust of the new policies
was the expansion of Peking's formal diplomatic ties with non-Communist nations in both the developed and underdeveloped areas of the
world. The 1970 agreement with Canada to establish diplomatic relations was both a breakthrough and a watershed. For in agreeing to
exchange ambassadors with Canada, the Chinese made a significant
compromise; instead of insisting that the Canadians must openly recognize China's claim to Taiwan, a compromise formula was agreed upon
in which the Canadians simply "took note" of Peking's claim. This
important precedent stimulated many other nations to consider recognition of China on the same terms. After Chile's decision to recognize
Peking in late 1970, there was a rapid trend toward normalizing relations with Peking, and by the fall of 1971 China had established formal
relations with about sixty nations. By mid-1972 the number exceeded
seventy,[47] and by January 1973 it had reached eighty-five. In the new
diplomatic drive for recognition, ideological factors played little part;
from 1970 on, China showed a willingness to establish formal inter-
governmental ties with almost all countries—including monarchies such
as Ethiopia and Iran and military dictatorships such as Greece and
Turkey—so long as they were prepared to break relations with the
Nationalist regime on Taiwan. A climax was reached in Peking's efforts
to gain acceptance by the international community when the regime
was seated in the United Nations in the fall of 1971 in place of the
Nationalists. For the first time in more than two decades, Peking began
to play a direct role in the functioning of the world's major international institutions.

What was most striking about Peking's "turning outward" in 1969
was the flexibility and apparent lack of dogmatism that Chou En-lai
and Chinese professional diplomats showed. China did not by any
means abandon its long-run revolutionary goals, but the immediate
foreign policy objective was to expand ties and promote Chinese short-
run interests by conventional diplomatic, political, and economic means.
Peking continued to hold itself up as a model for revolutionaries elsewhere, to give overt backing to the Communists in the Vietnam war,

and to provide moral support and discreet assistance to some other revolutionary movements, but its priority aim now was to develop normalized state-to-state relations with existing governments, whatever their ideological coloring, and to expand Peking's role and influence in the established forums and channels of international political and economic intercourse.

A corollary objective continued to be to work toward a position of leadership among the underdeveloped nations of the Third World, and toward this end Peking took positions on one issue after another in support of those favored by Third World nations and in opposition to the views of the superpowers. Meanwhile, however, it also worked assiduously to improve and broaden China's relations with many industrialized nations in the "second intermediate zone," particularly in Europe. While neither of these goals represented any very significant departure from past objectives in conceptual terms, the energy with which Peking pursued them and the degree to which its tactics were now characterized by nonideological pragmatism, or opportunism, was the striking new element. While reminiscent of policy during the Bandung period, China in its foreign policy now showed an even greater willingness than in the mid-1950s to play the conventional roles of a major power and to promote its interests through accepted diplomatic, political, and economic means. Long-term revolutionary goals were clearly subordinate to immediate short-run considerations of national interest.

Détente with the United States and Japan

The most dramatic turnabout in China's approach to the world in recent years was unrelated, however, to its policies toward either the Third World or the "intermediate zone." It was Peking's decision to adopt an entirely new approach toward the United States and Japan. The shift in policy toward the United States, in particular, was an extraordinary development that resulted in a basic change in the pattern of big power relations in Asia and had far-reaching repercussions and implications.

The decision by the Chinese to invite the President of the United States—long regarded as the symbolic leader of the "imperialist camp" —to visit Peking in 1972 demonstrated convincingly that Chinese leaders had decided to give highest priority to the working out of new relationships with the major powers in Asia, for reasons relating above all to national security concerns rather than ideological concepts. While Peking continued to assert that it was opposed to any "balance of power policy" and denied any superpower ambitions, Chinese policy implicitly recognized the emergence of a complicated new four-power relationship in Asia involving China, the Soviet Union, the United States, and Japan, and the need for a high degree of flexibility and maneuverability on China's part in dealing with the new situation.

Many factors doubtless contributed to Peking's decision to adopt a new policy toward the United States. First and foremost, there was the belief that it was now the Soviet Union rather than the United States which posed the greatest immediate threat to China's security. As anxiety about Moscow's intentions grew, Chinese leaders concluded that their interests could best be served by improving relations with both the United States and Japan, even though this would require pushing ideological considerations into the background and adopting a less doctrinaire position on the Taiwan problem and other issues.

In more concrete terms, Peking's new policy toward the United States was undoubtedly a response to several specific developments. During 1968–69, tension caused Sino-Soviet relations to deteriorate to the point that Peking's leaders apparently worried about the possibility of an actual Soviet military attack, perhaps a preemptive strike against major Chinese urban centers or nuclear installations. Chinese leaders probably concluded that improving relations with the United States would be the best way to impose constraints on Moscow and increase Peking's room for political maneuver. Japan was seen to be emerging as an influential new force in Asia, both economically and politically, and Chinese leaders were wary about Japan's future role, particularly after the Nixon-Sato communiqué of late 1969 which hinted that Tokyo might become directly involved in security responsibilities relating to Korea and Taiwan. Peking's warnings at that time about the dangers of Japanese remilitarization probably exaggerated its concern for political effect, but there is little question that it was genuinely anxious about what Japan would do with its growing power. The Chinese may have concluded that if they did not improve relations with Tokyo, Japan might move in directions that would pose new dangers to China. A more conciliatory posture toward Tokyo as well as Washington might help check trends in Japan toward increased militarization, and support pressures for accommodation with China. Moreover, if Sino-Japanese relations could be normalized, this could also improve Peking's ability to deal with Moscow.

A third, and extremely important, influence on Chinese policy was the significant change that U.S. policy in Asia was undergoing. China's sense of immediate threat from the United States apparently reached a peak in 1965–66, when U.S. intervention in Vietnam escalated sharply. Thereaefter, its fears declined, in part because Washington took direct steps to reassure Peking that, despite intensified fighting in Vietnam, the United States had no desire or intention to threaten China. Equally or more important, the Chinese perceived that the United States—because of domestic as well as foreign pressures—was moving toward military disengagement from Vietnam, and was now committed to a reduction of the American military presence in Asia. The President's announcement in 1969 of his "Nixon doctrine" promised a gradual but steady pullback of the American military presence throughout the region.

The Chinese apparently recognized that both the U.S. government and American public opinion were moving gradually toward a basic reassessment of China policy. From 1969 on, Washington began to take small but significant steps—beginning with liberalized travel and trade restrictions and removal of American naval patrols from the Taiwan Strait—that were almost certainly seen by Peking for what they were, namely "signals" of increased American flexibility.[48] Peking's leaders now had more reason than at any time in the past for believing that, if China were to adopt a more flexible stance toward the United States, Washington might well be responsive.

Exactly when the Chinese began to reassess their policy toward the United States is not known, but it may have been as early as the fall of 1968. They indicated at that time a willingness to reopen the ruptured U.S.-Chinese ambassadorial talks at Warsaw and proposed discussion with the United States of an "agreement on the Five Principles of Peaceful Coexistence."[49] Little progress was made during the next two years, however. Both Peking and Washington were feeling their way cautiously, and several developments slowed the process. The Warsaw talks were postponed by Peking in early 1969, ostensibly because of the defection to the United States of a Chinese Communist diplomat in the Netherlands. This defection may have been only a pretext, however; the real explanation was probably related to policy disputes within China and Chinese reactions to U.S. policy in Vietnam. In any case, the talks resumed in early 1970. But they were broken off again after U.S. military intervention in Cambodia. Finally, in the spring of 1971, Peking signaled a major change in its policy by inviting an American table tennis team to China—the first such American visit since 1949. A few months later, in July 1971, the President's National Security Adviser, Henry Kissinger, made a dramatic secret visit to Peking, after which the United States and China announced to a startled world that President Nixon would visit Peking.

The Nixon-Chou summit meeting in Peking in February 1972 climaxed this series of events. The resulting "Shanghai communiqué"[50] symbolized, in many respects, the emergence of a new pattern of relations among the major nations of Asia. In specific terms, it called for the development of direct trade and cultural exchanges and improved diplomatic contacts (without, however, opening up formal diplomatic relations). More important even than the specific agreements was the fact that the communiqué demonstrated, in a dramatic fashion, the determination of both Washington and Peking to move toward mutual accommodation. Both sides pledged to work toward eventual "normalization" of relations. Even though long-held positions on many major issues were reiterated by both signatories, the results were extremely important, and the communiqué clearly marked the start of a very new kind of Sino-American relationship. On the crucial issue of Taiwan, which for two decades had posed a insuperable barrier to U.S.–China contacts, both sides showed a significant degree of flexibility, without abandoning the essentials of their past positions. In effect, they indicated a willingness to set the Taiwan issue aside for the present. For Peking, this meant reversing a long-held position that no real improvement in U.S.–China relations would be possible until the Taiwan problem was resolved.

The repercussions of the meeting between President Nixon and Premier Chou En-lai were immediate and far-reaching. All nations involved in Asian affairs, large and small, were compelled to reassess their positions and policies, and most of them began modifying their policies in varied ways.

Most important, the groundwork was laid for rapid moves toward normalizing Sino-Japanese relations. Peking began in late 1971, after the initial visit by Kissinger to China and before the Nixon-Chou summit meeting, to play down its propaganda about the dangers of Japanese remilitarization, signaling its eagerness to establish formal relations with whoever might be Premier Eisaku Sato's successor in Japan. In Japan—where the President's trip to China was labeled "the Nixon shock," in part because he had not consulted with Japanese leaders beforehand—pressure mounted in the wake of the Shanghai communiqué for rapid steps to improve relations with China, as well as for efforts to define a more independent Japanese foreign policy. Debate intensified on the appropriate role for Japan in Asia and the world. When elections were finally held in Japan in 1972, and Kakuei Tanaka replaced Sato as Premier, the pace of events in Sino-Japanese relations quickened. In his first major act as Premier, Tanaka made his promised pilgrimage to Peking, and the Chinese and Japanese quickly agreed to establish formal diplomatic relations.[51] Tokyo acceded to Peking's demand that it cut formal relations with the Nationalist regime on Taiwan and proceeded to do so, but Peking indicated that it would not object to the continuation of Japan's economic interests in Taiwan or to the maintenance by the Japanese of an informal mission there.

The Soviet Union responded to these developments by attempting to improve relations with both the United States and Japan. Foreign Minister Andrei Gromyko visited Japan in early 1972; discussions on a Japanese-Soviet peace agreement were reopened; and exploration of the possibilities for Japanese-Soviet economic cooperation in Siberia and the Soviet Far East intensified. In late 1972, the first U.S.–Soviet summit meeting in Moscow was held, resulting in several important agreements on arms control and other matters.

Many smaller nations in Asia also sought to adjust to the new situation in various ways. Several made tentative moves in the direction of accommodation with China. To cite a few examples, Malaysia dispatched a trade mission to Peking, the Thais sent a ping-pong team, and even the Philippines decided to allow increased travel and contacts. Some Southeast Asian nations also began to broaden contacts with the Soviet Union. Most of them already had developed extensive economic relationships with Japan, and in fact were beginning to worry about the dangers of economic dependency on the Japanese. Prime Minister Lee Kuan Yew of Singapore probably set an example likely to be followed in time by others when he adopted a policy of attempting to balance the four major powers' influence against each other. China, on its part, stepped up its efforts to expand its diplomatic and political activities not only in Southeast Asia but globally. With its political position strengthened by its acceptance into the United Nations, as well as by its new relationship with the United States, China rapidly assumed an increasingly prominent and active role in the international community.

Continuing Issues and Persistent Patterns of Behavior

It is no simple matter to sort out the variables from the constants in the patterns of behavior characterizing Peking's approach to the world since 1949. The problem is to differentiate between short-term tactics and the underlying motivations, perceptions, assumptions, goals, and behavior patterns that shape long-range policy. Tactical change has itself been a constant in China's foreign as well as domestic policy. The sharp contrasts between its militancy in the early and late 1950s, its isolationism in the late 1960s, and its relatively moderate and pragmatic activism in both the mid-1950s and early 1970s is so striking that one must search closely to discern continuing patterns. Yet, despite all the changes, there have been significant continuities and persistent patterns of Chinese behavior that it is important to identify and analyze.

The Interplay of Ideological Factors and Nonideological Constraints

The fact that China since 1949 has been a Communist nation ruled by first generation revolutionary leaders dedicated to Marxist-Leninist and specifically Maoist values has clearly been an important influence on Peking's foreign policy. But exactly how, and to what extent, requires careful examination.

The ideological assumptions, messianic goals, and revolutionary experience of the Chinese Communist leaders—and in particular of Mao—have obviously shaped their views of the world in numerous ways. Like many revolutionaries elsewhere in the past, these men have had a vision that transcends national boundaries, and they have been committed to promote basic revolutionary values and goals that they believe to have universal validity. Their sense of mission and commitment to support certain preconceived patterns of change in the world have been major factors inducing them to look outward and think in universalistic terms.

Peking's leaders have also shown a strong propensity to regard their own revolutionary experience as a model for revolutionaries elsewhere —a propensity that, while varying over time, significantly increased as their faith in other models, and specifically that provided by the Soviet Union, declined.[52] In their analysis of forces at work on the world stage, moreover, they have tended to base many of their judgments about international relations on images, perceptions, and assumptions acquired during their own struggle for power in China. The ways in which ideologically based assumptions have influenced the outlook of Chinese leaders and their approach to foreign relations have been probed at length by numerous students of Chinese affairs. Only a few require emphasis here.

Communist China's leaders have viewed the world as being in a state of constant flux, undergoing a process of worldwide revolutionary change. In such a world, the task of revolutionary leaders is to understand the changing nature of the contending forces, identify friends, foes, and potential short-term allies, build as broad a united front of "progressive" elements as possible, and struggle persistently to shift the balance of forces in favor of eventual revolution.

Some of the strategic concepts deriving from these assumptions appear to have persisted with relatively little change. What has undergone constant adjustment since 1949 is Peking's analysis of the world balance of forces and the changing realities of international relations. Starting with a concept of a bipolar struggle between Communist and non-Communist forces, the Peking leadership became increasingly aware of the complexities of the international situation; by the early 1970s, they viewed the world as being divided into at least three major categories of nations and "forces"—Communist, non-Communist, and uncommitted—and also saw each of these as internally divided. Within the Communist world, true "Marxist-Leninists" now confronted "revisionists." In the capitalist world, the interests of the "second intermediate zone" were seen to diverge significantly from those of the United States. And in the Third World, certain forces were viewed as part of a worldwide process of "national liberation," while others were regarded as nonrevolutionary or even reactionary. In this situation, the goal of policy was to build, to the extent possible under Chinese Communist leadership, a broad united front directed against the principal centers of both "imperialism" and "revisionism" and to promote, first, "national liberation" struggles and, ultimately, Communist-led revolutions on the basis of "correct" Marxist-Leninist principles.

As revolutionaries, Peking's leaders have believed that foreign policy should be conducted on several different levels and that many different instruments of policy should be used to promote change in the world. A revolutionary nation should not simply rely on diplomacy and other traditional instruments of state-to-state relations; it should also, through "people's diplomacy" and the support of national liberation and revolutionary movements abroad, attempt to encourage forces within other countries that are likely to strengthen long-term revolutionary trends.

On the basis of their own experience in the takeover of China, Peking's leaders have believed that military power is an essential element in policy both at home and abroad, but they have not believed that military power alone is the crucial determinant of overall power and influence. Political and psychological forces are regarded as vitally important too. Because this is so, the political and psychological "balance of forces" rather than simply the military balance of power has often been seen to be of overriding significance in the long run, and Mao has repeatedly asserted his faith that militarily weaker forces can overcome forces that appear to be stronger if sound strategy and flexible tactics are pursued.

While ideologically inspired concepts such as these have unquestionably influenced Peking's foreign policy in important ways over the past two-plus decades—especially at the strategic level—numerous constraints have severely limited Peking's revolutionary activities abroad in practice. More often than not, China has acted primarily as a modern nation-state, much as other powers do, rather than as a headquarters for world revolution.

Even in its ideological pronouncements, Peking has strongly emphasized that all revolutionary struggles must be essentially indigenous and that revolutions cannot, therefore, be "exported"—although revolutionary ideology, concepts, and values can be. Even when its rhetoric has been most militant, therefore, Peking has circumscribed its support of revolutionary movements abroad, and it has not shown any predisposition to intervene with Chinese military forces to support revolutions in other countries.

Consequently, although China has periodically adopted a strongly revolutionary stance and has consistently given moral support to revolutionaries elsewhere, its concrete support for struggles outside its borders has been carefully limited. In some situations, training, advice, and—occasionally—discreet matériel support have been provided on a small scale, but in most cases its assistance has consisted mainly of moral support and verbal exhortation. Korea, and perhaps Vietnam, might seem to be exceptions to this generalization, but China's involvement in the internal wars of these countries was viewed primarily by Peking in terms of its national security interests rather than its revolutionary goals, although obviously both factors have been involved. Elsewhere, the constraints on Peking's support for revolutionary activities have been greater. Even in Burma—a small, weak, and highly vulnerable country on China's immediate border—Peking's intervention in internal revolutionary struggles has been much more limited than one might have expected, judging from Chinese values, rhetoric, and military capabilities in the area. While China continues to give material support as well as training assistance to the White Flag movement in Burma and while on occasion Chinese personnel may participate in certain of its operations, the support is still far less than Peking could easily provide at no great risk.

In fact, not once since coming to power in 1949 has the Peking regime intervened abroad on a large scale with its own forces primarily to try to create a new revolutionary regime, even in areas on China's immediate periphery, and to date not a single new Communist state has emerged anywhere as a result of Chinese support. The Communist regimes in both North Vietnam and North Korea were established before the Chinese Communists came to power. On numerous occasions, moreover, Peking has pursued policies toward particular countries—for example, India after 1959—that have harmed rather than helped the cause of the local Communist party. While Peking's leaders may have rationalized their policies in these instances as being in the interest of revolution "in the long run," short-run policy clearly put China's own national interests first.

This does not mean, of course, that the kind of moral support and limited assistance Peking has given to Communist movements abroad has not created serious problems and major anxieties for the non-Communist countries affected. Especially in Asian nations fairly close to China—such as Thailand, Malaysia, Indonesia, and Burma—Peking's foreign policy strategy and rhetoric have been extremely disturbing during periods of Chinese militancy. Overall, however, Peking's support of revolutions abroad has generally been limited as well as covert, and the impact has tended to be marginal rather than decisive.

The fundamental problems for most countries in Asia attempting to cope with Communist-led forces have been essentially domestic rather than foreign, even when the local Communists have received some Chinese support. And in virtually all such countries, nationalism has to date proved to be the strongest internal political force; external backing for local Communist movements frequently has harmed rather than helped the local Communists' cause. Only in Vietnam have the Communists had significant success in their effort to link Communism with the main force of nationalism; the basic explanation for the Vietnamese Communists' strengths and successes is not the external support given by China and the Soviet Union, but Vietnamese nationalism (although Chinese and Soviet aid has obviously been extremely important to Hanoi just as U.S. aid has been to Saigon).

Looking ahead, one can have little doubt that the revolutionary element in Chinese thinking will continue to influence the country's approach to the world, but there is also good reason to expect that Peking's support for revolutionaries abroad will continue to be primarily verbal. As in the past, moreover, the degree of China's emphasis on revolutionary goals will doubtless vary, as Peking's broad foreign policy strategies change, in inverse proportion to China's emphasis on normal state-to-state relations. The Chinese can be expected to continue operating abroad on various levels—through Party and nonofficial channels as well as through official government action. But Peking cannot give equal stress to revolutionary activity and "normalized" state-to-state relations with any hope of success, because the unavoidable conflicts of interests that result are frequently self-defeating. If Peking's past performance is any guide, support of revolutionary activities will tend to diminish when Chinese leaders believe their overall strategy requires primary emphasis on the promotion of immediate national interests through state-to-state relations. This is clearly the main trend in Chinese policy at present—and has been since the end of the Cultural Revolution.

Even if China places emphasis again on revolutionary objectives at some point in the future, the same constraints that have operated in the past will probably limit the action China takes. It is already evident that as China becomes increasingly involved in the international community—for example, in the United Nations—it will be under pressure to act more and more as a conventional power and less and less as a revolutionary state. And as Mao and the other surviving members of the first generation of leaders pass from the scene and a second generation takes over, the force of ideology and revolutionary interests as determinants of Chinese foreign policy will probably decline, even if the rhetoric of revolutionary struggle persists.

If one attempts to look into the more distant future, prediction is more difficult. One cannot exclude the possibility that China might make a stronger effort to establish the predominance of its political influence in adjacent areas such as Southeast Asia. But one should not assume that an effort by China to establish clear predominance is inevitable or, if attempted, would necessarily be successful.

Of course, even if one accepts the proposition that Chinese support is likely to be a marginal rather than a decisive factor in the period immediately ahead in determining the success or failure of most Communist struggles for power elsewhere in Asia—particularly in areas beyond the Indochina states—this does not rule out the possibility that the rise to power of a Communist regime in one or more Asian countries that are neighbors of China's could have considerable political impact on the region which might well significantly enhance Peking's influence. At the same time, one cannot assume that any new Asian Communist regime would inevitably be a satellite of Peking or that a Communist takeover in one country would necessarily make Communist successes elsewhere in the region more likely.

Tradition and Modern Nationalism

To understand the mainsprings of Chinese foreign policy, one must look beyond Communist ideology and take full account of attitudes and patterns of behavior deeply rooted in long-standing Chinese traditions and powerful nationalistic impulses. In one sense, China's present leaders are still grappling with a basic problem that has preoccupied the country's leaders for more than a century—determination of how, and how much, China should accommodate to the modern international state system and what roles China should play in it.

Before the nineteenth century, China had not been incorporated at all into the modern international state system and had had only minimal contacts with it. The Chinese lived to a large extent in a world of their own. Ruling an empire of continental proportions, Chinese leaders had almost unlimited faith in their country's cultural superiority and regarded it as the center of the civilized world. All peoples and political entities outside the Sinic cultural area were treated as both inferior and subordinate. Even though the Chinese cultural area gradually expanded over the centuries through migration and spreading acculturation, and the territorial base of the Chinese empire periodically contracted and expanded, in a basic sense the Chinese remained inward-looking and isolationist. Believing in the self-sufficiency of Chinese society, they opposed extensive contacts with the rest of the world and tried to keep foreigners at arm's length.

The impact of the technologically superior, dynamic, and expansionist Western nations in the nineteenth century fundamentally changed this situation. China was forced, against its will, to open its doors. Isolation was no longer possible. Confronted with Western (and Japanese) military superiority, the Chinese were humiliated, forced to grant numerous concessions to foreigners, and compelled to accept a subordinate status. Moreover, the traumatic Western impact challenged traditional Chinese values and helped to undermine the entire Confucian political and social system in China, setting in motion powerful new forces for revolutionary change and modernization.

The modern nationalist movement in China began to develop soon after the Sino-Japanese War of 1894–95 and then exploded with tremendous force after World War I. Since that time, all important Chinese political leaders have been motivated by a determination to oppose colonialism and imperialism and to achieve full national independence. All have been committed to building China into a powerful modern nation-state, achieving great-power status, and playing a major role in the contemporary international community.

Like other Chinese leaders of the modern period, the Communists have been moved by nationalist impulses at least as much as by ideology. In fact, it is futile to try to distinguish clearly between nationalistic and ideological motivations in Chinese policy today, since they are so closely intertwined and in a basic sense usually tend to be mutually reinforcing. On balance, though, nationalism has molded Peking's ideology as much—and probably more—than ideology has shaped Chinese nationalism.

Both nationalism and ideology have been forces impelling the Chinese to look outward in recent decades, but in a particularistic rather than a universalistic way. Like the leaders of other large modern states, Peking's leaders have been concerned above all with protecting China's security and promoting its basic rights and interests. They have been determined to play a major role in the international community, as the leaders of other great powers do, as a means of increasing China's power and influence as a nation and ensuring its "rightful place" in the world. Highest priority has repeatedly been given to the protection of China's security and other "national interests," even when this has clearly involved compromising or subordinating ideological considerations and long-term revolutionary aims.

In some respects, however, Peking's leaders have been ambivalent about China's increasing involvement in the world. Throughout much of the 1960s, the impulse to play an influential role in world affairs was paralleled by a determination to maintain a posture of militant "self-reliance" and limit China's contacts with the international community. Disillusioned with their alliance policy of the 1950s, Chinese leaders—especially Mao—turned inward in the late 1950s, and during the Cultural Revolution they pursued policies of extreme isolation. Peking's stress on self-reliance in the late 1960s was accompanied by outbursts of xenophobia somewhat reminiscent of the Boxer Rebellion of 1900. Some Chinese leaders seemed determined to act once again as if China constituted a self-sufficient universe of its own, morally and politically superior to the rest of the world and capable of solving its problems by itself with minimal real involvement in the international community. Since the end of the Cultural Revolution, this trend has obviously been reversed; Peking has turned outward again and developed the most activist foreign policy in modern Chinese history. Yet the ambivalence continues: Peking still wants to keep the outside world at a distance and control all contacts between Chinese and foreigners, even while expanding its diplomatic and economic activities on the broad international stage.

Territorial Disputes

Peking's decision makers have been deeply concerned, like the leaders of every modern nation-state, with all matters relating to China's national security, and they have been extremely sensitive on matters relating to sovereignty and national integrity. Since 1949, China has repeatedly been involved in clashes with other nations—both major powers and smaller countries—over territorial issues.[53] And because territorial disputes are among the most explosive in international relations, these have been a major cause of tension and conflict in Peking's foreign relations. While only minor border claims have been involved in some instances, in others the Chinese have hinted at possible claims to large "lost territories." Whatever the specific causes of a particular dispute, Peking has tended to be more militant in its approach to territorial issues than toward other foreign policy problems. These disputes have not only been a major factor influencing China's foreign policy; they have also helped to shape the world's view of China, sometimes fostering the image of China as a dangerous and aggressive force.

A careful examination of Peking's foreign policy record since 1949 suggests that even on territorial issues, which have obviously on occasion aroused strong feelings of Chinese nationalism, Peking has been less inflexible than is often assumed to be the case. While the Chinese have on a number of occasions pushed irredentist claims in ways that have appeared threatening to others, Peking has been willing in many instances to compromise when China's broad national interests have so dictated.

In the early 1960s, Peking signed agreements with several nations on China's periphery, including Burma, Nepal, Pakistan, Afghanistan, and Mongolia, to settle outstanding territorial issues and formally demarcate China's borders with these states.[54] Even though in some of these border disputes—for example, in the case of Burma—Peking had exerted threatening pressures in earlier years, the stance China now adopted was notably conciliatory. Its new willingness to compromise some claims quite clearly was traceable to broad foreign policy considerations, which argued for general efforts to improve relations with these small countries, in part as a means of competing with and exerting political pressures on India or, in the case of Mongolia, the Soviet Union. These instances highlighted the fact that China is quite capable of showing flexibility, even on very emotion-laden issues, when the nation's broad interests demand it.

In regard to two specific territorial issues, Peking's flexibility was particularly remarkable. Few observers would have predicted in 1949 that any vestige of Western colonialism would be tolerated by the Chinese two decades later. Yet the British colony of Hong Kong and the Portuguese colony of Macao have continued to exist and to thrive. Peking has repeatedly made clear that it regards both as Chinese territory and that they should ultimately revert to China, but it has taken no steps to press for their return, has set no timetable, and has carefully avoided moves that would seriously upset the status quo.

The explanation obviously lies in Peking's pragmatic evaluation of its immediate economic interests. In the case of Hong Kong, Peking has been able to earn large amounts of badly needed foreign exchange from trade with and through the colony, and this is deemed more important at present to China's interests than the immediate exercise of Chinese political control. This is a realistic and valid assessment, but it has required toleration of a major symbol of nineteenth century colonialism, and one that was the target of intense Chinese nationalism before 1949.

It is widely assumed that Peking will reassert China's sovereignty and control over Hong Kong at least by the end of this century, by which time the British lease of the New Territories attached to Hong Kong will have expired. This could prove to be a correct assumption. But it is at least conceivable that if at that time Hong Kong continues to be of great importance to the Chinese economically, Peking might consider some special status for it. The ultimate Chinese position may depend on whether, by the time a decision must be made, Peking believes that other Chinese ports, such as Shanghai, can take over the vital functions that Hong Kong has performed in the past.

The case of Macao is less clear, since it is not important economically to China. The most plausible explanation for the continued toleration of the existence of Macao as a Portuguese colony is that the Chinese recognize that a Communist takeover there would have seriously adverse effects in Hong Kong, arousing fears that would reduce the latter's economic stability and utility to China.

While these cases illustrate Peking's ability to be flexible on certain territorial questions when other national interests are overriding, its posture on some other territorial issues that have embroiled it in conflicts with the major powers in Asia has tended to be more uncompromising. Even in these cases, however, the degree to which the territorial issues themselves or broader policy considerations have been the crucial factors dictating Peking's posture and policies requires close examination.

The Taiwan Issue

The most important irredentist issue for China ever since 1949 has clearly been Taiwan.[55] Chinese leaders—both on the mainland and Taiwan—have consistently asserted that Taiwan is simply a province of China, on the grounds that its population is Chinese, that Chinese rule over Taiwan was established many years ago, and that the Potsdam and Cairo agreements after World War II promised its return to China. Peking has considered it essential to "liberate" Taiwan, both to complete the reunification of China and to eliminate a competitor regime. It has adamantly opposed any moves that might suggest Taiwan could be permanently separated from China.

Peking was preparing to invade Taiwan in early 1950, but the U.S. decision to reintervene at the time of the Korean war—and the subsequent American commitments to defend Taiwan against attack—barred a military takeover. Since then, Peking's leaders have periodically pledged, with considerable passion, to "liberate" Taiwan. But even in regard to this irredentist claim, the Chinese have shown notable realism, and in recent years they have demonstrated—to the surprise of many —that when their national interests demand it, they can relegate even such an issue to the background. For some time it has been clear that although Peking has not, and doubtless will not, renounce the "right" to use force, the problem is now viewed by the Chinese Communist leaders in relatively long-run terms. Since the failure of their two off-shore island probes in the 1950s, they appear to have recognized that reunification will have to be accomplished by political rather than military means. They now seem prepared to tolerate the status quo, probably for a prolonged period of time, at least if overall trends do not appear to be moving toward ultimate independence for the island. Although Peking reiterated its claim to the island in the Nixon-Chou "Shanghai communiqué"[56] of February 1972, it agreed in effect to lay the Taiwan issue aside in order to improve Sino-American relations. This implicit acceptance that reunification will have to be accomplished by peaceful political means involved a major compromise of its previous rigid position.[57]

The United States, on its part, also altered its stand to adjust to new realities. While reaffirming its intention to continue its defense commitment to Taiwan, as well as to maintain diplomatic relations with the island government, Washington stated in the Shanghai communiqué that it does "not challenge" Peking's claims and "acknowledges" that "all Chinese on either side of the Taiwan Strait maintain that there is but one China and that Taiwan is a part of China." In the communiqué, the United States also reaffirmed "its interest in a peaceful settlement of the Taiwan question by the Chinese themselves" and pledged to "reduce" U.S. forces on Taiwan "as tension in the area diminishes," and to "withdraw" them "ultimately," if and when there is a "prospect" for a solution of the Taiwan problem by the "Chinese themselves." The meaning of the reference to diminishing tensions in the area was not explained, but presumably it meant, among other things, after the fighting in Vietnam had ended. Despite the deliberate ambiguity of these statements, they did, in effect, constitute a pledge by Washington that it would not itself actively promote the permanent separation of Taiwan from the mainland.

Peking's new flexibility on the Taiwan issue has clearly been dictated by the priority it has placed on improving Sino-American relations in order to strengthen its political and security position vis-à-vis the Soviet Union. Several other factors are doubtless also involved. China now lacks—and will probably lack indefinitely—sufficient naval and amphibious strength to carry out a military attack on the island. It obviously hopes, moreover, that the United States will gradually disengage from Taiwan, that the Nationalist regime will be progressively isolated and weakened, and that over time both internal and external pressures will mount for Taiwan to accommodate to, and ultimately rejoin, the mainland. Peking cannot be certain, however, that this will take place. Although it is possible that pressures will operate in favor of eventual reunification, it is also possible that they will push in the opposite direction. The great economic and social as well as political differences between Taiwan and the mainland, the apparent sentiment of many people in Taiwan at present favoring a separate status, and the fact that Taiwan's economy appears to be strong and independently viable despite its weakened international political position are all factors that could work for long-term separation.

Although the present prospect is that the status quo will persist in Taiwan, essentially unchanged, in the years immediately ahead, the unresolved problems relating to the island's future may yet pose some difficult policy questions for Peking and for others as well. If pressures were to grow for formal independence, Peking might consider adopting a more militant stance again—particularly if it had by then built up its naval and amphibious capabilities and if the United States had substantially disengaged from Taiwan. But even under those circumstances, there would probably be strong inhibitions against a large-scale military attack, not only because of the strength of Taiwan's own military forces, but also because any major military action by Peking against the island would alarm the other major powers involved in Asia, and China could not be certain of their response. What seems most likely, therefore, is that Peking will try to woo Taiwan into closer association, perhaps even offering to grant some special status involving a degree of real autonomy as a quid pro quo for formal political reassociation with the mainland. China's past flexibility toward Hong Kong and Macao provides precedents if Peking wishes to pursue a more moderate rather than a militant course to bring Taiwan into its orbit. In 1973, there were stong indications that Peking might be moving slowly in this direction, although how far it might be willing to go was not yet clear. Nor could one predict whether, in time, impatience might propel Peking toward a more militant stance again.

Sino-Soviet and Sino-Indian Border Problems

Apart from the Taiwan problem, the most dangerous territorial issues involving Peking during the past two decades have been those between China and the Soviet Union. The existence of a 4,500-mile Chinese-Russian border virtually guaranteed that, as overall relations between Peking and Moscow deteriorated, there would be serious Sino-Soviet border tensions and conflicts. Incidents began to occur in the early 1960s, and thereafter they steadily increased until they resulted in a major border crisis in 1969.

Disputes over territory have not, however, been the basic causes of Sino-Soviet tension, but rather symptoms and symbols of it. It is true that the Russians have shown genuine concern that the Chinese might push irredentist claims affecting large portions of territory in the Soviet Far East and Siberia, in areas that were once considered to be loosely a part of the Chinese empire, and Chinese leaders have been quite willing to hint at such a possibility. They first did so during 1963–64, and although subsequently Peking has never demanded, clearly or formally, the retrocession of any large territories, neither has it attempted to ease Moscow's fears. There is good reason to believe that Peking's position, which is in many respects one of deliberate ambiguity about questions affecting these sizable Soviet territories, has been a deliberately adopted form of political warfare against the Russians rather than an indication of any serious Chinese intention to try to recover "lost territories." The Chinese certainly know that no major territorial adjustment would be possible without unacceptable risks of major war, and, recognizing their relative weakness, they have tried to avoid provoking major war with any large power.

Since the initiation of the Sino-Soviet negotiations on border problems in 1969, it has become evident, in fact, that settlement of the specific border disputes would probably involve only minor border rectifications,[58] if broader security and political conflicts between the two countries could be moderated. For the present, however, Peking has taken a rigid position of "principle" that, before any settlement can be reached, the Russians must acknowledge that past Sino-Russian treaties affecting boundaries and territories were all "unequal treaties." This Moscow has refused to do, in part because of fears that it might open the door to future Chinese claims and in part because the precedent could complicate Soviet relations with nations in Eastern Europe and elsewhere that would also like to obtain border adjustments. As a consequence, the negotiations have dragged on with no significant results to date.

The most important reason for Chinese rigidity is almost certainly not the territorial problems themselves, but rather the huge and continuing Soviet military buildup on China's borders and China's fear of military attack. In early 1973 knowledgeable cadres in China told me that Kosygin and Chou reached an "understanding" in 1969 that border negotiations should proceed without "any threat of force" and that, as they put it, the Russians have violated that understanding repeatedly by taking steps to increase their military forces near China. (This "understanding" cannot be confirmed by any documentary source, but it is plausible.) In any case, the Chinese seem unlikely to alter their position significantly until the Russians show a willingness to cut back their forces on China's borders and reduce the pressure that the presence of such forces implies. If this were to occur, it is quite conceivable that Chinese leaders could decide that limited steps toward détente with Moscow would be in China's interests. Under such circumstances, disputes over relatively minor border territories might be susceptible to fairly rapid compromise if China were willing to drop its insistence that Moscow admit that all past treaties were "unequal." So far, however, neither side appears inclined to make the necessary concessions, and thus the border dispute and Sino-Soviet tensions seem likely to continue. Moscow may be waiting until Mao dies and the succession occurs, hoping that the new leadership in China will be either more amenable to conciliatory moves or more susceptible to Soviet pressures. Peking seems apprehensive that the Russians may use any pretext available to try to meddle in Chinese affairs at the time of the succession.

The Sino-Indian border dispute has been second only to the Sino-Soviet dispute as an issue creating tension between China and a neighboring power. In this instance, however, one can argue that border problems were a cause—rather than simply a symptom and symbol—of conflict. Yet even in this case the evidence suggests that the border problems and territorial issues have been subordinate to broader policy considerations in the calculations of both Peking and New Delhi.

The first incidents along the Sino-Indian border in the 1950s were relatively minor; in fact, they were not even publicized at the time. It was only in 1959, when overall relations between the two countries began to deteriorate, that the border incidents increased in seriousness, came into the open, and became a focus of intense dispute and hostility. On both sides, national security became a serious concern. The Chinese were worried about instability in Tibet and the maintenance of important supply lines between Tibet and Sinkiang, while the Indians were apprehensive about the security of their whole northern border. To India's dismay, Peking asserted that the entire border was undefined and put forward extensive claims to territory in both the eastern and western portions of the frontier regions. The 1962 "border war" exacerbated tension between the two countries, and despite prolonged discussion and debate since then, in which both sides have put forward detailed historical and other justifications for their conflicting claims, no progress has been made to date toward a compromise solution.

Both China and India have maintained fairly rigid positions on the validity of their border claims, in part because each has believed its national prestige to be at stake and in part for bargaining purposes. Nevertheless, some hints of areas of possible compromise have emerged. Peking has indicated that it would probably be willing to give up most of its claims in the east if New Delhi were willing to accept Peking's claims to certain territories in the west—in particular the Aksai Chin region, where Peking maintains an important strategic road linking Tibet and Sinkiang.[59] There is little prospect that such a compromise can be reached, however, unless and until the overall climate of Sino-Indian relations improves, and this would require major policy adjustments in both Peking and New Delhi. While it is not impossible that this will occur, there are few signs as yet of a breakthrough, and therefore the immediate prospect is for continued low-level friction and tension in the Sino-Indian border region. One cannot entirely rule out the possibility that Peking might, under certain circumstances, again decide to undertake limited military probes in the region, to exert new pressures on the Indians. However, this does not seem likely in the near future for a number of reasons. New Delhi's increased self-confidence, improved military preparedness, and strengthened ties with the Soviet Union, as well as China's preoccupation elsewhere and its current predisposition to reduce rather than to heighten tension in the area of foreign policy all operate to reduce the likelihood of renewed Sino-Indian military conflict in the period ahead. For the present, Peking's tendency to give a relatively low priority to India and its resentment of Soviet-Indian cooperation also argue against Chinese initiatives toward settlement. However, the recent improvement of relations between Pakistan and India might induce the Chinese to reexamine their policy. And if there were to be a significant loosening of Soviet-Indian ties, the prospects for a change in Peking's policy toward India would definitely improve.

One other territorial issue that deserves brief mention concerns the Tiao Yu Tai or Senkaku Islands lying between Okinawa and Taiwan. These uninhabited islands, which Tokyo contends reverted to Japanese sovereignty along with Okinawa in 1972, are also claimed by both Peking and Taipei. The conflicting claims of these three governments have aroused considerable emotion, in part because large offshore oil deposits are believed to be located in the vicinity of the islands. The situation has not reached crisis proportions, nor does it seem likely to do so in the period immediately ahead, but it looms as a potentially inflammatory issue for the future that could involve both Chinese regimes and Japan. Here again, however, broad policy considerations rather than narrow territorial issues will probably determine whether it remains a relatively minor issue or becomes a serious focus of conflict.

These territorial issues have been discussed at some length not only because they have played such a prominent role in China's relations with its neighbors, but also because the conflicts over them have been a major factor influencing the views of Communist China held by other countries. Analysis of China's policies toward border and territorial issues in general leaves little doubt that such issues have been important to Peking in ways that have little or no relation to ideological considerations. And, on balance, it seems clear that China's approach to territorial issues—particularly during periods when Peking's broad foreign policy strategy has stressed militancy and above all when the disputes have involved conflicts with other major powers—has frequently exacerbated international tensions in Asia.

However, the record does not support the view that China has pursued recklessly aggressive or expansionist policies, even in regard to disputed territories, or the view that it has been consistently militant or intransigent. Although Peking has at times put forward inflated territorial claims, its specific territorial objectives appear in fact to be quite limited. The magnification of territorial disputes has generally occurred in the context of much broader strategic and political issues affecting China and an adversary. Peking's handling of territorial problems has frequently appeared to be unwise, not so much because of irredentist passions as because of the broad foreign policy strategies involved. However, when tensions have been high, Peking has generally shown caution in not pressing a border crisis to the point of major conflict; and when broad policy considerations have dictated compromise, it has shown a notable capacity for flexibility.

Will China's remaining territorial disputes—above all with the Soviet Union, but with India as well—decline in importance in the period ahead and become susceptible to solution? This will probably depend less on the details of the territorial disputes themselves than on the degree to which China's priority national interests and overall strategy argue for compromise and the degree to which Moscow and New Delhi are willing to adopt more flexible overall policies toward China. Even if the disputes are not resolved, Peking is likely to try to limit them in order to avoid major war.

An Essentially Defensive Posture

The bulk of available evidence strongly indicates that Peking's leaders, in their overall approach to foreign policy, do not think in terms of broad territorial expansion, in the way that Germany and Japan, for example, did in the 1930s or that the major colonial powers did before that. In part this reflects an acceptance by Chinese leaders of the limitations of their power. It also reflects the facts that nothing in their ideology or world outlook impels them at present to think in terms of broad territorial expansionism and that China's domestic problems are so great that its leaders are strongly inclined to avoid high-risk commitments or excessive involvements abroad.

Overall, China's basic military-security stance has been essentially defensive ever since the Communists came to power, and there are good reasons to believe that this will continue to be the case in the period immediately ahead. Even though some of Peking's neighbors have periodically believed China's posture to be actually or potentially threatening to them, it is equally true that Peking itself has felt periodically threatened by the major powers pressing in on China. Chinese fears in the early years after 1949 focused almost entirely on the United States. Then, in the 1960s, Peking increasingly saw itself as "encircled" and subject to hostile pressures from the United States and the Soviet Union and potentially—though to a much lesser degree in any immediate sense—from India (linked to the Soviet Union) and Japan (linked to the United States). However, by the end of the 1960s Chinese fears clearly focused primarily on the Soviet Union. In sum, there has probably been no time since 1949 in which Peking has not felt that its security was directly threatened by at least one major hostile power.

Chinese rhetoric has often stressed self-confidence in China's power, but in practice Peking has been very realistic in assessing real power relationships, recognizing its own military weakness and vulnerability, especially in relation to the United States and the Soviet Union, and in general it has pursued policies reflecting acceptance of China's limited military capabilities. This helps to explain why Peking has emphasized that, while China should "despise" the stronger powers "strategically" (over the long run), it must respect their power "tactically" (in the short run). In essence, China's problem—from Peking's perspective—has been to try to convert weakness (in military terms) into strength (in political and psychological terms). Often it is has appeared that the more vulnerable and threatened by outside powers Peking has felt, the more it has stressed militant rhetoric and an unyielding political stance.

Recognizing its weakness relative to the superpowers, Peking has put a high priority on building up China's military power, and the strength and effectiveness of China's military establishment have steadily improved since 1949. Both in the buildup of its forces and in the military doctrine governing their use, however, Peking has stressed defensive rather than offensive considerations. China's armed forces, totaling close to 3 million men, are among the three largest military establishments in the world, but the bulk of these forces (perhaps about 2.5 million men) still consists of conventionally armed ground troops with relatively limited firepower and mobility. China has developed a respectable—though untested—air force with over 4,000 planes, but it has concentrated overwhelmingly on fighter rather than bomber aircraft; only in recent years have the Chinese begun to produce a limited number of medium-range bombers. Its navy remains small; it has perhaps thirty or more diesel-powered submarines, a number of destroyers, and a sizable number of coastal patrol craft, but it still lacks any significant amphibious capability. There is no evidence, in short, that China has acquired in its military buildup the kind of matériel that would be needed by a nation planning for large-scale offensive operations outside its borders.

Aside from the fact that the nature of China's conventional forces severely limits Peking's ability to consider major military action abroad, Chinese thinking on military-strategic problems, to the extent that it can be judged from open debates, has focused almost wholly on defense issues. There have been important publicly aired differences about whether China should pursue an "active" or a "passive" defense in a particular situation, but no evidence is available of debate over whether —and, if so, how—China should consider a policy of active military expansionism. This does not mean, of course, that Peking's conventional forces do not have a considerable capability to operate at short distances beyond China's borders on the Asian mainland; they obviously do, as was demonstrated in Korea. It does suggest, however, that what is known about China's military capabilities and what can be inferred about its military intentions reinforce the conclusion that Peking's leaders have thought—and continue to think—primarily in defensive terms.

China's determination to acquire the military underpinning for major power status is clear, however, both from its buildup of conventional forces on land and in the air and from the priority it has placed on developing an independent nuclear capability. The progress it has made since the late 1950s in developing both nuclear weapons and missile delivery systems has been impressive.[60] But the evidence available about China's nuclear as well as its conventional programs at present again reinforces the conclusion that Peking's motives are primarily defensive rather than offensive. The Chinese obviously wish to acquire the political prestige that a nuclear capability can bring, but in purely military terms their major aim in developing a nuclear and missile capability appears to be the achievement of a credible minimal deterrent that can prevent the Soviet Union and the United States from posing nuclear threats to China. The determination to acquire such a deterrent is understandable in light of the implicit or explicit nuclear threats from the two superpowers to which China has been exposed on several occasions.

China does not have any realistic possibility of achieving, in the foreseeable future, a "first strike capability" against either superpower, or for that matter anything approaching "parity" with them, and Peking's leaders probably recognize this. China can hope to acquire a credible deterrent, but any attempt to use nuclear weapons as a means of exerting overt pressures on and threatening its neighbors would probably be both dangerous and counterproductive. Chinese leaders seem to recognize this too. At present, in fact, they probably believe that the possession of a relatively small nuclear arsenal could increase the dangers to which China is exposed for the next several years, and this may impose additional constraints on Peking's policies for some time. Certainly, Chinese leaders have gone to considerable lengths to avoid any "bomb-rattling," and China is the only nuclear power to date to make a general "no first use" pledge.[61] All of these facts suggest that, despite the priority being given to the strengthening of Chinese military forces, nuclear as well as conventional, China will probably continue, in the period ahead, to stress goals that are basically defensive rather than offensive.

Reactive Responses or Positive Goals?

Peking's military-security policies not only have been essentially defensive; to a considerable degree they have also been reactive. China is not unique in this respect. Reactive responses have been key elements in the development of the military-security policies of both the superpowers—toward each other and toward China as well. In the case of China, however, Peking's militant rhetoric and its desire to preserve the image of a dynamic nation pursuing positive revolutionary goals have sometimes obscured the realities of the situation. Even when the Chinese have appeared to be most militant, they have often been reacting, from a sense of weakness and vulnerability, to moves by others that they have perceived as threats or pressures immediately endangering the security of China or of the non-Chinese states on China's immediate periphery.

In analyzing China's involvement in conflicts on its periphery—in Korea, the Indochina states, and the Sino-Soviet and Sino-Indian border areas—the conclusion in each instance is that Chinese behavior has not been the result of Peking's initiatives alone.[62] The Chinese have not only made threats but have taken military actions, it is true, in all these instances, but in all of them they have also reacted to military actions or threats by others. These conflicts can only be understood, therefore, if one analyzes them as a process of *interaction*, in which a sense of threat has motivated both sides.

It would be misleading and incorrect, however, to portray China as a country that merely reacts to external developments interpreted as threatening by its leaders. As indicated earlier, Peking has initiated military pressures and probes on a number of occasions to pursue certain of its goals, and some of these have precipitated major crises. The offshore islands crises of 1954–55 and 1958 are notable examples; others include Peking's border pressures on Burma in the 1950s, the Chinese attack against India in 1962, and the initial Chenpao island clash with the Soviet Union in 1969. Even in these cases, however, Peking's use of military power was not reckless, adventurist, or expansionist, but rather a calculated, controlled application of limited military pressure to achieve quite restricted objectives.

In broad terms, Peking's general approach to situations posing important military-security problems can be characterized in the following terms. Even though it is true that the Chinese have tended to think in terms of ambitious long-range objectives, in the short run they have repeatedly been willing to accommodate to situations that have not fulfilled their hopes. While determined to expand China's power and international influence, they have not been committed to broad territorial expansion. And while determined to build China into a military power, they have consistently given priority to defensive rather than offensive considerations. Viewing military force primarily as an adjunct to political strategy, they have relied principally on ideological, political, and psychological means, rather than on military action, to pursue their aims. They have, in general, favored relatively low-risk, low-cost policies and have been strongly predisposed to keep Chinese military forces within China's borders. The exceptions have been when the security of China itself or of adjacent buffer areas considered crucial to China's security has appeared to them to be seriously and directly threatened by a foreign power, as was the case in Korea. In crisis situations, they have generally acted with prudence and caution, and when local conflicts have threatened to expand, they have usually moved to check the process of escalation in order to avoid major war. Repeatedly, they have demonstrated that they are very aware of the enormous dangers of any large-scale war, whether conventional or nuclear, that involved China with another major power, and one of their high priority goals seems to have been to avoid such a war.

Probable Future Trends

Do these characterizations of China's foreign policy behavior during
the past quarter-century provide a basis for projecting its policies in
the period ahead? The answer must be tentative. The persistence of
certain basic patterns of behavior reveals a considerable degree of continuity. Yet there are enormous imponderables as one looks ahead to
the succession period, and the possible effects on China's foreign relations—above all, on Sino-Soviet relations.

Significant shifts in Chinese strategies and tactics have occurred
periodically in the past, even when there has been continuity in China's
leadership, and the uncertainties about who will lead China after Mao
inevitably pose new and extremely difficult questions about the future.
Moreover, if major changes occur in the emerging power balance in
Asia or in the policies of other major nations toward Peking, they
could impel future Chinese leaders, whoever they are, to reassess their
policies. Because of imponderables such as these, one can do no more
than estimate possibilities—or, at best, probabilities; there are no cer-
tainties.

Within these limitations, what now appear to be the likely patterns
and directions of Chinese foreign policy in the next few years? More
specifically, if one assumes that many of the overall patterns of the
past, as well as the general directions of policy that have been taking
shape since the end of the Cultural Revolution, will continue without
sudden or fundamental change for some time to come, what will
China's foreign policy be in the period immediately ahead?

On the basis of these assumptions, it seems likely that Peking will continue to pursue relatively flexible and pragmatic policies abroad as well
as at home for some time to come. Its major preoccupation will probably continue to be what it is today: China's national security, in particular the "Soviet threat" to it as perceived in Peking. Revolutionary
goals will have a lower priority than concrete national interests, specifically those national interests involving relations with the major
powers.

There is little reason to believe that Peking will try to align itself
with any one major power against the others. Rather it seems more
likely to maintain an essentially self-reliant and independent stance and
attempt to achieve maximum room for maneuver in its relations with
all the major powers. For some time, however, China may continue to

place special stress on improving relations with the United States, in part because it is the strongest but also because it is the most distant of the major powers involved in Asia. Because of Peking's desire for effective counterweights to balance and restrain Moscow, it will probably be at least tolerant of, and may actually approve, American military-strategic ties with Japan and Western Europe during the next few years. As times passes, however, the Taiwan problem, as well as other troublesome questions in Southeast Asia and elsewhere, could again become issues of contention between Washington and Peking.

The Chinese will probably continue to be ambivalent about their developing relationship with Japan, on the one hand hoping to develop broader economic relationships and other ties with Tokyo, and on the other hand worrying about Tokyo's expanding influence in Korea, Taiwan, and Southeast Asia as well as its relationships with Moscow. In fact, although Sino-Japanese cooperation will probably increase in many fields, the two countries seem likely, gradually, to become increasingly competitive in much of the region, especially in Southeast Asia. Exactly how such competition might develop and what forms it might take are difficult to predict, since the Chinese will have to rely primarily on political influence whereas Japanese influence will be above all economic.

China's latent fear of major Japanese remilitarization, including the possibility that Tokyo will decide to "go nuclear," will probably persist. A decision by Japan to rearm in a major way would doubtless lead to a reassessment by Peking of its present policies. Even though it does not seem likely that the Japanese will move in this direction in this decade, the Chinese desire to prevent Japanese rearmament will probably argue, in the minds of Peking leaders, for the avoidance of policies that might increase pressures within or on Japan for expanding its military strength. This will probably reinforce other factors supporting the continuation of Peking's present relatively conciliatory approach toward Japan for some years.

Even assuming that fear of the Soviet Union continues to be a fundamental—perhaps *the* fundamental—motivating factor behind Chinese policy for some time, the question of how to deal with Moscow could nevertheless become at some point a major focus of foreign policy debate in China. Many will probably argue that China should persist in its present policy of trying to counterbalance Moscow by strengthening relations with other powers, competing against the Russians on a worldwide basis, and maintaining an uncompromising stand on the major issues dividing Peking and Moscow. Sooner or later, however, some policy makers will probably argue that greater flexibility is desirable to try to break the present stalemate and reduce the present high level of tension. Some might even press for a major shift of emphasis in Chinese policy, from détente with the United States to reconciliation with the Soviet Union, arguing on security as well as ideological grounds that China's interest can better be served by close Sino-Soviet cooperation.

It would be an error, therefore, to exclude the possibility of some relaxation of Peking-Moscow tensions. If open Sino-Soviet conflict can be avoided and if—it is a big if—the Russians are willing to adopt a more conciliatory stance, reducing their military pressures on China's borders, it is quite possible—after Mao's death if not before—that Chinese policy makers may consider a more flexible and conciliatory policy toward Moscow.

In light of the suspicions and fears that have developed on both sides after more than a decade of political conflict, however, there seems relatively little possiblity of a dramatic swing of the pendulum, leading to any far-reaching Sino-Soviet reconciliation that would restore the close alliance of the 1950s. What seems likely is that, at best, any movement toward Sino-Soviet détente would be cautious, gradual, and probably fairly limited. There is no basis for certainty about this, however, and what will happen in Sino-Soviet relations at the time of the succession is one of the most important unanswered questions about the future.

Even if Peking's primary concern remains big power relations, it will almost certainly also continue an active policy toward the Third World designed to expand China's influence throughout Asia, the Middle East, Africa, and Latin America. Although it will doubtless continue to support some insurrectionary movements in those areas, it will probably stress, here as elsewhere, policies that strengthen China's ties with existing governments. Africa will probably remain, as it is today, a priority area of Chinese interest and a beneficiary of considerable Chinese aid, while in the Middle East the Chinese will probably continue to support radical Arabs, in part to embarrass the Soviet Union. As the self-proclaimed champions of underdogs everywhere, the Chinese can be expected to give strong political support—and some economic aid—to many Third World countries, and to back them diplomatically in conflicts of interest with either or both of the superpowers, but perhaps especially with the Soviet Union. Everywhere, China can be expected to compete actively against the Russians for influence over local Communist parties and movements.

In areas close to its borders, China will try to compete against the influence of all of the other major powers, probably for the most part by political rather than military means. As long as Peking gives top priority to the competition against Moscow and is concerned about the possibility of Japanese rearmament, it may press considerably less strongly that it has in the past to achieve an elimination of American influence or a total withdrawal of the U.S. military presence from Asia.

In Northeast Asia, while giving strong political support to North Korea, Peking will probably throw its weight in favor of policies that contribute to military stability and oppose moves that might result in renewed conflict on the Korean peninsula. So long as North Korea continues as a buffer, so long as the Soviet Union does not substantially increase its influence, and so long as neither the United States nor Japan seems immediately threatening in the region, Peking will probably itself avoid threatening or destabilizing moves that might upset the status quo.

In Southeast Asia as well, China seems likely, in the aftermath of the Vietnam war, to adopt a more flexible and less threatening overall posture, with emphasis on increased diplomatic activity and regional trade. Peking will probably give some backing to the idea of neutralizing the area, hoping that moves in this direction would enhance China's influence and reduce (not necessarily totally eliminate) U.S. influence and the American military presence without creating a vacuum into which the Soviet Union could somehow move. China will certainly insist on maintaining a viable buffer next to its southern border—in North Vietnam—but barring a serious new security threat in the region, the Chinese seem likely to avoid threatening moves themselves and to oppose sudden or dramatic moves by others (including North Vietnam) that might risk provoking new big power confrontations and conflicts. Over time, China's concerns in Southeast Asia may focus primarily not on the Americans or even the Russians but rather on the Japanese because of their economic dominance.

For some time, Peking may continue to give relatively low priority to South Asia, in part because its leverage in the area has substantially declined as a result of recent trends and developments: India's growing influence, Pakistan's mounting internal problems, and the cementing of Soviet-Indian ties. But there is little basis for predicting how long Peking will continue its present fairly inflexible and hostile policy toward India. The major determinant of Peking's policy may well be what the Chinese conclude will be the most effective means of countering Soviet influence in the region. Another crucial factor affecting the course of Sino-Indian relations could be whether or not India decides to "go nuclear."

In Western Europe, China will almost certainly continue its present efforts to improve and extend relations with as many nations as possible. The Sino-Soviet conflict will provide a principal motive. Peking will not only try to expand trade but will also try to obtain political support from European countries to strengthen its hand in dealing with Moscow. The Chinese have clearly indicated that they would be apprehensive about any far-reaching East-West détente in Europe, especially if it involved the withdrawal of U.S. forces there, fearing that this would enable Moscow to divert more forces eastward and exert even stronger pressures than at present on China. In Eastern Europe, Peking can be expected to focus its attention on the Communist nations—such as Yugoslavia and Rumania—that show the greatest independence in relations with Moscow.

On the broad international stage, the Chinese can be expected during the next few years to become increasingly active in the United Nations and other international bodies. While Peking has been on occasion highly ambivalent about the international community as it is presently organized, and has even intimated at times that it was more interested in changing the basic ground rules than in "joining the club," the record shows that China more often than not has felt it necessary to conform to accepted international law and practice.[63] Since its seating in the United Nations, there has been growing evidence that the Chinese will accommodate to accepted patterns of behavior (in about the same degree that other major powers do), and will view the United Nations and similar bodies as important political arenas in which to pursue China's national interests, increase its international influence (especially among Third World countries), and compete against the influence of the superpowers. Over time, this increased participation in international bodies will probably strengthen the pressures on China to emphasize state-to-state relations and deemphasize support of revolutionary activities against established governments. While Peking can be expected to take some actions within the United Nations and other international bodies that will exacerbate existing problems (probably, for example, it will oppose most international peacekeeping operations), it probably will also be drawn gradually into an increasing number of cooperative international activities as well. It will certainly work hard to assume a leadership position in relation to the Third World.

In sum, Chinese policy in the period immediately ahead is likely to continue to focus primarily on immediate national interests rather than long-range ideological goals, and on state-to-state relations more than support of revolutionary movements. Its military-security posture will probably continue to be essentially defensive and cautious. However, it is highly likely to pursue activist and relatively outward-looking political and economic policies, rather than the isolationist and inward-looking policies characteristic of past extremist phases. These trends are likely not simply because they are consistent with China's current policies but more fundamentally because they appear to reflect major imperatives rooted in China's perceptions of its basic national interests at this stage of the country's development and in the context of the present world situation.

For a long time to come, Chinese leaders will probably continue to recognize China's relative military weakness and vulnerability in relation to the superpowers and operate within the constraints that this fact imposes. The present preoccupation with domestic problems will almost certainly increase during the succession period, and this will add new constraints to those already existing on their foreign policy. Moreover, the actual potentialities for promoting China's interests through support of revolutionaries abroad seems to be declining rather than increasing at present.

Economic pressures at home should reinforce pragmatic, nonrevolutionary trends in foreign policy, since the need to import new technology will probably increase and, as stated earlier, China's involvement in major international organizations will exert new pressures in favor of policies that are relatively nonrevolutionary and reflect practical national interest considerations. Finally, the indisputable, and in some instances dramatic, foreign policy successes achieved by Peking since the end of the Cultural Revolution through pursuing nondoctrinaire policies will probably argue, at least for some time to come, against any radical shifts in strategy or tactics; so long as the supporters of present policies can point to continuing growth in China's prestige, critics who may wish to change—or even reverse—present strategy will find the going difficult.

Premier Chou En-lai's political report to the Tenth Party Congress in late 1973 suggested that, even though aspects of his foreign policy may be under continuing challenge from either the "right" or the "left," or both, in China, there have been no fundamental recent changes in his assessment of the world situation and of China's basic security problems, particularly vis-à-vis the Soviet Union.[64] The report suggests, in fact, that he intends to continue developing the main lines of policy that he has been evolving since the end of the Cultural Revolution.

Predictably, Chou reiterated China's support for the "struggles" of the "peoples" in the Indochina states and elsewhere. Describing the present international situation as one of "great disorder," he reaffirmed the faith of China's leaders that "revolution . . . in the world will eventually triumph." But he actually had very little to say about promoting revolutionary struggles now. His rhetoric on the subject was kept to a minimum, and he made it clear that this is not China's priority concern at the moment.

The report developed a number of basic themes in the area of foreign policy. One important one was opposition to the two superpowers' alleged desire for "hegemony." Another was China's strong support of the interests of Third World countries. In regard to Japan, Chou simply noted that Sino-Japanese relations have been "normalized." To the Europeans, however, he said, in effect: beware of Soviet intentions.

Broadly speaking, Chou called for an expanded international "united front" and indicated that this should be directed against both of the superpowers. His pro–Third World, antisuperpower themes suggested that China will continue, in the future as in the past, to oppose both the Soviet Union and the United States on many issues, particularly those affecting Third World countries. But both the overall tone of the speech and the specifics in it made it clear that China's primary concern in the area of foreign policy is with what it regards as the Soviet threat to Chinese security and that, partly for this reason, Peking continues to be committed to the development of a new relationship with the United States.

Chou did not accuse the United States of posing any direct threat to Chinese security today. Instead, he pointed out that "Sino-American relations have been improved to some extent." However, the fact that this was a rather restrained statement conceivably may reflect continuing pressure from domestic critics of his policy toward the United States. Chou may also have had such critics in mind when he discussed at some length the importance of what he called "necessary compromises between revolutionary countries and the imperialist states," a phrase that obviously encompassed his compromises with the United States. On Taiwan, Chou's statements were notably moderate. Taiwan "must be liberated," he said, and it will have a "bright future"; but he made no threats against it and instead simply said, "Let us strive together" for reunification. He carefully avoided putting any overt pressure on the United States in regard to the Taiwan issue. However, Chou made a point of characterizing détente as essentially a tactic. "Relaxation," he asserted, "is a temporary phenomenon, and great disorder will continue." It is difficult to judge whether this reveals his actual thinking about the period ahead or whether it was intended to placate those who may criticize him for putting détente ahead of revolution. One suspects the latter may have been an important consideration.

Chou's discussion of Sino-Soviet relations was quite different. A sizable portion of his report was devoted to criticism of the Russians, some of it fairly harsh and even shrill. He accused the Russians of unjustified intervention in Czechoslovakia and in many other specific places. He charged that Brezhnev had been pursuing a policy of "subverting the leadership of the Chinese Communist party," and attempted at several points in his report to link the Russians with the Lin Piao affair. Labeling Lin a "super-spy," Chou said that he had "wanted to capitulate to Soviet revisionist social-imperialism" and had then "fled as a defector to the Soviet revisionists in betrayal of the Party and the country." Finally, Chou warned the Chinese people to "be fully prepared . . . particularly against surprise attack on our country" by the Russians.

While the overall tone was bitter, Chou left the door slightly open to some change in the state of Sino-Soviet relations. He made it clear, however, that China would require compromises on Moscow's part first. Sino-Soviet "controversy on matters of principle should not," he said, "hinder the normalization of relations between the two states." The boundary question could and should be "settled peacefully through negotiations," but negotiations would have to be "free from any threat."

All political reports at major Party congresses in China are intended to provide important guidelines on policies for the period ahead. Chou's report at the Tenth Congress did not point to any major shifts in basic assessments of China's problems or any important new policy directions fundamentally different from those he has been developing ever since the Cultural Revolution. Above all, the report highlighted China's continuing concern about Soviet intentions—and fear of possible Soviet attack or subversion. This obviously remains at the forefront in the thinking of China's leaders, particularly as the succession approaches. Although some of Chou's statements provided hints, as already indicated, that he may feel compelled to defend his policy toward the United States against actual or potential criticism, there was nothing in his report to suggest that Peking will not continue developing its new relationship with Washington in the period immediately ahead. In sum, most of the major themes in his report confirmed policy directions that have been apparent for some time.

Continuing Uncertainties

Although the trends suggested above seem likely, not only because they are consistent with past patterns of Chinese behavior but because of the major domestic and international factors currently shaping Chinese policies, the outlook could be altered, perhaps even suddenly, as a result of dramatic changes either within China or in the international environment affecting it. The succession process in China and the uncertainties about Sino-Soviet relations, especially at the time of the succession, are the crucial variables in the immediate future.

All available evidence suggests that the development, in the period since the end of the Cultural Revolution, of relatively flexible and nondoctrinaire policies has been strongly supported not only by Premier Chou En-lai but also by Mao Tse-tung. Chou's role is in no way surprising; in fact, on the basis of all that is known about him, it is reasonable to believe that he has generally favored policies of this sort in the past. Mao's endorsement of such policies is more surprising, since China's current posture is very different both from the militant, ideologically motivated approach to the world that he strongly advocated at certain times in the past and from the inward-looking isolationism that characterized the Cultural Revolution period. What makes his support understandable is his preoccupation—one might even say his obsession—with what he has perceived for more than a decade to be a broad political as well as military threat to China from the Soviet Union, and his frequently demonstrated ability, ideological considerations notwithstanding, to be extremely realistic in assessing power relationships and adjusting policy to fit them.

There is good reason to believe, however, that there have been influential leaders in China who on several occasions since 1949 have disagreed with Mao's outlook on foreign policy—including, specifically, his inflexible stance toward the Soviet Union—and that some of them may have opposed the general direction of Peking's overall foreign policy since the Cultural Revolution. Less is known about foreign policy debates in China than about disputes over domestic policy, and it is a plausible inference that there have been fewer of them and that in general they have been less divisive than differences over domestic policy. Some have been important, however. Significantly, the most divisive of those we know about have focused on China's policy toward the Soviet Union and the United States and have involved some of China's top military leaders. These have contributed significantly to some of the serious political crises ending in purges, including those of Minister of National Defense P'eng Teh-huai in 1959, Chief of Staff Lo Jui-ch'ing on the eve of the Cultural Revolution, and Minister of National Defense Lin Piao in 1971.

In none of these cases are the full details known, but there is a basis for believing that in each instance the officials purged had at least questioned, partly on the grounds of China's national security requirements, the wisdom of Mao's persistently intransigent and hostile attitude toward the Soviet Union from the late 1950s on. In the late 1950s, not only P'eng but some other Chinese leaders as well are believed to have argued that Mao was pushing the Sino-Soviet dispute too far and that China's security interests demanded greater efforts to find some basis for cooperation with Moscow. In the mid-1960s, Lo and others apparently argued that the expanding U.S. role in neighboring Vietnam required that Peking repair its relations with Moscow to permit "united action" by the Communist powers against American intervention in Southeast Asia. And it is reasonable to believe, even though the evidence is fairly fragile, that Lin Piao also favored steps to improve Sino-Soviet relations and questioned the wisdom of giving priority to an improvement of Sino-American relations.

There is little basis, however, for speculating on the specific alternative courses of action urged by critics of Mao's foreign policies. The implications, in Maoist charges, that what they advocated was not only pro-Soviet but also subversive in terms of China's interests are not convincing. But it is not known whether they argued for a dramatic and far-reaching reconciliation with Moscow, for modest attempts to reduce tensions, or simply for a more even-handed Chinese approach to all the major powers including the Soviet Union. One can assume that at a minimum, however, some have urged a more flexible policy aimed at reducing rather than heightening the tensions and conflicts of interest in Sino-Soviet relations—and, in the case of Lin and his allies, they probably questioned the Mao-Chou initiatives toward the United States.

Conceivably, the most recent purges in China may have ousted many of the strongest and most prominent critics of Peking's current policies toward Moscow and Washington—and silenced most of those who may have secretly sympathized with the criticism. Yet one cannot exclude the possibility that some Chinese leaders will attempt to change policies in the future—especially when the leadership enters the succession period. The speed with which Mao and Chou have moved since 1971 to consolidate their new U.S. policy has been interpreted by some as a sign of determination to bulwark their policy sufficiently before the succession so that it cannot be easily changed at that time. The agreement in early 1973 to establish Liaison Offices—which are embassies in all but name—in both Peking and Washington, despite the continuation of U.S. diplomatic relations with the Chinese Nationalists, tends to support such an interpretation.

In foreign policy as well as in domestic policy, much depends in the period immediately ahead on whether Chou survives Mao and is able to manage a relatively smooth succession and create a viable collective leadership amenable to the broad lines of policy that have gradually evolved since the Cultural Revolution. If not and military leaders were to assume dominant positions, it is not inconceivable that previous military criticism of Mao's foreign policies might find new spokesmen in positions of power. Or if the influence of militant ideologues were to rise significantly in the post-Mao leadership, pressures might rise for a return to the kind of ideologically motivated revolutionary posture favored by Mao at certain periods in the past. Such a shift might or might not involve major changes in China's approach to the Soviet Union, but it almost certainly would create pressures for significant modifications of China's current polices toward the United States and other non-Communist nations.

A variable of equal importance is Soviet policy toward China at the time of the succession—and the responses it will evoke from the Chinese. There is every reason to believe that the Russians regard the succession period in China as one of critical importance, because they long ago abandoned any hope of a Sino-Soviet rapprochement as long as Mao lives, because they have become increasingly uneasy over time about Chinese intentions, and because they may believe that there are some within the Chinese leadership who secretly favor policies toward Moscow and Washington quite different from the present ones.

Whether the Russians believe that they might have a significant influence on the succession's outcome is difficult to say. Conceivably they may, but it would not be surprising if this is now a subject of serious debate in Moscow.

The Russians could consider several options at the time of the succession. They could adopt a more conciliatory posture, using concessions to try to induce post-Mao leaders, whoever they might be, to change China's policies. Or they might attempt to exert pressures of various sorts, backed by explicit or implicit threats, especially in border regions and neighboring areas, to try to compel Chinese leaders to be more compliant. Or they might, as many Chinese probably fear, attempt by various direct or indirect means to "meddle" in Chinese politics, backing certain Chinese leaders against others, in order to try to influence the outcome of the succession struggle. If the succession were to deteriorate into a serious struggle that produced a state of political confusion and weakness, some Russian leaders might be tempted to use their forces on China's immediate periphery to exert pressure on Peking, and perhaps even to seize territory in certain key Chinese border areas. Not all of these theoretical options are mutually exclusive, of course, and Soviet policy conceivably could combine both the carrot and the stick and both direct and indirect means of manipulation and pressure.

It is impossible to predict how the Chinese might respond if the Russians were to adopt more active strategies of any of the kinds suggested—i.e., whether they would respond positively to conciliatory gestures, submit to pressures, react strongly against attempted manipulation, or try to retaliate against Soviet threats or intervention.

From the point of view of other nations, probably the most dangerous situation would be one in which, as a result of internal struggles, China appeared relatively weak and vulnerable and Moscow decided to exert stronger pressures, tried to manipulate political forces in China, or decided on direct intervention. In such a situation, the Chinese, in a mood of anger, fear, or even desperation, might try somehow to retaliate. The risk then would be that fear, miscalculation, or simply passion might impel both sides to take actions that could escalate and lead to overt Sino-Soviet conflict. The outbreak of war between these two vast nations could have far-reaching and potentially extremely dangerous effects on the stability of the entire balance in Asia. Even if the United States and Japan were to try to keep aloof in such a situation, each would be compelled to undertake a fundamental reassessment of its policies. Japan might embark on major remilitarization, and the United States would probably have to reexamine its entire "Nixon doctrine" approach to Asia. The present areawide trend toward lowered tension might be reversed, and new fears would doubtless arise in areas such as Korea and Southeast Asia. Worldwide efforts toward détente and arms control would probably also be very seriously damaged and perhaps set back for years.

If, on the other hand, China were to experience a relatively smooth succession, and both the new leadership in Peking and the leadership in Moscow were to adopt more conciliatory, restrained policies—perhaps taking cautious steps designed to break the present stalemate in their relations and to reduce tensions, or at least avoiding new provocative actions that would exacerbate the situation—the prospects for the gradual evolution of a more stable pattern of relationships in Asia would improve. If, however, a post-Mao leadership were to go even further, and a dramatic swing of the pendulum occurred, in which China adopted a strongly pro-Soviet stance paralleled by more hostile policies toward the United States or Japan, or both, this—while not being as immediately destabilizing as a major Sino-Soviet conflict— would nevertheless have far-reaching and adverse implications and repercussions, requiring fundamental reappraisals of broad policy by both Washington and Tokyo.

An even broader and more diffuse question can be raised about China's overall approach to the world in the post-Mao period. How far are future Chinese leaders likely to be prepared to go in involving China in the world community, in participating in the multiple and ever-expanding channels of present-day international intercourse, and in exposing the Chinese people to increased external foreign contacts and influences from abroad?

Although the policies that Peking has been developing since the end of the Cultural Revolution have involved a significant turning outward and a new international activism, in marked contrast to the militantly isolationist policies in the late 1960s, the process of developing broad intercourse between Chinese society and foreign societies has not really gone very far to date. The Chinese people are almost certainly still the most isolated and the most protected from extensive foreign contacts of those of any major nation. Travel, trade, and intellectual, scientific, and cultural exchanges have been increasing, but in comparison to other major nations (including other Communist nations) China has really only begun to develop broad international intercourse. Clearly, there are still many leaders in the Chinese hierarchy who continue to believe that contacts between China and the rest of the world—especially intellectual contacts—must be tightly controlled and severely restricted to minimize the dangers of importing corrupting influences from abroad.

China's economy is probably still, despite recent trends, the most autarkic of any major nation. Peking permits no foreign investment, for years has accepted no long-term loans, and has perhaps the smallest volume of trade in per capita terms of any large country. In 1973 China's total foreign trade will probably be less than $7 billion. Although this will represent some increase over the level of the recent past, it will be less than the foreign trade of Taiwan, which has roughly one-fiftieth of mainland China's population.

A short while ago—certainly in the late 1960s while the Cultural Revolution was under way—one would have said that no great increase in political, economic, intellectual, and cultural intercourse between China and the outside world should be expected in the foreseeable future. Events of the past three years have changed this prospect, but how much? There is no basis as yet for concluding that Chinese leaders are now ready to abandon their concept of self-reliance and move toward much greater economic and other involvement in the world community; but they are nevertheless now moving, slowly and cautiously, away from the extreme isolationism of the recent past.

How far China should go down this road will probably be a subject of major and continuing debate in Peking in the years ahead. There will be pressures, some of which may increase after Mao's death, to expand China's relationships, especially in the economic field. But there will also be strong inhibitions against going too far or too fast, and some Chinese leaders will undoubtedly oppose steps that seem to compromise China's self-reliance. In the broadest sense, this will be one of the most fundamental issues with which future Chinese leaders will have to wrestle. How it is resolved will influence almost every aspect of domestic as well as foreign policy—and the interrelationships between the two—in ways that will affect the interests of most key groups within China. Ideologues can be expected to resist broadening intellectual and economic intercourse with the world community, partly on the grounds that relative isolation is necessary to preserve ideological purity and defend the integrity of Maoist policies within China. Many scientists, professionals, and intellectuals will almost certainly urge increased international contacts, on the grounds that such contacts are crucial if they are to perform at a level comparable to their professional colleagues and competition elsewhere. Many of China's top planners and bureaucrats responsible for economic development will probably press for expanded trade and economic relationships generally. The attitudes of China's military leaders—at various levels and in different service areas—are much more difficult to predict.

Perhaps the area in which this issue will be most pressing in the immediate future is the economy. Debate is likely to revolve around several questions: How far can or should China go in permitting or encouraging increased contacts between Chinese scientists and technical experts and their counterparts abroad in order to import scientific and technological knowledge needed for Chinese economic development? How much and how fast should China's foreign trade be increased? Should China seek sizable long-term credits from abroad, and if so to what extent? To what extent should it be prepared to adjust domestic economic priorities in order to orient its economy toward foreign trade and develop much broader international economic intercourse?

The strongest arguments in favor of greater involvement in the international economy will come from those who argue it is necessary to achieve a more rapid rate of economic growth in China. The strongest resistance is likely to come from those who fear the political and ideological repercussions within China of increased involvements abroad. The debate will involve, implicitly if not explicitly, fundamental questions concerning China's self-image, its basic values and priorities, and its broad world outlook. The outcome will significantly influence, therefore, the kind of country China will become in the period ahead, as well as its overall relationship to the world community. Will China live largely in a world apart, independent, militantly self-reliant, and in many respects isolationist, determined to act as a world power but in a way that protects its domestic institutions and basic values from significant foreign contamination? Or will it decide to become more fully assimilated into the world community, increasingly involved in the complex networks of contemporary transnational intercourse, and increasingly drawn into more—and more cooperative as well as competitive—international relationships?

These questions will create continuing dilemmas and tensions within China, as well as in its relations with the outside world. The direction in which Chinese leaders actually move will be influenced not only by competing pressures from different groups within China but also by varied influences and pressures from abroad. Given present trends, it now appears likely that China will continue to move cautiously in the direction of greater involvement in the world community. The process will probably be both gradual and difficult, primarily because of continuing opposition and fears at home. But it seems likely to continue nevertheless, in part because of internal pressures in favor of more rapid economic growth, and in part because of subtle external pressures on China. In the world today, the broader processes of modernization and development are not easily confined within national boundaries, and the dynamics of change work powerfully toward increased international interaction and interdependence. It is difficult for any nation to isolate itself in an extreme fashion from such forces.

Yet, while this projection is plausible, there is no certainty about the direction in which China will move. It will not only depend, like so much else about China's future, on the outcome of the succession, but will also be significantly influenced by the policies of other countries toward China. To the extent that post-Mao leaders believe they are confronted by a world that is essentially threatening and hostile, the process of fully incorporating China into the international community will be seriously impeded. To the extent that they continue to see concrete benefits from expanding international intercourse, and believe that they can do this without excessive danger to their security, their values, or their institutions, the process will be significantly encouraged.

VI

Summary and Implications for U.S. Policy

How can one sum up China's present situation and its problems and prospects in the period immediately ahead? During the past few years China has experienced great turmoil and change, and today it is still in the process of political recovery and reconstruction. As it looks forward to the post-Mao succession, it faces another period of great potential change, and the country is pervaded by an atmosphere of uncertainty and tentativeness about the future. This is a difficult transition period, in which there are more questions than answers about the future. Many of the questions will remain unanswerable until the succession actually occurs—and probably for some time thereafter.

The future character of the regime and the direction in which it moves will be determined to a large extent by how effectively the Chinese are able to cope with a number of basic unresolved problems. One of the most important is the problem of rebuilding and consolidating the regime's new leadership. After Mao dies, the leadership must find a new basis for unity and for establishing its legitimacy and authority. In a fundamental sense, the entire future of the regime during the next few years hinges to a large extent on the ability of its leaders to manage the succession with a minimum of divisive struggle and to form a stable post-Mao leadership—whether it is a collective leadership or some other viable form. If the succession is relatively smooth, the regime's prospects for coping successfully with the other major problems facing China will be greatly improved. If not, the problems of transition after Mao will be enormously complicated.

A related problem, also still to be resolved, concerns the role of the

316

military establishment in China and the future relationship between military and civilian leaders and institutions. During the Cultural Revolution, the relatively stable military-civil relationship that existed during the regime's early years broke down, propelling military men into positions of political ascendancy throughout much of the country. Although the political roles of the military have been gradually reduced since the end of the Cultural Revolution and the pendulum has swung slowly back toward civilian control, this process is far from complete, and to date no stable civil-military balance comparable to that in the past has been achieved. Whether a stable pattern will emerge, and if so when and how, will depend to a considerable extent on the nature and outcome of the succession.

How to cope with China's economic problems and resolve dilemmas relating to both production and distribution will be another basic determinant of the country's prospects in the period ahead. The search for optimal developmental policies has been under way since the earliest days of the regime, and the degree of success and failure in stimulating growth has varied greatly, depending on the strategies pursued. There have been some periods of impressively rapid growth, but in other periods China has suffered severe economic setbacks. One fundamental question underlying many of the debates within the Chinese leadership over economic policy issues has been that of priorities: should the regime stress rapid growth per se or egalitarian values and rapid revolutionary social change? Since the setbacks of the Cultural Revolution period, China's leadership appears to have been evolving policies based on compromises between these two poles, and the process of development has resumed. If the regime's current policies are continued without radical change, the prospect is for continued growth, at a not unimpressive but nevertheless relatively modest rate.

If the Chinese shift course in economic policy, the move could be in either of two directions—toward policies that put increased stress on more rapid growth even at the expense of revolutionary values or toward policies that put greater emphasis on revolutionary egalitarian values even at the expense of economic growth. The consequences in either case would be quite different from what I have projected for both the regime and the society. Which path China chooses in the economic field as in most other areas will depend in considerable part on the kind of leadership that emerges from the post-Mao succession. In any case, the regime's success, or lack of it, in solving China's basic economic problems and dilemmas will significantly affect the country's prospects for political and social stability in the future.

Restoration of a stable ideological consensus concerning the regime's and the society's fundamental values and priorities is another basic problem China still faces. The Cultural Revolution reflected—and exacerbated—a tendency toward ideological polarization within the leadership, and it seriously weakened the previously existing basis for consensus. While an effort to create a new consensus is now under way, considerable ideological confusion and latent ideological conflict persist. Consequently, the nature and the roles of ideology in China in the post-Mao period are still not wholly predictable.

Yet another problem that the regime still faces is that of completing the process of political reconstruction now under way—the task of rebuilding a viable and stable institutional structure. While China's principal civilian political institutions have been gradually rebuilt since the direct and violent attacks on them during the Cultural Revolution, it will take some time to achieve a genuinely stable institutional structure once again and to work out a viable new pattern of relationships among the regime's principal power centers and institutional hierarchies. There are many questions still to be answered about the probable institutional structure and relationships among the Party, military, state, and mass organizations in the period immediately ahead. A wide variety of developments in the post-Mao era must be considered within the realm of possibility—leading either to serious political, and possibly even military, conflicts that could result in major economic and social as well as political setbacks, or to a fairly rapid restoration of national cohesion and dynamism that could result in a renewed surge forward toward the regime's major long-term goals.

In the main body of this study, the background and nature of these problems have been described at some length; numerous factors that could affect the outcome have been analyzed; and various developments that seem conceivable, possible, or probable have been considered. Because so many unpredictable internal and external variables are involved, there is no "scientific" basis for determining whether, broadly speaking, one should have a relatively sanguine or a comparatively pessimistic view of China's prospects for resolving its problems without another great and destructive internal upheaval. After all the evidence is in, one must still, in looking ahead, fall back upon judgments that are at least in part subjective.

Although I am impressed by the great difficulty of the problems that China's leaders now confront and would not rule out the possibility that pessimistic projections about their ability to handle these problems could prove to be correct, I nevertheless tend to believe, as should be evident from the discussion in previous chapters, that there is considerable basis for taking a cautiously sanguine view of China's ability to handle the succession without violent struggles that would have far-reaching adverse consequences. If the leaders are able to do this, and can create a reasonably stable post-Mao leadership, I believe their other problems, while extremely complex and clearly not subject to quick or easy solutions, are not likely to be insoluble. It is obvious, however, that under the best of circumstances these problems will involve painful dilemmas for a long time to come.

Above all, a cautiously sanguine view of China's future prospects must rest on the assumption that at the time of the succession a viable post-Mao leadership composed of men who are reasonably practical, realistic, and flexible can be established. There can be no certainty that such a leadership will emerge, but it now seems definitely possible. Despite the many existing tensions and conflicts within the leadership, China's top elite will probably be powerfully motivated to try to prevent destructive power struggles and to stabilize a new leadership situation as rapidly as possible after Mao goes. This should be a major factor operating in favor of resolving differences through compromise. As has been emphasized earlier, the chances for a relatively smooth post-Mao transition will probably be greatest if Premier Chou En-lai is in a position to manage the process and has a reasonable period of time in which to consolidate the situation before he passes from the scene.

The most likely outcome of a relatively smooth succession—certainly if Chou still occupies a key position, but conceivably even if he does not—would seem to be a new kind of collective leadership. To succeed, this would have to be built on numerous policy compromises and workable power balances among civilian and military leaders, central and local authorities, and varied bureaucratic interests, and it would have to include individuals representing a variety of political and ideological outlooks. Under any circumstances, the building of such a leadership will involve enormous difficulties, but the motivation to do so in the post-Mao period will probably be strong, above all because of the potentially disastrous consequences that could result if intense conflict occurs. Even if the task falls to leaders other than Chou En-lai, many of the same motives and pressures will probably be operative.

If it is assumed that what emerges is a workable collective leadership, composed of practical men who are inclined to compromise and able to focus their attention on China's pressing immediate problems, what would then seem to be likely or possible trends affecting major problem areas?

In the field of military affairs, it seems probable that there will be increasing stress over time on modernization and professionalization of the armed forces of China. Continuing concern about potential threats to China's security, especially from the Soviet Union, will argue for a steady buildup of China's military capabilities. Although Peking will face many difficult choices regarding the allocation of resources—not only between the civilian and military sectors of the economy but also between different sectors in the military establishment itself—the regime will doubtless continue to give high priority to the development of both its conventional and its nuclear forces. In the period immediately ahead, the principal emphasis will probably be, as it has been in the recent past, on developing China's defensive rather than offensive capabilities. The modernization process seems likely to reinforce other pressures toward increased professionalism within the military. There will probably also be continuing efforts to increase central control over the military, but such efforts will doubtless meet significant resistance from powerful regional military commanders, and the balance between central and regional power will continue for some time to be a delicate, and in some respects potentially unstable, one. Over time, however, centralized control seems very likely to increase.

In relation to the society as a whole, the People's Liberation Army (PLA) will probably continue to play a variety of political, economic, and social roles for a fairly long time to come. Yet over time its nonmilitary roles seem likely to be reduced, at least gradually, as China's civilian political institutions regain their strength, and as military leaders place increased emphasis on national defense tasks and problems of military modernization and professionalization.

In relation to the key question of who holds power in China, the military will obviously continue for a fairly long time to occupy a crucial position. For the foreseeable future, military leaders—both at the center and at the regional level—will almost certainly occupy many important leadership and decision-making positions, and what these military leaders decide to do at the time of the post-Mao succession could be decisive in determining the outcome. One prerequisite for a relatively nonviolent succession and the building of a stable post-Mao leadership will be a willingness on the part of China's top military and civilian leaders to compromise, share power, and form workable political alliances. There should be compelling reasons for them to try to avoid overt conflict, however. If one takes a sanguine view of the prospects, the emergence of a new pattern of complex alliances between military and civilian personnel at all key levels of the regime seems likely.

In economic policy, it appears at present that the most likely prospect under a post-Mao collective leadership is the continuation, broadly speaking, of current trends toward fundamentally pragmatic, nonideological approaches. To succeed, such approaches will require continued efforts to achieve workable compromises between competing pressures to stress either agriculture or industry, rural development or urban development, labor-intensive projects or capital-intensive projects, decentralization or centralization, nonmaterial or material incentives, and "redness" or "expertness." The current stress on agricultural and rural development, decentralized small-scale labor-intensive projects, nonmaterial incentives, and "redness" will doubtless continue to have some influence on future policies, but over time this seems likely to shift gradually toward somewhat greater emphasis on the development of large urban industries, the use of material incentives, and the importance of "expertness."

If China suffers no prolonged period of major disasters—either political or natural—during the next few years, a period of continuing growth at a moderate but nevertheless respectable rate—perhaps close to 4 percent a year (or somewhat higher or lower) seems likely. Growth of this kind would enable the Chinese regime to continue building the foundations of national power and to maintain—and conceivably even improve very gradually—the current standard of living. It would have a generally positive effect on the prospects for future social and political stability. It would not, however, transform China into an economic superpower in the foreseeable future or result in any rapid rise in living standards. A much more rapid growth rate would probably require significant changes in some current policies, including a substantially greater involvement in the international economy. China may move in this direction in the period ahead, but this movement will probably be relatively slow and cautious because of many inhibitions and obstacles.

Marxism-Leninism and the Thought of Mao will almost certainly continue to provide the basic ideological underpinnings of the regime, but the present uncertainty and confusion about ideological issues and about how to resolve numerous concrete conflicts of values may continue for some time. Over the longer run, however, the intensity and force of ideology are likely to decline gradually. Post-Mao leaders will doubtless attempt to achieve a new ideological consensus, which will have to be based on numerous compromises and a somewhat different mixture of Maoist and non-Maoist values than any in the past. Purist Maoist values may well continue to define the society's basic code of revolutionary morality and ethics. However, Mao's successors, while unlikely to reject Mao's Thought openly or to carry out any clear-cut de-Maoification policy, will almost certainly try to reinterpret the Thought of Mao in order to adapt it to their own new needs. It seems likely that many of Mao's most extreme egalitarian and populist concepts will have a declining influence on the regime's actual policies. The main thrust of any effort to reinterpret Mao's Thought will probably be in the direction of pragmatic flexibility, to help justify the leadership's tendencies—already apparent today—to pursue relatively nonideological and practical policies focused on the country's most pressing immediate problems.

The importance of nationalism as a motivating force will probably rise steadily. In fact, many of the regime's policies will probably be shaped more by a combination of strong nationalism and flexible pragmatism than by extreme Maoist revolutionary values such as those that underlay the dramatic upheavals of the Great Leap Forward and the Cultural Revolution. After Mao goes, great revolutionary upsurges or outbursts of this sort seem much less likely than in the past.

If the succession is relatively smooth—and here again one must emphasize the *if*—the regime's institutional structures will probably be gradually rebuilt and stabilized in the post-Mao period. The achievement of institutional stability will require the resolution of some extremely difficult issues regarding the respective roles and relationships of the Party, army, and government, but these should not be insoluble if bitter power struggles can be avoided—or at least can be minimized. After Mao goes, it seems likely that trends toward a depersonalization of decision making and a strengthening of the regime's institutions will occur in parallel and that gradually there will be renewed emphasis on regularized operation of the regime's bureaucracies and relatively routinized administration. While mass mobilization, in which Mao had such great faith, does not seem likely to be totally rejected, it probably will become less important in the future. In sum, the process of institutionalizing the revolution—a process greatly set back by the Cultural Revolution—will probably resume.

Projections of domestic trends along the general lines outlined above are plausible if Chinese leaders are able to put larger national interests above narrow personal, group, and local concerns, and if they are able to contain or minimize the potentially explosive tensions that will clearly exist at the time of the succession. No one can argue, however, that these represent the only possible outcomes. In fact, if the regime were to experience a bitter struggle for power instead of a smooth succession, China could enter a period of great political confusion once again.

In considering the future, therefore, one cannot exclude possibilities quite different from the most sanguine ones suggested above. A violent power struggle could have far-reaching effects that at worst could seriously destabilize and weaken the regime and the society as a whole. One conceivable extreme result could be the emergence of a relatively ineffectual central leadership and a substantial diffusion of power to regional and provincial authorities, especially local military leaders. Even if this occurred, however, the reemergence of old-style "warlordism" would not seem likely, because of many factors now at work in China, including the force of modern nationalism and the strength of the Chinese desire for national prestige and power.

Another very different outcome could be the emergence, in a period of conflict and confusion, of a new central leadership clearly dominated by military officers who might try to assert overt military primacy in the political arena and expand the PLA's influence once again throughout the society. At worst, China might then face the danger that its political system could develop into a Communist form of military oligarchy or dictatorship.

Another possibility would be the emergence at the top of militantly revolutionary and ideologically oriented "leftists" or "radicals" who, either by themselves or in alliance with others, might attempt (conceivably, even within the context of a collective leadership) to shift the regime back toward extreme "Maoist" policies of the sort manifested in the Great Leap Forward or the Cultural Revolution. Such a shift does not, at present, seem likely, but if it were to occur, trends in all the fields already discussed could move in directions very different from—and possibly even opposite to—my projections. Any attempt to duplicate the Great Leap Forward or the Cultural Revolution would probably result in extreme ideological and political polarization once again, which could lead to renewed political and social conflict of an intense sort and would probably result in serious economic setbacks.

In any of the above alternative circumstances, the formation of a broadly based and stable leadership, the establishment of a viable civil-military relationship, the definition of workable and effective economic policies, the building of a new ideological consensus, and the achievement of a stable institutional structure would all probably be significantly delayed. While conflict conceivably might be contained at the leadership level (as it was at the time of the Lin Piao purge), one could not exclude the possibility that it might also lead to widespread instability and social disorder at the grassroots level (as it did during the Cultural Revolution), with extremely costly consequences for the society and population as a whole.

These are merely a few of the adverse outcomes within China that can be envisaged if the succession process should be extremely violent rather than relatively orderly; it would be easy to speculate about other possibilities and about many variations in each case. If China should enter a period of bitter power struggles and widespread domestic turmoil at the time of the succession, in fact, the conceivable outcomes are so numerous that it is difficult even to speculate about them.

In view of the possibilities—and uncertainties—about what may occur domestically in China in the immediate post-Mao period, what can be said about the directions of China's foreign policy in the period ahead? Here too, either a relatively sanguine or a comparatively pessimistic view is arguable, with projections varying accordingly. If one is sanguine—as I am inclined to be at present—several trends and developments appear likely.

There is little doubt that post-Mao leaders, whoever they are, will continue to give high priority to the buildup of China's national power and to the expansion of China's international influence. The speed with which they can strengthen the country's foundations for modern power will obviously be significantly affected by the regime's success in solving its domestic problems—i.e., in preserving unity, achieving political stability, and spurring economic growth. However, even if the post-Mao transition is difficult, as long as the country does not experience extreme political and economic setbacks, the military-industrial basis for modern power in China can be expected to grow steadily in the future as in the past.

On balance, it seems highly likely that China, after Mao, will continue to pursue activist policies abroad, diplomatically, politically, and economically. The extreme isolationism of the Cultural Revolution period does not seem likely to be soon repeated. The benefits that have accrued to China—not only in security terms but in relation to its broad political and economic interests—as a result of its outward reach since the Cultural Revolution have been substantial, and consequently it would be difficult for any post-Mao leaders, whatever their ideological preferences on strategy and tactics might be, to argue persuasively that the country should turn inward once again in any extreme fashion.

Serious internal turmoil would obviously impose limits on China's ability to pursue activist policies abroad. Not only would the country's leaders be heavily preoccupied with domestic problems; they would also be greatly constrained by domestic weaknesses. But internal problems would not necessarily prevent the leadership from continuing to pursue many of its goals through low-cost low-risk diplomacy and policies of political maneuver. (Even the impotent Peking government of the Republican warlord period attempted this with some success.)

Chinese foreign policy will doubtless continue to be motivated by a mixture of ideological goals and practical considerations of national interest, and the mixture may vary over time. However, in the years immediately ahead, under the kinds of leadership that now seem most likely to emerge, the main thrust of China's foreign policy will probably be—as it has been since 1969—in the direction of increased flexibility and pragmatism. Abroad, as at home, priority will probably be given to the solution of immediate and pressing concrete problems rather than to the demands of any ideologically motivated grand design, and in practical terms China's foreign policy is therefore likely to focus primarily on state-to-state relations rather than on support of foreign revolutions or on ideological goals.

The overriding foreign policy concern of Chinese leaders, whoever they are, will almost certainly continue to be—in the period ahead as in recent years—the enhancement of China's national security. Accordingly, priority will probably continue to be placed, in practice if not in theory, on the problems of dealing with the other major powers that are involved in Asian affairs. The Chinese may continue to denounce "power politics" and abjure any desire to achieve superpower status, but they will almost certainly focus their primary attention on their relationships with the Soviet Union, the United States, and Japan.

In their propaganda as well as in their diplomacy and foreign aid programs, they can be expected to try both to expand China's activities and influence in the Third World and to broaden China's relationships with the developed nations in Europe and elsewhere; but the realities of evolving big power relationships in the new multipolar situation in Asia will probably be the most important factor shaping their broad foreign policies.

In dealing with other powers, China can be expected to continue pursuing an essentially independent and flexible policy, striving to achieve maximum room for maneuver and avoiding any clear-cut alliances or alignments with other major powers. Moreover, confronted by several powers that are clearly stronger than China (militarily or economically or both), and constrained by serious internal problems, the Chinese leadership seems highly likely, at least throughout the rest of this decade, to continue to maintain a military-security posture that is essentially defensive and to pursue cautious, low-risk policies designed to avoid large-scale military conflict. Even if new leaders after Mao should decide to adopt a more revolutionary, militant, and ideological posture, such as the regime did in the late 1950s and again in the late 1960s, it is reasonable to assume they will continue to be fairly realistic, as Chinese leaders have been in the past, in assessing the realities of power relationships and in recognizing that China's military inferiority—as well as its domestic problems—dictate prudence in its policies abroad. This will not necessarily preclude, of course, the possibility of pressures (or even small-scale low-risk intervention) in areas on China's immediate periphery. However, the likelihood of reckless adventurism seems fairly remote.

One of the most important questions for all concerned about China's external relations in the period ahead is whether or not radical changes are likely to occur in Peking's policy toward one or more of the other major powers involved in Asia. More specifically, will post-Mao leaders make drastic changes in China's policy toward the Soviet Union, paralleled by major changes in policy toward the United States or Japan or both? Will the present pattern of Sino-Soviet relations undergo dramatic change as a result of actions taken by either Peking or Moscow, or both, at the time of the succession? The trend in these big power relationships will have profound effects on the basic issues of war and peace in Asia and on the prospects for stability in the entire region during the rest of this decade.

One cannot exclude any of several possible developments in Sino-Soviet relations. If the succession in China is relatively smooth and the resulting leadership is led by Chou En-lai or others who think like him, no drastic or radical change seems likely. Under such leadership, China can be expected to continue its efforts to improve relations with the United States and Japan in order to increase its area for maneuver and strengthen its position in countering what is now perceived to be a serious Soviet threat to China's security. It is very possible, however, that even a leadership of this sort might at some point decide to adopt a more flexible policy toward Moscow in order to explore the possibilities for reducing the present level of tension. If it were to do so, and Moscow were to be conciliatory in its response, a process of limited Sino-Soviet détente might be set in motion. Such a limited détente would probably not be seriously destabilizing in its effects on the region as a whole; in fact, if it substantially reduced the danger of a Sino-Soviet war, it could contribute positively to the evolution of a more stable four-power relationship in Asia in the years ahead.

Other possibilities could, however, have seriously destabilizing effects. One would be a decision by post-Mao Chinese leaders who disagree with the main thrust of the foreign policy strategy evolved by Mao and Chou since 1969 to attempt a major reorientation of Chinese policy toward full-scale reconciliation with the Soviet Union. If such a reorientation were accompanied by a more hostile policy toward the United States or Japan, as it well might, it would clearly create new fears throughout East Asia, and would necessitate fundamental reassessments by the United States and Japan of their policies toward China, the Soviet Union, and the East Asian region as a whole.

The most dangerous possibility of all would be a major Sino-Soviet military conflict. Conceivably, a situation of extreme confusion in China at the time of the succession might tempt the Russians to consider any of several policies designed to try, through military pressures, political manipulation, or even direct intervention, to influence the succession outcome. In such a situation, Chinese passions as well as fears would doubtless increase greatly. The result would probably be heightened tension, which could provoke actions and reactions that might eventuate in overt Sino-Soviet conflict. Even if such a conflict did not spread in such a way as to involve others directly, it would probably have profoundly adverse effects throughout East Asia and worldwide.

There is relatively little reason to believe at present that a major Sino-Soviet conflict is inevitable, or even that it is likely. On the contrary, there is good reason to assume that, even if tensions were to rise, both sides would operate under severe constraints, and neither would be likely deliberately to try to provoke major conflict—above all because of mutual fears of nuclear disaster. Nevertheless, the potential for conflict certainly exists, and the danger is that it could erupt as a result of miscalculation. The danger will probably be at its height during and immediately after the succession occurs in China. No matter how one assesses the possibility or probability of open Sino-Soviet military conflict, the very fact that such a conflict is conceivable highlights one of the greatest potential dangers to peace and stability in the Asian region in the period immediately ahead.

Implications for U.S. Policy

Since the focus of this study has been on China itself, not on U.S. problems in dealing with China, it would not be appropriate to conclude it with a brief and therefore superficial discussion of the detailed issues that are likely to arise in future U.S. policy toward China; such issues are too complex for such a treatment. It is appropriate, however, to examine briefly some of the broad implications for U.S. policy toward China of the foregoing analysis of China's basic problems and prospects.

The most important point is an elementary one. To deal with China effectively in the years ahead, it is clearly necessary that the U.S. government and the American public have a better understanding than in the past of the basic forces at work in China, the changing character of the regime and the society, and the competitive pressures that will shape trends in the future. The starting point for this should be a recognition that China is engaged in a historic and difficult struggle to modernize, develop, and define its role in the world and that, as the Maoist era draws to a close, the Chinese face an array of unresolved problems that create great uncertainties about the future.

The tendency of Americans has been to shape their images of China to fit their own preconceptions and mood of the moment, with minimal understanding of the realities of the situation. During the past quarter-century, many Americans have tended to view China either as an aggressive colossus about to overrun Asia or as a crippled giant on the verge of internal collapse. Recently, since the sudden improvement of Sino-American relations began in 1971, the tendency has been to view it as a country with few visible problems, surging ahead at breakneck pace toward achieving a model "new China" at home and superpower status abroad. All of these images have badly distorted the realities of the situation.

A rational policy toward China must be based on a more realistic and sophisticated view of the enormous complexity of the forces shaping the nature of the Chinese regime and Chinese policies both at home and abroad. Because of the basic uncertainties that China's transition from the Maoist era to the post-Mao era involves, it is essential to be prepared for change. It is also necessary, however, to understand the parameters of likely change and the factors that will determine the direction of change. Understanding these parameters and factors will enable the United States to avoid an irrational response to change—whether it takes the form of unjustifiable alarm or unrealistic euphoria.

For the foreseeable future—at least during the remainder of this decade—the China with which the world will have to deal is not likely to be an aggressive colossus, and it certainly will not suddenly become a superpower. While conceivably it could become a crippled giant, the probability is that it will not—if it can avoid extreme conflict at the time of the succession. Nor is it likely to be a model "new China" of the kind that some of the currently fashionable euphoric descriptions of the country seem to imply. The reality will be much more complex.

Assuming it does matter to the rest of the world what kind of China emerges in the post-Mao period, what should the world hope for? A China that, as a result of succession struggles, is severely weakened, politically unstable, and highly vulnerable? Or a China that is able to make a relatively smooth transition to a comparatively stable post-Mao leadership, and is able not only to maintain national unity, ensure social order, foster continued economic development, and guarantee China's security, but also to play an increasing role in the normal patterns of international relations?

If one were to assume that a unified, stable, developing China in the post-Mao period would be likely to pose an imminent aggressive threat of serious proportions in the period immediately ahead, one might well argue that it would be better for all concerned if China were to become a crippled giant. However, as argued earlier, there is good reason to believe that a threatening China of this sort is not likely to emerge in the foreseeable future. The greater danger would probably be posed by the existence of an extremely weak, vulnerable, and fearful China. If a China of this sort were to emerge, the chances of conflict that could endanger the stability of East Asia would probably increase.

To what extent can other countries have a significant influence on the kind of China that develops in the post-Mao period? There is no doubt that the nature of the post-Mao regime and the direction of its policies will be determined above all by powerful domestic forces now at work in China, rather than by decisions made in foreign capitals. This does not mean, however, that the policies of other nations will have no effect on the regime's future leadership and policies. China, like other nations, reacts to external as well as internal pressures, and even relatively marginal influences resulting from actions taken by foreign nations could be extremely important, in either a positive or a negative sense, in the period ahead.

Any attempt by other major powers—in particular the United States or the Soviet Union or both—to pursue at the time of the succession in China manipulative policies designed to try to influence the outcome of the interplay of domestic forces would probably be counterproductive for the external power or powers involved and threatening to the stability and prospects of peace in the area. On the other hand, if the major powers exercise restraint when the succession in China occurs, maintain a conciliatory posture, and demonstrate their desire not only to establish workable relations with Mao's successors but also to help China's future leaders cope with the country's fundamental problems, the prospects that China will be inclined to pursue relatively moderate policies in the post-Mao period are almost certain to be improved, and the dangers of conflict are likely to be reduced.

Few Americans would question, in the light of recent improvements in Sino-American relations, that it is currently in the interest of the United States for Washington to continue its efforts to reduce tensions, broaden ties with Peking, and work toward "normalized" relations. But what are the implications for U.S. policy of the uncertainties posed by the approaching succession? Uncertainty about the future argues, in my view, for making every possible effort now—just as the Mao-Chou leadership in China today appears to be doing—to strengthen and consolidate the new Sino-American relationship before the succession actually occurs, to try to minimize the chance of any drastic reversal after Mao dies. The United States should also emphasize that it will continue to strive to cement good relations with China no matter who holds the reins of power in Peking.

A less obvious but nevertheless important proposition is that, because a Sino-Soviet conflict would pose great dangers, it is very much in the U.S. interest not to try to manipulate or exacerbate tensions between Peking and Moscow but rather to encourage restraint and moderation on both sides in the Sino-Soviet relationship. The U.S. hope should be that after Mao goes there will be no drastic sudden change in Sino-Soviet relations, whether toward close alignment by China with the Soviet Union or toward escalation of Sino-Soviet tensions to the point where they could result in overt military conflict. Instead, it should be the U.S. hope that leaders in both Peking and Moscow will decide to try to reduce tensions gradually, in ways that will contribute not only to their mutual security but also to the stability of the entire East Asian region. The leverage that the United States possesses to work directly for such an outcome may be limited, but the potential influence that might be exercised by Washington simply as a result of the basic posture it adopts toward both powers should not be underestimated. If the United States were to pursue a deliberate manipulative policy, attempting to "use" Peking to balance Moscow or Moscow to balance Peking, or were to allow itself to be manipulated even in a subtle fashion by one or the other of these powers, the dangers inherent in the situation would increase. However, if American policy makers follow an even-handed course, continuing to seek improved relations with both Peking and Moscow and using whatever influence they can to encourage restraint in the approaches of China and the Soviet Union toward each other as well as in their relations with the United States, this should reinforce those forces working for stability and peace in the region.

It is essential that in the context of the changing four-power relationships in East Asia the United States continue to maintain a very close relationship with Japan. It should also do what it can to encourage cooperation rather than conflict between Peking and Tokyo. The U.S.–Japanese alliance is clearly the focal point at present of American security and economic interests in East Asia, and if the United States were forced to "choose" today between friendly relations with China or friendly relations with Japan, it would have to choose Japan. But the aim of U.S. policy should be to prevent the necessity for such a choice by working to improve relations with both.

In bilateral relations with China, the United States can and should attempt to develop a range of concrete policies toward China that will at least indirectly support those in Peking who argue that it is in China's interest not only to continue developing an improved relationship with the United States but also to play an increasingly moderate and cooperative role in the broader international community. Through increased exchanges and expanded trade relations, and conceivably by providing certain types of aid as well, the United States (and other countries) should try to assist China's post-Mao leaders to solve some of the country's most pressing economic and other problems. To the extent that this is feasible, and successful, it may help to strengthen, at least to some extent, the hand of those Chinese who, broadly speaking, favor relatively flexible, pragmatic, and moderate approaches to problems both at home and abroad.

The United States should also strive persistently to engage China's present and future leaders, whoever they are, in serious discussions of the basic military-security problems in Asia and to involve them in cooperative efforts to deal with such vital issues as arms control and disarmament. Many important military-security problems will persist for years to come in East Asia, and China's participation will be essential to any serious attempt to deal with them. The need to involve China in nuclear arms control efforts will clearly grow as China's nuclear capabilities improve, and there will come a point when Peking's cooperation will be essential to ensure progress in this field.

The need to engage China's leaders in efforts to solve such problems will exist whoever the country's future leaders may be. But the prospects for dealing effectively with Peking and working toward solution of such problems will be significantly influenced by the type of leadership that emerges in the future and the general direction of post-Mao domestic trends, as well as by future Chinese attitudes toward all the major powers involved in Asia.

One basic U.S. goal should be the creation of a more stable relationship among all the major powers in Asia—the United States, China, Japan, and the Soviet Union—and India as well, without ignoring the interests of the smaller nations. To work toward this end, the United States must, as already emphasized, continue to place high priority both on the continuation of a close American-Japanese relationship (in both the economic and military-security areas) and on the maintenance of a stable relationship with the Soviet Union (especially in the military-security field). But it must also work steadily to cement and broaden bilateral U.S.–China ties, and try to ensure that the trend toward improved relations with China will continue into the post-Mao period despite the uncertainties that the succession in China will inevitably bring.

To this end, the United States should use its influence in whatever ways it can to reduce rather than increase the likelihood that China will encounter major disasters either at home or abroad. The overall aim should be to improve the prospect that China will emerge from the post-Mao succession with a regime that is capable of maintaining internal stability and coping with the nation's enormous domestic problems and willing, in its dealings with the outside world, to go even further than it has in the period since the Cultural Revolution in developing more extensive and more constructive relationships with other nations. While no one can be certain that this will be the outcome of developments in the period ahead, it is what the United States should hope for, and should use whatever influence it can bring to bear to support.

Notes

THE CONCLUSIONS in this volume are based on analysis for more than two decades of published Chinese materials, above all articles in the Chinese Communist press, plus monitored radio broadcasts from China. My perspective in studying post-1949 developments has been influenced also, however, by several years of study and residence in China before 1949, half a year of observation of the Chinese Communist regime at the time of its takeover of power in 1949, and several years of research in Hong Kong in the 1950s and 1960s, and by insights obtained on the present situation and current trends on a visit to China in the winter of 1972–73.

Every judgment in this book could be bolstered with citations from the Chinese press and radio broadcasts, but it has seemed neither desirable nor appropriate to burden an essentially interpretive essay with an elaborate apparatus of documentation of this sort. I have therefore restricted such citations to a minimum.

My notes are intended to serve several different purposes. Whenever I have included quotations or statistics in the text, I have cited either primary or secondary sources for them. I have also cited sources for my data on specific points that I believe some readers might consider controversial. In addition, I have included a number of general bibliographical notes, especially at the start of chapters or sections of chapters, but at various other points in the discussion as well, to guide interested readers to useful background and supportive data. Finally, I have tried to give credit to at least some of the authors of important secondary sources on China that have been of particular value to me—and whose work should, I believe, be of interest to readers who may wish to pursue certain topics or points further.

I have been highly selective in all this; the literature on contemporary China is now extensive, and to have cited any significant portion of the relevant writings would have required documentation far beyond what seems appropriate for a volume of this sort. Readers wishing to explore the secondary literature further will find bibliographies in many of the books that I cite; in addition I would recommend to them a very useful topically organized bibliography on contemporary Chinese politics: Michel C. Oksenberg, Nancy Bateman, and James B. Anderson, *A Bibliography of Secondary English Literature on Contemporary Chinese Politics* (Columbia University, East Asian Institute, no date.)

Perhaps a brief comment is desirable on several of the sources that are cited frequently in the notes. *Survey of China Mainland Press, Current Background*, and *Selections from China Mainland Magazines* are publications that contain English translations of Chinese Communist materials. All three are produced by the American Consulate-General, Hong Kong, and are distributed by the National Technical Information Service, U.S. Department of Commerce. The *Foreign Broadcast Information Service* and the *Joint Publications Research Service* are also produced by the U.S. government and are available from the same source. The latter contains translations of varied types of written Chinese Communist material; the former contains transcriptions of Chinese Communist radio broadcasts. *Peking Review* is an official Chinese Communist journal published in several foreign languages for foreign audiences. *Current Scene* is a journal published by the American Consulate-General in Hong Kong that contains articles by both government analysts and private scholars. The former, especially those labeled "The Editor," are often of special value, since they reflect careful research by members of the Consulate-General drawing on the extensive information available to them. The *China Quarterly* (Contemporary China Institute, London) and *Asian Survey* (University of California Press) are the two English-language journals that probably contain the largest number of useful scholarly articles on contemporary China.

Although—like other students of China—I have had to rely heavily in this study on what one can learn from official Chinese data and statements, I was able, as already noted, to gain useful insights as well as new information on my trip to China, in December 1972 to January 1973, as a member of a delegation sent by the National Committee on United States–China Relations. In this intensive month-long visit, we were able to travel fairly extensively, and in eight major cities and nearby suburban and rural areas we visited factories of all sizes, communes of several types, and educational institutions at all levels. Equally important, we had numerous interviews and discussions with Chinese officials of many sorts, both in Peking and at provincial and lower levels. I have not felt it appropriate, except in a very few instances where detailed facts obtained from the formal briefings are used, to cite specific sources for data and impressions derived from this trip, but in varied ways, both concrete and intangible, my judgments about the "reality" of existing conditions today and the direction of major current trends, as well as about continuity and change over the past twenty-three years, were clearly influenced by what I was able to see and learn in China on that trip.

Chapter I

1. General studies of the Chinese Communist regime as it evolved in the immediate post-1949 period include W. W. Rostow (ed.), *The Prospects for Communist China* (Technology Press of M.I.T. and Wiley, 1954), a broad-ranging analytical study that attempts to look to the future and project probable trends; and A. Doak Barnett, *Communist China: The Early Years, 1949–55* (Praeger, 1964), a volume of contemporary reports on major developments. Richard L. Walker, *China Under Communism: The First Five Years* (Yale University Press, 1955), and Peter S. H. Tang, *Communist China*

Today, Vol. 1 (Research Institute on the Sino-Soviet Bloc, 1957 and 1961) are detailed studies of the regime in the 1950s, both of which pay considerable attention to the influence of the Soviet Union and the Soviet model on China, as seen at that time by the two authors. The concepts associated with a "totalitarian" model were clearly a major influence on much of the analysis of China in that period, as a number of recent critics of that model have stressed. In my view, while some analysis in the 1950s may have pushed the use of the totalitarian model too far, the tendency recently has probably gone too far in rejecting, rather than simply modifying, the totalitarian model in retrospective analyses of China in the early 1950s.

2. The most important primary source for study of ideology in contemporary China is, of course, Mao Tse-tung, *Selected Works of Mao Tse-tung*, 4 vols. (Peking: Foreign Languages Press, 1961–65). An excellent recent volume analyzing many facets of ideology in China is Chalmers Johnson (ed.), *Ideology and Politics in Contemporary China* (University of Washington Press, 1973). Among the most useful analyses of the Thought of Mao Tse-tung are Benjamin I. Schwartz, *Communism and China: Ideology in Flux* (Harvard University Press, 1968); and Stuart R. Schram, *The Political Thought of Mao Tse-tung* (rev. ed., Praeger, 1969); there are also numerous journal articles of value by these two authors. James Chieh Hsiung, *Ideology and Practice: The Evolution of Chinese Communism* (Praeger, 1970), contains a stimulating discussion of contemporary Chinese Communist ideology and its Chinese roots; and Arthur A. Cohen, *The Communism of Mao Tse-tung* (University of Chicago Press, 1964), traces the Marxist-Leninist origins of and precedents for many Chinese Communist ideological positions. For discussion of the "two lines," see sources listed in Chapter 3, note 2. Some other particularly useful journal articles discussing special aspects of Mao's Thought are listed in subsequent notes in this chapter.

3. In the late 1960s Mao's supporters argued that early differences on concrete policy questions actually reflected basic ideological conflicts that trace back even to the pre-1949 period; see, for example, "Outline of the Struggle Between the Two Lines from the Eve of the Founding of the People's Republic of China through the 11th Plenum of the 8th CCP Central Committee," *Current Background*, No. 884 (July 18, 1969). Although I do not find this convincing, this is not to say there were not important differences of outlook even in the early years. Chang Kuo-t'ao (one of the dozen founders of the Chinese Communist Party), in the source cited in note 21 in Chapter 4, argues provocatively that from the start Chinese Communist leaders were identifiable as belonging to one of two general groups: those oriented primarily toward "ideology and theory" and those oriented primarily toward "action and practice." But it is another matter to say that these were really basic differences in ideology. In my opinion they were not, and the Maoists have had to rewrite, and distort, history to try to link early policy differences to basic ideological differences.

4. In a "Speech At a Work Conference of the Central Committee" on October 25, 1966, Mao stated that, after the division of the leadership into a

first front and second front, "it looked as though many independent kingdoms were set up. . . . I did not take charge of routine work. . . . I then felt [by the fall of 1965] that in Peking my suggestions could not be put into practice." (*Current Background*, No. 891, Oct. 8, 1969, p. 75.) At a "Report meeting" on the previous day, he had said: "Teng Hsiao-p'ing . . . has never consulted me about anything since 1959" (*Current Background*, No. 891, Oct. 8, 1969, p. 71); this statement obviously cannot be taken literally, but it doubtless does reflect a real feeling on Mao's part about his inability to control China's bureaucracies.

5. There are numerous studies that illuminate the multiple "causes" of the Cultural Revolution; some very useful ones are Philip Bridgham, "Mao's 'Cultural Revolution': Origin and Development," *China Quarterly*, No. 29 (January–March 1967), pp. 1–35; Richard Baum and Frederick C. Teiwes, *Ssu-Ch'ing: The Socialist Education Movement of 1962–1966* (University of California, Center for Chinese Studies, China Research Monograph 2, 1968); J. D. Simmonds, *China: Evolution of a Revolution, 1959–66* (Australian National University, Department of International Relations, Working Paper 9, 1968); Charles Neuhauser, "The Chinese Communist Party in the 1960s: Prelude to the Cultural Revolution," *China Quarterly*, No. 32 (October–December 1967), pp. 3–36; W. F. Dorrill, *Power, Policy, and Ideology in the Making of China's "Cultural Revolution,"* Memorandum RM 5731-PR (Rand Corp., August 1968); Lucian W. Pye, "Coming Dilemmas for China's Leaders," *Foreign Affairs*, Vol. 44, No. 3 (April 1966), pp. 387–402; Roderick MacFarquhar, "Mao's Last Revolution," *Foreign Affairs*, Vol. 45, No. 1 (October 1966), pp. 112–24; and A. Doak Barnett, *China After Mao* (Princeton University Press, 1967).

6. The most prevalent view now among China scholars, and one that I share, is that the Lushan Party plenum in 1959 was a watershed that can be regarded in many respects as the starting point of the polarization in the leadership that laid the groundwork for the Cultural Revolution, and that the concrete steps that led to the Cultural Revolution itself began at a meeting of the Politburo Standing Committee in September 1965.

7. See A. Doak Barnett (with a contribution by Ezra Vogel), *Cadres, Bureaucracy, and Political Power in Communist China* (Columbia University Press, 1967), especially pp. 38–47 and 187–90. By the mid-1960s Mao was in open opposition to these trends; on January 29, 1965, for example, in a "Comment of [*sic*] Comrade Ch'en Cheng-jen's Report on Staying at a Selected Spot," Mao stated bluntly: "The bureaucratic class is a class sharply opposed to the working class and the poor and lower-middle peasants." *Current Background*, No. 891 (Oct. 8, 1969), p. 49.

8. A sophisticated analysis of the influence of bureaucratic politics on policy making in China is Michel C. Oksenberg, "Policy Formulation in Communist China: The Case of the 1957–8 Mass Irrigation Campaign" (Ph.D. dissertation, Columbia University, 1969).

9. Mao Tse-tung, *On the Correct Handling of Contradictions Among the People* (Peking: Foreign Languages Press, 1959), p. 43.

10. Some observers are inclined to believe that Mao has had a strong disposition to view any opposition to his values and policies as a sign of plotting to undermine his position or overthrow him. It is difficult, however, to obtain data that would either confirm or refute such a hypothesis.

11. The eleventh plenum of the Central Committee (which in August 1966 adopted Mao's program for the Cultural Revolution) was apparently "packed" with outsiders (including many students)—something unprecedented in the history of Central Committee meetings—and a speech by Chiang Ch'ing, Mao's wife, not long thereafter stressed that adoption of a "correct" line was more important than legal niceties concerning "majority" and "minority" views, suggesting that Mao's views were probably really minority views at that time. See Dorrill, *Power, Policy, and Ideology*, pp. 141–42.

12. In recent years, and especially during the Cultural Revolution, the dominant leadership in China has tended to define the values in Mao's Thought as immutable and universally valid truths. Actually, to understand fully Mao's Thought, one must understand its evolution over time. In the discussion in this chapter, however, it has not been possible to discuss its evolution. For this, the reader is referred to sources such as those listed in note 2; one of the best and most succinct summaries of the historical development of Mao's Thought is Schram, *The Political Thought of Mao Tse-tung*; see especially the Introduction, pp. 15–144, but also the explanatory text in each chapter.

13. The Chinese Communists themselves, it should be noted, have consistently, since Yenan days, referred to Mao's concepts and ideas as "The Thought of Mao Tse-tung" and have avoided labeling them an "ism." There are various interpretations concerning why this has been so; see, for example, Hsiung, *Ideology and Practice*, especially pp. 126–65, and Franz Schurmann, *Ideology and Organization in Communist China* (rev. ed., University of California Press, 1968), pp. 17–57. I believe, however, that the use in English of the terms "Maoism" and "Maoist" is justifiable, and it is now sanctioned by general usage.

14. The Chinese phrase, *pu-tuan ko-ming*, can be and often is translated as "continuous revolution" or "permanent revolution." For a discussion of the concept, see Stuart R. Schram, "Mao Tse-tung and the Theory of the Permanent Revolution, 1958–69," *China Quarterly*, No. 46 (April–June 1971), pp. 221–44. See also John Bryan Starr, "Conceptual Foundations of Mao Tse-tung's Theory of Continuous Revolution," *Asian Survey*, Vol. 11, No. 6 (June 1971), pp. 610–28.

15. A good discussion of the concept of contradictions in Mao's Thought and its effect on his behavior is in Schurmann, *Ideology and Organization*, pp. 73–104. See also, for analysis of Mao's ideas regarding contradictions, Vsevolod Holubnychy, "Mao Tse-tung's Materialistic Dialectics," *China Quarterly*, No. 19 (July–September 1964), pp. 3–37.

16. John Wilson Lewis, *Leadership in Communist China* (Cornell University Press, 1963), is a detailed analysis by an American scholar of the "mass line" and its operation, especially in the 1950s.

17. See Maurice Meisner, "Leninism and Maoism: Some Populist Perspectives on Marxism-Leninism in China," *China Quarterly*, No. 45 (January-March 1971), pp. 2–36.

18. See Ezra F. Vogel, "Voluntarism and Social Control," in Donald W. Treadgold (ed.), *Soviet and Chinese Communism: Similarities and Differences* (University of Washington Press, 1967), pp. 168–84.

19. Stuart R. Schram, "Chinese and Leninist Components in the Personality of Mao Tse-tung," *Asian Survey*, Vol. 3, No. 6 (June 1963), p. 268.

20. See *On Khrushchov's* [sic] *Phoney Communism and Its Historical Lessons for the World* (Peking: Foreign Languages Press, 1964); the text is also available in the appendixes of Barnett, *China After Mao*, pp. 123–95. Published as a joint editorial in *People's Daily* and *Red Flag* on July 14, 1964, this important statement can be assumed to reflect Mao's views at that time. It is extremely revealing of the concerns that led Mao to initiate the Cultural Revolution. After condemning the Soviet Union under Khrushchev, the editorial goes on: "Is our society today thoroughly clean? No, it is not. Classes and class struggle still remain . . . degenerates do their utmost to find protectors and agents in the higher leading bodies. We . . . must keep fully alert." It then summarizes Mao's "theories and policies" to prevent "the restoration of capitalism" in China.

21. The text of this, from which the following quotations are drawn, is in "Chairman Mao Discusses Twenty Manifestations of Bureaucracy," *Joint Publications Research Service*, JPRS 49826 (Feb. 12, 1970), *Translations on Communist China*, No. 90, "Selections from Chairman Mao," pp. 40–43.

22. On August 1, 1966, Mao wrote a letter to middle school students in Peking stating "it is right to rebel," and when he issued his "first big-character poster" on August 5, 1966, he did so under the slogan "bombard the headquarters." See *Current Background*, No. 891 (Oct. 8, 1969), p. 63. The glorification of the Paris Commune at this stage of the Cultural Revolution, moreover, had strong anarchist undertones. Mao himself states that he was much influenced by anarchism before turning to Marxism (see Stuart Schram, *Mao Tse-tung* [Penguin Books, 1966], p. 49), and in the early stages of the Cultural Revolution this strain in his thought appeared to have a strong influence on his actions. In a talk before a Central Committee Work Conference on August 23, 1966, Mao stated, "a few months of disturbances will be mostly for the good" (*Current Background*, No. 891, Oct. 8, 1969, p. 891).

23. See Schram, *The Political Thought of Mao Tse-tung*, pp. 331–71; and Jerome Ch'en (ed.), *Mao* (Prentice-Hall, 1969), pp. 98–111.

24. On September 6, 1944, Mao made a now-famous speech on "Serve the People"; for the text of this, see *Peking Review* (Sept. 6, 1968), p. 5. And in the section of the "little red book" of quotations from Mao, almost all of the ones in the section on "serving the people" are from statements by Mao in the 1944–45 period; see Mao Tse-tung, *Quotations from Chairman Mao Tse-tung* (Praeger, 1967), pp. 95–97. It was not until the Cultural Revolution, however, that this slogan achieved the prominence it now enjoys.

25. Many of Mao's statements reveal these biases. They are also well

illustrated in his June 26, 1965, "Instruction on Health Work." In this he stated: "The Ministry of Public Health is not that of the people, and it is better to rename it as the Ministry of Urban Health ... or the Health Ministry of the Urban Lords. ... Medical education must be reformed. Basically there is no need to read so many books. ... The method of training doctors [now] is ... for the purpose of serving the cities. ... Only some doctors who have been out of college for one or two years and are not very proficient should be kept by hospitals in the cities. All the rest should go to the countryside. ... In medical and health work, put the stress on rural areas." See "Collection of Statements by Mao Tse-tung (1956–1967)," in *Current Background*, No. 892 (Oct. 21, 1969), p. 20.

26. During the Cultural Revolution, almost all those whose values differed from Mao's were labeled "revisionists" and supporters of "the capitalist road." Neither of these terms—nor others, such as "Liuists," which many non-Chinese observers have adopted—is really accurate or adequate; hence I will simply label those who have differed from Mao on many (but by no means all) issues "non-Maoists."

27. Many political scientists, including myself, who have been concerned with the major value conflicts between Mao and others have focused primary attention on Mao's differences with bureaucratic and technocratic groups. The clashes between his values and those of many writers, artists, and intellectuals have been of equal importance, however. These are analyzed with insight and skill by Merle Goldman, in *Literary Dissent in Communist China* (Harvard University Press, 1967); and in "Party Policies Toward the Intellectuals: The Unique Blooming and Contending of 1961–2," in John Wilson Lewis (ed.), *Party Leadership and Revolutionary Power in China* (Cambridge University Press, 1970), pp. 268–303.

28. Michel Oksenberg, in "China, The Convulsive Society," Foreign Policy Association, *Headline Series*, No. 203 (December 1970), pp. 5–19, discusses in an illuminating way five "belief systems" that he believes to be in conflict in contemporary China. The five are: the traditional, the revolutionary, the technological, the bureaucratic, and the totalitarian.

29. P'eng Teh-huai's "Letter of Opinion" of July 14, 1959, criticizing the Great Leap Forward, is one eloquent statement of a view that was probably shared by many. "Petty-bourgeois fanaticism renders us liable to commit 'Left' mistakes," he said. "In the course of the great leap forward of 1958, like many comrades, I was bewitched by the achievements of the great leap forward and the passion of the mass movement. Some 'Left' tendencies developed to quite an extent; we always wanted to enter into communism at one step. Our minds swayed by the idea of taking the lead, we forgot the mass line and the style of seeking truth from facts which the Party had formed over a long time. So far as our method of thinking was concerned, we often confused strategic planning with concrete measures, the long-term policies with immediate steps, the whole with the part, and the big collective with the small collective. ... As a result, divorced from reality, we failed to gain the support of the masses. ... In the view of some comrades, putting politics in

command could be a substitute for everything. . . . To correct these 'Left' manifestations is generally more difficult than to get rid of the Rightist conservative ideas." See Union Research Institute, *The Case of Peng Teh-huai 1959–1968* (Hong Kong: Union Press Limited, 1968), pp. 11–12.

30. This was the dominant tone, for example, in Liu Shao-ch'i's "Political Report" to the Eighth Party Congress, on September 15, 1956; see *Eighth National Congress of the Communist Party of China*, Vol. 1, Documents (Peking: Foreign Languages Press, 1956), pp. 15–111. During the Cultural Revolution the Maoists accused Liu of having "propagated," at that time, "the theory of the extinction of class struggle and publicized that the class character of the bourgeoisie had changed"; see "The Defender of Capitalist Economy," in *Current Background*, No. 836 (Sept. 25, 1967), p. 36.

31. One of the best discussions of this subject is in Joseph R. Levenson, *Confucian China and Its Modern Fate: The Problems of Intellectual Continuity* (University of California Press, 1958).

32. See "Talk at the Hangchow Conference," Dec. 21, 1965, in *Current Background*, No. 891 (Oct. 8, 1969), p. 51.

33. Some of the complex mixtures of values that have affected Chinese policy making and organizational behavior are discussed in Harry Harding, *Maoist Theories of Policy Making and Organization*, Report R-487-PR (Rand Corp., September 1969).

34. The basic documents on the Tenth Party Congress and its results are the following: "Press Communique on CCP 10th National Congress Held 24–28 Aug.," and "List of the 319 members and alternate members of the Tenth Central Committee of the Communist Party of China," *Foreign Broadcast Information Service*, FBIS-Chi-73-168 (Aug. 29, 1973), pp. B1–B6; "Additions to Namelists in Communique on 10th CCP Congress," *Foreign Broadcast Information Service*, FBIS-Chi-73-169 (Aug. 30, 1973), pp. B1–B4; "Chou En-lai's Report to the 10th CCP National Congress," *Foreign Broadcast Information Service*, FBIS-Chi-73-170 (Aug. 31, 1973), pp. B1–B13; "Report by Wang Hung-wen 24 Aug on Revision of the CCP Constitution," pp. B1–B16, and "Constitution of CCP Adopted at the 10th National Congress," pp. B7–B11, both in *Foreign Broadcast Information Service*, FBIS-Chi-73-171 (Sept. 4, 1973).

35. In his famous May 7, 1966, letter to Lin Piao (from which the May 7 schools get their title) Mao declared that "education should be revolutionized." The term "revolution in education" came into usage not long thereafter; see "Chairman Mao on Revolution in Education," *Current Background*, No. 888 (Aug. 22, 1969), pp. 17 and 20. At the universities I visited in China in December 1972–January 1973, all aspects of current educational policies were described and analyzed under this rubric.

36. One of many official accounts of May 7 schools is "Liuho 'May 7' Cadre School Provides New Experience in Revolutionizing Organizations," *Peking Review*, (Oct. 11, 1968), pp. 23–24. A useful observer's account of such a school is Alexander Casella, "The Nanniwan May 7th Cadre School," *China Quarterly*, No. 53 (January–March 1973), pp. 153–57. A general dis-

cussion of the development of May 7 schools is in "The 'May 7' Cadre School and the 'May 7' Movement," *Issues and Studies*, Vol. 6, No. 11 (August 1970), pp. 14–15. Ten articles on these schools from the *People's Daily* are collected in "Operation of 'May 7' Cadre Schools," *Current Background*, No. 899 (Jan. 19, 1970).

37. Two stimulating, provocative, and controversial studies of China's "political culture" and the impact of Maoist Thought on it are Lucian W. Pye, *The Spirit of Chinese Politics* (M.I.T. Press, 1968), and Richard H. Solomon, *Mao's Revolution and the Chinese Political Culture* (University of California Press, 1971).

38. Any judgment of this sort must, of course, be highly subjective. Even though some recent visitors to China appear to have concluded that a very far-reaching "transformation" of values has occurred, on my own 1972–73 trip to China, I was impressed as much by apparent continuities of thought and behavior as by changes. Nevertheless, I am prepared to believe that the behavior of many Chinese has been significantly influenced by the enormous stress on the need to "serve the people" and some of the effects of this tremendous emphasis on social responsibility may well be lasting.

39. It is significant that as of early 1973 virtually all of the ranking systems in China for cadres, workers, teachers, professional people, and others were essentially the same as they had been before the Cultural Revolution. To a visitor, the degree to which, even today, rank-based protocol affects relationships is striking.

40. See Schram, *The Political Thought of Mao Tse-tung*, p. 42.

41. For readers who may be interested, some of the most useful broad studies of the Chinese Communist political system and the structure and operation of its organizations and institutions prior to the Cultural Revolution are Schurmann, *Ideology and Organization in Communist China*; Ezra F. Vogel, *Canton Under Communism* (Harvard University Press, 1969); Barnett, *Cadres, Bureaucracy, and Political Power in Communist China*; John Wilson Lewis, *Leadership in Communist China* (Cornell University Press, 1963); James R. Townsend, *Political Participation in Communist China* (University of California Press, 1967); John M. H. Lindbeck (ed.), *China: Management of a Revolutionary Society* (University of Washington Press, 1971); and A. Doak Barnett (ed.), *Chinese Communist Politics in Action* (University of Washington Press, 1969).

42. By the mid-1950s, when the regime adopted a state constitution (in 1954) and a new Party Constitution (in 1956), the general pattern of institutional structures, roles, and relationships appeared to have been firmly established. As will be discussed below, however, the dynamic of real political as well as economic and social change continued thereafter.

43. Much of the best analysis of the Cultural Revolution has appeared in journal articles. There are, however, several very useful books and monographic studies that deal wholly or in part with this period. See Thomas W. Robinson (ed.), *The Cultural Revolution in China* (University of California Press, 1971); Stanley Karnow, *Mao and China: From Revolution to Revolution* (Viking, 1972); Edward E. Rice, *Mao's Way* (University of California

Press, 1972); Michel Oksenberg and others, *The Cultural Revolution: 1967 in Review* (University of Michigan, Center for Chinese Studies, Michigan Papers in Chinese Studies, Nov. 2, 1968); Ping-ti Ho and Tang Tsou (eds.), *China in Crisis*, Vol. 1, Books 1 and 2 (University of Chicago Press, 1968); John Wilson Lewis (ed.), *Party Leadership and Revolutionary Power in China* (Cambridge University Press, 1970); Parris H. Chang, *Radicals and Radical Ideology in China's Cultural Revolution* (Columbia University, Research Institute on Communist Affairs, 1973); and Richard Baum (ed.), *China in Ferment: Perspectives on the Cultural Revolution* (Prentice-Hall, 1971). Useful articles written from varied perspectives include Philip Bridgham, "Mao's Cultural Revolution: The Struggle to Consolidate Power," *China Quarterly*, No. 41 (January–March 1970), pp. 1–25; Charles Neuhauser, "The Impact of the Cultural Revolution on the Chinese Communist Party Machine," *Asian Survey*, Vol. 8, No. 6 (June 1968), pp. 465–88; Richard M. Pfeffer, "The Pursuit of Purity: Mao's Cultural Revolution," *Problems of Communism*, Vol. 18, No. 6 (November–December 1969), pp. 12–25; Parris H. Chang, "Mao's Great Purge: A Political Balance Sheet," *Problems of Communism*, Vol. 18, No. 2 (March–April 1969), pp. 1–10; Victor C. Falkenheim, "The Cultural Revolution in Kwangsi, Yunnan, and Fukien," *Asian Survey*, Vol. 9, No. 8 (August 1969), pp. 580–97; Melvin Gurtov, "The Foreign Ministry and Foreign Affairs during the Cultural Revolution," *China Quarterly*, No. 40 (October–December 1969), pp. 65–102; and Barry Burton, "The Cultural Revolution's Ultra-Left Conspiracy: The 'May 16 Group,'" *Asian Survey*, Vol. 11, No. 11 (November 1971), pp. 1029–53. A number of first-person accounts of the Cultural Revolution, by Chinese and foreigners, have been written; among the best are Gordon A. Bennett and Ronald N. Montaperto, *Red Guard* (Doubleday, 1971), and Neale Hunter, *Shanghai Journal* (Praeger, 1969).

44. On October 24, 1966, in a "Speech at a Report Meeting," Mao Tse-tung stated: "Nobody had thought—not even I—that a single big character poster, the Red Guards and the large-scale exchange of revolutionary experiences would lead to the demise of various provincial and municipal committees." On the following day, in a speech at a Central Committee Work Conference, Mao commented on the initial effects of the Cultural Revolution: "the impact was quite violent. It was also beyond my expectation that the broadcast of the big-character poster of Peking University would stir up the whole country. . . . I myself had caused this big trouble and I cannot blame you if you have complaints against me." See "Long Live Mao Tse-tung Thought (A Collection of Statements by Mao Tse-tung)," *Current Background*, No. 891 (Oct. 8, 1969), pp. 70 and 75.

45. See Neuhauser, "The Impact of the Cultural Revolution," regarding the Cultural Revolution's effects on the Party; and Gurtov, "The Foreign Ministry and Foreign Affairs," regarding the impact on one major state agency. As will be noted below, however, small Party "core groups" continued in existence in at least some places despite the fact that Party Committees, as such, ceased operating.

46. Before my visit to China in December 1972–January 1973, I had been

aware, from Chinese publications, that such "core groups" or "leading groups" were widely established toward the end of the Cultural Revolution but not that they had existed, in at least some places, throughout the Cultural Revolution. In interviews in China, however, some cadres told me how such "core groups" had operated, even at the height of the Cultural Revolution turmoil, in their particular units.

47. This fact is highlighted in many first-person accounts, such as the story of a Red Guard member presented in Bennett and Montaperto, *Red Guard*. By 1968 a major theme of the regime's propaganda output was the need to combat "factionalism" and the so-called theory of many centers; see, for example, "Make a Class Analysis of Factionalism," *Peking Review* (May 10, 1968), pp. 2–3; and "Unite Under the Leadership of the Proletarian Headquarters Headed by Chairman Mao," *Peking Review* (Aug. 9, 1968), pp. 7–8.

48. See *Peking Review* (April 30, 1969) for the full official account of the Congress.

49. The 1969 Party Constitution had only twelve articles (in contrast to sixty in the 1956 Party Constitution); for texts, see *Peking Review* (April 30, 1969), pp. 36–39, and *The Constitution of the Communist Party of China* (Peking: Foreign Languages Press, 1956), pp. 9–49.

50. From conversations in December 1972–January 1973 with numerous cadres in China, many of whom had themselves spent time at May 7 schools, I learned that a high percentage of the very large numbers of cadres who were sent to such schools in the initial phase of the program from late 1968 and early 1969 on stayed at the schools for two or three years—although a few had shorter stays, and some have not yet returned to full-time regular work. Cadres who had not yet spent time at May 7 schools were still being sent to them in 1973 but generally for a few months rather than several years.

51. See Fang Chun-kuei, "An Analysis of the Current Status of Chinese Communist Party and Government Organs," *Issues and Studies*, Vol. 6, No. 4 (January 1970), pp. 50–55.

52. Examples of both general and specific discussions of this process at lower levels are Yü Wen, "Resolutely Taking the Road of Better Troops and Simpler Administration as Pointed Out by Chairman Mao," *People's Daily*, Dec. 11, 1969, in *Survey of China Mainland Press*, No. 4565 (Dec. 29, 1969), pp. 1–4; and Chin P'ing, "Pay Attention to Consolidating the Fruits of Better Troops and Simplified Administration," *Red Flag*, No. 12 (Nov. 29, 1969), in *Selections from China Mainland Magazines*, No. 669 (Dec. 29, 1969), pp. 12–16.

53. No official text has ever been published. However, a text released by the Nationalist regime (presumably one smuggled out to Taiwan from the mainland) is widely believed to be genuine. See *Foreign Broadcast Information Service*, FBIS-Chi-70-216 (Nov. 5, 1970), pp. B1–B6. See also "The PRC Draft Constitution," *Current Scene*, Vol. 8, No. 18 (Dec. 7, 1970), pp. 25–26.

54. The unofficial version of the new draft state constitution contains 30 articles, compared to 106 in the 1954 constitution. See first source cited in

note 53, pp. B1–B6, and *Constitution of the People's Republic of China* (Peking: Foreign Languages Press, 1961).

55. Article 2, in the text released by the Nationalists in 1970, cited in note 53 for this chapter.

56. See "The Case Against Lin Piao," *Chinese Law and Government*, Vol. 5, No. 3–4 (Fall–Winter 1972–73), p. 6.

57. A series of annual year-end review articles in the *Asian Survey* provide a useful picture of the evolution of the general situation in China from the end of the Cultural Revolution to the present. Richard Baum, "China: Year of the Mangoes," *Asian Survey*, Vol. 9, No. 1 (January 1969), pp. 1–17; Gordon A. Bennett, "China's Continuing Revolution: Will It Be Permanent?" *Asian Survey*, Vol. 10, No. 1 (January 1970), pp. 2–17; Harry Harding, "China: Toward Revolutionary Pragmatism," *Asian Survey*, Vol. 11, No. 1 (January 1971), pp. 51–67; Harry Harding, Jr., "China: The Fragmentation of Power," *Asian Survey*, Vol. 12, No. 1 (January 1972), pp. 1–15; and Thomas W. Robinson, "China in 1972: Socio-Economic Progress Amidst Political Uncertainty," *Asian Survey*, Vol. 13, No. 1 (January 1973), pp. 1–18. There has been some excellent reporting by newspapermen of developments in this period, also; see, for example, Seymour Topping, *Journey Between Two Chinas* (Harper and Row, 1972), and Tillman Durdin, "The New Face of Maoist China," *Problems of Communism*, Vol. 22, No. 5 (September–October 1971), pp. 1–13. Although a great many of the recent books by other sorts of visitors are insubstantial, some have been perceptive, including Ross Terrill, *800 Million Chinese: The Real China* (Atlantic Monthly Press, 1971), and Klaus Mehnert, *China Returns* (Dutton, 1972).

My discussion below of conditions as of 1973 draws upon my observations in China, and interviews with cadres in Communes, Street Committees, and factories in December 1972–January 1973, as well as reports by other visitors. The basis for all impressions is inevitably limited, and one cannot assume that the places and institutions one is allowed to visit are "typical," but since it is impossible to conduct research in depth, all judgments about the institutional situation at the grassroots level in China today must be based on this kind of evidence.

58. To cite three specific examples of the numbers of people classified as members of the "four [bad] elements" in various types of institutions, leading cadres in the Huai Hai Street Revolutionary Committee in Shanghai stated that 1.2 percent of the 68,000 people under its administration were so classified as of December 1972; in the Lo Tung Brigade of the T'ang T'ang Commune in Fo Kang Hsien in Kwangtung Province, 12 household heads, out of a total of 325 households in the Brigade, were so classified (i.e., between 3.5 and 4 percent); and in the Shanghai No. 31 Cotton Textile Mill, there were 67 persons classified as members of the "four [bad] elements" out of a total of 7,300-plus workers and staff members (or just under 1 percent). Members of the "four [bad] elements" are subjected to many kinds of special controls and restrictions.

59. The following discussion also relies heavily on information gathered from observation and interviews with cadres when I was in China in December 1972–January 1973. At that time the cadres I met emphasized that the process of rebuilding the national structures of the mass organizations would be accelerated in 1973, and developments since then have confirmed this.

60. My analysis of Party-Revolutionary Committee (government) relations, and of the nature of the merged structure now existing under the Party Committees and Revolutionary Committees, is based primarily on interviews in December 1972–January 1973 in China with leading cadres at provincial, municipal, and lower levels. Before I visited China, I had read Chinese press and journal accounts that suggested the possibility of such a merger. For example, an article published in early 1970 stated: "Since most of the members of the revolutionary committee are members of the Party committee, the administrative organs of the revolutionary committee are at the same time administrative organs of the Party committee; the Party committee does not establish separate administrative organs." See "Great Victory for Chairman Mao's Proletarian Line on Party Building," *Peking Review* (Jan. 2, 1970), p. 12. A New China News Agency article in December 1969 stated, "The working organization of the revolutionary committee is also that of the party committee; the party committee does not establish separate administrative organs." See *Foreign Broadcast Information Service*, FBIS-Chi-69-243 (Dec. 17, 1969), p. B5. However, only after interviewing numerous cadres at several levels in China did it become clear that this new pattern is now generally followed and that it has very significant implications for overall Party-government relations, as is discussed below.

61. This information was provided in a briefing by a "Leading Member" of the Secretariat of the Shanghai Municipal Revolutionary Committee, December 30, 1972.

62. Often the way cadres explained this to me was that China is still engaged, domestically, in a process of "struggle, criticism, and transformation," and as long as this—and in particular the "transformation" process—is not completed, all institutional structures must be regarded as experimental and provisional.

63. Chou En-lai made this statement in an interview with Edgar Snow; see Edgar Snow, "Talks with Chou En-lai, The Open Door," *The New Republic* (March 27, 1971), p. 21.

64. In a briefing on December 30, 1972, a "Leading Member" of the Secretariat of the Shanghai Municipal Revolutionary Committee stated that the Shanghai government then had "about 40" bureaus, or equivalents, and he listed 33 of them, placing them in six major categories: (1) *Administration*: Civil Affairs Bureau, Industrial and Commercial Administration Bureau, and Public Security Bureau; (2) *Education, Culture, and Health*: Education Bureau, Culture Bureau, Public Health Bureau, and Film Bureau; (3) *Management of Industry*: Metallurgical Industry Bureau, Machinery and Electrical Equipment Bureau, Chemical Industry Bureau, Meters and Instruments Bureau, Textile Industry Bureau, Light Industry Bureau, Handcraft Industry

Bureau, Electric Management Bureau, and Supply of Materials Bureau; (4) *Communications*: Civil Aviation Bureau, Maritime Transport Bureau, Harbor Administration Bureau, Railways Bureau, Construction Engineering Bureau, Municipal Construction Bureau, Public Utilities Bureau, Housing Bureau, Postal Bureau, and Telecommunications Bureau; (5) *Finance and Trade*: Commerce Bureau No. 1, Commerce Bureau No. 2, Foreign Trade Bureau, Food Bureau, and Finance and Tax Bureau; and (6) *Agriculture*: Agriculture Bureau, and Aquatic and Marine Products Bureau. Obviously, bureaucratic complexity and specialization have continued, despite the Cultural Revolution.

65. The source for this was a cadre I interviewed who was on the payroll of one of the "groups" under the Shanghai Revolutionary Committee and Party Committee.

66. Chou En-lai stated to Edgar Snow: "In the past there were 90 departments directly under the central government. . . . Now there will be only 26"; Snow, "Talks with Chou En-lai." As of the end of 1972, twenty-three ministry-level bodies and thirteen other agencies under the State Council had been mentioned in Chinese Communist publications or in oral statements by Chinese Communist Party cadres. The ministry-level organs were: Ministry of Agriculture and Forestry, Ministry for Allocation of Materials, Ministry of Building Construction, Ministry of Building Materials, Ministry of Commerce, Ministry of Communications, Ministry of Economic Relations with Foreign Countries, Ministry of Finance, Ministry of Foreign Affairs, Ministry of Foreign Trade, Ministry of Fuel and Chemical Industry, Ministry of Light Industry, First Ministry of Machine Building, Ministry of Metallurgical Industry, Ministry of National Defense, Ministry of Public Health, Ministry of Public Security, Ministry of Water Conservancy and Electric Power, Physical Culture and Sports Commission, State Capital Construction Commission, State Planning Commission, Scientific and Education Group, and Cultural Group. The other agencies were: Central Broadcasting Administration, Central Meteorological Bureau, China Civil Aviation General Administration, China Travel and Tourism Bureau, Foreign Affairs Bureau, Government Offices Administration Bureau, New China News Agency, People's Bank of China, Publishing Department, Small Group of the State Council for the Supervision and Guidance of Libraries, Museums, and Work on Cultural Relics, State Council Staff Office, State Oceanographic Bureau, and the Telecommunications General Bureau. See "Restructuring of Bureaucracy Nearly Complete," *Current Scene*, Vol. 10, No. 7 (July 1972), pp. 12–16, which mentions all of these except the Ministry for Allocation of Materials. (In China, one cadre I met stated that the Nationalities Affairs Commission has also been reconstituted, although I have not seen any confirmation of this.) The above listing represents a cut of roughly half in the number of organs at this level before the Cultural Revolution.

67. See, in addition to the *Current Scene* article cited in note 66, an article by Tillman Durdin, in *New York Times*, Dec. 31, 1972.

68. These estimates were given to me by a fairly senior cadre of the Ministry, in a conversation on December 25, 1972.

69. Interview in Peking on December 22, 1972, with a "Responsible Person" from the General Office of the Science and Education Group.

70. For the text of the new constitution, see the last FBIS source cited in note 34 for this chapter.

Chapter II

1. The most comprehensive and useful single volume on the Chinese Communist military establishment in the context of domestic politics is William W. Whitson (with Chen-hsia Huang), *The Chinese High Command: A History of Communist Military Politics, 1927–71* (Praeger, 1973). The best general monograph on the military prior to the Cultural Revolution is John Gittings, *The Role of the Chinese Army* (London: Oxford University Press, 1967). Other monographic and book-length studies that have provided useful background material for this chapter include Samuel B. Griffith II, *The Chinese People's Liberation Army* (McGraw-Hill, 1967); Alexander L. George, *The Chinese Communist Army in Action* (Columbia University Press, 1967); Ellis Joffe, *Party and Army: Professionalism and Political Control in the Chinese Officer Corps, 1949–1964* (Harvard University Press, East Asian Monographs, 1965); and Alice Langley Hsieh, *Communist China's Strategy in the Nuclear Era* (Prentice-Hall, 1962). Chester J. Cheng (ed.), *The Politics of the Chinese Red Army* (Hoover Institution Publications, 1966), contains translated issues of a secret Chinese military journal for an eight-month period in 1961, which provide many insights into internal military organization, operations, and problems.

There is now a fairly wide range of useful articles on Chinese military affairs in varied journals. One good collection is contained in a special issue on "Chinese Military Affairs" of *China Quarterly*, No. 18 (April–June 1964). Also very useful for any analysis of the relationships of military and political affairs, which is the primary focus of the discussion in this chapter, are several articles by Ralph L. Powell, including "The Military Affairs Committee and Party Control of the Military in China," *Asian Survey*, Vol. 3, No. 7 (July 1963), pp. 347–56; "Commissars in the Economy: 'Learn from the PLA' Movement in China," *Asian Survey*, Vol. 5, No. 3 (March 1965), pp. 125–38; "Communist China's Mass Militia," Parts 1 and 2, *Current Scene*, Vol. 3, No. 7 (Nov. 15, 1964), pp. 1–7, and Vol. 3, No. 8 (Dec. 1, 1964), pp. 1–8; and "The Increasing Power of Lin Piao and the Party-Soldiers 1959–1966," *China Quarterly*, No. 34 (April–June 1968), pp. 38–65. Another valuable analysis is in Chalmers Johnson, "Lin Piao's Army and Its Role in Chinese Society," Parts 1 and 2, *Current Scene*, Vol. 4, No. 13 (July 1, 1966), pp. 1–10, and Vol. 4, No. 14 (July 15, 1966), pp. 1–10. I have also profited from several unpublished papers by Angus M. Fraser, including "The Changing Role of the PLA Under the Impact of the Cultural Revolution" (Institute for Defense Analyses, Research Paper P-524, July 1969).

2. Two factors made the Communist leadership significantly different from the Nationalists in this respect. One was the crucial importance of ideology,

which placed military affairs in the context of the broader political struggle. The other was the guerrilla and mobile character of the Communists' struggle, which necessitated close contact between military personnel and the civilian population. Many Nationalist leaders were military men who were involved in politics, but the fusion of military and political functions was much greater among Communist leaders.

3. The pioneer study of conflicts between professionalism and politics after 1949 was Joffe, *Party and Army*; it is still very useful, especially for its analysis of trends in the 1950s. Gittings, *The Role of the Chinese Army*, in dealing with the problem, carries the analysis of professionalization, modernization, and the reaction against them up to the period immediately before the Cultural Revolution; see especially pp. 119–75 and 225–62. See also Ellis Joffe, "The Conflict between Old and New in the Chinese Army," *China Quarterly*, No. 18 (April–June 1964), pp. 118–40.

4. In some countries, large-scale military demobilization at the end of a wartime period is taken for granted; in China, however, no systematic orderly demobilization on any sizable scale had really been undertaken since the period when modernized armies had first begun to take shape. The Communists' success in carrying out a major demobilization rapidly and smoothly was, therefore, an extremely impressive achievement.

5. The degree of centralized control of Chinese Communist military units has been, and remains today, a matter of debate in some respects. There is no room for debate, however, about the fact that the situation since the Communist takeover has been entirely different from that in the pre-1949 period. Up until the end of Nationalist rule on the mainland, a large portion of the military forces in China consisted of locally based armies controlled by semiautonomous provincial leaders who were merely allied with the Nationalist government in Nanking, and were subject to minimal central control. One of the first steps taken by the Communists was to destroy all these semiwarlord armies, either demobilizing their troops or incorporating them into the Communists' own forces.

6. See Cheng, *The Politics of the Chinese Red Army*. Many issues of the secret military journal *Kung-tso T'ung-hsun* (variously translated as *Bulletin of Activities* or *Work Correspondence*) document this point in considerable detail. See also John Wilson Lewis, "China's Secret Military Papers: 'Continuities' and 'Revelations,'" *China Quarterly*, No. 18 (April–June 1964), pp. 68–78, which summarizes many of the problems revealed in the journal.

7. See Powell, "The Military Affairs Committee," pp. 347–56.

8. See Gittings, *The Role of the Chinese Army*, pp. 102–06.

9. See John Gittings, "The 'Learn from the Army' Campaign," *China Quarterly*, No. 18 (April–June 1964), pp. 153–59.

10. See Powell, "Commissars in the Economy.

11. This was highlighted by the issuance of Lin Piao's article, "Long Live the Victory of People's War," in September 1965, which was a major explication of Mao's Thought. For text, see A. Doak Barnett, *China After Mao* (Princeton University Press, 1967), pp. 196–262.

12. See Donald Zagoria, "The Strategic Debate in Peking," and Uri

Ra'anan, "Peking's Foreign Policy 'Debate' 1965–66," both in Tang Tsou (ed.), *China in Crisis* (University of Chicago Press, 1968), Vol. 2, on pp. 237–68 and 23–71, respectively. Most Chinese accounts, however, stress domestic factors behind Lo's purge; see "Report on the Question of the Errors Committed by Lo Jui-ching," *Issues and Studies* (Taiwan), Vol. 5, No. 11 (August 1969), pp. 87–101. In "Basic Differences Between the Proletarian and Bourgeois Military Lines," *Peking Review* (Nov. 24, 1967), pp. 11–16, in the context of an attack on Lo, there is a discussion of active defense versus passive defense, but in terms quite different from those used by foreign scholars. In many respects, reconstruction of the debate must rely on circumstantial evidence; the analyses by Zagoria and Ra'anan are very plausible, in my view, despite the fact that they have been challenged by some China scholars.

13. "Decision of the Central Committee of the Chinese Communist Party Concerning the Great Proletarian Cultural Revolution," in Union Research Institute, *CCP Documents of the Great Proletarian Cultural Revolution, 1966–1967* (Hong Kong: Union Press Limited, 1968), pp. 42–54, especially pp. 53–54.

14. "Decision of the CCP Central Committee, the State Council, the Military Commission of the Central Committee and the Cultural Revolution Group under the Central Committee Concerning the Resolute Support of People's Liberation Army for the Revolutionary Masses of the Left," in Union Research Institute, *CCP Documents*, pp. 195–97.

15. Such details are scattered throughout the sources cited in this chapter's note 1. Of particular value is Whitson, *The Chinese High Command*, pp. 364–415. For the early period of the Cultural Revolution, see also Jürgen Domes, "The Cultural Revolution and the Army," *Asian Survey*, Vol. 8, No. 5 (May 1968), pp. 349–63.

16. A good detailed analysis of the Wuhan incident is in Thomas W. Robinson, "The Wuhan Incident: Local Strife and Provincial Rebellion during the Cultural Revolution," *China Quarterly*, No. 47 (July–September 1971), pp. 413–38.

17. "Order of the CCP Central Committee, the State Council, the Central Military Commission and the Central Cultural Revolution Group Concerning the Prohibition of the Seizure of Arms, Equipment, and Other Military Supplies from the PLA," Sept. 5, 1967, in Union Research Institute, *CCP Documents*, pp. 507–10.

18. See Stanley Karnow, *Mao and China: From Revolution to Revolution* (Viking, 1972), pp. 444 ff.

19. See Harvey Nelsen, "Military Forces in the Cultural Revolution," *China Quarterly*, No. 51 (July–September 1972), pp. 444–74.

20. See article by Tillman Durdin, in *New York Times*, Dec. 31, 1972.

21. The most valuable analysis of subgroups within the Chinese military establishment is contained in the writings of William W. Whitson, especially *The Chinese High Command*, on which this discussion draws heavily.

22. This discussion draws heavily on the sources listed in notes 1 and 3

for this chapter, especially Joffe, *Party and Army*, Gittings, *The Role of the Chinese Army*, and Whitson, *The Chinese High Command*. One succinct Chinese Communist statement on some of the key issues is in "Basic Differences Between the Proletarian and Bourgeois Military Lines," *Peking Review* (Nov. 24, 1967), pp. 11–16. "Within our Party and army," the article asserts, "in recent decades and in all historical stages of the development of the Chinese revolution, there have [*sic*] always been a sharp and acute struggle between two diametrically opposed military lines. . . . In the last forty years, the struggle between Chairman Mao's line and the bourgeois line in army building has always focused on the fundamental question of whether to put politics or military affairs first, whether prominence should be given to politics or to military affairs."

23. Mao's major writings on military affairs are in Mao Tse-tung, *Selected Military Writings of Mao Tse-tung* (Peking: Foreign Languages Press, 1963). The classic exegesis of Mao's concepts of people's war is in Lin Piao's article, "Long Live the Victory of People's War," cited in this chapter's note 11. Two succinct summaries of Mao's military doctrines and theories are in Ralph L. Powell, "Maoist Military Doctrines," *Asian Survey*, Vol. 8, No. 4 (April 1968), pp. 239–62, and Griffith, *The Chinese People's Liberation Army*, pp. 235–50.

24. See Gittings, *The Role of the Chinese Army*, pp. 288–91.

25. See "Report on the Question of the Errors Committed by Lo Jui-ching." This excerpts a Chinese Communist pamphlet containing a document purported to have been prepared as a report to the Central Committee; while it is impossible to verify this attribution, the document seems authentic. It accuses Lo Jui-ch'ing of many different kinds of "errors," including attempts to usurp power; many of the charges focus, however, on his opposition to Mao's stress on the priority of politics in military affairs and his tendency toward a professional, "purely military viewpoint."

26. See Nelsen, "Military Forces," especially pp. 446–48.

27. In addition to Gittings, *The Role of the Chinese Army*, Chapter 5, pp. 99–118, see also George, *The Chinese Communist Army in Action*, which contains a detailed analysis of the political control system in the army, based on interviews with prisoners of war in Korea; and Ying-mao Kau and others, *The Political Work System of the Chinese Communist Military, Analysis and Documents* (Brown University, East Asian Language and Area Center, 1971).

28. I have profited from unpublished work on the public security system and the PLA by Stanley Lubman of the University of California at Berkeley. For general data on the public security system and its operation in the period before the Cultural Revolution, see Jerome Alan Cohen, *The Criminal Process in the People's Republic of China 1949–1963: An Introduction* (Harvard University Press, 1968), and Victor Li, "The Operation of a Public Security Station" (paper prepared for delivery at the Columbia University Seminar on Modern East Asia: China, Oct. 21, 1970; processed). For an analysis of army-public security relations during the Cultural Revolution, see Ralph L.

Powell and Chong-Kun Yoon, "Public Security and the PLA," *Asian Survey*, Vol. 12, No. 12 (December 1972), pp. 1082–1100. The authors of this article state that circumstantial evidence indicates that by 1971–72 there was a partial withdrawal of the PLA from direct involvement in police activities. How far this has gone is difficult to determine, however; as I stated earlier in this chapter, PLA Military Control Committees were still in direct charge of the police in most cities I visited in December 1972–January 1973.

29. Gittings, *The Role of the Chinese Army*, pp. 202–24, contains an excellent discussion of the militia forces, and major policy shifts regarding them. Details about the militia organization as it evolved in the early years of the regime are in Li Ting, *Militia of Communist China* (Hong Kong: Union Research Institute, Communist China Problem Research Series No. EC-7, 1954).

30. This discussion of Field Army groups is based on Whitson, *The Chinese High Command* (Chapter 12, "The Field Army in Chinese Communist Military Politics"), pp. 498–517.

31. This discussion of generational groups is also based on Whitson, *The Chinese High Command* (Chapter 9, "Military Generations in Communist China"), pp. 416–35.

32. The tightness of Chinese control over information about internal debates that involve interservice rivalries is such that only speculative and inferential views are possible at present. One of the few debates concerning development priorities relevant to civilian versus military demands, and possibly to competing military demands as well, that has been brought into the open in recent years was the electronics versus steel controversy, publicized in 1971. Although the precise significance of this debate was not made clear in the somewhat cryptic public statements about it, these statements indicated the existence of important general differences as to priorities regarding basic economic industries versus relatively exotic industries of special relevance to advanced weapons systems. Note especially *People's Republic of China: An Economic Assessment*, A Compendium of Papers Submitted to the Joint Economic Committee, 92 Cong. 2 sess. (1972), p. 57. For Chinese articles on the issues, see "Develop Iron and Steel Industry in China Under Guidance of Mao Tse-tung's Thought," *People's Daily*, May 12, 1971, in *Survey of China Mainland Press*, No. 4904–4907, CMP-SCMP-71-21 (May 24–27, 1971), pp. 64–75; "Machinery Industry Must Support Mining," Peking Radio Broadcast, June 13, 1971, in *Foreign Broadcast Information Service*, FBIS-Chi-71-118 (June 18, 1971); and "Liu Shao-ch'i's Overemphasis on Electronics Criticized," *People's Daily*, Aug. 12, 1971, in *Foreign Broadcast Information Service*, FBIS-Chi-71-160 (Aug. 18, 1971).

33. The data are not available for accurate estimates of the People's Republic of China's military expenditures. One U.S. government estimate, however, suggests that they rose from $4 billion in 1961 to $10 billion in 1970, calculated in current U.S. dollars, generally averaging between 7 and 8 percent of GNP. If correct, that would put its expenditures, as a percentage of GNP, close to those of the United States and the USSR and considerably above

those of most developing nations. There is little doubt that China can bear its present burden of military expenditures, and probably could increase it, but even the present level strains the country's resources and involves a price in terms of potential civilian development. See U.S. Arms Control and Disarmament Agency, *World Military Expenditures 1971* (Washington, July 1972), especially pp. 19 and 27, for estimates of military expenditures.

34. A useful analysis of this is in Carol Gillespie Tryon, "The Role of Demobilized Soldiers in the People's Republic of China 1955–1965" (unpublished paper for Columbia University, East Asian Institute Certificate, 1969).

35. See Gittings, *The Role of the Chinese Army*, pp. 176–201, and Ralph L. Powell, "Soldiers in the Chinese Economy," *Asian Survey*, Vol. 11, No. 8 (August 1971), pp. 742–60.

A telegram, written by Mao and sent to Chinese Field Armies and Party bureaus in 1949, contains an excellent statement of Mao's view about the responsibility of the army for undertaking multiple—including economic—functions, which has apparently continued to motivate his actions in recent years: "The army is not only a fighting force, it is mainly a working force. All army cadres should learn how to take over and administer cities. In urban work they should learn how to be good at dealing with the imperialists and Kuomintang reactionaries, good at dealing with the bourgeoisie, good at leading the workers and organizing trade unions, good at mobilizing and organizing the youth, good at uniting with and training cadres in the new Liberated Areas, good at managing industry and commerce, good at running schools, newspapers, news agencies and broadcasting stations, good at handling foreign affairs, good at handling problems relating to the democratic parties and people's organizations, good at adjusting the relations between the cities and the rural areas and solving the problems of food, coal and other daily necessities and good at handling monetary and financial problems." *Selected Works of Mao Tse-tung*, Vol. 4 (Peking: Foreign Languages Press, 1961), p. 337.

36. Gittings, *The Role of the Chinese Army*, p. 182.

Chapter III

1. The most useful and comprehensive recent analyses of trends in the Chinese economy are those made by a group of U.S. government specialists, contained in *People's Republic of China: An Economic Assessment* (hereafter cited as *An Economic Assessment*), A Compendium of Papers Submitted to the Joint Economic Committee, 92 Cong. 2 sess. (1972). Other studies, dealing with economic institutions and policies that have been particularly valuable to me in the preparation of this chapter include Alexander Eckstein, *Communist China's Economic Growth and Foreign Trade* (McGraw-Hill, 1966); Nai-Ruenn Chen and Walter Galenson, *The Chinese Economy Under Communism* (Aldine, 1969); Alexander Eckstein, Walter Galenson, and Ta-chung Liu (eds.), *Economic Trends in Communist China* (Aldine, 1968); Audrey Donnithorne, *China's Economic System* (London: Allen and Unwin, 1967);

and Barry M. Richman, *Industrial Society in Communist China* (Random House, 1969). Among the earlier studies that are of basic importance for understanding the Chinese Communist economy are Ta-chung Liu and Kung-chia Yeh, *The Economy of the Chinese Mainland: National Income and Economic Development, 1933–1959* (Princeton University Press, 1965); Choh-ming Li, *Economic Development of Communist China* (University of California Press, 1959); Alexander Eckstein, *National Income of Communist China* (Free Press, 1961); Yuan-li Wu, *The Economic Potential of Communist China* (Stanford Research Institute, 1963); and Dwight H. Perkins, *Market Control and Planning in Communist China* (Harvard University Press, 1966). Official Chinese statistics for the 1950s are collected in Nai-Ruenn Chen, *Chinese Economic Statistics* (Aldine, 1967).

2. Useful data on economic issues and debates are scattered through the sources listed in note 1 for this chapter, and those cited later in Chapter 4, note 8, as well as sources that will be mentioned in later notes in this chapter. A brief but good general summary of several major issues and debates is in Richard Diao and Donald Zagoria, *The Nature of Mainland Chinese Economic Structure, Leadership and Policy (1949–1969) and Prospects for Arms Control and Disarmament*, U.S. Arms Control and Disarmament Agency, Report ACDA/E-124 (February 1972), Chapter 3, "Some of the Major Debates and Disputes on Economic Issues," pp. 121–80. (Diao was employed by the Ministry of Finance in Peking during the 1950s.) A succinct summary of the polarization of views over agricultural policies is in Parris H. Chang, "Struggle Between the Two Roads in China's Countryside," *Current Scene*, Vol. 6, No. 3 (Feb. 15, 1968), pp. 1–14. The official "Maoist" view on the development of "two lines" was articulated in a mass of publications during the Cultural Revolution. A few of the most useful of these are Ch'i Pen-yu, "Patriotism or National Betrayal?" in *Selections from China Mainland Magazines*, No. 571 (April 10, 1967), pp. 1–16; "A Chronicle of Events in the Life of Liu Shao-ch'i," *Current Background*, No. 834 (Aug. 17, 1967), pp. 1–29; "More Accusations Against Liu Shao-ch'i," *Current Background*, No. 836 (Sept. 25, 1967), pp. 1–55; "Six Anti-Liu Shao-ch'i Lectures for Rural Youths," *Current Background*, No. 847 (Feb. 16, 1968), pp. 1–29; "Selected Edition on Liu Shao-ch'i's Counter-revolutionary Revisionist Crimes," *Selections from China Mainland Magazines*, No. 651 (April 22, 1969), pp. 1–41, No. 652 (April 28, 1969), pp. 1–39, and No. 653 (May 5, 1969), pp. 1–41; and "Outline of the Struggle Between the Two Lines from the Eve of the Founding of the People's Republic of China Through the 11th Plenum of the 8th CCP Central Committee," *Current Background*, No. 884 (July 18, 1969), pp. 1–31.

3. In attempts to separate economic policy into periods, the question is not really whether there have been four *or* six periods; as will be clarified subsequently in the text, in some respects there have been six, in other respects four.

4. Choh-ming Li, *Economic Development*, contains an excellent general survey of this period.

5. Surprisingly, there is no adequate monograph that focuses on the Great Leap and analyzes it in all its complex dimensions. However, every major study of the Chinese economy that has been written since the 1958 period analyzes that period. For one succinct summary, see Alexander Eckstein, *Communist China's Economic Growth*, pp. 29–37. Franz Schurmann, *Ideology and Organization in Communist China* (rev. ed., University of California Press, 1968), pp. 464–500, is a good analysis by a political sociologist of rural organizational developments during the period.

6. Perceptive articles about trends in the early 1960s written as they were occurring include Edwin F. Jones, "The Impact of the Food Crisis on Peiping's Policies," *Asian Survey*, Vol. 2, No. 10 (December 1962), pp. 1–11; and Franz Schurmann, "China's 'New Economic Policy'—Transition or Beginning?" *China Quarterly*, No. 17 (January–March 1964), pp. 65–91. The attacks on Liu Shao-ch'i cited in note 2 of this chapter distort reality in some respects but nevertheless reveal much about trends in economic policy during the period. A succinct retrospective summary of post-Leap trends can be found in Eckstein, *Communist China's Economic Growth*, pp. 37–40.

7. A book-length study by two Western economists that analyzes Chinese Communist policies of the Cultural Revolution period in terms of a new "Chinese road" is E. L. Wheelwright and Bruce McFarlane, *The Chinese Road to Socialism* (Monthly Review Press, 1970). In my view, however, it reflects theory more than practice and rhetoric more than reality. More realistic analyses of policies as they evolved after the Cultural Revolution are The Editor, "Peking's Program to Move Human and Material Resources to the Countryside," *Current Scene*, Vol. 7, No. 18 (Sept. 15, 1969), pp. 1–17; and The Editor, "China's Economy in 1969: Policy, Agriculture, Industry, and Foreign Trade," *Current Scene*, Vol. 8, No. 11 (June 1, 1970), pp. 1–17.

8. This is discussed enthusiastically by Wheelwright and McFarlane in *Chinese Road to Socialism*.

9. See Charles Hoffman, *Work Incentive Practices and Policies in the People's Republic of China, 1953–1965* (State University of New York Press, 1967).

10. See Arthur G. Ashbrook, Jr., "China: Economic Policy and Economic Results, 1949–71," in *An Economic Assessment*, pp. 46–47. The charts here indicate a rise in per capita GNP from $104 in 1952 to $150 in 1971.

11. The salary and wage figures used in this chapter were obtained through direct interviews in China in December 1972 and January 1973 with government officials, factory managers, workers, cadres, and educational administrators. The budget estimates are based on discussions I had with middle-level cadres. The prices are ones I obtained directly from price tags in department stores in Peking, Shanghai, and Anshan (except for the lowest figure for thermos jugs and the higher figure for bicycles, which I obtained from prices checked by Robert A. Scalapino on the same trip).

12. Schurmann, *Ideology and Organization*, Chapter 3, pp. 173–219; and Dwight H. Perkins, "Centralization Versus Decentralization—Mainland China and the Soviet Union," *Annals of the American Academy of Political and*

Social Science, Vol. 349 (September 1963), pp. 70–80, discuss some of the complexities of issues relating to centralization versus decentralization.

13. See the discussion in Peter Schran, "Economic Management," Part 3, in John M. H. Lindbeck (ed.), *China: Management of a Revolutionary Society* (University of Washington Press, 1971), pp. 193–220.

14. See, for example, the charge that in 1962 Teng Hsiao-p'ing "advocated giving production quotas to the individual household," in "Selected Edition on Liu Shao-ch'i's Counter-revolutionary Revisionist Crimes," p. 6.

15. See "Vigorous Development of Small Local Industry," *Peking Review* (Feb. 6, 1970), p. 10. See also "China's Road of Socialist Industrialization," *Peking Review* (Oct. 24, 1969), pp. 7–13; and "New Leap in China's National Economy," *Peking Review* (Jan. 14, 1972), pp. 7–8.

16. "Local Industry in China," *Peking Review* (Sept. 24, 1971), pp. 9–11.

17. "New Leap in China's National Economy," p. 8.

18. "Local Industry in China," p. 9.

19. Ibid. For examples of discussions in the Chinese press of *hsien*-level industrial development, see "Honan County Develops Small Industries," *Foreign Broadcast Information Service*, FBIS-Chi-69-242 (Dec. 16, 1969), pp. D1–D3; and "A *Hsien* in Honan Province Self-Reliantly Sets Up Small But Complete System of Local Industries," *Survey of China Mainland Press*, No. 4564 (Dec. 24, 1969), pp. 1–3.

20. See Carl Riskin, "Small Industry and the Chinese Model of Development," *China Quarterly*, No. 46 (April–June 1971), pp. 245–73; and Jon Sigurdson, "Rural Industry—A Traveller's View," *China Quarterly*, No. 50 (April–June 1972), pp. 315–32. I myself visited a number of small rural and urban factories in China in December 1972–January 1973; my judgment was that while some of those I observed might be of questionable viability in the long run (especially if rigorous cost criteria are applied), others clearly were viable operations that made eminently good economic sense.

21. See, for example, "Whither the God of Plague, Criticizing and Repudiating the Reactionary Essence of Sun Yeh-fang's 'Theory of Profit in Command,'" *Current Background*, CMP-CB-70-07 (April 29, 1970), pp. 18–27.

22. For useful general discussions of the priority given agriculture and general rural policies since the early 1960s, see Alva Lewis Erisman, "China: Agricultural Development, 1949–71," in *An Economic Assessment*, especially pp. 126–46; and The Editor, "Peking's Program to Move Human and Material Resources to the Countryside," *Current Scene*, Vol. 7, No. 18 (Sept. 15, 1969).

23. See "The First Five Year Plan," *Current Background*, No. 335 (July 12, 1955), pp. 1–67, which contains the text of a 1955 speech by Chairman of the State Planning Commission Li Fu-ch'un summarizing the plan; see also A. Doak Barnett, *Communist Economic Strategy: The Rise of Mainland China* (National Planning Association, 1959), pp. 8, 89, 90–91, and 102, which compares official claims on plans and actual performance (and gives sources and the basis for calculation of dollar figures).

24. Erisman, "China: Agricultural Development, 1949–71," pp. 140–41.

25. Ibid., p. 138.

26. Ibid., p. 139. Despite the increase in tractor production, the process of agricultural mechanization in China has obviously just begun; the overwhelming majority of tasks in the fields are still done by traditional land labor, as I observed on my 1972–73 trip to China.

27. In a conversation with me in December 1972, a leading Chinese geneticist at Futan University in Shanghai stated that the Chinese had tested high yield seeds from abroad and found most of those tested unsuitable for their needs. The Chinese themselves have been developing their own high yield seeds, he said, but they have not yet been put into very wide use. See also ibid., pp. 136–38, 142–43.

28. Estimates vary widely. The author of "Peking's Program to Move Human and Material Resources to the Countryside" makes an estimate (obviously based on information available to the American Consulate-General, Hong Kong) of a possible maximum of 25 million.

29. This figure was used by a "Leading Member" of the Shanghai Revolutionary Committee Planning Group in a briefing given to the American delegation to which I belonged, in December 1972. Specifically, he stated that "about 900,000 educated young people have gone [from Shanghai] to interior areas in the past four to five years, to factories in the interior, to state farms, and to Communes."

30. One of the most perceptive analyses of Maoist educational values and the dilemmas caused by conflicting goals affecting education in China is Donald J. Munro, "Egalitarian Ideal and Educational Fact in Communist China," in Lindbeck, China: Management of a Revolutionary Society, pp. 256–301. Two useful general sources on education in China since 1949 are Stewart Fraser (ed.), Chinese Communist Education (John Wiley, 1965), and R. F. Price, Education in Communist China (Praeger, 1970). Educational trends during the Cultural Revolution and in the period since 1969 are discussed in The Editor, "Educational Reform in Rural China," Current Scene, Vol. 7, No. 3 (Feb. 8, 1969), pp. 1–17; S. Garrett McDowell, "Educational Reform in China as a Readjusting Country," Asian Survey, Vol. 11, No. 3 (March 1971), pp. 256–70; and Suzanne Pepper, "Education and Political Development in Communist China," Studies in Comparative Communism, Vol. 3, No. 3–4 (July–October 1970), pp. 198–223. One example of the Maoist attacks against educational policies before the Cultural Revolution is Shih Yen-hung, "Down with the Chief Backer of the Revisionist Educational Line," People's Daily, July 18, 1967, in Current Background, No. 836 (Sept. 25, 1967), pp. 11–19. For some trenchant comments by Mao on the educational system in China before the Cultural Revolution, see "Long Live Mao Tse-tung Thought (A Collection of Statements by Mao Tse-tung)," Current Background, No. 891 (Oct. 8, 1969), pp. 42–47.

31. A highly laudatory account of recent health and medical policies is in Joshua S. Horn, Away With All Pests: An English Surgeon in People's China, 1954–1969 (Monthly Review Press, 1969). Useful analytical articles on these

policies include Bruce J. Esposito, "The Politics of Medicine in the People's Republic of China," *Bulletin of the Atomic Scientists* (December 1972), pp. 4–9; The Editor, "Mao's Revolution in Public Health," *Current Scene*, Vol. 6, No. 7 (May 1, 1968), pp. 1–10; The Editor, "The Mao-Liu Controversy Over Rural Public Health," *Current Scene*, Vol. 7, No. 12 (June 15, 1969), pp. 1–18.

32. Virtually all writers on the Chinese economy agree that the goal of achieving fuller utilization of China's labor force was a primary motivation for both the Great Leap policies and many of the policies adopted after the Cultural Revolution. Christopher Howe, *Employment and Economic Growth in Urban China 1949–1957* (Cambridge University Press, 1971), analyzes how problems of urban unemployment and labor absorption in the 1950s contributed to the new emphasis on labor utilization in policies from the late 1950s on.

33. These and the following comments are based in part on my interviews and observations in China in December 1972–January 1973.

34. The publication, during the Cultural Revolution, of previously unpublished statements by Mao was particularly revealing concerning his suspicions of and disillusionment with many of China's intellectuals, his strong opposition to intellectual elitism, and his emphasis on the need for "redness." The following are examples of Mao's statements, quoted in "Long Live Mao Tse-tung Thought": "The economists and technicians who pay no attention to ideological and political affairs but are busy with work all day will go astray" (p. 28, from "Instruction on the Question of 'Redness' and Expertness," Jan. 31, 1958); "Problems abound in all forms of art . . . in many departments very little has been achieved so far in socialist transformation. The 'dead' still dominate in many departments" (p. 41, from "Comment on Comrade K'o Ch'ing-shih's Report," Dec. 12, 1963); "when the intellectuals came into power under the reign of Chia-ch'ing, the country was poorly run. Too much education is harmful. . . . Scholastic philosophy . . . is doomed to become extinct. . . . Marxist books should be read, but we also cannot read too many of them . . . should one read too many of them, one would proceed to the negative side and become a bookworm, a dogmatist or a revisionist" (pp. 42–44, from "Instructions Given at the Spring Festival Concerning Educational Work," Feb. 13, 1964); "Broadly speaking, the intellectuals of the industrial field are better because they are in contact with reality. Those in the scientific field, that is in the field of pure science, are poorer, but they are somewhat better than those dealing with arts. Those who are most divorced from reality are the ones in departments of arts be they students of history, philosophy or economics. They are so divorced from reality that they know nothing about world affairs" (p. 46, from "Talk with the Nepalese Educational Delegation on Educational Problems," 1964); "One who goes to school for several years becomes more stupid as he reads more books" (p. 52, from "Talk at the Hangchow Conference," Dec. 21, 1965).

35. On the basis of the available information, it is extremely difficult to judge how true this is. A general impression, obtained by a number of Western scientists visiting China recently, and supported in general terms by

my own observation and impressions in December 1972 and January 1973, is that advanced work in the institutes of the Chinese Academy of Sciences may have been relatively little affected by political disruptions, but that advanced work at universities has been much more adversely affected. Leo A. Orleans, "China's Science and Technology: Continuity and Innovation," in *An Economic Assessment*, pp. 185–219, stresses that the emphasis on applied science predated the Cultural Revolution, which is true, but I myself learned of specific cases in which more theoretically oriented work was continued right up to the Cultural Revolution but was then stopped and has yet to be resumed; what is hard to judge is how widespread this was, and is.

36. The discussion of universities in this chapter is based in considerable part on my interviews and observations in December 1972 and January 1973 at four major universities: Peita and Tsinghua Universities in Peking, Futan University in Shanghai, and Chungshan University in Canton.

37. See, for example, an enthusiastic analysis of this by a scientist specializing in Chinese science, in C. H. Geoffrey Oldham, "The Scientific Revolution and China" (New York: Institute of Current World Affairs, Newsletter CHGO-37, Dec. 2, 1964; processed), and a somewhat more restrained analysis by the same author in "Science in China," *Encyclopaedia Britannica, 1973 Yearbook*, pp. 32–49.

38. See a brief discussion of this in A. Doak Barnett, "Mao Versus Modernization," *M.I.T. Technology Review* (October–November 1968), pp. 30–33.

39. China's population is in many respects an enigma. See Leo A. Orleans, "China's Population Statistics: An Illusion?" *China Quarterly*, No. 21 (January–March 1965), pp. 168–78. Many statements by Chinese leaders themselves indicate uncertainty about the situation. See, for example, Li Hsien-nien's statement quoted in the source cited in note 48 below. Periodic tantalizing statements about population by Chinese leaders include, for example, those quoted in The Editor, "The Food and Population Balance: China's Modernization Dilemma," *Current Scene*, Vol. 9, No. 6 (June 7, 1971), pp. 1–7; and The Victor-Bostrom Fund and The Population Crisis Committee, *Population and Family Planning in the People's Republic of China* (Washington, 1971), pp. 1–35. There has been extensive analysis, however, of existing Chinese population data. The most detailed have been the studies of John S. Aird, including *The Size, Composition, and Growth of the Population of Mainland China*, U.S. Department of Commerce, Bureau of the Census, Series P-90, No. 15 (1961); *Estimates and Projections of the Population of Mainland China: 1953–1986*, Bureau of the Census, Series P-91, No. 17 (1968), and "Population Policy and Demographic Prospects in the People's Republic of China," in *An Economic Assessment*, pp. 220–34. In my view, the last-named study is one of the best up-to-date analyses of both data and Chinese policy—but there can be no certainty that its estimates are correct. I have found very valuable, also, a number of writings by Pi-chao Ch'en, including "Population Planning in China: Policy Evolution and Action Program" (paper prepared for the Conference on Public Health in the People's Republic of China, Ann Arbor,

Mich., May 1972; processed); "The Prospects of Demographic Transition in a Mobilization System: China," in Richard L. Clinton and R. Kenneth Godwin (eds.), *Research in the Politics of Population* (Lexington Books, 1972), pp. 158–82; and "China's Population Program at the Grassroots Level," in Harrison Brown and Alan Sweezy (eds.), *Population: Perspective, 1972* (Freeman, Cooper, 1973). The range of estimates of present population made by careful Western scholars is from around 750 million to close to 850 million, and estimates of rates of growth range from 1.5 percent to 2.3 percent; see U.S. Department of State, *Issues in United States Foreign Policy*, No. 4, "People's Republic of China," Publication 8666 (October 1972), p. 24. Edgar Snow stated that in 1970–71 he was authoritatively told that the growth in rate of population in China had by 1966 been brought down below 2 percent; see Edgar Snow, "Population Care and Control," *The New Republic* (May 1, 1971), p. 21. There is no question that Chinese policy now stresses population control and the goal of reducing net growth as rapidly as possible. Chou En-lai has stated that China's aim is to reduce the growth rate to under 1 percent before the end of the century; see *Population and Family Planning*, p. 34. Many recent visitors to China have returned with fragmentary data, but on the basis of my own interviews in China in December 1972 and January 1973, I believe such data must be used with great caution. Until new census data are available, it will be difficult to improve present estimates or to resolve present differences in interpretation of them. In 1973 I saw posters in Shanghai stating that a new national census was to be undertaken (and mentioning not only the known 1953 census but also a 1964 census that was previously rumored but not officially revealed at the time); however, officials denied any knowledge of a new national census. (Chou En-lai has mentioned to visitors, however, a 1964–65 census; see Ch'en, "China's Population Program at the Grassroots Level," p. 1.)

40. Aird, "Population Policy and Demographic Prospects," p. 328.

41. Ibid., pp. 328–29. Even though the mathematics of these projections is fairly convincing, one is left with the feeling that factors or developments now difficult to foresee—including perhaps more stringent and effective population controls, dictated by both political and economic necessity—might alter the situation at least somewhat.

42. Ch'en, "The Prospects of Demographic Transition," p. 176.

43. U.S. Central Intelligence Agency, *People's Republic of China Atlas* (1971), p. 68.

44. See A. H. Usack and R. E. Batsavage, "The International Trade of the People's Republic of China," in *An Economic Assessment*, p. 343.

45. China's foreign trade in 1971 was $4.6 billion; see The Editor, "China's Foreign Trade in 1971," *Current Scene*, Vol. 10, No. 10 (October 1972), p. 1. In March 1973 a member of the Bureau of East Asian and Pacific Affairs, Department of State, stated in an interview that a preliminary estimate for 1972 was $5.5 billion. (Since roughly $500 million of the estimated increase in dollar terms was due to the dollar devaluation, the level, in terms of pre-devaluation dollars comparable to those used in estimating the dollar value of 1971 trade, would have been about $5 billion.)

46. Hints that Peking's leaders were considering whether China should involve itself more in the international economy came earlier. See, for example, "China's Road of Socialist Industrialization," *Peking Review* (Oct. 24, 1969), p. 9. This article emphasized self-reliance but also stressed that "we do not reject learning from other countries." By late 1972, when I visited China, high officials in Peking were emphasizing China's desire to import foreign technology; by early 1973, the Chinese were accepting sizable medium-term credits.

47. Certainly no other major nation has failed to publish any general national statistics for a period of more than a decade. Because of the nature and size of its economy, China would have difficulty building a sound statistical system under any conditions. Choh-ming Li, *The Statistical System of Communist China* (University of California Press, 1962), analyzes the development and then political disruption of the statistical system in the 1950s. The system has obviously been rebuilt since then, but it doubtless still has serious shortcomings. The only national output figures publicly announced since the Cultural Revolution have been a few figures such as those for steel and grain output. Most of the quantitative analyses of the Chinese economy, therefore, have had to be based on complicated estimates and elaborate interpolations. Most of the major studies listed in note 1 for this chapter discuss the statistical problems faced by the authors, and how they have tried to meet them.

48. *Foreign Broadcast Information Service*, FBIS-Chi-71-230 (Nov. 30, 1971), p. A8.

49. Arthur G. Ashbrook, Jr., "China: Economic Policy and Economic Results, 1949–71," in *An Economic Assessment*, p. 39. This article is an excellent discussion based on U.S. government estimates of China's GNP growth. The general order of magnitude of Ashbrook's estimates is supported by other leading economic specialists in China; Alexander Eckstein, for example, also estimates that from 1949–69 the "average annual growth rate was about 4 percent and on a per capita basis around 2 percent"; see Alexander Eckstein, "Mainland China and U.S. Policy," paper prepared as testimony for hearings before the Subcommittee on Foreign Economic Policy of the Joint Economic Committee, 91 Cong. 2 sess. (Dec. 9, 1970; processed). There is a less widely held view, however, that the rate has been higher: John W. Gurley, for example, believes that "China's real GNP has risen on the average by at least 6 percent since 1949, or by at least 4 percent on a per capita basis." See John W. Gurley, "Maoist Economic Development: The New Man in The New China," *The Center Magazine* (Center for the Study of Democratic Institutions), Vol. 3, No. 3 (May 1970), p. 32.

50. See U.S. Arms Control and Disarmament Agency, *World Military Expenditures 1971* (July 1972), pp. 3–4. These figures are based on economic growth estimates provided to ACDA by other U.S. government agencies.

51. Nai-Ruenn Chen and Walter Galenson, *The Chinese Economy Under Communism* (Aldine, 1969), pp. 56–57.

52. Eckstein, *Communist China's Economic Growth*, p. 48.

53. Chen and Galenson, *The Chinese Economy*, p. 59.

54. Ashbrook, "China: Economic Policy and Economic Results," p. 27.

55. Robert Michael Field, "Chinese Industrial Development: 1949–70," in *An Economic Assessment*, p. 63.

56. See data in Eckstein, *Communist China's Economic Growth*, p. 48; and Field, "Chinese Industrial Development," p. 63.

57. See chart in Chen and Galenson, *The Chinese Economy*, p. 89. The figures here are based on official claims and, as indicated in this chart, some non-Communist estimates are considerably lower.

58. The official figure used for Chinese grain output in 1972 is 240 million tons; see *Peking Review* (Jan. 5, 1973), p. 12. The Chinese also state, however, that grain output in 1972 dropped 4 percent from 1971 which would imply a 1972 output of 236 million tons. U.S. government analysts state that a high Chinese official has indicated in a private conversation that 240 million is a rounded figure; they therefore believe that the correct 1972 figure is probably closer to 236 million tons.

59. See Leo Tansky, "Chinese Foreign Aid," in *An Economic Assessment*, pp. 371–82; Eckstein, *China's Economic Growth*, especially Chapters 5 and 6, pp. 135–241; and Sidney Klein, *Politics Versus Economics: The Foreign Trade and Aid Policies of China* (Hong Kong: International Studies Group, 1968).

60. The quotations from the text of Chou En-lai's report are taken from *Foreign Broadcast Information Service*, FBIS-Chi-73-170 (Aug. 31, 1973), pp. B1–B13.

61. In an interesting unpublished paper, written at the U.S. Army War College ("Economic Possibilities for Communist China, 1970–80," no date; processed), Harley M. Roberts uses Shigeru Ishikawa's economic model of the Chinese economy, introduces a variety of policy possibilities, and then attempts to estimate various possible rates of growth in China for the period 1970–80, depending on whether China (1) is politically fractionalized, (2) is under overt military rule, (3) follows essentially pragmatic, "revisionist" policies, or (4) pursues "Maoist" policies. He projects four different rates, according to the above scheme: 3 percent, 7.4 percent, 5.5 percent, and 4.3 percent. The third of his "models," assuming relatively pragmatic policies that might produce an average growth rate of perhaps 5.5 percent, is probably the closest to the assumptions in this chapter.

Chapter IV

1. The basic materials for much of the analysis in this chapter have come from several biographical dictionaries and directories. The outstanding English-language work of this sort that focuses entirely on Chinese Communist leaders is Donald W. Klein and Ann B. Clark, *Biographic Dictionary of Chinese Communism, 1921–1965*, Vols. 1 and 2 (Harvard University Press, 1971); it does not, however, cover the far-reaching changes that have occurred since the start of the Cultural Revolution. Also of great value is Howard L. Boorman (ed.), *Biographical Dictionary of Republican China*, Vols. 1, 2, 3,

and 4 (Columbia University Press, 1967, 1968, 1970, and 1971); while this work deals primarily with the period 1911–49, some of the biographies of major Chinese Communist leaders who were already prominent at that time are the best ones available. Particularly useful for data on leaders who came to the fore in the years after the Cultural Revolution in China began, and who are therefore not listed in either Klein and Clark or Boorman, is Union Research Institute, *Who's Who in Communist China*, Vols. 1 and 2 (rev. ed. Hong Kong: Union Press Limited, 1969).

A series of unclassified documents issued by the Department of State and Central Intelligence Agency, which list leading Chinese Communist officials and their organizational positions, has also provided essential material for this chapter. Although unpublished, these mimeographed documents are available in most major American libraries with special collections on China. Those used in the research for this study have included "Directory of Party and Government Officials in Communist China," Vol. 1, Biographic Directory 234 (Aug. 1, 1953); "Directory of Party and Government Officials of Communist China," Vols. 1 and 2, Biographic Directory 271 (Nov. 23, 1960); "Directory of Chinese Communist Officials," Vols. 1 and 2, BA63-7 (May 1963 and October 1963); "Directory of Party and Government Officials of Communist China," Vol. 1, Biographic Directory 271 (July 20, 1960); "Directory of Chinese Communist Officials: Provincial, Municipal, and Military," A69-5 (April 1969); "Directory of Chinese Communist Officials: Party, Provincial, Municipal and Military," A70-13 (May 1970); "Chinese Communist Party Central Committee Members," A70-14 (May 1970); "Directory of Chinese Communist Officials," A71-14 (May 1971); "Chinese Communist Party Central Committee Members," A72-11 (May 1972); and "Directory of Officials of the People's Republic of China," A72-21 (August 1972). (The first, second, and fourth of these are identified as documents prepared by the Department of State; the others, in the form distributed outside the government, do not carry any agency identification.)

Useful statistical and biographical data on top leadership groups that emerged from the Ninth Party Congress of 1969 can be found in a number of journal articles including the following: Donald W. Klein and Lois B. Hager, "The Ninth Central Committee," *China Quarterly*, No. 45 (January–March 1971), pp. 37–56; Jürgen Domes, "The Ninth CCP Central Committee in Statistical Perspective," *Current Scene*, Vol. 9, No. 2 (Feb. 7, 1971), pp. 5–13; "The 9th Party Congress," *China News Analysis*, No. 756 (May 9, 1969), and No. 757 (May 16, 1969); "The Politbureau," *China News Analysis*, No. 758 (May 23, 1969), No. 759 (May 30, 1969), No. 761 (June 20, 1969), No. 762 (June 27, 1969), and No. 763 (July 4, 1969); Chang Ching-wen, "An Analysis of the Newly Elected 9th CCP Central Committee," *Issues and Studies*, Vol. 5, No. 10 (July 1969), pp. 31–37. Data on the Central Committee, Politburo, and Standing Committee selected by the Tenth Congress are in *Foreign Broadcast Information Service*, FBIS-Chi-73-169 (Aug. 30, 1973), pp. B2–B4.

An extremely valuable general volume that discusses numerous aspects of leadership in China is Robert A. Scalapino (ed.), *Elites in the People's*

Republic of China (University of Washington Press, 1972). It includes a perceptive analysis of the Eighth and Ninth Central Committees by Robert A. Scalapino, "The Transition in Chinese Party Leadership: A Comparison of the Eighth and Ninth Central Committees," Part 2, pp. 67–148.

2. Three particularly valuable book-length studies that focus on the career and character of Mao Tse-tung are Stuart Schram, *Mao Tse-tung* (London: Pelican Book-Penguin Books, 1966); Jerome Ch'en, *Mao and the Chinese Revolution* (London: Oxford University Press, 1965); and Benjamin I. Schwartz, *Chinese Communism and the Rise of Mao* (Harvard University Press, 1951). Edgar Snow, *Red Star Over China* (Random House, 1938), remains an essential source on Mao.

3. See, for example, Jerome Ch'en, *Mao and the Chinese Revolution*, pp. 188–89. Some recent analyses, however, stress that Mao's "victory" at Tsunyi was "incomplete" and "limited," and that it took a good many years thereafter for him to consolidate his position of primacy; see Noriyuki Tokuda, "Mao Tse-tung's Ideological Cohesion With the Party and the Revolutionary Movement, 1935–1945" (paper prepared for delivery at the Conference on Ideology and Politics in Contemporary China of the Joint Committee on Contemporary China, American Council of Learned Societies and Social Science Research Council, Santa Fe, N.M., Aug. 2–6, 1971; processed).

4. Tokuda, "Mao Tse-tung's Ideological Cohesion," especially p. 71.

5. Whereas the concentration of governmental powers in Mao's hands was clear and unambiguous from 1949 to 1954, the 1954 constitution appeared to prescribe a greater division of powers, among Mao as State Chairman, Liu Shao-ch'i as head of the Standing Committee of the National People's Congress, and Chou En-lai as head of the State Council (Premier). Mao continued, however, to hold the post of Chairman of the Party, the post in which ultimate decision-making power rested. See A. Doak Barnett, *Communist China: The Early Years, 1949–55* (Praeger, 1964), p. 315.

6. See source cited in note 10 in this chapter for analysis of the Kao-Jao affair.

7. Mao's deep-rooted commitment to promote mass mobilization and oppose bureaucracy helps to explain his lack of desire to become a bureaucratic administrator. For historical background on this see Mark Selden, "The Yenan Legacy: The Mass Line," pp. 99–151, and Ilpyong J. Kim, "Mass Mobilization Policies and Techniques Developed in the Period of the Chinese Soviet Republic," pp. 78–98, in A. Doak Barnett (ed.), *Chinese Communist Politics in Action* (University of Washington Press, 1969). For one insightful interpretation of the complex factors that have influenced Mao's role and his performance as a leader see Michel C. Oksenberg, "Policy Making Under Mao, 1949–68: An Overview," in John M. H. Lindbeck (ed.), *China: Management of a Revolutionary Society* (University of Washington Press, 1971), pp. 79–115.

8. There is now a fairly extensive literature of analysis of policy formulation and policy disputes in China, from the 1950s on. A selection of some of the most useful ones on domestic issues would include Robert R. Bowie and

John K. Fairbank (eds.), *Communist China, 1955–1959: Policy Documents with Analysis* (Harvard University, Center for International Affairs and East Asian Research Center, 1962); Roderick MacFarquhar, "Communist China's Intra-Party Dispute," *Pacific Affairs*, Vol. 31, No. 4 (December 1958), pp. 323–35; Harold Hinton, "Intra-Party Politics and Economic Policy in Communist China," *World Politics*, Vol. 12 (July 1960), pp. 509–24; Michel C. Oksenberg, "Policy Formulation in Communist China: The Case of the 1957–8 Mass Irrigation Campaign" (Ph.D. dissertation, Columbia University, 1969); Parris Chang, "Patterns and Processes of Policy Making in Communist China, 1955–1962: Three Case Studies" (Ph.D. dissertation, Columbia University, 1969); Franz Schurmann, *Ideology and Organization in Communist China* (rev. ed., University of California Press, 1968); Merle Goldman, *Literary Dissent in Communist China* (Harvard University Press, 1967); David A. Charles, "The Dismissal of Marshal P'eng Teh-huai," *China Quarterly*, No. 8 (October–December 1961), pp. 63–76; Philip Bridgham, "Mao's 'Cultural Revolution': Origin and Development," *China Quarterly*, No. 29 (January–March 1967), pp. 1–35; Richard Baum and Frederick C. Teiwes, *Ssu-Ch'ing: The Socialist Education Movement of 1962–1966* (University of California, Center for Chinese Studies, China Research Monograph 2, 1968); Charles Neuhauser, "The Chinese Communist Party in the 1960s: Prelude to the Cultural Revolution," *China Quarterly*, No. 32 (October–December 1967), pp. 3–36; J. D. Simmonds, "P'eng Te-huai: A Chronological Re-examination," *China Quarterly*, No. 37 (January–March 1969), pp. 120–38; Tang Tsou, "The Cultural Revolution and the Chinese Political System," *China Quarterly*, No. 38 (April–June 1969), pp. 63–91.

9. In a speech delivered at a work conference of the Party Central Committee on October 25, 1966, Mao stated: "Originally, for the sake of state security and in view of the lessons in connection with Stalin in the Soviet Union, we created the first front [line] and second front. I was with the second front while others were with the first front." See "Long Live Mao Tse-tung Thought (A Collection of Statements by Mao Tse-tung)," *Current Background*, No. 891 (Oct. 8, 1969), p. 75. It has never been clear who, besides Mao, belonged to the so-called second line. A plausible hypothesis is that it consisted of Mao and some close personal followers. To what extent Mao regarded the establishment of a "first line" and "second line" as a real sharing of power is debatable. One can argue that he may well have tended to some extent to regard himself, as monarchs previously had, as being outside of and above the institutional structure. Yet Mao apparently did try to differentiate his functions and those of China's top bureaucratic leaders; as the quotation above suggests, he was probably influenced by the belief that some of the post-Stalin difficulties in the Soviet Union had been due to Stalin's failure adequately to prepare for the succession.

10. See Frederick Carl Teiwes, "Rectification Campaigns and Purges in Communist China, 1950–61" (Ph.D. dissertation, Columbia University, 1971), p. 248.

11. Although the available texts of P'eng Teh-huai's speeches and his

"Letter of Opinion" issued at the time of the Party's 1959 Lushan meeting indicate that he was very critical of many of Mao's policies, there is no evidence he attempted directly to challenge Mao's leadership. See Union Research Institute, *The Case of P'eng Teh-huai: 1959-1968* (Hong Kong: Union Press Limited, 1968), especially pp. 1-38.

12. There have been numerous attempts to analyze and explain this pattern. Some stress the existence of an inherent dynamic within the leadership as a whole leading to alternating periods of revolutionary upsurge and periods of retreat or consolidation. Others emphasize shifts in the balance of power and influence within the leadership. Useful discussions of this phenomenon from substantially different perspectives include Tang Tsou, "The Cultural Revolution and the Chinese Political System," pp. 63-91; G. William Skinner and Edwin A. Winckler, "Compliance Succession in Rural Communist China: A Cyclical Theory," in Amitai Etzioni (ed.), *Complex Organizations: A Sociological Reader* (2d ed., Holt, Rinehart and Winston, 1969), pp. 410-38; and Chang, "Patterns and Processes of Policy Making."

13. For Chinese data published during the Cultural Revolution that shed considerable light on the interactions between Mao Tse-tung and other leaders, and especially Liu Shao-ch'i, see "Long Live Mao Tse-tung Thought (A Collection of Statements by Mao Tse-tung)," *Current Background*, No. 891 (Oct. 8, 1969); "Outline of the Struggle Between the Two Lines from the Eve of the Founding of the People's Republic of China Through the 11th Plenum of the 8th CCP Central Committee," *Current Background*, No. 884 (July 18, 1969); "Collection of Statements by Mao Tse-tung (1956-1967)," *Current Background*, No. 892 (Oct. 21, 1969); and "Selections from Chairman Mao," Joint Publications Research Service, *Translations on Communist China*, No. 90, JPRS 49826 (Feb. 12, 1970), and No. 109, JPRS 50792 (June 23, 1970); Union Research Institute, *Collected Works of Liu Shao-ch'i: 1958-1967* (Hong Kong: Union Press Limited, 1968), pp. 357-77; and "Selected Edition on Liu Shao-ch'i's Counter-revolutionary Revisionist Crimes," *Selections from China Mainland Magazines*, No. 651 (April 22, 1969), No. 652 (April 28, 1969), No. 653 (May 5, 1969).

14. Liu Shao-ch'i is said to have stated, in a speech to a January 27, 1962, Party meeting, that "the economy is on the brink of collapse," that the regime's construction projects had been "too many" and "the demands too high and drastic," and that "command was exercised blindly." He also reportedly charged that "the people's communes were premature." See "Selected Edition on Liu Shao-ch'i's Counter-revolutionary Revisionist Crimes," *Selections from China Mainland Magazines*, No. 652 (April 28, 1969).

15. On the growth of the Mao cult, see Tokuda, "Mao Tse-tung's Ideological Cohesion," pp. 58-76. The 1945 Party constitution stated: "The Chinese Communist Party guides its entire work by the teachings which unite the theories of Marxism-Leninism with the actual practice of the Chinese Revolution—the Thought of Mao Tse-tung—and fights against any dogmatist or empiricist deviations." See Liu Shao-ch'i, *On the Party* (Peking: Foreign Languages Press, 1950), p. 157.

16. It simply stated: "The Communist Party of China takes Marxism-Leninism as its guide to action." See John Wilson Lewis, *Major Doctrines of Communist China* (Norton, 1964), p. 115.

17. In a January 9, 1965, interview with Edgar Snow, Mao not only admitted that a cult of personality had developed in China but, contrasting Khrushchev with Stalin, asked, "Was it possible that Mr. Khrushchev fell because he had no cult of personality at all?" See Edgar Snow, "Interview with Mao," *The New Republic* (Feb. 27, 1965), p. 21.

18. This is discussed later in this chapter. See also Chalmers Johnson, "The Changing Nature and Locus of Authority in Communist China," in Lindbeck, *China: Management of a Revolutionary Society*, pp. 34–76, for a broad analysis of the changing basis of legitimacy and authority.

19. Jerome Ch'en, "The Development and Logic of Mao Tse-tung's Thought," in Chalmers Johnson (ed.), *Ideology and Politics in Contemporary China* (University of Washington Press, 1973), p. 113.

20. It is not a simple matter to evaluate Mao's "egalitarianism." There is no question that he put great stress on the need for others to conform to egalitarian values, but the extent to which such values determined his relationships with his closest associates and immediate subordinates is certainly arguable.

21. For one fascinating account of the circumstances under which Mao Tse-tung and Liu Shao-ch'i are said to have first formed a close political alliance see Chang Kuo-t'ao, "Introduction," in Union Research Institute, *Collected Works of Liu Shao-ch'i before 1944* (Hong Kong: Union Press Limited, 1969), pp. i–x. That Liu's role was second only to Mao's was already clear when he gave the major political report at the Seventh Party Congress in 1945. By the time of the Eighth Party Congress in 1956, when he again gave the principal political report, it was almost indisputable.

22. The 1969 Party constitution stated explicitly, "Comrade Lin Piao is Comrade Mao Tse-tung's close comrade-in-arms and successor." See text in *Peking Review* (April 30, 1969), p. 36.

23. See Thomas W. Robinson, "Lin Piao as an Elite Type," in Scalapino, *Elites*, pp. 149–95.

24. See "The Case Against Lin Piao," *Chinese Law and Government*, Vol. 5, No. 3–4 (Fall–Winter 1972–73), pp. 3–144.

25. In recent years Chou En-lai himself has said that China will have a collective leadership after Mao dies. See, for example, a report of his interview in October 1972 with a delegation from the American Society of Newspaper Editors. Warren H. Phillips, "Collective Leadership Will Eventually Succeed Mao, Chou En-lai Says," *Wall Street Journal*, Oct. 9, 1972.

26. A good analysis of Chou's characteristics and talents and how they affected and guided his actions during the Cultural Revolution is available in Thomas W. Robinson, "Chou En-lai and the Cultural Revolution in China," in Thomas W. Robinson (ed.), *The Cultural Revolution in China* (University of California Press, 1971), pp. 165–312.

27. Several studies that analyze broader leadership groups in the military

establishment and civilian hierarchies are mentioned in later notes in this chapter and in the notes in Chapter 2. Scalapino, *Elites*, contains several good studies of subnational and functional elites. Two good studies of provincial elites are Frederick C. Teiwes, *Provincial Party Personnel in Mainland China, 1956–1966* (Columbia University, East Asian Institute, 1967), and Frederick C. Teiwes, "Provincial Politics in China: Themes and Variations," in Lindbeck, *China: Management of a Revolutionary Society*, pp. 116–89.

28. Teng was actually first identified as Secretary-General (*mi-shu-chang*) of the Party in May 1954; the post was then redesignated General Secretary (*tsung-shu-chi*) in 1956. While Teng was closely associated with Liu Shao-ch'i, especially from this time on, it is significant that his rapid rise nationally during 1952–54 was first in governmental posts (he became Vice Premier in 1952) which suggested close ties with Chou En-lai. Teng's surprising political rehabilitation in 1973 (after seven years of eclipse during which he had been closely linked to Liu Shao-ch'i as a major enemy of Mao's) may perhaps be explained in part by such ties. See Boorman, *Biographical Dictionary*, Vol. 3, pp. 252–54, and Klein, *Biographic Dictionary*, Vol. 2, pp. 819–26.

29. This group apparently crystallized in the spring of 1968, probably after the March purge of Chief of Staff Yang Ch'eng-wu. In May and thereafter its members appeared together on a number of public occasions; the term "Mao's proletarian headquarters" came into use later in the year.

30. There are now many accounts revealing various facets of the current official Chinese Communist version of the Lin Piao affair. Chou En-lai's political report at the Tenth Party Congress dealt with it, but only briefly. An account that obviously reflects details that Peking now wishes to publicize as part of its official version is by an Australian correspondent who has long had special access to the Chinese Communists: Wilfred Burchett, "Lin Piao's Plot—The Full Story," *Far Eastern Economic Review* (Aug. 20, 1973), pp. 22–24. Another detailed analysis based on the public record and possibly on U.S. government information is Charles J. V. Murphy, "Who Killed Lin Piao?" *National Review* (June 8, 1973), pp. 625–46. See also "The Case Against Lin Piao," *Chinese Law and Government*, Vol. 5, No. 3–4 (Fall–Winter 1972–73).

31. I am indebted to Donald W. Klein for some of the results of his research, provided to me in private communications dated Dec. 22 and 23, 1970, and Jan. 15, 1971, for my conclusions regarding the Politburo membership as of 1949.

32. *Bol'shaya Sovetskaya Entsiklopedya (Large Soviet Encyclopedia)*, Vol. 35 (1955), p. 393. I am indebted to Donald W. Klein for this reference.

33. Both Boorman, *Biographical Dictionary*, Vol. 2, p. 227, and Union Research Institute, *Who's Who*, Vol. 1, p. 325, state that K'ang Sheng was elected to the Politburo in 1945, but Donald W. Klein states that the first date that K'ang's membership can be definitely documented is 1954.

34. See Parris H. Chang, "Research Notes on the Changing Loci of Decision in the Chinese Communist Party," *China Quarterly*, No. 44 (October–December 1970), pp. 169–94.

35. See *Peking Review* (April 30, 1969), pp. 48–49, for the new membership.

36. The articles on the leadership groups elected by the 1969 Party Congress listed in note 1 for this chapter include various attempts to categorize the new membership.

37. In September 1955, the title of Marshal was conferred by Mao on ten military leaders: Chu Teh, P'eng Teh-huai, Lin Piao, Liu Po-ch'eng, Ho Lung, Ch'en Yi, Lo Jung-huan, Hsu Hsiang-ch'ien, Nieh Jung-chen, and Yeh Chien-ying. Continuing support from some of these "old Marshals" has been of great importance to Mao, but the falling out, over time, with others has tended to weaken Mao's position. The 1969 Central Committee included seven of them (all but P'eng and Ho, who had been purged, and Lo, who had died), but the new Politburo included only four of them: Chu, Lin, Liu, and Yeh. In the Tenth Politburo, selected in 1973, Yeh was a Standing Committee member and Liu and Chu were Politburo members, but Lin had been purged and Hsu and Nieh, although still Central Committee members, were not on the Politburo.

38. For the membership of the Politburo selected in August 1973, see *Foreign Broadcast Information Service*, FBIS-Chi-73-169 (Aug. 30, 1973), pp. B2–B4.

39. For general discussion of the Central Committee, see the sources listed in note 1 of this chapter, especially Klein and Hager, "The Ninth Central Committee," and Scalapino, "The Transition in Chinese Party Leadership"; for lists of the 1956 and 1969 Central Committees, respectively, see *Survey of China Mainland Press*, No. 1381 (Oct. 1, 1956), pp. 4–5, and *Peking Review* (April 30, 1969), pp. 47–48. For the composition of the 1973 Central Committee, see *Foreign Broadcast Information Service*, FBIS-Chi-73-169 (Aug. 30, 1973), p. B4.

40. This continued to be true of the Eighth Central Committee elected in 1956; see Franklin W. Houn, "The Eighth Central Committee of the Chinese Communist Party: A Study of an Elite," *American Political Science Review*, Vol. 51, No. 2 (June 1957), p. 400; and Derek Waller, "The Evolution of the Chinese Communist Elite, 1931–1956," in Scalapino, *Elites*, p. 55.

41. This was highlighted in one of the pioneer studies of Chinese Communist leaders: Robert C. North, *Kuomintang and Chinese Communist Elites*, Hoover Institute Studies (Stanford University Press, 1952).

42. See Scalapino, *Elites*, pp. 70–71. Scalapino categorizes both Mao Tse-tung and Liu Shao-ch'i as "petty intellectuals" rather than "intellectuals," because of their educational background when they entered the Party. He uses the term "intellectuals" to refer to journalists, writers, and professors at higher levels, and "petty intellectuals" to refer to those with lesser educational backgrounds or achievements. Some scholars may question this distinction; however, I believe it is valid to distinguish between persons whose principal orientation has been toward careers dealing with ideas and those who, while they may have been recruited as students into revolutionary movements, have subsequently been, above all, political activists, organizers, and so on.

43. See the discussion in Houn, "The Eighth Central Committee."

44. See, especially, the discussion in Scalapino, "The Transition in Chinese Party Leadership," for analysis in great detail of many facets of the Ninth Central Committee.

45. For one estimate as high as 45 percent, see Ralph L. Powell, "The Role of the Military in China's Transportation and Communication Systems," *Current Scene*, Vol. 10, No. 2 (Feb. 7, 1972), p. 6. Any figure must be viewed as approximate, however, in view of incomplete data on both the backgrounds and current activities of some of the new Central Committee members.

46. See note 39 to this chapter for a basic source on the new Central Committee. I am indebted to several U.S. government analysts, interviewed in September 1973, for assistance in identifying individuals and providing data on them.

47. *Foreign Broadcast Information Service*, FBIS-Chi-73-169 (Aug. 30, 1973), p. D5.

48. Parris H. Chang, "Provincial Party Leaders' Strategies for Survival During the Cultural Revolution," in Scalapino, *Elites*, p. 501.

49. See Donald W. Klein, "The State Council and the Cultural Revolution," in John W. Lewis, *Party Leadership and Revolutionary Power in China* (Cambridge University Press, 1970), pp. 351–72.

50. See Richard Diao and Donald Zagoria, *The Nature of Mainland Chinese Economic Structure, Leadership and Policy (1949–1969) and the Prospects for Arms Control and Disarmament*, U.S. Arms Control and Disarmament Agency, ACDA/E-124 (February 1972), pp. 181–83.

51. The estimates in this chapter are based on unpublished U.S. Department of State reports analyzing the scale of purges in the Chinese military establishment in 1966–67—provided to me orally in interviews in 1971.

Chapter V

1. Several general studies on China's foreign policy and foreign relations since 1949 attempt to analyze the subject in fairly comprehensive terms, and some of them include detail relevant to most of the questions discussed in this chapter. They include Harold C. Hinton, *Communist China in World Politics* (Houghton Mifflin, 1966), and by the same author, *China's Turbulent Quest* (Macmillan, 1970); A. Doak Barnett, *Communist China and Asia: Challenge to American Policy* (Harper, 1960); Vidya Prakash Dutt, *China's Foreign Policy 1958–62* (Bombay: Asia Publishing House, 1964); Peter Van Ness, *Revolution and Chinese Foreign Policy* (University of California Press, 1971); J. D. Simmonds, *China's World: The Foreign Policy of a Developing State* (Columbia University Press, 1970); Ishwer C. Ojha, *Chinese Foreign Policy in an Age of Transition: The Diplomacy of Cultural Despair* (Beacon Press, 1969); Arthur Huck, *The Security of China* (Columbia University Press, 1970); R. G. Boyd, *Communist China's Foreign Policy* (Praeger, 1962); and

H. Arthur Steiner, *Communist China in the World Community* (*International Conciliation*, No. 533, May 1961). Among the numerous useful collections of writings on Chinese foreign policy are Tang Tsou (ed.), *China in Crisis* (University of Chicago Press, 1968), Vol. 2, *China's Policies in Asia and America's Alternatives*; King C. Chen (ed.), *The Foreign Policy in China* (East-West Who? Inc. Publishers, 1972); and Jerome Alan Cohen (ed.), *The Dynamics of China's Foreign Relations* (Harvard University Press, East Asian Monographs, 1970). Other major works on China's foreign relations with particular countries and areas, including the Soviet Union, Korea, Southeast Asia, South Asia, Africa, and Latin America, and on specific facets of Chinese foreign policy, will be mentioned in later notes. Among the large number of noteworthy articles on broad Chinese foreign policy, a few deserve special mention. These include Allen S. Whiting, "The Logic of Communist China's Policy: The First Decade," *Yale Review* (Autumn 1960), pp. 1–17; Allen S. Whiting, "The Use of Force in Foreign Policy by the People's Republic of China," *Annals of the American Academy of Political and Social Science*, Vol. 402 (July 1972), pp. 55–66; Allen S. Whiting, "China and East Asian Security," in *Strategy for Peace: Thirteenth Conference Report* (Stanley Foundation, October 1972), pp. 60–66; A. M. Halpern, "Communist China and Peaceful Coexistence," *China Quarterly*, No. 3 (July–September, 1960), pp. 16–31; A. M. Halpern, "The Chinese Communist Line on Neutralism," *China Quarterly*, No. 5 (January–March 1961), pp. 90–115; A. M. Halpern, "The Foreign Policy Uses of the Chinese Revolutionary Model," *China Quarterly*, No. 7 (July–September 1961), pp. 1–16; A. M. Halpern, "China in the Postwar World," *China Quarterly*, No. 21 (January–March 1965), pp. 20–45; Tang Tsou and Morton H. Halperin, "Mao Tse-tung's Revolutionary Strategy and Peking's International Behavior," *American Political Science Review*, Vol. 59, No. 1 (March 1965), pp. 80–99; Michael B. Yahuda, "China's New Era of International Relations," *Political Quarterly*, Vol. 43, No. 3 (July–September 1972), pp. 295–307.

2. The two "camps" idea was elaborated in detail in a long article written by Liu Shao-ch'i in November 1948. See *Internationalism and Nationalism* (Peking: Foreign Languages Press, March 1951), pp. 1–51.

3. Mao Tse-tung, "On the People's Democratic Dictatorship," *Selected Works of Mao Tse-tung*, Vol. 4 (Peking: Foreign Languages Press, 1961), p. 415. This theme had already been emphasized by Liu in the article cited in note 2 above.

4. See *Foreign Relations of the United States, Diplomatic Papers, 1944*, Vol. 6: *China* (Washington, 1967), August 23 memorandum on John Stewart Service conversation with Mao Tse-tung, pp. 604 ff., and *Foreign Relations of the United States, Diplomatic Papers, 1945*, Vol. 7: *The Far East, China* (Washington, 1969), March 13 John Stewart Service interview with Mao Tse-tung, pp. 273 ff.

5. Data recently published in a book by Seymour Topping reveal that U.S. Ambassador John Leighton Stuart was invited to visit Mao Tse-tung in Peking in early 1949. (Ambassador Stuart had been accredited to the Na-

tionalist government but stayed in Nanking at the time of the Communist takeover.) Many students of that period, including myself, have been inclined to believe that the Chinese had probably decided as early as 1948 to align closely with Moscow. The new data about the invitation to Stuart raise a question as to whether the Chinese Communists were more open-minded than has generally been assumed and whether they might have been willing to adopt a more flexible and less hostile posture toward the United States if Stuart had made the visit. See Seymour Topping, *Journey Between Two Chinas* (Harper and Row, 1972), pp. 83–90.

6. Text in *Sino-Soviet Treaty and Agreements* (Peking: Foreign Languages Press, 1951), pp. 5–8. The text states that each would render military and other assistance to the other if the other were "attacked by Japan or any state allied to it"—a phrase that clearly referred to the United States.

7. See, for example, Liu Shao-ch'i's November 16, 1949, statement; text, *New China News Agency*, Nov. 23, 1949.

8. China's decision to enter the Korean war has been carefully analyzed in an excellent study: Allen S. Whiting, *China Crosses the Yalu* (Macmillan, 1960). For general background on the war, and China's participation in it, see David Rees, *Korea: The Limited War* (St. Martin's Press, 1964, Pelican Books, 1970); see also Dean Acheson, *Present at the Creation* (Norton, 1969), especially Chapters 44, 45, 47–49, 53–55, and 68.

9. See Whiting, *China Crosses the Yalu*, especially p. 45 and Chapter 4, pp. 47 ff.

10. See *Current Affairs Handbook*, Nov. 5, 1950, in *Current Background*, No. 32 (Nov. 29, 1950), and the statement made by a leading Chinese general to the Indian Ambassador to Peking, in K. M. Panikkar, *In Two Chinas* (London: Allen and Unwin, 1955), p. 108.

11. See "Diplomatic Relations of Communist China," *Current Background*, No. 440 (March 12, 1957). This gives information up to March 1, 1957. The later evolution of Peking's diplomatic relations is summarized in Donald W. Klein, "The Management of Foreign Affairs in Communist China," in John M. H. Lindbeck (ed.), *China: Management of a Revolutionary Society* (University of Washington Press, 1971), pp. 315–16.

12. See Barnett, *Communist China and Asia*, pp. 97–98 and 147–71; and Herbert Passin, *China's Cultural Diplomacy* (Praeger, 1962).

13. The Sino-Indian agreement of April 1954, followed by a joint Sino-Burmese communiqué in June of the same year, highlighted this new approach to the neutralist nations. See *Survey of China Mainland Press*, No. 786 (April 29, 1954), for the text of the Sino-Indian agreement and *Survey of China Mainland Press*, No. 841 (July 3–4, 1954), for data on the Sino-Burmese statements. The "five principles of peaceful coexistence" were articulated on both of these occasions.

14. See Melvin Gurtov, *The First Vietnam Crisis* (Columbia University Press, 1967), and King C. Chen, *Vietnam and China, 1938–1954* (Princeton University Press, 1969).

15. Barnett, *Communist China and Asia*, pp. 102–03.

16. See Fred Greene, *U.S. Policy and the Security of Asia* (McGraw-Hill, 1968), Part 2, pp. 71–123.

17. See George McT. Kahin, *The Asian-African Conference, Bandung, Indonesia* (Cornell University Press, 1956); and A. Doak Barnett, "Chou En-lai at Bandung," *American University Field Staff Reports*, No. ADB-1955-4 (May 4, 1955), pp. 1–15.

18. *Survey of China Mainland Press*, No. 841 (July 3–4, 1954), p. 2.

19. For Mao Tse-tung's November 18, 1957, speech in Moscow, see "Mao Tse-tung on Imperialists and Reactionaries," *Current Background*, No. 534 (Nov. 12, 1958).

20. Donald S. Zagoria, *The Sino-Soviet Conflict, 1956–61* (Princeton University Press, 1962), pp. 160–61.

21. See Arthur Lall, *How Communist China Negotiates* (Columbia University Press, 1968), and Kenneth T. Young, *Negotiating with the Chinese Communists: The United States Experience, 1953–67* (McGraw-Hill, 1968), pp. 248–49.

22. See Tang Tsou, "Mao's Limited War in the Taiwan Strait," *Orbis*, Vol. 3, No. 3 (Fall 1959), pp. 332–50; and Tang Tsou, "The Quemoy Imbroglio: Chiang Kai-shek and the United States," *Western Political Quarterly*, Vol. 12, No. 4 (December 1959), pp. 1075–91.

23. There had been earlier border incidents, and exchanges of notes over differing maps, but it was only after the 1959 Tibetan revolt and the flight of the Dalai Lama to India that the border disputes became tense and were brought into the open; thereafter, Sino-Indian relations began to undergo fundamental change. See Barnett, *Communist China and Asia*, pp. 313–15.

24. A thorough study of this is Neville Maxwell, *India's China War* (Pantheon, 1970). Maxwell places a large share of the blame for the conflict on India's "forward policy." See also Kuang-sheng Liao and Allen S. Whiting, "Chinese Press Perceptions of Threat: The U.S. and India, 1962," *China Quarterly*, No. 53 (January–March 1973), pp. 80–97. Not surprisingly, Indian interpretations of the motivations for Peking's policy toward India are substantially different; see, for example, Dutt, *China's Foreign Policy*, pp. 195–271.

25. The best single volume on the origins of the Sino-Soviet dispute is Zagoria, *The Sino-Soviet Conflict*. The literature on the dispute and on Chinese-Russian relations is, however, extensive—more extensive, in fact, than on any other facet of China's foreign relations—and only a few of the useful studies will be mentioned here. Zbigniew K. Brzezinski, *The Soviet Bloc— Unity and Conflict* (Harvard University Press, 1960), and Alexander Dallin (ed.), *Diversity in International Communism* (Columbia University Press, 1963), analyze the early periods of the dispute in the broad context of developments affecting all the Communist states and parties. John Gittings, *Survey of the Sino-Soviet Dispute* (Oxford University Press, 1968); two volumes by William E. Griffith, *The Sino-Soviet Rift* (M.I.T. Press, 1964), and *Peking, Moscow, and Beyond* (Georgetown University, Center for Strategic and International Studies, 1973); and Harold C. Hinton, *The Bear at the Gate*

(Washington: American Enterprise Institute for Public Policy Research, 1971), focus directly on Sino-Soviet relations and carry the story up to the recent period. Richard Lowenthal, *World Communism: The Disintegration of a Secular Faith* (Oxford University Press, 1964), analyzes broad developments affecting the entire "bloc." Kurt London (ed.), *Unity and Contradictions: Major Aspects of Sino-Soviet Relations* (Praeger, 1962), contains a number of useful chapters on Sino-Soviet relations and competition. A study that is very useful for the historical background to recent developments in relations between the two countries is O. Edmund Clubb, *China and Russia: The "Great Game"* (Columbia University Press, 1971).

26. *Long Live Leninism* (Peking: Foreign Languages Press, 1960).

27. On September 1, 1963, the Chinese asserted that although the Soviet Union had made statements supporting China on September 7 and 19, 1958, during the second offshore island crisis, it only did so "when there was no possibility that a nuclear war would break out and no need for the Soviet Union to support China with its nuclear weapons." See "A Comment on the Soviet Government's Statement, August 21, 1963," in Griffith, *The Sino-Soviet Rift*, p. 382. See also Morton H. Halperin, *China and the Bomb* (Praeger, 1965), pp. 55–62; and the papers by Harold C. Hinton, Malcolm Mackintosh, and George Quester on "Sino-Soviet Relations in a U.S.-China Crisis," in Morton H. Halperin (ed.), *Sino-Soviet Relations and Arms Control*, Vol. 2, *Collected Papers* (Harvard University, East Asian Research Center and Center for International Affairs, 1966).

28. "Statement by the Spokesman of the Chinese Government—A Comment on the Soviet Government's Statement of August 3," *Peking Review* (Aug. 16, 1963), p. 14.

29. This joint editorial in *People's Daily* and *Red Flag* was the last of nine "Comments on the Open Letter of the Central Committee of the CPSU," which constituted a sweeping polemical attack on the Khrushchev regime during 1963–64. For text, see *Peking Review* (July 17, 1964), pp. 7–28.

30. See the discussion in Chapter 1, pp. 6 ff., and especially p. 12.

31. Thomas W. Robinson, *The Sino-Soviet Border Dispute: Background, Development, and the March 1969 Clashes*, Report RM-6171-PR (Rand Corp., August 1970).

32. See Griffith, *The Sino-Soviet Rift*, especially pp. 177–206; Gittings, *Survey of the Sino-Soviet Dispute*, especially pp. 200–11; and Robert A. Scalapino, "Moscow, Peking, and the Communist Parties of Asia," *Foreign Affairs*, Vol. 41, No. 2 (January 1963), pp. 323–43.

33. Most writing on China and the Third World has been in the form of articles. However, most of the general studies listed in note 1 for this chapter deal with the topic. In addition, there have been several very useful book-length studies dealing with China's relations with particular regions, including Bruce Larkin, *China and Africa, 1949–1970* (University of California Press, 1971); Cecil Johnson, *Communist China and Latin America, 1959–1967* (Columbia University Press, 1970); and Melvin Gurtov, *China and Southeast Asia: The Politics of Survival* (Heath Lexington Books, 1971).

34. In addition to the work by Larkin cited in note 33, see Robert A. Scalapino, "Sino-Soviet Competition in Africa," *Foreign Affairs*, Vol. 42, No. 4 (July 1964), pp. 640–54; George T. Yu, "Peking versus Taipei in the World Arena: Chinese Competition in Africa," *Asian Survey*, Vol. 3, No. 9 (September 1963), pp. 439–53; and Zbigniew Brzezinski (ed.), *Africa and the Communist World* (Stanford University Press, 1963).

35. *Peking Review* (Feb. 14, 1964), p. 6.

36. In addition to the work by Cecil Johnson cited in note 33 for this chapter, see Ernst Halperin, "Peking and the Latin American Communists," *China Quarterly*, No. 29 (January–March 1967), pp. 111–54; and Joseph J. Lee, "Communist China's Latin American Policy," *Asian Survey*, Vol. 4, No. 11 (November 1964), pp. 1123–34.

37. For the interaction of China, India, Pakistan, and the Soviet Union, see Bhabani Sen Gupta, *The Fulcrum of Asia: Relations Among China, India, Pakistan, and the U.S.S.R.* (Pegasus, 1970). See also, for background, Wayne Wilcox, *India, Pakistan and the Rise of China* (Walker, 1964).

38. See Robert A. Holmes, "Chinese Foreign Policy Toward Burma and Cambodia: A Comparative Analysis" (Ph.D. dissertation, Columbia University, 1969).

39. The first reference to the concept of a second intermediate zone was in an editorial in the *People's Daily*, Jan. 21, 1964. See "All the World's Forces Opposing U.S. Imperialism, Unite!" reprinted in *Peking Review* (Jan. 24, 1964), p. 7.

40. *China, The United Nations and the United States* (United Nations Association of the U.S.A., 1966), p. 21; and Lincoln P. Bloomfield, "China, the U.S. and the U.N.," *International Organization*, Vol. 20, No. 4 (Autumn 1960), p. 673.

41. See D. P. Mozingo and T. W. Robinson, *Lin Piao on "People's War": China Takes A Second Look At Vietnam*, Memorandum RM-4814-PR (Rand Corp., November 1965).

42. For different interpretations of the coup and China's involvement, see David Mozingo, "China's Policy Toward Indonesia," in Tang Tsou, *China in Crisis*, Vol. 2, pp. 333–52; Daniel S. Lev, "Indonesia 1965: The Year of the Coup," *Asian Survey*, Vol. 6, No. 2 (February 1966), pp. 103–10; Arthur J. Dommen, "The Attempted Coup in Indonesia," *China Quarterly*, No. 25 (January–March 1966), pp. 144–70; and John O. Sutter, "Two Faces of 'Konfrontasi': 'Crush Malaysia' and the 'Gestapu,' " *Asian Survey*, Vol. 6, No. 10 (October 1966), pp. 523–46.

43. Charles Neuhauser, *Third World Politics* (Harvard University, East Asian Research Center, 1968), pp. 49–60.

44. See sources cited in note 12 for Chapter 2.

45. As Melvin Gurtov makes clear in "The Foreign Ministry and Foreign Affairs during the Cultural Revolution," *China Quarterly*, No. 40 (October–December 1969), pp. 65–102, the worst period was over by the fall of 1967, and thereafter the Foreign Ministry gradually resumed normal operations; but it was not really until late 1968 or early 1969 that it was operating again

with effectiveness comparable to the past and began pursuing an active foreign policy on a state-to-state level.

46. Anthony R. Dicks, "The Hong Kong Situation I: Impasse" (Institute of Current World Affairs, Newsletter ARD-19, Sept. 5, 1967; processed).

47. *Issues in United States Foreign Policy*, No. 4, "People's Republic of China" (Department of State Publication 8666, October 1972), p. 31, is the source for the mid-1972 figure. The January 1973 figure is based on the author's compilation of data on subsequent developments in China's diplomatic relations.

48. For data on recent U.S.-China policy and U.S.-China interaction, see Roderick MacFarquhar and others, *Sino-American Relations, 1949–71* (Praeger, 1972); A. Doak Barnett, *A New U.S. Policy toward China* (Brookings Institution, 1971); and Richard Moorsteen and Morton Abramowitz, *Remaking China Policy: U.S.-China Relations and Governmental Decision Making* (Harvard University Press, 1971). Some of the most useful material relevant to recent U.S. China policy also is in several volumes of congressional hearings, including *United States Relations with the People's Republic of China*, Hearings before the Senate Committee on Foreign Relations, 92 Cong. 1 sess. (1971); *United States-China Relations: A Strategy for the Future*, Hearings before the Subcommittee on Asian and Pacific Affairs of the House Committee on Foreign Affairs, 91 Cong. 2 sess. (1970); and *U.S. Policy With Respect to Mainland China*, Hearings before the Senate Foreign Relations Committee, 89 Cong. 2 sess. (1966).

49. "Statement by Spokesman of Information Department of Chinese Foreign Ministry," *Peking Review* (Nov. 29, 1968), p. 31.

50. See text in *New York Times*, Feb. 28, 1972.

51. See text of "Joint Statement of the Government of the People's Republic of China and the Government of Japan," in *New York Times*, Sept. 30, 1972.

52. See Halpern, "The Foreign Policy Uses of the Chinese Revolutionary Model." The Chinese, after stressing the relevance of their "model" to others in the early 1950s, downplayed this theme in the mid-1950s, but then greatly increased stress on it in the late 1950s. In 1965, in "Long Live the Victory of People's War," Lin Piao stated that "Comrade Mao Tse-tung's theory of and policies for people's war have creatively enriched and developed Marxism-Leninism" and that it "has become an urgent necessity for the people in many countries to master and use people's war."

53. In addition to the sections in the sources cited in this chapter's note 1 that discuss territorial and border problems, see for additional details Dennis J. Doolin, *Territorial Claims in the Sino-Soviet Conflict* (Hoover Institution Publications, 1965); Tai Sung An, *The Sino-Soviet Territorial Dispute* (Westminster Press, 1973); George N. Patterson, *The Unquiet Frontier* (Hong Kong: International Studies Group, June 1966); and Francis Watson, *The Frontiers of China: A Historical Guide* (Praeger, 1966).

54. The dates of these treaties, and sources for their texts, are to be

found in Douglas M. Johnston and Hungdah Chiu (eds.), *Agreements of the People's Republic of China, 1949–1967: A Calendar* (Harvard University Press, 1968).

55. For brief studies useful for background on some of the legal and foreign policy issues relating to Taiwan, see Joseph W. Ballantine, *Formosa: A Problem for United States Policy* (Brookings Institution, 1952); Jerome Alan Cohen and others, *Taiwan and American Policy: The Dilemma in U.S.-China Relations* (Praeger, 1971); and William M. Bueler, *U.S. China Policy and the Problem of Taiwan* (Colorado Associated University Press, 1971).

56. In the communiqué, "The Chinese side reaffirmed its position: The Taiwan question is the crucial question obstructing the normalization of relations between China and the United States; the Government of the People's Republic of China is the sole legal government of China; Taiwan is a province of China which has long been returned to the motherland; the liberation of Taiwan is China's internal affair." On its part, "The U.S. side declared: The United States acknowledges that all Chinese on either side of the Taiwan Strait maintain there is but one China and that Taiwan is a part of China. The United States does not challenge that position. It reaffirms its interest in a peaceful settlement of the Taiwan question by the Chinese themselves." The United States did not explicitly state its own position and did not break relations with the Nationalist regime or abandon the U.S. defense commitment to it, so the communiqué fell short of what Peking had previously stated would be required for any improvement of U.S.-China relations.

57. During my visit to China in December 1972 and January 1973, this was evident in many conversations with Chinese officials on foreign affairs. A posture of this sort can, of course, be rapidly modified, but there are many reasons to believe that it may persist at least for a considerable period of time.

58. Chinese Communist diplomats state that the basic positions outlined in Peking's May 24, 1969, and October 7, 1969, statements are still operative; for texts of these statements, see *Peking Review*, May 30, 1969, pp. 3–9, and Oct. 10, 1969, pp. 3–4. In the former, which spells out the Chinese positions in considerable detail, the Chinese state that the treaties relating to the present Sino-Soviet boundary should be taken "as the basis" for settling the boundary question and that "necessary adjustments at individual places on the boundary can be made in accordance with the principles of consultation on an equal footing and of mutual understanding and mutual accommodation."

59. No one can be certain, of course, about what final positions Peking will accept until concrete Sino-Indian agreements are reached. I would judge, however, on the basis of official Chinese statements which are adamant about Aksai Chin but strongly imply a willingness to compromise on other areas that are subject to conflicting claims, that Peking will insist on keeping Aksai Chin but may accept essentially the McMahon line in the east. See, for example, the Chinese government's October 24, 1962, and other official statements in *The Sino-Indian Boundary Question* (2d enlarged ed. Peking: Foreign Languages Press, 1962). Others share this judgment. See, for ex-

ample, John Wilson Lewis, "Communist China's Invasion of the Indian Frontier: The Framework of Motivation," *Current Scene*, Vol. 2, No. 7 (Jan. 2, 1963), pp. 1–10.

60. See Jonathan D. Pollack, "Chinese Attitudes Toward Nuclear Weapons, 1964–9," *China Quarterly*, No. 50 (April–June 1972), p. 271, for data on the characteristics of Chinese nuclear and thermonuclear detonations. For data on recent Chinese missile development, see three articles by William Beecher in the *New York Times*: "Shift in Strategy by Peking Is Seen," July 25, 1972; "China Said To Add Missile Strength," Nov. 8, 1972; and "Chinese ICBM Bid Reported by U.S.," March 4, 1973. Except for ICBM development, which has lagged somewhat behind U.S. government predictions of recent years, Chinese nuclear weapons development has generally been faster than foreign observers expected.

61. In earlier years, when the Soviet Union was relatively weak in nuclear terms, its position was that all nuclear powers should adopt a "no use" policy as part of broad disarmament policies. It is debatable how much China's present positions are traceable to its comparative weakness, and might change when its nuclear capabilities have substantially expanded. There seems little possibility, however, that its relative nuclear position will change so much in the period we are discussing—i.e., the 1970s—to make this very likely.

62. This theme is stressed in a number of the studies cited already, including Whiting, *China Crosses the Yalu*, Maxwell, *India's China War*, Robinson, *The Sino-Soviet Border Dispute*, and Gurtov, *China and Southeast Asia*. Several studies of less well-known crises or disputes make the same point; see, for example, A. M. Halpern and H. B. Fredman, *Communist Strategy in Laos*, Research Memorandum RM-2561 (Rand Corp., June 14, 1960).

63. See the discussion in James Chieh Hsiung, *Law and Policy in China's Foreign Relations: A Study of Attitudes and Practices* (Columbia University Press, 1972).

64. The following quotations are from the text of Chou's report, *Foreign Broadcast Information Service*, FBIS-Chi-73-170 (Aug. 31, 1973), pp. B1–B13.

Index

Abramowitz, Morton, 376n
Acheson, Dean, 372n
Afghanistan, 267
Agriculture: collectivization of, 122, 148; Communes and, 148, 149; growth rate, 149; investment in, 147-48; modernization of, 125, 127, 148; output, 123, 125, 168-69, 173, 177, 178, 182; priority to development of, 124, 126, 128, 147, 149
Aird, John S., 359n, 360n
Anderson, James B., 334
An, Tai Sung, 376n
Armed forces, 3, 107, 296. *See also* Military establishment; People's Liberation Army
Arts, revolutionizing the, 14, 24
Ashbrook, Arthur G., Jr., 355n, 361n
Australia, 253; trade with China, 268

Ballantine, Joseph W., 377n
Bandung period, 254-55
Bangladesh, 267
Barnett, A. Doak, 355n, 337n, 339n, 342n, 349n, 356n, 359n, 364n, 370n, 372n, 373n, 376n
Bateman, Nancy, 334
Batsavage, R. E., 360n
Baum, Richard, 337n, 343n, 345n, 365n
Beecher, William, 378n
Behavior, of Chinese, 32-33
Bennett, Gordon A., 343n, 344n, 345n
Birth control, 159-62
Boorman, Howard L., 362n, 363n, 368n
Bowie, Robert R., 364n
Boyd, R. G., 370n
Bridgham, Philip, 337n, 343n, 365n
Brown, Harrison, 360n
Brzezinski, Zbigniew K., 373n, 375n
Bueler, William M., 377n
Burchett, Wilfred, 368n
Bureaucracy, 16, 19, 41, 189; Communist Party, 54; Mao's indictment of, 11-13, 35, 45, 67; restrictions imposed by, 7; structure of (*1973*), 61

Burma, 271, 282; border dispute, 267, 287, 299
Burton, Barry, 343n

Cadres, 26, 59, 61, 62, 160; classification of, 133; Communist Party, 7, 42, 50, 54-55, 71, 84, 119, 137, 186, 241; economic planning by, 139, 140; effect of Cultural Revolution on, 62-63; indoctrination of, 25, 40, 45, 56-58; military, 83; revolutionary, 41
Cambodia, 257, 267
Canada, 268, 273
Capital goods, production of, 147
Casella, Alexander, 341n
Castro, Fidel, 266
Cement production, 174-76
Central Committee, 43, 186; eighth (*1956*), 231-32; ideology of, 235; membership of, 203, 228-36; ninth (*1969*), 233-35; provincial representation in, 237, 238; purges of, 234, 235, 236; representation by the masses in, 233, 238; role of military in, 22, 203, 230, 237, 240; seventh (*1945*), 229-31; tenth (*1973*), 236-38
Central People's Government Council, 187
Centrist policy, 27, 28, 201, 206, 211
Ceylon, 267
Chang Ch'un-ch'iao, 209, 210, 211, 218, 220, 222, 223, 226, 227, 243
Chang Kuo-t'ao, 187, 336n, 367n
Chang, Parris H., 343n, 354n, 365n, 366n, 368n, 370n
Chang Wen-t'ien, 213, 214, 216, 217
Charles, David A., 365n
Cheng, Chester J., 348n, 349n
Ch'en Hsi-lien, 87, 88, 210, 222, 226, 243
Ch'en, Jerome, 339n, 360n, 361n, 364n, 367n
Chen, King C., 371n, 372n
Chen, Nai-Ruenn, 353n, 354n, 361n, 362n
Ch'en, Pi-chao, 359n

Ch'en Po-ta, 207, 208, 214, 215, 217, 218, 219, 220, 223, 224, 225, 226
Ch'en Tsai-tao, 87
Ch'en Yi, 214, 216, 219
Ch'en Yun, 204, 206, 207, 208, 216, 218
Chiang Ch'ing, 59, 210, 218, 219, 220, 223, 226, 338n
Chiang Kai-shek, 195
Chile, 273
China, People's Republic of: anti-imperialist policy of, 251, 255–56, 263, 264, 280; confrontation over offshore islands, 75, 252, 261; efforts to recover Taiwan, 252–53, 256, 261; foreign relations, see Foreign policy; foreign revolutionary movements and, 248, 250–51, 281–82; intervention in Korean war, 71–72, 73, 110, 248–50, 282, 297; national defense, 110–12, 114, 247, 249, 253, 263–64, 282, 286; nineteenth century reforms, 19, 20; nuclear capability, 75, 76, 107, 109, 111, 262; succession problem in, see Succession; trade, see Foreign trade; and United Nations, 269, 273, 278, 283, 304, 305
Ch'in Dynasty, 152
Chinese Communist Party: bureaucracy of, 12, 54–55, 60; constitution of 1973, 64; draft constitution of 1970, 46; effect of Cultural Revolution on, 40–41, 56; efforts at reorganization of, 44–45, 48–50, 54–55; Eighth Party Congress, 190, 214; influence on institutions, 37–38; influence on military, 69–70, 71, 76, 83–84, 92, 98, 99; Ninth Party Congress, 22, 43, 44, 207, 208; Provincial Committees of, 44; relationship with government, 55–56; Seventh Party Congress, 187; Tenth Party Congress, 1, 23, 24, 26, 29, 47, 55, 56, 57, 64, 116, 181, 186, 200, 209, 224, 242, 306, 308, 341n; top leaders of, 203–11. See also Central Committee; Military Affairs Commission; Party Committee; Politburo; Revolutionary Committees; Standing Committee
Ch'ing Dynasty, 20, 69
Chin P'ing, 344n
Ch'in Shih-huang, Emperor, 24
Ch'i Pen-yu, 354n
Chi Teng-k'uei, 223, 227
Ch'iu Hui-tso, 222, 224
Chiu, Hungdah, 377n
Chou En-lai, 22, 47, 56, 59, 60, 61, 64, 69, 86, 116, 185, 200, 204, 207, 209, 210, 216, 218; on Africa, 266; centrist policy of,

206, 211, 228; defense of bureaucracy by, 63, 189, 219, 241; and foreign policy, 306; political report (1973), 23–24, 57, 181, 306–08; and Sino-American relations, 306–07; and Sino-Soviet relations, 307–08; as successor to Mao, 198, 201, 242–43, 310, 319; summit meeting with President Nixon, 277
Chu Teh, 69, 203, 205, 206, 207, 209, 210, 216, 218, 220, 222, 225
Clark, Ann B., 362n, 363n
Clinton, Richard L., 360n
Clubb, O. Edmund, 374n
Coal production, 174–76
Cohen, Arthur A., 336n
Cohen, Jerome Alan, 351n, 371n, 377n
Cold war, 246, 247
Collective leadership, 192, 195, 199, 202, 203
Collectivization, 2, 13, 17, 121, 122, 148
Commissar system, 98–100, 103
Commune program, 6, 21, 51, 141, 181, 191, 255, 262; in rural areas, 49, 125, 134, 148, 149
Communist bloc, 251, 259, 268
Communist Party of China. See Chinese Communist Party
Confucius, 24, 25, 26
Consumer goods, 133–34, 148
Consumption, 125, 135; guaranteed minimum levels of, 130
Cuba, 266
Cultural Revolution, 1, 3, 13, 29, 33, 90, 91, 180, 191, 197, 206, 324; causes of, 6–8; economic development during, 127–28, 137; effect on bureaucracy, 62–63; effect on institutions, 35–36, 38–39, 45–46; effect on leadership, 185, 186, 239–41; foreign policy during, 271–72; General Political Department, 100; impact on Chinese Communist Party, 40–41, 56, 78, 86; Mao and, 8–9, 22, 191, 193–94; propaganda campaign of, 20–21; Public Security system during, 101; role of ideology in, 6, 21, 318; role of military in, 78, 79–84, 88, 89, 97, 317
Cultural Revolution Group, 27–28, 207, 209, 219, 220, 223
Culture, revolutionizing, 21, 25

Dallin, Alexander, 373n
de Gaulle, Charles, 269
Developing nations. See Third World nations
Dialectic approach, 9, 17
Diao, Richard, 354n, 370n

Dicks, Anthony R., 376n
Domes, Jürgen, 350n, 363n
Dommen, Arthur J., 375n
Donnithorne, Audrey, 353n
Doolin, Dennis J., 376n
Dorrill, W. F., 337n, 338n
Dulles, John Foster, 253
Durdin, Tillman, 347n, 350n
Dutt, Vidya Prakash, 370n, 373n

Eckstein, Alexander, 353n, 354n, 355n, 361n, 362n
Economic development, 7, 117; and centralization versus decentralization, 136–43, 182; during Cultural Revolution, 127–28, 137; during Great Leap Forward, 124–26; foreign trade and, 313, 314; major issues relating to, 118–19; non-Maoist emphasis on, 17, 18; People's Liberation Army role in, 113; reliability of statistics, 166–67; self-reliance and, 119, 162–65; six stages in, 120–21; trends in, 317, 321; variations in approach to, 118
Education, 63; fees, 132, 133; higher, 156–58; for the masses, 150; medical, 340n; revolutionizing, 14, 21, 24, 25, 30, 156, 157; rural, 151, 179
Egalitarianism, 14, 15, 18, 33, 125, 154, 179, 182; economic, 130–36; in military, 69, 92
Electric power production, 174–76
Elitism, 17, 18, 19, 33, 131
Erisman, Alva Lewis, 356n, 357n
Esposito, Bruce J., 358n
Ethiopia, 273
Etzioni, Amitai, 366n

Fairbank, John K., 365n
Falkenheim, Victor C., 343n
Fang Chun-kuei, 344n
Fertilizer, chemical: production, 172, 173, 174–76; use, 127, 148
Field Armies, 71, 72, 73, 104–06
Field, Robert Michael, 362n
Fiscal policy, 121
Five Anti-Campaign, 121
Five-Year Plans: first, 122–24, 137, 138, 140, 170, 172, 173, 255; fourth, 139
Food imports, 127, 268
Foreign policy: adoption of "hard line" (1957), 255–56; and African nations, 265–66, 302; and Communist bloc nations, 251, 260, 265, 271; defensive approach to, 295–97; diplomatic relations with non-Communist nations, 250, 251,

255, 269, 273; during Cultural Revolution, 271–72; and India, 258–59, 267, 292–94, 304; influence of ideology on, 246, 247, 259, 260–61, 265, 279–84, 325; isolationism in, 269–72, 285, 286, 313; and Japan, 110, 111, 163, 183, 230, 247, 248, 257, 268, 275–78, 296, 301, 303, 312, 327; and Latin America, 266, 269, 302; and Pakistan, 259, 266–67, 287, 304; pragmatic approach to, 272–75; revolutionary interests and, 280–81, 283, 284; self-reliance and, 162–65, 264, 300, 313; and Soviet Union, 71, 75, 86, 95, 110, 162–63, 246, 247–48, 256, 259–65, 291–92, 296, 300, 302, 307–08, 312, 326–28, 331; territorial disputes, 258–59, 261, 286–95, 298; and Third World nations, 254, 262–63, 265–68, 270, 271, 274, 302, 326; trends in, 324–25; and United States, 75, 86, 110, 111, 246, 249, 253, 256, 274–77, 296, 301, 312, 328–33
Foreign trade, 123; efforts to expand, 165, 254, 314; with non-Communist nations, 125, 127, 163; volume of, 165, 168–69, 313, 360n
France, 230, 269
Fraser, Angus W., 348n
Fraser, Stewart, 357n
Fredman, H. B., 378n

Galenson, Walter, 353n, 361n, 362n
General Political Department (GPD), 79, 87, 209, 222; commissar system under, 81, 99–100, 103; effect of Cultural Revolution on, 82
George, Alexander L., 348n, 351n
Germany, 268
Gittings, John, 348n, 349n, 351n, 352n, 353n, 373n
GNP. See Gross national product
Godwin, R. Kenneth, 360n
Goldman, Merle, 340n, 365n
GPD. See General Political Department
Grain production, 168–69, 173, 177, 178
Great Leap Forward, 6, 9, 21, 29, 74, 76, 162, 180, 191, 206, 324; agricultural production during, 173; criticism of, 340n; economic policies during, 124–26, 137, 138, 146, 180; failure of, 125; foreign policy during, 255; Politburo membership during, 215
Greece, 273
Greene, Fred, 373n
Griffith, Samuel B., II, 348n, 373n, 374n
Gromyko, Andrei, 278

Gross national product (GNP): foreign trade as proportion of, 165; growth rate of, 152, 167–70, 179, 183, 184, 362n
Gupta, Bhabani Sen, 375n
Gurley, John W., 361n
Gurtov, Melvin, 343n, 372n, 374n, 375n, 378n

Hager, Lois B., 363n, 369n
Hainan, 246
Halperin, Ernst, 375n
Halperin, Morton H., 374n
Halpern, A. M., 371n, 376n, 378n
Harding, Harry, Jr., 341n, 345n
Health care, 24, 125, 150, 160; fees, 132, 133; in rural areas, 151, 179
Hinton, Harold C., 365n, 370n, 373n, 374n
Hoffman, Charles, 355n
Holmes, Robert A., 375n
Holubnuchy, Vsevolod, 338n
Ho Lung, 105, 214, 216
Hong Kong, 271, 287, 288–89
Ho, Ping-ti, 343n
Horn, Joshua S., 357n
Houn, Franklin W., 369n, 370n
Howe, Christopher, 358n
Hsiao Hua, 100
Hsieh Fu-chih, 217, 218, 222, 225, 227
Hsiung, James Chieh, 336n, 338n, 378n
Hsu Hsiang-ch'ien, 217, 219, 220
Hsu Shih-yu, 87, 88, 210, 222, 226, 243
Hua Kuo-feng, 227, 243
Huang K'o-ch'eng, 76
Huang Yung-sheng, 81, 86, 218, 222, 224
Hu Ch'iao-mu, 239
Huck, Arthur, 370n
Hundred Flowers Campaign, 26, 191
Hungary, 260
Hunter, Neale, 343n

Ideological pluralism, 32
Ideology, 1, 3; as cause of Sino-Soviet dispute, 260–61; changing role of, 20–22; compromise over, 29–31; conflicts over, 4–6, 27–28, 34; declining influence of, 25–26, 31, 322; effect on foreign policy, 246, 247, 259, 260–61, 265, 279–84; interaction of nationalism and, 285–86; Maoist, 4, 9–15, 29, 30, 154, 155; non-Maoist, 15–19; of Politburo, 223–24, 226; role of, in post-Mao period, 318, 322
Imperialism, 251, 255–56, 280; social, 263, 264
Income: differentials, 131–36; per capita, 132

India, 173; relations with China, 261–62, 304
Indochina, 248, 252. See also Cambodia; Laos; Vietnam
Indonesia, 270, 282
Industry, 124, 126; capital goods, 122, 124, 147; expansion of, 18, 122; local, 145; management policies of, 123; production, 121, 125, 143, 163, 165, 168–69, 171–73, 174–76, 180, 182; small-scale, 128, 141, 143–46, 152
Inflation, 121
Institutions, 1, 3; Communist Party and, 37–38; during first Five-Year Plan, 122; during Great Leap Forward, 124–25; effect of Cultural Revolution on, 35–36, 38–39, 318; instability in, 35–36, 42, 45, 63, 65–66; Mao's attitude toward, 11, 35, 45; methods for changing, 13–14; reconstruction of, 36, 43, 47–48, 65–66, 318, 322
Intellectuals, 26, 30, 155
Investment, 125, 135, 183; "capital construction," 147; foreign, 164
Iran, 273
Isolationism, 269–72, 285, 286, 313

Jao Shu-shih, 188, 213
Japan, 111, 163, 183; growth rate, 170; relations with China, 230, 247, 268, 275, 296, 301, 327; relations with United States, 253, 327, 332; remilitarization of, 110, 301, 303
Jen Pi-shih, 212, 214
Joffe, Ellis, 348n, 349n, 351n
Johnson, Cecil, 374n, 375n
Johnson, Chalmers, 336n, 348n, 367n
Johnston, Douglas M., 377n
Jones, Edwin F., 355n

Kahin, George McT., 373n
K'ang Sheng, 207, 208, 209, 210, 213, 214, 215, 217, 218, 219, 220, 222, 223, 225, 239
Kao Kang, 188, 213, 214
Karnow, Stanley, 342n, 350n
Khrushchev, Nikita, 261, 262; destalinization program, 256, 260
Kiangsi Soviet, 229
Kim, Ilpyong J., 364n
Kishi, Nobusuke, 257
Klein, Donald W., 362n, 363n, 368n, 369n, 370n, 372n
Klein, Sidney, 362n
Kissinger, Henry, 277
K'o Ch'ing-shih, 215, 216

Korean war, 71-72, 73, 110, 248-50, 282, 297, 299
Kuomintang, 229

Labor: emphasis on manual, 130; mass mobilization of, 2, 123, 125, 127, 128, 152, 182; material incentives for, 134–35, 181, 182; productivity, 154; transfer of, from urban to rural areas, 150, 152, 154
Labor unions, 40, 51
Lall, Arthur, 373n
Land reform, 121, 148
Langley, Alice, 348n
Laos, 257, 267
Larkin, Bruce, 374n
Leadership: collective, 192, 195, 199, 202, 203, 241, 242, 319; from Communist Party elite, 3; Communist versus Nationalist, 348-49n; effects of Cultural Revolution on, 185, 186, 239-41; future role of military in, 317; for post-Mao era, 316, 317, 319; purges, 43, 239-41, 309, 310; top level of, 43, 203-11. See also Succession
Lee, Joseph L., 375n
Lee Kuan Yew, 278
Lei Feng, 77
Lev, Daniel S., 375n
Levenson, Joseph R., 341n
Lewis, John Wilson, 338n, 340n, 342n, 343n, 349n, 367n, 370n, 378n
Liao, Kuang-sheng, 373n
Li Ching-ch'uan, 57, 215, 239
Li, Choh-ming, 354n, 361n
Li Fu-ch'un, 214, 216, 218, 239, 356n
Li Hsien-nien, 160, 210, 214, 216, 219, 220, 223, 227, 239
Li Hsueh-feng, 217, 223, 224, 225, 239
Lindbeck, John M. H., 342n, 364n, 367n, 372n
Lin Piao, 23, 24, 60, 62, 207, 213, 217, 218, 349n; alliance with Mao, 78-79, 205; attempted coup by, 208; as Mao's successor, 22, 43-44, 46, 197; the military and, 76-77, 95, 96, 100, 216, 219, 222; purge of, 47, 59, 64, 86, 87, 105, 185, 197, 199, 224, 225, 309; on self-reliance, 270; and Soviet revisionists, 307
Lin Po-ch'u, 212, 216
Li Teh-sheng, 87, 100, 209, 210, 211, 222, 225, 243
Literature, revolutionizing, 24
Li Tso-p'eng, 222, 224
Liu Lan-t'ao, 239
Liu Po-ch'eng, 214, 216, 218, 222, 225

Liu Shao-ch'i, 30, 77, 120, 144, 187, 189, 201, 204, 206, 207, 215, 217; as Mao's successor, 196; ouster of, 60, 197, 199
Liu, Ta-chung, 353n, 354n
Li, Victor, 351n
Localism, economic, 140-42, 145
Lo Jui-ch'ing, 76, 78, 95, 101, 217, 218, 239, 309, 350n
Lo Jung-huan, 214, 216
London, Kurt, 374n
Lowenthal, Richard, 374n
Lubman, Stanley, 351n
Lushan plenum, 76, 206, 216, 337n
Lu Ting-yi, 214, 215, 217, 220, 239

Macao, 271, 287, 288
McDowell, S. Garrett, 357n
McFarlane, Bruce, 355n
MacFarquhar, Roderick, 337n, 365n, 376n
Machine tools production, 174-76
Mackintosh, Malcolm, 374n
Malaysia, 278, 282
Malnutrition, 125, 160
Maoism, 8-15; as a secular religion, 22, 159, 193, 194
"Mao's Proletarian Headquarters," 203, 207, 218
Mao Tse-tung, 5, 6, 20, 23, 25, 28, 31, 40, 59, 60, 69, 86, 99-100, 126, 127, 191, 204, 207, 217, 233, 336n, 339n, 351n, 358n; alliance with Lin Piao, 78-79, 205; anti-imperialist policy of, 255-56; attack on institutions, 35, 39, 65; and bureaucracy, 11-13, 35, 45, 67, 189, 337n; on contradictions, 9-10; and Cultural Revolution, 8, 22, 191, 193-94, 207; and détente with U.S., 261; economic policy of, 120, 180, 181; and egalitarianism, 14-15; emphasis on politics, 14, 21, 155; and first Five-Year Plan, 123-24; foreign policy of, 247, 261, 308-09; and General Political Department, 99-100; ideology of, 8-14, 21, 154, 155, 158, 180, 182, 188, 279; impact on China, 186-87; and the military, 69, 74, 76-77, 80, 81, 94-95; as a "populist," 10-11; relations with Communist Party, 38-39, 187, 192; resistance to policies of, 190-91; and revolution, 10, 13-15, 34, 264; successors to, see Succession; on voluntarism, 11. See also Thought of Mao
Marxism-Leninism, 3, 4, 5, 16, 32, 157, 192, 235, 261, 279, 280, 321; Maoist approach to, 9, 13, 20, 23, 32

Masses: potentiality of, 10, 17; representation in Central Committee, 233
Mass organizations, 38, 40, 42, 49, 51, 52, 83, 84, 137, 322–23
Maxwell, Neville, 373n, 378n
May 7 schools, 25, 45, 56, 58
Mehnert, Klaus, 345n
Meisner, Maurice, 339n
Middle East, 251, 256, 265
Military Affairs Commission, 96, 100, 214, 216, 222; function of, 73, 219
Military Control Commissions, 71, 72, 82, 85; police functions of, 101
Military establishment: centralization of, 70, 73, 97, 349n; Communist Party and, 69–70, 71, 83–84, 92, 98, 99; dual command structure of, 98–100; effect of Korean war on, 73–74; elite subsystems in, 104–05; emphasis on defense by, 295–97; future role of, 88–91; generational differences in, 106; interservice rivalry in, 107; main forces of, 94, 95–96, 115; modernization of, 70, 72, 74, 93–95, 99, 107–08, 114, 320; multiple functions of, 353n; nationalism in, 97; political role of, 53, 67–68, 71, 72–73, 77, 83–84, 91–92, 103; potential role of, in post-Mao period, 87–88, 320–21; professionalization of, 73, 74, 75, 93–95, 99, 114, 320; purges in, 240–41; regional forces of, 95, 96, 115; role in society, 67–68, 106, 112, 320. See also Militia; People's Liberation Army
Militia: army-Party control of, 102–03; expansion of, 74–75; future role of, 115
Modernization programs, 7, 15, 19, 20, 158, 159, 183. See also Military establishment
Montaperto, Ronald N., 343n, 344n
Moorsteen, Richard, 376n
Mozingo, D. P., 375n
Munro, Donald J., 357n
Murphy, Charles J. V., 368n

Nationalism, 2, 25, 34, 97, 284, 322, 323; interaction of ideology and, 285–86; territorial issues and, 287
Nationalist government, 69, 70, 71, 247, 252, 290. See also Taiwan
National liberation, 280, 281
National People's Congress (NPC), 48, 61, 215; efforts to stabilize government, 46–47, 64–65
National security, 93, 108–09, 295–99, 309, 325

Nehru, Jawaharlal, 254
Nelson, Harvey, 350n, 351n
Nepal, 267, 287
Neuhauser, Charles, 337n, 343n, 365n, 375n
New Zealand, 253
Nieh Jung-chen, 217, 219
Nixon, Richard M., 274, 276, 277, 289
Nixon doctrine, 276, 312
Non-Maoists: emphasis on economics, 17, 18; ideology, 15–19
North Africa, 251
North, Robert C., 369n
NPC. See National People's Congress
Nuclear capability and development, 75, 76, 107, 109, 111, 269, 297–98; Soviet Union and, 262

Ojha, Ishwer C., 370n
Oksenberg, Michel C., 334, 337n, 340n, 343n, 364n, 365n
Oldham, C. H. Geoffrey, 359n
Orleans, Leo A., 359n

Pakistan, 259, 287, 304
Panikkar, K. M., 372n
Paper production, 174–76
Party Committee, 49, 50, 56
Passin, Herbert, 372n
Pathet Lao, 267
Patterson, George N., 376n
Peaceful coexistence, 251, 254, 276
P'eng Chen, 30, 189, 212–13, 215, 217, 239
P'eng Teh-huai, 76, 95, 105, 213, 216, 217, 309, 340n
People's diplomacy, 251, 253, 281
People's Liberation Army (PLA), 53, 57, 320, 323; Field Armies, 71, 72, 73; formation of, 70; ideological indoctrination in, 77–78, 92, 112; leadership training in, 112–13; Military Control Commission, 71, 72, 82, 85, 101; political role of, 71, 74, 77, 78, 80, 82, 88, 89, 91–92, 112, 115, 116; problems in, 76; propaganda teams of, 81, 83; role in Communist takeover, 70–71; role in economic development programs, 113; social role of, 68, 77. See also General Political Department
Pepper, Suzanne, 357n
Perkins, Dwight H., 354n, 355n
Petroleum production, 174–76
Pfeffer, Richard M., 343n
Philippines, 253, 278
Phillips, Warren H., 367n
PLA. See People's Liberation Army

Poland, 260

Polarization, ideological, 5, 6, 8, 27, 28, 34

Police. *See* Public Security system

Politburo, 60, 62, 73, 192, 215; of *1969*, 217, 220, 221–24; during the Cultural Revolution, 212, 217–18; functions of, 211; ideology of, 221, 223–24, 226; membership of, 59, 212–17, 224–25; provincial leaders in, 227; purges of members, 216, 217, 220, 224, 225; reorganization (*1973*), 186, 224; role in economic affairs, 139, 216; role of "leftists" in, 218, 219, 222, 226, 227; role of military in, 116, 216, 222, 226; role of women in, 223

Political system, 32; breakdown of, 3; centralization in, 214; effect of nationalism on, 34; restructuring of, after Cultural Revolution, 22–23, 47–48, 59, 63; role of military in, 67–68, 72–73, 77, 78, 80, 88; and Soviet Union, 2, 3

Political values, 14, 32–33, 118, 182; impact on education, 156; Maoist emphasis on, 14, 92, 128, 155, 180

Pollack, Jonathan D., 378n

Population, 168–69; accuracy of statistics on, 166–67; efforts to limit, 159–62; growth rate, 160–62

Populism, 10–11

Powell, Ralph H., 348n, 349n, 351n, 352n, 353n, 370n

Po Yi-po, 214, 216

Pragmatism: economic, 180, 287, 321; in foreign policy, 264–74, 300, 305, 325

Price, R. F., 357n

Production: agricultural, 123, 125, 173, 177, 178, 182; industrial, 121, 125, 143, 163, 165, 171–73, 174–76, 180, 182

Professionalism, 7, 15, 16, 18, 69; military, 73, 74, 75, 76, 93–95, 108, 114, 226

Public Security system, 49; during Cultural Revolution, 101: military supervision of, 83, 100–01; relationship with Communist Party, 102–03

Public works projects, 152

Pye, Lucian W., 337n, 342n

Quemoy, 252

Quester, George, 374n

Quotations from Chairman Mao Tsetung, 22, 25, 339n

Ra'anan, Uri, 350n

Rationing, 132

Red Guard, 35, 40, 41, 79, 82, 83, 84, 194, 271

Rees, David, 372n

Rents, 132, 133

Revisionism, 260, 263, 280, 307

Revolutionary Committees: establishment of, 41, 42, 43, 44, 46; functions of, 41, 49, 50, 56; role of military in, 83–85

Revolutionary process, 9–10, 13–14, 17, 264–65, 280, 281, 283, 300

Revolutionary Rebels, 35, 40, 41, 194

Rice, Edward E., 342n

Richman, Barry M., 354n

Riskin, Carl, 356n

Roberts, Harley M., 362n

Robinson, Thomas W., 342n, 345n, 350n, 367n, 374n, 375n

Rostow, W. W., 335n

Rumania, 304

Rural development, 147, 182; transfer of urban resources for, 149–52

Saifudin, 227

Sato, Eisaku, 278

Scalapino, Robert A., 363n, 367n, 368n, 370n, 375n

Schram, Stuart R., 336n, 338n, 339n, 342n, 364n

Schran, Peter, 356n

Schurmann, Franz, 338n, 342n, 354n, 365n

Schwartz, Benjamin I., 336n, 364n

Selden, Mark, 364n

Self-reliance: economic development and, 119, 162–65; foreign policy and, 162–65, 264, 300, 313; foreign trade and, 125

Senkaku Islands (Tiao Yu Tai Islands), 294

Service, John Stewart, 371n

Shanghai, Communist Party organization in, 48, 54

Shanghai Municipality, 58; organization of, 346–47n

Shanghai Revolutionary Committee, 209, 210, 222

Shih Yen-hung, 357n

Sigurdson, Jon, 356n

Sihanouk, 267

Simmonds, J. D., 337n, 365n, 370n

Sino-Indian agreement (*1954*), 254

Sino-Indian border crises, 258–59, 261, 292–94

Sino-Soviet differences, 75, 110, 258, 275;

border problem, 291–92; issues involved in, 260–61; origins of, 259–60
Sino-Soviet military alliance (1950), 71, 247, 248, 253
Skinner, G. William, 366n
Snow, Edgar, 346n, 347n, 360n, 364n, 367n
Social institutions, 2, 13–14
Socialist Education Campaign, 191
Socialization, 13, 121, 122
Society: role of military in, 67–68, 106; stratification of, 34
Solomon, Richard H., 342n
Southeast Asia, 267–68
Southeast Asia Treaty Organization, 253
South Korea, 253
Soviet Union, 2, 3, 95, 123, 183; agricultural output, 173; Chou En-Lai's policy toward, 23, 307–08; destalinization program, 261, 262; and Korean war, 249; military aid to India, 261–62; nuclear test ban treaty, 263; potential post-Mao relations with China, 311–12, 326–28, 331; relations with China, 75, 86, 123–24, 162, 163, 246–48, 259–65, 291–92, 296, 300, 302; space achievements, 256; succession problem in, 190; training of Chinese in, 213, 230
Specialization, 7, 15, 18, 19, 69, 155; military, 73, 94
Stalin, Josef V., 190, 196
Standard of living, 131–32, 134, 135
Standing Committee, 192, 203, 211, 225; in 1969, 43, 209, 219; function of, 207; membership of, 205–06; role of military in, 116
Starr, John Bryan, 338n
State Council, 61–62
State Planning Commission, 139
Statistics: population, 168–69; reliability of, 166–67
Steel production, 168–69, 174–76
Steiner, H. Arthur, 371n
Student groups, 40–41, 51–52
Succession, 87–88, 115, 116, 184, 208, 308, 310, 316; collective leadership, 192, 195, 199, 202, 242, 319; ideology and, 322; leaders considered, 22, 43–44, 46, 197–98, 242–43; Mao's plans for, 196–97; predictions, 199–202, 243–44; role of military, 320–21; Soviet attitude toward, 311; Tenth Party Congress and, 186
Su Chen-hua, 226
Sugar production, 174–76
Sukarno, 267–68

Sung Jen-ch'iung, 239
Sun Yat-sen, 195
Sutter, John O., 375n
Sweezy, Alan, 360n

Taiwan, 111, 246, 249, 252–53, 256, 288–90, 307
Tanaka, Kakuei, 278
T'an Chen-lin, 57, 215, 216, 239
Tang, Peter S. H., 335n
Tansky, Leo, 362n
T'ao Chu, 217, 220, 239
Teams: production, 49–50, 126, 138; propaganda, 81, 83, 156
Teiwes, Frederick C., 337n, 365n, 368n
Teng Hsiao-p'ing, 57, 77, 189, 205, 206, 207, 213, 215, 239, 356n
Teng Tzu-hui, 215
Terrill, Ross, 345n
Territorial claims, 286–87; Burma, 287, 299; Hong Kong, 281–89, 291; Macao, 287, 288, 291; Senkaku (Tiao Yu Tai) Islands, 294; Sino-Indian border, 258–59, 261, 292–94, 298; Sino-Soviet border, 291–92, 298; Taiwan, 111, 246, 249, 252–53, 288–90
Thailand, 282
Third World nations, 254, 265–68, 270, 274, 302, 326; national liberation movements in, 280; Sino-Soviet competition for, 262, 303
Thought of Mao, 30, 31, 187, 192, 194, 197, 321; impact of, 32–33; and the military, 77, 78, 92, 156; repudiation of, 27, 29; in Soviet Union, 193
Tibet, 246, 258
Timber production, 174–76
Tokuda, Noriyuki, 364n, 366n
Topping, Seymour, 345n, 371n, 372n
Townsend, James R., 342n
Tryon, Carol Gillespie, 353n
Tsou, Tang, 343n, 350n, 365n, 366n, 371n, 373n
Tung Pi-wu, 60, 209, 210, 212, 216, 218, 220, 223, 225
Turkey, 273

Ulanfu, 214
Unemployment, 122, 123, 153, 154
United Kingdom, 251
United Nations, 269, 273, 278, 285, 304, 305
United States, 75, 86, 183; and China's national security, 110, 111; détente with China, 261, 274–77; future policy toward China, 328–33; intervention in

Vietnam, 270, 276; and Korean war, 248–49; Nixon doctrine, 276, 312; nuclear test ban treaty, 263; relations with Japan, 258, 327, 332; relations with Soviet Union, 261, 333; relations with Taiwan, 247, 252, 253, 289–90
Universities, 156–58
Urbanization, 19, 123, 147
Usack, H. H., 360n

Values, 1; consensus on, 31, 34; Maoist, 15–16, 26, 27, 30, 34, 91; non-Maoist, 15–16, 27, 34; political, 14, 118, 180, 182; professional, 91; revolutionary, 13–14; social, 118, 135, 180, 182. See also Ideology
Van Ness, Peter, 370n
Vietnam, 267, 270, 273, 276, 282, 283, 303
Vietnam war, 273, 276
Vogel, Ezra F., 339n
Voluntarism, 11

Walker, Richard L., 335n
Waller, Derek, 369n
Wang Chia-hsiang, 239
Wang Hung-wen, 24, 209, 210, 211, 225, 226, 227, 243
Wang Ming, 187
Wang Tung-hsing, 218, 222, 226, 243
"Warlordism," 97, 323
Watson, Francis, 376n
Weapons development, 75, 76, 107, 109, 111, 297–98

Wei Kuo-ch'ing, 227
Wen Yu-ch'eng, 218
Wheelwright, E. L., 355n
Whiting, Allen S., 371n, 372n, 373n, 378n
Whitson, William W., 348n, 350n, 351n, 352n
Winckler, Edwin A., 366n
Women's groups, 40, 52
Wu Fa-hsien, 218, 222, 224
Wuhan incident, 80, 82, 87, 97
Wu Teh, 227
Wu, Yuan-li, 354n

Yahuda, Michael B., 371n
Yang Ch'eng-wu, 81, 220
Yang Shang-k'un, 217, 239
Yao Wen-yuan, 59, 210, 218, 220, 223, 226
Yeh Chien-ying, 60, 87, 209, 217, 219, 222, 225
Yeh Ch'un, 218, 222, 225
Yeh, Kung-chia, 354n
Yoon, Chong-Kun, 352n
Young Communist League, 51
Young, Kenneth T., 373n
Yu, George T., 375n
Yugoslavia, 250, 251, 259, 304
Yü, Wen, 344n

Zagoria, Donald, 349n, 350n, 354n, 370n, 373n